Laurence Gardner, a Fellow of the Society of Antiquaries of Scotland, is a constitutional historian and Professional Member of the Institute of Nanotechnology. Distinguished as the Chevalier de St Germain, he is attached to the European Council of Princes (a constitutional advisory body established in 1946) as the Jacobite Historiographer Royal. In the artistic domain, he has been Conservation Consultant to the Fine Art Trade Guild, and in the world of music his libretto compositions have been performed at London's Royal Opera House. He is also Executive Producer for a Hollywood movie company. Prior of the Knights Templars of St Anthony (1561) and of the Sacred Kindred of St Columba, he is the internationally bestselling author of *Bloodline of the Holy Grail*, *Realm of the Ring Lords*, *Genesis of the Grail Kings*, *Lost Secrets of the Sacred Ark* and *The Magdalene Legacy*.

LAURENCE GARDNER

BESTSELLING AUTHOR OF *BLOODLINE OF THE HOLY GRAIL*

THE SHADOW OF SOLOMON

THE LOST SECRET OF THE FREEMASONS REVEALED

WEISER BOOKS

San Francisco, CA / Newburyport, MA

Also by Laurence Gardner:

Bloodline of the Holy Grail
Genesis of the Grail Kings
Realm of the Ring Lords
Lost Secrets of the Sacred Ark
The Magdalene Legacy

This edition first published in 2007 by
RED WHEEL/WEISER, LLC
With offices at:
500 Third Street, Suite 230
San Francisco, CA 94107
www.redwheelweiser.com

Originally published in 2005 by HarperElement,
an imprint of HarperCollins*Publishers*, ISBN: 0-00-720760-3.

ISBN-10: 1-57863-404-0
ISBN-13: 978-1-57863-404-0

Typeset in Palatino.
Cover photograph © Fox Photos/Getty Images.

Printed and bound in China by
Imago

10 9 8 7 6 5 4 3 2 1

The mason poor that builds the lordly halls,
Dwells not in them; they are for high degree.
His cottage is compact in paper walls,
And not with brick or stone, as others be.

Edward de Vere, Earl of Oxford, 1573

Contents

Colour Plates   XII

Illustrations   XIV

Acknowledgements   XVII

Introduction   XIX

PART I

1	ANCIENT SECRETS	3
	A Magical Heritage	3
	The Riddle of the Lost Archive	5
	Setting the Stage	6
	The Revolution	10
	Religion and the Great Lights	15

2	MASONIC ORIGINS	19
	Secret Signs	19
	The Old Charges	20
	Antients and Moderns	26
	Old Masters	30
	The Key	32

3	ROYAL SOCIETY	35
	The Transition	35
	Heresy	38
	The Invisible College	40
	A Royal Charter	48

4	LEGACY OF INVENTION	51
	The Georgian Movement	51
	The Gresham Days	53
	Fraternal Disputes	57

Fire and Pestilence   60
Gravity on a Plate   63
Genius of the Few   65

5   POWER AND POLITICS   67
         Builders and Bees   67
         The New Foundation   71
         Divided Loyalties   73
         The Dunkerley Episode   77
         Legal Exemption   78
         The Sussex Years   80

6   IMPERIAL CONQUEST   84
         The Celtic Realms   84
         Edict of Rome   88
         Missing Documents   91
         The Great Divide   95
         The Latter Years   98

PART II

7   KNIGHTS OF THE TEMPLE   103
         The Children of Solomon   103
         The Scottish Connection   105
         A Sovereign Order   109
         The Royal Secret   111
         Persecution   113
         The Rosy Cross   116
         The Cathedral Builders   119

8   HIRAMIC LEGEND   122
         The Masonic Apron   122
         The Widow's Son   124
         The Death of the Builder   127
         Time and the Virgin   129

The Master Craftsman 132
Tracing Boards 135

9   THE TRANSITION 140
     Early Guilds 140
     Outlaws of the Privy Seal 141
     The Riches of Salomon 145
     Statutes and Charters 149
     The Art of Memory 153

10   ROSSLYN 159
     Heritage of St Clair 159
     The Mystery of the Chapel 163
     Truth and the Temple 167
     Sinclair in America 172

11   MYSTERIOUS SCIENCE 176
     The Portable Lodge 176
     The Kirkwall Scroll 179
     A Golden Philosophy 182
     Noah and the Ark 184
     Seeds of Life 189

12   THE TEMPLE OF LIGHT 194
     Pillars and Obelisks 194
     Moses of Egypt 199
     The Power of Tchām 200
     House of Gold 204

13   THE LOST WORD 213
     The Quest 213
     Behind Closed Doors 215
     The Secret of the Stone 219
     The Light Bearer 223
     Divine Food 226

PART III

14	ANTI-MASONRY	233
	Reformation	233
	The Biblical Satan	236
	Horns and Hooves	238
	The Demons of Taxil	242

15	THE TUDOR STAGE	248
	Secret Service	248
	Shakespearean Masonry	252
	The Bohemian Connection	255
	Fine Devices	259
	The House of Salomon	261

16	GUILDS AND TRADITIONS	264
	The Mysteries	264
	The Soul of the City	267
	A Parcel of Rogues	270
	The Jacobite Scene	272
	Stuart Masonry	275
	France and the Feminine	279

17	INTO AMERICA	282
	Scottish Rite	282
	The Franklin Foundation	286
	Oglethorpe's Georgia	290
	Washington and Revere	291
	Scots and the New World	293
	The Masonic Tea Party	295
	The Crown of America	298

18	DEBATES AND MONUMENTS	300
	Conspiracies	300
	The Great Seal	302

	The *Illuminati*	307
	Masonic Memorials	312
19	THE ROYAL ART	317
	A Loss of Context	317
	A Masonic Code	318
	The Powder of Projection	325
	The Ark of the Covenant	328
20	DISCOVERING THE SECRET	333
	Hell Fire!	333
	The Magic of *Ormus*	336
	Elements of Construction	340
	The Lord of Light	342
	Ark of Gold	345
	The Levitical Solution	346

Notes and References	351
Masonic and Monarchical Timeline	376
Bibliography	388
Picture Credits	398
Index	399

COLOUR PLATES

1   *The Ancient of Days*
2   *Jacob's Ladder*
3   *Allegory of the Liberal Arts*
4   *Supper at Emmaus*
5   *Constitutions of the Free-Masons*, 1723
6   Obelisks in Alexandria and London
7   *Constitutions of the Free-Masons*, 1784
8   The 12th-century Round Church of the Knights Templars
9   Rosicrucian image depicting the *Boaz* and *Jachin* pillars
10 Masonic summons of the 18th-century Globe Lodge
11 Rosicrucian image with the Point within a Circle
12 Thomas Sprat's *History of the Royal Society of London*
13 *Freemasonry Instructing the People* (the Masonic Marianne)
14 Edward, Prince of Wales, and the Victoria Jubilee Grand Lodge
15 *King Solomon of Judah*
16 The Kirkwall Scroll – Ark of the Covenant
17 St Bernard and the 12th-century Chapter House Lodge
18 First Degree Tracing Board
19 Second Degree Tracing Board
20 Third Degree Tracing Board
21 *King Solomon and the Temple*
22 Egyptian obelisk at Luxor
23 Irish Round Tower at Glendalough
24 *The Ark of the Covenant in Jerusalem*
25 The Fire of London Monument
26 Site of the *Goose and Gridiron* tavern in 1870
27 *Sir Francis Dashwood – The Conversation*
28 Masons' Window at Chartres Cathedral
29 *Viennese Masonic Lodge Initiation*
30 *Ars Magna Lucis et Umbrae* (The Great Art of Light and Darkness)

31 Prince Charles Edward Stuart and the Count of St Germain
32 Fire of London plaque on the Fish Hill Street Monument
33 *Benn's Club* – The Jacobite Aldermen of London
34 *Knights Templars at the Paris Chapter House on 22 April 1147*
35 *Prince Charles Edward Stuart in Edinburgh, 1745*
36 Ark of the Covenant – George Washington Masonic National Memorial
37 *Drafting the Declaration of Independence*
38 *Benjamin Franklin at the Court of Louis XVI and Marie Antoinette*
39 *George Washington as a Freemason*
40 *The Boston Tea Party*
41 *Allegory of Masonic Support*
42 *Liberty Displaying the Arts and Sciences*

ILLUSTRATIONS

1   The Three Great Lights and Working Tools
2   Liberal Arts of Geometry, Astronomy, Logic and Arithmetic
3   The old city of Oxford
4   Sir Francis Bacon (1561–1626), Grand Master of Rosicrucians
5   The 1917 proclamation of King George V
6   Geometry of the Philosophers' Stone
7   The masonic beehive
8   The Hon. Elizabeth St Leger
9   Prince Charles Benedict James Stuart, 4th Count of Albany
10 A Knight Templar Initiation
11 The Virgo Constellation and *Notre Dame* Cathedrals of France
12 King Solomon, architect of the Temple
13 Time and the Virgin (The Freemason's Rest)
14 First and Second Degree Tracing Boards
15 Third Degree Tracing Board
16 Seal of the Knights Templars and Canons of St Anthony of Leith
17 The *Wedjat* Eye of Horus
18 Rosslyn Chapel
19 Arms of the United Grand Lodge of England
20 The Zerubbabel inscription of Sir William Sinclair
21 Noah and his sons building the Ark
22 Nîn-kharsag and Enki at the House of Shimtî
23 The masonic pillars of *Boaz* and *Jachin*
24 The barge *Cleopatra* in London, and the New York obelisk
25 A sandpaper Round Tower
26 Moses burns the Golden Calf at Mount Horeb
27 God the Architect (from the *Bible Moralisée*, 1245)
28 A *benben* pyramidion with winged disc
29 The Rose-Cross seal of Martin Luther
30 Frontispiece from Léo Taxil's *Mysteries of the Freemasons*
31 *The Mirrour of Policie* – An English Freemason, 1598

32   Baconian pillars and the ship *Argo*
33   *The Theater of Fine Devices*
34   Seal of the *Chapitre Primordian de Rose Croix*
35   Thirty-three degrees of the Scottish Rite
36   Great Seal of the United States of America
37   Thomas Jefferson's original drawing for the Great Seal
38   Hermes in the *Apotheosis of Washington*
39   Aerial view of the Washington Monument
40   Section of the Egyptian treasure relief of Tuthmoses III
41   Robert Fludd's 16th-century drawing of the Great Light
42   The Royal Arch, by Laurence Dermott, 1783
43   Commanders of the Temple of Carcassonne, 1786
44   Graphic of single *Ormus* atoms attached to short-strand DNA
45   Masonic Lewis tackle, and modern superconductive levitation

ACKNOWLEDGEMENTS

The compilation of this book would not have been possible without the direct or indirect assistance of Masonic Grand Lodges world-wide, and for the publications made available by them, especially those issued by Lewis Masonic of London. In this regard, I should make specific reference to the United Grand Lodge of England, the Grand Lodge of Antient, Free and Accepted Masons of Scotland, and the Grand Lodge of Ireland. For access to European archives, I must add my special thanks to the Grand Orient de France, and for assistance in America I am most grateful to the directors of the Library Company of Philadelphia, and the curators of the George Washington Masonic National Memorial.

Also, for their valued assistance, I am indebted to archivists and librarians at the British Library, the British Museum, the Bibliothèque Nationale de France, the Ashmolean Museum, the Bodleian Library, the National Library of Scotland, and the Royal Irish Academy. Services and provisions must also be acknowledged as provided by Oxford and Cambridge Universities, the Royal Society of London, Gresham College, London, the Southern Jurisdiction Scottish Rite of the United States of America, along with the Society of Antiquaries of Scotland, the Rosslyn Chapel Trust, and the Corporation of London.

For information concerning artwork, I am grateful to the Guildhall Library, London, the Musée des Beau-Arts, Caen, the Musée Conde, Chantilly, the City of Edinburgh Museums, the Bridgeman Art Library, London, Château de Versailles, Galleria degli Uffizi, Florence, Historiches Museum de Stadt, Vienna, and the Library and Museum of Freemasonry, London.

As always, I am thankful to my wife Angela for her tireless support, and to my son James for his continued encouragement. I am also beholden to the Royal House of Stewart, the Order of Knights Templars of St Anthony, and the Noble Order of the Guard of St Germain. And particular recognition is due to

HRH Prince Michael of Albany for affording privileged access to Household archives.

My express gratitude is similarly due to my literary agent Andrew Lownie, publicity agent Jennifer Solignac, foreign rights agent Scarlett Nunn, website manager Karen Lyster, technical advisor Tony Skiens, and business manager Colin Gitsham. My thanks also to Carole Tonkinson, Katy Carrington, and the directors and staff of Thorsons-Element and HarperCollins Publishers, together with editor Matthew Cory, and artistic consultant Sir Peter Robson.

Special appreciation is due on this occasion for help provided by Niven Sinclair, James Foote, Peter Williams, and Edmund Marriage of the Patrick Foundation – and for aiding my work in general to Nigel Blair of the Wessex Research Group and Octavia Kenny of the College of Psychic Studies. For their continued support of my work internationally, my ongoing thanks to Eleanor and Steve Robson of Peter Robson Studio, to Duncan Roads, Ruth Parnell, Marcus and Robyn Allen of Nexus. Adriano Forgioni of Hera, JZ Knight and all at Ramtha's School of Enlightenment, Christina Zohs of Yes News, Nancy and Mike Simms of Entropic Fine Art, and all the media hosts and journal editors who have been so supportive of this series.

Finally, I must convey my gratitude to all those readers who have followed and encouraged my work over the years, especially those who have written to me with so many useful comments and contributions.

Laurence Gardner

The Graal Studio
http://www.graal.co.uk

Introduction

For close to 300 years since the foundation of England's premier Grand Lodge in 1717, many books have been published concerning Freemasonry. They appear with some regularity, and masonic libraries are extensive in Britain, America, France and other countries. These books reside in two clearly defined camps: they are either written by masons, or they are written by non-masons. In the latter case, there are further subdivisions in that the publications might be pro-masonry or anti-masonry but, either way, their contents are based on hearsay. In comparison, books written by masons are generally written for masons. Though perhaps authoritative, they are largely concerned with in-house doctrines, and often relate to specific aspects that are of little interest to outsiders.

In *The Shadow of Solomon*, I have approached the subject from an objective standpoint since I am able to call upon long-term experience as a Freemason, while also now being an equally long-term Past Mason. Initiated into a City of London lodge in 1966, and subsequently progressing through the Craft degrees, my active regular involvement as a Master Mason continued for around 20 years. By the middle 1980s, however, it became necessary to review my situation because the requirements of lodge membership were potentially limiting to my occupation as an independent researcher. Consequently, I tended my formal resignation at the United Grand Lodge of England.

Since that time, while taking neither a pro nor anti-Freemasonry stance, I have continued to investigate masonic history, structure and practice in the course of general studies which often have loose or close associations with masonry. These include matters that concern chivalric institutions, philosophical societies and other groups that have influenced monarchical and governmental structure over the centuries. In the course of this, I have met with both approval and disapproval from masonic quarters. As in any walk of life, it is not possible to please everybody all of the time – and Freemasons are no exception in this regard. The majority are tolerant, fair-minded individuals with an aptitude for discussion, but for some there is no debating ground beyond the recognized teachings. Hence, although Freemasonry is not a religion, it is similar in certain respects since its defence mechanisms can operate in much the same way if there is a perceived challenge to the accepted dogma.

Numerous Grand Lodges worldwide have websites on the Internet, and these often present an intriguing scenario. Their purpose is to be informative – and many are – but there is also a good deal of defensive content. Pages of official replies are given to what are taken to be harmful assaults against the masonic establishment. No other organization suffers from such a proliferation of accusations, nor feels the need to respond with guarded explanations in every case. But why, if the Fraternity is loyal and mutually supportive, should they even care what outsiders think? It is the masonic choice to be secretive – it is not forced on them.

It is often stated in official literature that Freemasonry is not a secret society, and this is true to a point because its existence is hardly a secret; neither is there any requirement for secrecy of membership. But, in reality, this is splitting hairs since the masonic charge is that members must 'conceal and never reveal' aspects of learning from within the lodge environment. Thus, although not a secret society, it is indeed a *secretive* society and, to outsiders, this amounts to the same thing.

The basic precepts of Freemasonry have much in their favour, but the most anomalous feature is that masonic practice derives from certain ancient sciences which are never actually taught. Ceremonies are performed and rituals are learned, but it is stated that, for all this pageantry, the secrets on which the Brotherhood was founded were lost long ago.

The most devastating loss of primary manuscripts in respect of ancient philosophical thought was caused by the Church of Rome's burning of the Library of Alexandria in AD 391. Subsequent to this, numerous other records were destroyed throughout the Roman Empire. Some discoveries of the utmost significance were made in the Middle Ages when the Knights Templars excavated the Jerusalem Temple vaults after the First Crusade. But, again, much was destroyed in the 14th-century Inquisition against the Order. Remnants of documentation were preserved outside the Papal States, particularly in Scotland, and philosophers of the emergent Royal Society (such as Isaac Newton, Christopher Wren and Robert Boyle) used what was available to make some of the greatest ever scientific discoveries (or, as we shall learn, re-discoveries). Earlier in the 17th century, however, many valuable papers had been burnt during the Cromwellian Protectorate, with further losses incurred in the Great Fire of London. Following this, a change of reigning dynasty and parliamentary affiliation saw even more documentation sidelined, while many key adepts of the masonic tradition were dispersed into European exile.

Freemasonry, in its current form, was established in the 18th century as a questing fraternity that would endeavour to retrieve and collate what could be salvaged of the scattered archive, but it was a short-lived enterprise. Within a very short time the movement changed its emphasis to become a charity-based social institution, although electing to maintain aspects of ritual that would satisfy the original philosophical ideal. These days – although ostensibly perceived as a secret society – it is fair to say that modern Freemasonry's best kept secret is that it actually holds no secrets of any genuine substance. Contained within the surviving Renaissance annals, however, are numerous pointers which, although perhaps vague and incomprehensible 300 years ago, are becoming thoroughly meaningful as modern science catches up with its ancient past.

In *The Shadow of Solomon*, we shall follow an investigative trail of documented record, accessing some of the archival material that the Masonic *Constitutions* claimed to have been lost more than three centuries ago. We shall consider modern lodge workings in comparison with those of the past, to ascertain how latter-day Freemasonry was shaped and manipulated so as to cause its own original precepts to be forgotten. *The Shadow of Solomon* is arranged in three parts: in Part I the focus is on power, politics and the conspiratorial intrigue that set the scene for masonic evolution; Part II deals more specifically with the ceremonies and alchemical heritage of Freemasonry – its connection to chivalric institutions and the philosophies that underpin the foundation; finally, in Part III, the puzzle condenses into a unified shape as we discover not only how the original secrets of the Craft were lost, but why this happened and – most importantly – what those secrets were.

There are many allegorical glyphs and symbols used in Freemasonry; some are well known, others are not. But of all these, the most potent is among the least familiar to outsiders – a point within a circle ⊙. As we shall see, the whole original purpose of Freemasonry rests with the definitive meaning of this device, which dates back to ancient times. We shall also discover that a time-honoured aspect of the Craft known as the Royal Arch Chapter holds the ultimate key to Freemasonry. Although the Chapter is optional to Brethren, it is within this particular ritual (as distinct from the three primary degrees) that the light of masonic heritage truly shines – yet the all-important Royal Arch was totally ignored by the Grand Lodge establishment for 96 years from its foundation. Many masons have wondered why the biblical Ark of the Covenant appears at the crest of the Arms of the United Grand Lodge of England, when it is not an item of significance in the Craft degrees. But clearly – as our investigation will reveal – it was once of the utmost significance, just as were the enigmatic Philosophers' Stone, and the Golden Calf that Moses burnt to a powder in Sinai.

Our task is to undertake precisely what formalized Freemasonry sought to achieve when it was established back in 1717. It is, in essence, the quest for a philosophical treasure, and for a lost Mason's Word which is the code to unlocking that treasure. The difference between our quest and that undertaken by the Fraternity itself is that we are not constrained by in-house preconceptions.

Hence, our approach will succeed where earlier efforts have failed. Many of the time-honoured mysteries are, in fact, perfectly trace- able, and emerge as being far more dramatically exciting than might be imagined.

Laurence Gardner

Exeter, March 2005.

PART I

Ancient Secrets

A Magical Heritage

Stories of the biblical King Solomon reside at the heart of modern Freemasonry. They relate especially to the building of his lavish Temple in Jerusalem, where the Ark of the Covenant was housed in the Holy of Holies. Famed for his extraordinary wealth and wisdom, this son of King David from around 950 BC presents an Old Testament enigma. He is greatly revered in Judaic lore, but also criticized for having a number of wives and for allowing many deities to be worshipped within his realm. Notable in the Solomon accounts are his relationships with the King of Tyre and the Queen of Sheba, each of whom supplied him with valuable gifts and a vast quantity of gold to enrich his kingdom of Judah (*see* page 261).

Outside the Bible, Jewish tradition holds that Solomon was a practitioner of divine technology, with a magic ring and a gem that could cut through stone with silent precision. And it was said that he kept the Ark mysteriously suspended above the ground. In such respects, King Solomon was regarded well beyond his era as a master magician, and he became a much revered figure in Renaissance Europe. As we shall see, the geometry of his Temple was considered to represent sacred perfection; the secret of his stone-cutting and his ability with levitation became subjects of scientific quest, and his passionate interest in gold was a source of constant fascination.

In figurative terms, Solomon holds the key to unlock the secrets of modern Freemasonry, but before the institution was formalized in 1717, the historical connection to his legacy rested with the Poor

Knights of Christ and the Temple of Solomon. Commonly known as the Knights Templars, this elite fraternity of Western European knights – a military legation with a monastic structure – was founded in the early 1100s as an ambassadorial fraternity after the First Crusade. The question arises, therefore: Did the masonic movement take its lead from the Templars? If so, how does a modern-day charitable fraternity reconcile with a medieval Order of warrior monks? Or did Freemasonry evolve from stonemasons' guilds, as is generally portrayed? Perhaps it began with the mystery schools of ancient Egypt, with which there are recognizable similarities. Whatever the case, the same question applies: How does the present institution equate with any of these?

The Bible's Old and New Testaments have been used for centuries as scriptures which underpin the Jewish and Christian faiths, but that is not how they were originally conceived; neither were the Testaments written as cohesive volumes. They consist of a series of individual works written by different people at different times, eventually brought together with common purpose. The books embody aspects of history which, in the Old Testament, encompass lengthy spans of time, but they have a greater value than history alone in that the inherent stories often relate to truly extraordinary events. The fact that modern Freemasonry (which is neither a faith nor a religion) should focus on certain of these events after such a period of time is intriguing in itself, but it has been an evolutionary process which has brought a variety of past disciplines within the wrap of a single ideal.

In researching pre-18th century Freemasonry in its various guises, it becomes clear that its constituent parts were more romantically exciting as individual subjects than they have become beneath a masonic umbrella which veils them with allegory. Most notable is the science and nature of alchemy – the art of material transposition, which is most commonly associated with gold – along with the manipulation of light waves and, not least in the equation, the techniques of levitation. As recorded in texts from Mesopotamia, Egypt and other countries from the 3rd millennium BC, there is abounding evidence that the technological capabilities of ancient civilizations were far superior to anything credited to them by latter-day educational establishments. The study of such documents not only confirms a good deal of biblical scripture, but sheds a whole new light on the history and origins of Freemasonry. It is time, therefore, to put aside conventional dogma and preconceptions, and to look afresh at the archival material that supports the masonic ideal. To help us in our quest, we should first look at Freemasonry as it exists today and, in particular, at what its formative *Constitution* has to say about the masonic secrets themselves.

The Riddle of the Lost Archive

Freemasonry is described by the United Grand Lodge of England as 'a peculiar system of morality, veiled in allegory and illustrated by symbols'. It is associated with the funding of schools, hospitals and care centres. But, worthy as these activities might be, it appears that they were introduced to give meaning and purpose to a brotherhood which apparently had no access to records of the tradition which it endeavoured to emulate. When the Presbyterian mason Rev James Anderson compiled and published *The Constitutions of the Free-Masons* in 1723, he wrote:

> Very little has come down to us that testifies the English masonic tradition before the latter 17th century. Many of the Fraternity's records of Charles II's and former reigns were lost in the next and at the Revolution of 1688; and many of them were too hastily burnt in our time for fear of making discoveries.

Anderson's reference to the 'English masonic tradition' is important because it reflects a commonly held view that Freemasonry is English by design. In loose terms, this is fair comment since the first Grand Lodge (as against separately run independent lodges) was instituted in London in 1717. Just six years after this, Anderson commented on the fraternity's records of a previous generation – an archive that had seemingly been lost. Were those records English, or were they perhaps Scottish, given that King Charles II Stuart (whom he mentions) was of the royal line of Scotland? The Knights Templars certainly had been prevalent in Scotland after being banished by the Pope from England and Europe in 1307, but the 12th-century origin of the Templars was a matter of French historical record before it was Scottish.

If Freemasonry evolved into England from Scotland, and prior to that from France, an interesting scenario would be presented. But it would still not explain how centuries of chronicles from before 1723 had been lost. It may be that they were not lost – merely that it suited the new style of English Freemasonry to pretend this was so. But since Freemasonry is founded on the principles of honesty and integrity, it would seem incongruous for the establishment to be constituted with a pointless falsehood from the outset.

Our task, therefore, is to search beyond Anderson's *Constitutions* and the founding of the first Grand Lodge of England – to look back as far as possible, tracing the story of Freemasonry as it evolved to become the secretive, charitable institution that exists today. In this regard, our search for the lost records must begin with Anderson's own statement that they went missing in the reign following King Charles II, and during the Revolution of 1688.

Setting the Stage

Freemasonry is officially described as a 'peculiar system of morality', conceived as a neighbourly institution of fraternity and goodwill – and it rests upon well-defined codes of 'brotherly love, faith and charity'. Indeed, these are all perfectly valid and admirable ideals, but they can exist perfectly well outside Freemasonry. No doubt there are other organizations which claim to support the same principles, but they are not covert and secretive. Any individual

may aspire to the same codes of practice, but it does not take knowledge of secret signs and handshakes to make them possible. So,
does Freemasonry confer some great and privileged secret to its
members over and above these aspirations? Not according to James
Anderson. He made it plain enough in the *Constitutions* that the
secrets (whatever they were) have been lost. More than that, he said
they had been burnt 'for fear of making discoveries'.

From this it is evident that there is a distinct difference between pre
and post-1688 Freemasonry, and that the earlier movement held
secrets which are not apparent in the modern lodge workings.
Candidates are advised on initiation that they will be 'admitted to the
mysteries and privileges of ancient Freemasonry', but in fact they are
not. They are admitted to the workings (and perhaps privileges) of
modern Freemasonry. Some quaint rituals and entertaining ceremony
have been preserved (or newly invented), but anything which made
the brotherhood worthy of a code of silence, with secret signs and
passwords of recognition, has long since been sidelined or forgotten.

So what happened in England in 1688 that was so dramatic as to
change everything? Anderson specifically mentioned 'the Revolution',
and it is with this that we should commence our investigation. From
1603 until 1688, the monarchy of Britain was the Royal House of
Stuart. They had previously reigned in Scotland for 232 years from
1371, beginning with King Robert II, the grandson of Robert the
Bruce. When Queen Elizabeth I Tudor of England died childless in
1603, her supposed nearest relative, King James VI Stuart of Scots,
was granted dual crown status and invited to London to become
James I of England.

James was succeeded by his son, who became Charles I of Britain
in 1625 but, following the puritanical uprising of the parliamentary
rebel, Oliver Cromwell, and the resultant Civil War, Charles was
executed in 1649. There ensued a short period of Commonwealth,
during which the late king's son and royal heir was crowned King
Charles II of Scots, at Scone, Perthshire, on 1 January 1651. Later that
year, Cromwell's army defeated the new King's troops at Worcester
in England, and Charles II fled to safety in France. Oliver Cromwell

then decided to rule the nation by martial force alone, establishing his Protectorate in 1653 and dissolving Parliament to facilitate his military dictatorship.

In 1660, Charles II was restored to the British crowns, taking his hereditary seat in London. Although a popular and diplomatic monarch, Charles died without a legitimate heir, and was succeeded in 1685 by his brother, the Duke of York, who became King James II of England, while also being James VII of Scots (*see* Masonic and Monarchical Timeline, page 376).

In collaboration with such famed colleagues as the diarist Samuel Pepys (then Secretary to the Navy), James had previously revitalized the British Fleet after its abandonment by Oliver Cromwell. And, as James, Duke of York, he had named the American settlement of New York in 1664.[1] But, despite all his expertise and former glory, James became a very unfortunate king. Plagued in the first instance by a challenge for the throne from his illegitimate nephew, the Duke of Monmouth, James ultimately fell foul of his old trading enemies, the Dutch. He and Charles II had declared war against Holland in 1665 and, during his reign as King James II of England (VII of Scots), this loomed large to confront him in 1688.

At that time there was a religious upheaval in Britain – mainly because of Quaker and Presbyterian movements whose popularity in the rural areas was undermining the supremacy of the Anglican Church. It was also not long since England had been a formally Catholic nation, and Catholics still constituted about a seventh of the population.[2] In addition to this, there were many Jewish people in Britain and, throughout the reign of Charles II, everyone had been treated with due accord. His reign had been such a relief following the church-banning Cromwellian Protectorate that no one cared which religion their neighbour might prefer. But the Anglican ministers of James's era were not so forbearing, and pressures (such as exclusion from trading opportunities) were brought to bear against those who did not conform to the Church of England doctrine.

James decided that, as King and Guardian of the Realm, he had a primary responsibility to the people before any allegiance to

Parliament and the Church. On 4 April 1687, he issued a *Declaration for Liberty of Conscience*. It conveyed the ideal of religious tolerance and freedom for all, stating:

> Conscience ought not to be constrained, nor people forced in matters of mere religion. It has ever been contrary to our inclination, as we think it is to the interests of governments, which it destroys by spoiling trade, depopulating countries and discouraging strangers. And finally, that it never obtained the end for which it was employed.
>
> We therefore – and out of our princely care for all our loving subjects (that they may live at ease and quiet), and for the increase of trade and encouragement of strangers – have thought fit, by virtue of our royal prerogative, to issue forth this declaration of indulgence ... and do straitly charge and command all our loving subjects that we do freely give them leave to meet and serve God after their own way and manner.[3]

It was one of the most public-spirited documentary pronouncements ever made by a reigning monarch, but it was more than the Anglican ministers could tolerate – a king who presumed to offer people freedom of religious choice. James had challenged their ultimate supremacy – he must be in league with the Catholics!

James had always been offended by the way in which the Church had abandoned his grandfather, Charles I, to the mercy of irreligious mobsters, and how the bishops had conformed so readily to Cromwell's closure of the churches. He was no Anglican conformist, neither was he raised as a Presbyterian in the manner of his great-grandfather James I. But, in attempting to grant an equality of conscience, he sought to repeal the restrictive *Test Acts* of 1673 and 1678, which bound those in public office to communion with the Church of England. His action, therefore, was seen to oppose the privileges of the Anglican clergy, as well as affording people a denominational choice over which Parliament had no control.

Much later, in 1828–9, England's *Test Acts* were finally repealed in

favour of Catholics (with the exception of the offices of monarch and
Lord High Chancellor). Then, in 1858, the provisions were relaxed in
respect of Jews, and the Scottish *Test Act* of 1681 was overturned in
1889. In Britain today, all religious denominations (Christian or otherwise) are afforded the right of worship according to their beliefs
and conscience – precisely as King James II (VII) envisaged over 300
years ago. James was way ahead of his time, but his public popularity counted for nothing in 1688, neither did his earlier courage on the
battlefields of France and Flanders, nor his years of relentless work
for the British Navy. Because of his liberal attitude in religious
affairs, the stage was set for James's regnal demise.

The Revolution

What has all this to do with Freemasonry? In actual fact, everything,
for when King James was sent into French exile in December 1688,
the traditional masonic inheritance of the Kings of Scots went with
him – as did his key masonic allies. This is one of the reasons
why today the 33-degree masonic working known as the *Scottish
Rite* (albeit, as we will see, now a contrived *Scottish Rite*) embodies
rituals that are unfamiliar to the three degrees of English Craft
Freemasonry (*see* page 282). For now, to complete the 17th-century
picture, we need to follow on with the drama of King James.

James had two daughters by his first wife, Anne Hyde of
Clarendon, as well as a young son by his second wife, the Italian
noblewoman Mary d'Este de Modena. The elder of the daughters,
Mary, was married to Prince William of Orange, Stadhouder (chief
magistrate) of the Netherlands. It had been hoped that this alliance
would calm the long-standing dispute between Britain and Holland
over international trading rights but, in the event, it worked to
the contrary.

Given the situation of religious unrest in Britain, William saw his
opportunity to dominate Britain's trade from within and, with

approval from the Anglican Church, he put together an invasion force. Meanwhile, the Westminster Parliament in London had denied King James the funds to maintain a standing army in times of peace, so when William's assault came he had no means of defence. What followed in this large-scale, but comparatively localized, revolution was as pictorially dramatic as any Hollywood screenplay.

With a substantial fleet of ships and around 6,000 troops, William of Orange disembarked at Torbay in south-west England on 5 November 1688. Almost immediately, he issued violent threats against James's family. Consequently, on 21 December, James's second wife, Mary de Modena (disguised as an Italian laundress), and their son, the infant Prince of Wales, were secreted from London by night. Taken by armed riders across the countryside to the coast in howling gales and driving sleet, they embarked a small boat for Calais. Mary then got word to her cousin, King Louis XIV of France, who sent courtiers to fetch her. Once in Paris, Mary was met by King Louis and presented with the keys to the Château de Saint Germain-en-Laye. (This royal palace had previously been the grand residence of Mary Stuart, Queen of Scots 1542–87, before she also became Queen of France in 1559.)

Meanwhile, back in London, James received an ultimatum from his son-in-law, William. It stated that if James did not give up his crown immediately, then his family would be at risk. William was unaware that Mary and the prince had already left the country. Resigned to the situation, King James made a final gesture by throwing the Great Seal of England (the constitutional device of the English monarchy) into the River Thames.[4] He then made his way to Paris and to the Stuart Palace of St Germain, which became his primary residence thereafter.

Following James's departure, the parliamentary House of Lords determined that since he had fled, but not formally abdicated, there remained a legal compact between the king and the people. The throne was, therefore, 'not vacant' (although not technically occupied either). It was suggested that a Regency (with an appointed state administrator) was the best way to preserve the kingdom during the remainder of James Stuart's lifetime, but William of Orange made it clear that he had no intention of becoming just a Regent – neither would he consent to sharing in government. His declaration was so forceful that there was an immediate fear of war, and many thought he would seize the crown regardless. A panic conference then ensued between the Houses of Lords and Commons, resulting in a decision that perhaps the throne was vacant after all.[5]

With the support of the Anglican Whig aristocracy,[6] Prince William convened an illegal Parliament at Westminster on 26 December 1688, and the politicians were held at gunpoint to vote in respect of a dynastic change, with the majority voting in favour (although it was still a very close contest). The press later reported that 'the Convention Parliament was in no way at liberty to vote according to conscience because Prince William's soldiers were stationed within the House and all around the Palace of Westminster'.[7] The press report illustrates the effect that this militarily-obligated Parliament had on the monarchical structure:

> King James was gone, and William was present with the Dutch Guard at Westminster to overawe, and with power to imperil the fortunes and lives of those who stood in the way of his advancement ... William employed actual intimidation which resulted in majorities of *one* vote, in two of the most important divisions in the history of Parliament ... In our time, governments have resigned when their majority over a censuring opposition has not been so small. Yet a majority of *one* is held to be adequate justification for a revolution involving the fundamental principle of primogeniture upon which our social fabric is based!

Not all the Church of England hierarchy in the House of Lords were in opposition to King James, however. His supporters included Archbishop Sancroft of Canterbury, and the Bishops of Bath and Wells, Ely, Gloucester, Norwich, Peterborough, Worcester, Chichester, and Chester. When James was deposed, they were all deprived of their sees and incumbencies. History has since been manipulated to suggest that James was displaced because he was a Catholic. In truth, he was deposed to guarantee power to a Parliament that was controlled by Anglican supremacists and not elected by a democratic vote of the people.

William did not get everything his own way though. He gained the crown as King William III only with the proviso that his wife, Mary (James's daughter), held equal rights as Queen Mary II, instead of being ranked Queen Consort was is the norm. Consequently, the reign is known in history as that of William and Mary. At the same time, the 1689 *Bill of Rights* was introduced, stating that future British monarchs could reign only with parliamentary consent, and that MPs should be freely elected. In reality, MPs of the era were certainly not freely elected. Only a very limited number of male property-owners who enjoyed high incomes were allowed to vote, and the House of Commons was far from characteristic of the populace it was supposed to represent. The monarchical situation remains the same today in that HM Queen Elizabeth II reigns only with governmental consent as a parliamentary monarch. She is not a constitutional monarch (appointed by the provisions of a people's written Constitution) as are other kings and queens in Europe.

The reason why the 1689 Act came into being was that, although Queen Mary was a devout Protestant, the ministers were concerned about William's personal relationship with Rome. Holland was the chief northern province of the independent Netherlands which had previously been attached to the Holy Roman Empire, and it was known that William's army consisted largely of Catholic mercenaries paid from the papal purse. King James II had assisted Louis XIV of France in his nation's opposition to the Catholic empire, and it was anticipated by the Pope that, with William in charge of Britain, this support would cease, thereby weakening the French position.

On 23 September 2001, Britain's *Daily Mail* newspaper ran an article entitled 'William of Orange funded by the Pope', explaining how documents discovered at the Vatican reveal that Pope Innocent XI had provided William with 150,000 scudi – equivalent to more than £3.5m today. This came as a surprise to the people of Northern Ireland, who always felt that William's Orangemen (who prevented James Stuart's restoration attempt at the Battle of the Boyne in 1690) were a Protestant army.[8] Cecil Kilpatrick, archivist for the Orange Order, acknowledged that there had already been embarrassing indications of ties between William and the Pope. He said that in the 1930s, when they discovered Pope Innocent XI depicted with Prince William in a portrait at Stormont (the Northern Ireland Parliament), they 'had to get rid of it'!

Despite William's outwardly routine aspirations in what his supporters called the Glorious Revolution, the Whig politicians determined that, having facilitated his invasion, they were in a position to impose certain restrictions for the future. Notwithstanding protests from Stuart adherents on the Tory benches, they laid immediate ground rules. The *Bill of Rights*, with its inherent *Declaration of Rights*, stipulated that Parliament retained absolute rights of consent over the monarchy, the judiciary and the people. Furthermore, it was henceforth illegal for a monarch to make or amend any laws of the land. So, although William made a great show of strength at his initial Convention Parliament, the politicians maintained the upper hand by granting his kingship on a conditional basis. These measures, coupled with Queen Mary's Protestantism, curtailed the papal ambitions, but following Mary's childless death in 1694 the inevitable dilemma of succession arose.

To establish fully the Anglican Parliament's supreme position over the monarchy during the balance of William's reign, the 1701 *Act of Settlement* was introduced to secure the throne of Britain for Protestants alone, and the Act remains in force today – even though it was passed in the House of Commons by a majority of only *one* vote (118 for, and 117 against). The earlier *Act of Abjuration* (requiring all government officials to renounce King James) was similarly passed by *one* vote (193 to 192), and there was no true parliamentary majority for either of these Acts which set the constitutional scene for everything that followed concerning the operational nature of the British monarchy.

Religion and the Great Lights

The much publicized Orange Order was founded in 1795 in the wake of the Williamite revolution and the continuing aggression between Catholics and Protestants in Northern Ireland. The Order is often portrayed as being a masonic lodge in Ulster, but it is not. Indeed, the very nature of its constitution provides us with a good example as to the contrasting religious stance taken by authentic Freemasonry.

The Orange Order is pseudo-masonic in its presentation, but stipulates that its members must be Protestant Christians. There is no such requirement, nor indeed any religious stipulation in legitimate Freemasonry. Those of any religion (or none) are welcomed into the ranks, and the godhead of Creation is defined not in religious denominational terms, but as the Great Architect of the Universe. The Three Great Lights of Freemasonry (the so-called 'furniture', without which no lodge can be convened) include a volume of the *Sacred Law*. This might be the Judaeo-Christian Bible, the Koran, the Torah, the Vedas or the Zend-Avesta, depending on the predominant culture of the lodge concerned. Each and all are acceptable to attendant or visiting masons since the volume is representative of an essential belief in some form of supreme authority, by whatever definition. Outside that, discussion of religious matters is not permitted within the lodge environment.

The other Great Lights of Freemasonry are the square and compasses, representing the psyche and spirit respectively. The configuration in which these physical items are displayed within an active lodge (for instance, with one, two or neither of the compass points revealed in front of the square) denotes the degree in which the prevalent meeting is being conducted. The Three Great Lights in unison denote the extent of a mason's qualifying achievement within an overall environment of divine consciousness, while the lodge itself is perceived as a bridge between the material and spiritual worlds.

The Three Great Lights and Working Tools

This aspect of lodge working demonstrates that there is something more to Freemasonry than is immediately apparent from its superficial image. The masonic hierarchy is always quick to assert that Freemasonry is not a religion – and indeed it is not – but something else is indicated here: divine consciousness and a recognition of different material and spiritual worlds. If not religious, then there is clearly a spiritual aspect to consider, and the concept of 'worlds' is somewhat kabbalistic in nature. In fact, the levels of masonic spiritual attainment between the mundane environment and the higher levels of enlightenment are represented by Jacob's Ladder from the Genesis story of Jacob's dream.[9] This was depicted in Georgian times by the Rosicrucian poet and artist, William Blake (b. 1757), in the masonic tradition of a winding staircase (*see* plate 2). His is also probably the best-known representation of the masonic Great Architect of the Universe – the *Ancient of Days* with his compasses (*see* plate 1). The staircase, in its final interpretation, defines seven levels of consciousness, and can be assigned to each of the seven officers of a lodge (*see* page 135).[10]

While the spiritual path in modern Freemasonry is a journey of allegory and symbolism in pursuit of self-improvement, that of the Stuart era was about the acquisition of scientific knowledge with a much bigger scale of practical involvement. Hence, current masonic teachings point members to a wealth of Renaissance literature, recommending that it should be studied, although those making the suggestions have rarely perused the material themselves. Instead, they are generally in pursuit of social recognition and personal fulfilment, not scientific accomplishment.

The fact remains that any amount of Renaissance literature in the public domain might be studied without revealing the secrets that were lost to the English masonic stage in 1688. Even though all the relevant documentation was not carried to France by King James's supporters, a good deal was burnt and destroyed as described in the Anderson *Constitutions* (*see* page 5).

Intellectuals of the era, such as Sir Christopher Wren (b. 1632) and Sir Isaac Newton (b. 1642), did their best to work with the information to hand. They knew that masonic lore was connected with Kabbalah wisdom philosophy (an ancient tradition of enlightenment based on material and spiritual realms of consciousness). They also knew that it was related to the culture of the biblical kings, and were aware of a scholarly existence before the days of the Roman Empire. They researched the technology of the ancient Babylonians, the philosophies of Pythagoras and Plato, and the mystery traditions of old Egypt, becoming thoroughly absorbed in history beyond the bounds of biblical scripture. But for all that, and despite their own considerable scientific achievements, they also knew that they lived only in the shadow of King Solomon, whom Newton called 'the greatest philosopher in the world'.[11] Newton viewed the design of Solomon's Temple as a paradigm for the entire future of mankind and, in referring to the great masters of old, he wrote in a letter to his Royal Society colleague, Robert Boyle, 'There are things which only they understand.'

Newton believed that the dimensions and geometry of the Jerusalem Temple floor-plan contained clues to timescales,[12] and he used these mathematics in his calculations when developing his theory of gravitation.[13] The Temple, he said, was the perfect micro-cosm of existence, and his diagrammatic *Description of the Temple of Solomon* is held at the Bodleian Library in Oxford. At the centre of the Temple, in the *Sanctum Santorum* (Holy of Holies) was kept the Ark of the Covenant, and Newton likened this heart of the Temple to a per-petual fire, with light radiating outwards in circles, while also being constantly attracted back to the centre. In line with this thinking, a point within a circle was indeed a symbol for Light in ancient Egypt and, in the lodge ritual of Freemasonry, there is a related conversation which takes place between the Worshipful Master and his Wardens concerning the lost secrets. The Master asks the *Question*: 'How do you hope to find them?' *Answer*: 'By the centre'. *Question*: 'What is a cen-tre?' *Answer*: 'That point within a circle from which every part of its cir-cumference is equidistant'. In due course we shall discover that a point within a circle ⊙ is the most important of all masonic devices.

Although the Temple of Solomon commands primary attention in modern Freemasonry, far older masonic documents than Anderson's *Constitutions* suggest that, for all his great wisdom, Solomon (*c.* 950 BC) was the inheritor of a much more ancient tradition. From this point, we shall travel back in time to trace the history of Freemasonry as it devel-oped through the ages. What we know at this stage, however, is that the majority of what existed in English masonic circles prior to the 1688 Revolution disappeared from Britain's shores with the deposition and exile of the House of Stuart. This was explained in 1723 by James Anderson, whose *Constitutions* formed a base for the development of Freemasonry thereafter. Indeed, it follows that the immediate answer to the question 'What is Freemasonry?' can be summed up by saying that it is not the same thing today as it once was.

Masonic Origins

Secret Signs

Masons, in the operative sense, are stoneworkers, but the term Freemason is not so readily understandable. Many views have been put forward as to what the word actually means, but even Freemasons tend to disagree. The best routes to the origin of words are good etymological dictionaries – these have no vested interest and do not need to slant their descriptions in any particular way. The most famous of such early works is the 1721 edition of *Nathan Bailey's Universal Etymological Dictionary*. This was published just two years before James Anderson's *Constitutions* and, interestingly, the word Freemason does not appear. Neither does it in the revised edition of 1736.

Writers such as John Hamill (librarian and curator for the United Grand Lodge of England in 1986) consider that 'freemason' is a contraction of 'freestone mason' – a worker in finely grained freestones such as limestone and sandstone, which have no flaws and are easily cut.[1] Although quite plausible, this is not in keeping with general masonic theory which suggests that the prefix *'free-'* relates to the realm of the 'speculative' rather than 'operative' – ie, not a working stonemason as such. However, the term 'freestone mason' is recorded as far back as 1375, while the epitaph of a freestone quarryman at St Giles Church, Sidbury, describes him as 'John Stone, free mason'. It is thought that he was the father of the celebrated sculptor Nicholas Stone, who became Master of Works in 1619 for the great architect Inigo Jones at London's Banqueting House in Whitehall. Among the noted achievements of Devonshire-born Nicholas Stone (1586–1647) is the gate at St Mary's Hall, Oxford, the monument to the poet John Donne at St Paul's Cathedral, and numerous tombs including that of Viscount Dorchester at Westminster Abbey. In 1625, he was appointed as Master Mason at Windsor Palace by King Charles I.

When entitling his *Constitutions*, James Anderson hyphenated the word as 'Free-Masons' and, in earlier times, two separate words were sometimes used – which may explain the non-existence of 'freemason' in old dictionaries. Another early use of the term comes from 1435, when 'John Wode, mason, contracts to build the tower of the Abbey of St Edmundsbury in all manner of things that longe to free masonry'.[2] In line with this, the Oxford Word Library explains that, in those times, stonemasons' guilds would emancipate (or *free*) their local members so that they might travel from place to place in order to gain work contracts. When arriving in unfamiliar surroundings, they would communicate their degrees of proficiency by way of secret signs known only to others of their craft.

This makes reasonable sense and certainly gives a valid reason for the use of signs and passwords in order to gain employment at the right level of attainment. However, latter-day Freemasons are, for the most part anyway, not operative stonemasons and do not require the signs for this purpose. Either way, it is clear that by the mid-1600s operative masonic guilds did afford membership to non-operatives[3] (for example, selected employers, who would need to know the signs and symbols when hiring their workmen). Thus, as is commonly believed in masonic circles, the structural framework of Freemasonry (even if not the inherent subject matter) does seem to emanate from the methods employed by the medieval workers' guilds.

The Old Charges

The two oldest known masonic documents held in Britain have traditions from around 1390 and 1450 respectively. The first, which is called the *Regius Manuscript*, is a vellum at the British Museum containing a rather long (and not very good) poem of rhyming couplets.[4] In 1757, a facsimile bearing the arms of King George II was produced for the Royal Library, and the original was discussed by Mr Halliwell-Phillips at the Society of Antiquaries in 1838. Subsequently, some transcribed copies were made, entitled *The Early History of Freemasonry in England*. The document makes no mention of King Solomon, but does feature the Alexandrian mathematician Euclid (*c.* 300 BC), along with an account of England's King Athelstan of Mercia (*c.* 930) and his precepts concerning the duties of master masons and apprentices.

Rather more informative and entertaining than the *Regius* is the 15th-century *Matthew Cooke Manuscript*, which is also listed in the British Museum catalogue.[5] Edited by a Matthew Cooke, it was published in London in 1891 and is believed to have originated in middle England. The two-part contents – known as the History and the Old Charges – formed part of the masonic *General Regulations* compiled in 1720, and were also used as reference material for James Anderson's *Constitutions* three years later.

From a prayer-like beginning, the document moves to an explanation of the Seven Liberal Arts: grammar, rhetoric, dialectic, arithmetic, geometry, music and astronomy. It then tells how the sciences which formed the bedrock of Freemasonry began with the biblical offspring of Lamech, namely Jabal, Jubal, Tubalcain and their sister Naamâh (Genesis 4:19–22). In line with the Bible, Tubalcain is featured in the 3rd degree of Craft masonry (the Masters degree) as an instructor of metal artificers, and historically this takes us back more than two millennia before Solomon to around 3500 BC when Tôbalkin the vulcan, son of Akalem (Lamech), was a prince in southern Mesopotamia.

Lamech was fourth in succession from Enoch (Henôkh), the son of Cain of Kish, and the manuscript relates that his offspring inscribed the sciences on two imperishable stones. They were of such virtue that one of them, called *marbyll*, would never burn – and the other, called *latres*, would not perish in water.

In part of the text the stones are referred to as 'pylers', and this has generally been assumed to relate to 'pillars'. The same definition was also given in a 19th-century English translation from the 1st-century work of Flavius Josephus of Galilee, who had related a version of the same story in his *Antiquities of the Jews*.[6] The translation from Josephus has been criticized by scholars because of its many inaccuracies, among which are the use of 'brick' and 'stone' for the Hebrew words equivalent to *marbyll* and *latres*. Similarly, the word 'pillar' was wholly misleading and led to the illusion of two great columns which appeared to have no geographical location. Given that Lamech and his sons lived before the biblical Flood, the stones became known as the Antediluvian Pillars.

In fact, there are two very distinct words used in old Hebrew, each of which has been translated to 'pillar' in the English version of the Old Testament – *ammud* and *mazzebah*.[7] The first denotes a pillar such as a column in architecture or a column of smoke, but the second has a rather different connotation. It might refer to a stela or altar stone, but was equally applied to the stone that Jacob used for a pillow (pyler) and established as a *mazzebah* at Beth-el (Genesis 28:18). The antediluvian stones of the *Matthew Cooke Manuscript* were therefore correctly designated (before the translatory errors) as *mazzebah* stones of *marbyll* and *latres*. The former might perhaps have been marble or some crystalline rock, while the other was corrupted in some writings to 'laterus' and then reckoned to be 'laterite' (a red iron-based clay used for bricks and road surfaces). The fact is that the nature of *latres* is obscure, although early masonic tradition presumes it to have been a type of metal.[8]

The Seven Liberal Arts (*artes liberales*) were branches of knowledge taught in medieval schools, and they were so named from the Latin *liber* meaning 'free'.[9] (This is another possible derivation of the prefix *'free-'* in Freemason, but again it is not the definitive source of the term as will become clear when we return to the subject in chapter 7.) The Liberal Arts were not so much taught as a means of preparing students to gain a livelihood, but to increase their awareness in the philosophical sciences. They were individually defined in 819 by the Benedictine scholar, Rabanus Maurus, Archbishop of Mayence (Mainz) and Abbé of Fulda, the greatest seat of learning in the Frankish Empire in the days of Charlemagne. Rabanus was renowned as the most learned sage of the era, and it was said that he had no equal in matters of scriptural knowledge, canon law and liturgy.[10] Among the most renowned works of Rabanus was his richly illuminated *Life of Mary Magdalene*.[11]

Geometry, Astronomy, Logic and Arithmetic:
Four of the Seven Liberal Arts

The Liberal Arts were, in effect, perceived as routes towards personal enlightenment in the finer things that were the keys to harmony and justice. In the 2nd degree of Craft masonry (the Fellow Craft degree), it is explained to the candidate that there are seven levels to the winding staircase that leads to the middle chamber of Solomon's Temple. They are important aspects of the journey to wisdom, and allude (among other things) to the Seven Liberal Arts. They are the abstracts of truth and, as Plato claimed, the steps of the universal whole. The painting *Allegory of the Liberal Arts* by the Italian artist Biagio d'Antonio (*c.* 1445–1510), shows the seven levels (reminiscent in concept to Blake's *Jacob's Ladder*), with scholars and philosophers receiving instruction in the respective Arts at each level, at the base of which is the Gate of Wisdom (*see* plate 3).

The *Matthew Cooke Manuscript* continues with the story of Noah and relates that after the Flood the *marbyll* and *latres* stones were found by Hermes and the Greek philosopher Pythagoras. In historical terms, this makes little sense given the enormous time span (around 3,000 years) between Noah and Pythagoras. However, the manuscript was produced in about 1450 – two centuries before Archbishop Ussher of Armagh compiled the first biblical chronology, and many such date anomalies are discovered in documents of the era. But this does not excuse the naive manner in which the story is recounted verbatim today.

Other versions of the account separate the Hermes and Pythagorean involvements. They explain that, in the first instance, Hermes Trismegistus (Hermes the Thrice Great) – revered as the founder of alchemy and geometry, and from whose name the definition 'hermetic' derives – transcribed the stones' content onto an emerald tablet. Then, in time, the emerald text of Hermes was inherited by Pythagoras.

The extent of truth in the story of Lamech's offspring is unknown, but Apollonius of Tyana, from the Temple of Asklepios in Aegae, is said to have discovered the emerald text in the 1st century. From that time, many notable philosophers have studied and made use of his transcription. Extant part-translations date from the 700s, beginning with that of the Islamic philosopher Jābir Ibn Hayyān, who also wrote of the alchemical School of Pythagoras (the *Ta'ifat Fthaghurus*). Prominent among later students of the *Emerald Tablet* was Sir Isaac Newton. He was so entrenched in the research of ancient hermetic writings that, in a Royal Society lecture by Lord Keynes in 1942, he was referred to as 'the last of the magicians; the last of the Babylonians and Sumerians'.[12] Unfortunately, Newton did not have the benefit of the thousands of Mesopotamian tablets discovered since his lifetime, so his efforts to produce a reliable chronology of events were substantially hampered.

Newton also translated the *Corpus Hermeticum* (attributed to Hermes Trismegistus), from the Florentine collection of Cosimo de Medici, and was especially interested in a unified theory of the law of the Universe (the *prisca sapienta*), which he referred to as the Frame of Nature. With Hermes' maxim 'as above, so below' at its heart, it denotes that the harmony of earthly proportion is representative of its universal equivalent. In other words, that earthly proportion is the mundane image of cosmological structure. From the smallest cell to the widest expanse of the galaxies, a repetitive geometric law prevails, and this was understood from the very earliest of recorded times.

Following the 'Wisdom of Lamech' theme, the *Matthew Cooke Manuscript* moves to the geometry of Euclid, although confusing his lifetime with that of Abraham some 1,700 years before. It explains how geometry and masonry were synonymous crafts in ancient Egypt, and makes the point that these crafts were learned by the Israelites during their 400-year sojourn in the Nile Delta before travelling with Moses to the promised Holy Land (*c.* 1360 BC). Subsequently, the crafts flourished in Phoenicia and Judah, leading to their inheritance by King Solomon and his artificer Hiram, sent to Jerusalem by the King of Tyre.

At this point in the *Matthew Cooke* text, there is a dramatic leap in historical context and, in the same paragraph that relates to Solomon, it is stated: 'And from thence this worthy science was brought to France.' The account continues with the notion that

Charles II of France (*c.* 885) was a mason before he became king. Then, flitting back in time, we are in England with the 3rd-century St Alban, followed (as in the *Regius Manuscript*) by the 10th-century King Athelstan and his council of stonemasons!

In all of this, the *Matthew Cooke Manuscript* centres on the fact that the precepts of masonry were first cemented when 40,000 masons were employed to build the Tower of Babel in Shinar (historically, the great ziggurat of Babylon in Mesopotamia). The masonic Charges, it states, were formulated by King Nimrod of Babel – the mighty hunter of Genesis 10:8–10 – when he sent 3,000 masons to build the city of Nineveh in Assyria (northern Mesopotamia). Again there is a major date anomaly here since there were more then 2,000 years between Nimrod and the building of Nineveh.

Authentic or not, this rambling and diverse account is a strange mixture of tales concerning philosophical mathematics and hermetic practice, interwoven with the artisan craft of straightforward stone-masonry, without actually detailing much about any of them. Although considered to relate to speculative Freemasonry (as against operative stoneworking) it does little more than establish the fact that there is a similarity in the guild-like structure of officers and workers in the lodge fraternity.

Antients and Moderns

The documented history of Craft Freemasonry in a form that might be recognized today starts in 1717. This was just three years after Georg, Elector of Hanover in Germany, was brought over by the Westminster politicians to become King George I of Britain, thus initiating the Hanoverian dynasty, which followed the Stuart and Orange reigns. On 24 June that year, the Grand Lodge of England was founded by an amalgamation of four London lodges, which met at different taverns, namely *The Goose and Gridiron*, St Paul's Churchyard, *The Crown*, Lincoln's Inn Fields, *The Rummer and Grapes*,

Channel Row, and *The Apple Tree*, Covent Garden.[13] (The *Goose and Gridiron*, as it was in 1870 before demolition, is shown in plate 26.)

Following the death of King William in 1702, his late wife's sister had reigned as Queen Anne for a while. But since Anne had no surviving children by her husband Prince George of Denmark, her own choice of successor was the German Electress, Sophia of Hanover. She was the daughter of Frederick V, Elector Palatine of the Rhine, whose wife was Elizabeth Stuart, a daughter of King James I (VI). Irrespective of the Stuart maternal connection, however, the Scots vigorously opposed the concept of a German ruler to the extent that the English Parliament implemented express trade limitations against the Scots. In March 1705, Westminster passed the *Alien Act*[14] which demanded that the Scots must accept Sophia of Hanover as Anne's successor or all trade between the North and South would cease. The importation of Scottish coal, linen and cattle into England would be forbidden and there would be no continued export of English goods into Scotland.

In order to give Westminster full powers north of the Border, the traditionally separate Scottish Three Estates Parliament in Edinburgh was terminated by the 1707 *Act of Union*. Many Scots would have preferred to install the son of the deposed King James as their monarch when Queen Anne died in 1714. But they had no say in the matter and, in the light of Sophia of Hanover's own demise, her son Georg von Brunswick duly arrived in London to receive the crown. Following the termination of Scotland's Parliament, all traditional Scottish Orders were taken over and reconstituted by the English establishment. These included The Most Ancient and Noble Order of the Thistle (previously equivalent to England's Most Noble Order of the Garter) and, in the course of the restructuring, Scottish Freemasonry was also subsumed. As a result, English Freemasonry rose to the fore, soon to be granted the Hanoverian patronage that persists today with Edward, Duke of Kent, as the overall Grand Master.

Meanwhile, with the four tavern lodges combined to form the premier Grand Lodge of England from 1717, John, 2nd Duke of Montagu, was installed as Grand Master in 1721. The frontispiece of James Anderson's *Constitutions* depicts Montagu passing the Constitutional Roll and the compasses (dividers) to his successor Philip, Duke of Wharton, in 1723 (*see* plate 5).

Having stated that the pre-1688 records of Freemasonry had been lost, Anderson set down a schedule of regulations concerning lodge appointments and activities as approved by Lord Montagu. His 1723 *Constitutions* also contained a list of Charges, described as being 'The Ancient Records of Lodges beyond the Sea, and of those in England, Scotland and Ireland' – though from where he obtained them in that particular form is unknown. In 1738, however, Anderson produced a revised set of *Constitutions* in which his (or someone's) imagination concocted a detailed history of English Freemasonry, which had supposedly begun with an assembly of stonemasons convened in York by a Prince Edwin in 926.[15]

To substantiate his dubious history of the masonic institution, Anderson explained how it had been neglected and sidelined by the previous Grand Master, Sir Christopher Wren, who had conveniently died since the 1723 *Constitutions* were published. This was in direct contrast to Anderson's earlier pronouncement that there had been no Grand Lodge, and therefore no Grand Master, prior to 1717, and Wren is certainly not listed as a documented Grand Masters after that date. So why did Anderson single out Christopher Wren for the blame? The reason, as will become clear, is that Wren had been a prominent mason of the Stuart fraternity of King Charles II, whose records Anderson claimed had been lost. With the Hanoverian Elector now reigning in Britain the chance came to reinvent the history of Freemasonry, and James Anderson was the foremost architect of this project, whose imaginative writings emerged like a holy writ.

In 1768, the decision was taken to build a central headquarters for Grand Lodge. A site was duly purchased in Great Queen Street, London, and on 23 May 1776 the foundation stone was laid for what was to become the first Freemasons' Hall (incorporating, of course, the *Freemason's Tavern* so as to maintain the traditional meeting environment). When producing the 1784 revision of

Anderson's *Constitutions*, the prestigious Hall was featured in the new frontispiece illustration (*see* plate 7). In this depiction, the figure of Truth is holding her mirror to illuminate the Hall, while accompanied by the other virtues of Freemasonry. (The larger Freemason's Hall complex used today in Great Queen Street was built in 1927–33.)

During the course of Anderson's revisions, a second Grand Lodge was founded on 17 July 1751. Calling themselves the 'Antients' (*Ancients*), they nicknamed the earlier Grand Lodge – which by then had around 200 member lodges – as the 'Moderns'. The full style of the new group was The Most Antient and Honourable Fraternity of Free and Accepted Masons. Whereas the Moderns used the old Company of Masons guild crest as their arms, the Antients used a quartered design of a lion, ox, man and eagle – the four 'living creatures' from the Old Testament book of Ezekiel.[16] (These visionary creatures are known in astrological circles as the Tetramorphs, representing Leo, Taurus, Aquarius and Scorpio respectively.) The Antient's Book of Constitutions, called the *Ahiman Rezon* (meaning, essentially, 'Brother Prince') was prepared by the Irish masonic artist Laurence Dermott, who became Grand Secretary of the Antients and the chief protagonist for their Royal Arch degree (of which more later).[17]

Claiming a more authentic Scots–Irish tradition, which they undoubtedly had by way of the Royal Arch ritual, the Antient Grand Lodge became significant competition for the premier Grand Lodge, especially since they warranted travelling lodges in regiments of the British Army, which eventually took the masonic concept to the colonies.

In 1727, a central charity fund had been established by the premier Grand Lodge to give the cause a common purpose and, following a programme of diversified contributions for some decades, a girls' school (funded by voluntary subscriptions) was founded in London in 1788. This established a more positive focus and soon afterwards, in 1798, the Antient Grand Lodge set up a charitable fund for boys. Now, not only was there competition over seniority and authenticity of ritual, but the two key Grand Lodges were competing in the arena of public relations and social recognition. To complicate matters even further, yet another lodge, the Grand Lodge of All England was established at York in 1761. And, in 1778,a breakaway group fromthe premier Grand Lodge was styled (by way of a warrant from York) as the Grand Lodge South of the River Trent.

The whole scene had become so argumentatively pointless within the course of a century that a necessary truce was called. Articles of Union were then agreed and signed by the respective Grand Masters and officers at Kensington Palace on 25 November 1813. Henceforth, the Antients and Moderns were amalgamated to form the United Grand Lodge of England which prevails today.

Old Masters

The legend of Hiram Abiff and the building of Solomon's Temple, which dominates the 3rd degree of modern Craft Freemasonry first appeared in print as late as 1730 in a treatise by the London mason Samuel Pritchard, entitled *Masonry Dissected.*[18] Its appearance in that work indicates that it was known earlier as part of the newly designed Grand Lodge ritual, although not mentioned by Anderson in 1723. The English scholar Thomas Paine (1723–1809) stated that Pritchard swore an oath before the Lord Mayor of London that his *Masonry Dissected* was a 'true and genuine copy of every particular' – but he did not say a copy of what! (Paine was personally famed for his works, *Common Sense, Age of Reason* and *The Rights of Man,* along with his part in the American Revolution.) We shall examine in detail the main Hiramic legend in chapter 8, but for now we can look at another account of Freemasonry's origins as it appeared soon after the foundation of United Grand Lodge.

In 1802, a Portuguese journalist named Joseph Hippolyte da Costa was imprisoned by the Catholic Inquisition for the crime of being a Freemason, as was denounced by papal decree. Following his escape after three years, in 1820 he wrote an essay entitled 'History of the Dionysian Artificers' which drew parallels between masonic initiation and the Orphic mysteries. (*See* chapter 5 for more on this Portuguese mason.)

In this account, Hiram Abiff is said to have belonged to an ancient society known as the Dionysian Artificers, who emerged around 1000 BC just before the building of Solomon's Temple.[19] They took their name from the Greek god Dionysus (Bacchus), and were associated with another group called the Ionians, who built the Temple of Diana at Ephesus. Apparently, when in Jerusalem, the Dionysian Artificers called themselves the Sons of Solomon, and used Solomon's six-pointed seal (two interlaced triangles) as their masons' mark. They were seemingly masters of sacred geometry and hermetic philosophy.

There is no reason to doubt the existence of the Dionysian Artificers. They were, in fact, cited by the Greek geographer Strabo in the 1st century BC. He wrote that they acquired their name because Dionysius was reckoned to be the inventor of theatres. Whether Solomon's artificer, Hiram of Tyre, was associated with this group is another matter. He might well have been if they had a presence in Phoenicia, but there is no mention of the Hiram connection that can be discovered prior to the 1820 treatise.

Another addition to the said masonic pedigree comes in the form of a college of architects called the Comacine Masters, who were based at Lake Como in Northern Italy during medieval times. The masonic link to this guild was said to have been referenced by a Lucy Baxter (pen-name Leader Scott) in her book *The Cathedral Builders*, published in 1899. The theme of a link between the Comacines and Freemasonry was subsequently taken up in a booklet called *The Comacines* that was serialized in the masonic journal, *The Builder*, in 1910.

From the architectural records of Lombardy, it can be deduced that the *Magistri Comacini* were indeed prominent in their day, and they made a good contribution to Italian design between the years

800 and 1000. But there is nothing whatever to associate them in any way with English masonic history. In fact, not even Leader Scott (who is widely misquoted) said there was a connection. Having investigated the possibility, she stated: 'There is no certain proof that the Comacines were the veritable stock from which the pseudo Freemasonry of the present day sprang.'[20]

The Key

The net product of all this research into the origins and history of post-1688 English Freemasonry is that it is about as weak and insubstantial as it could possibly be. Taken chronologically, the story begins with the biblical metal-worker Tubalcain of Mesopotamia (*c.* 3500 BC) and the wisdom of his father Lamech – a story that incorporates the later Hermes Trismegistus (Thoth of Egypt), and eventually the Greek philosopher Pythagoras.

From Tubalcain and his siblings, the history skips to King Nimrod of Babylon, who apparently instituted the masonic Charges (*c.* 3000 BC), and then leaps 1,000 years to Abraham, who somehow met with Euclid (*c.* 300 BC) in Egypt. Moving from Egypt to Israel with Moses (*c.* 1360 BC), we arrive with the Dionysian Artificers and Hiram of Tyre, who built Solomon's Temple in Jerusalem (*c.* 950 BC). After that we are in England with St Alban (AD *c.* 260); then with King Charles II of France (*c.* 850), and back again to England with Prince Edwin of York (*c.* 926), and King Athelstan of Mercia (*c.* 930).

At the end of all this, there is the unfortunate Sir Isaac Newton trying to fathom what he can from this chaotic mire. And to cap it all, James Anderson – the man responsible for most of the chaos – admits that there were no legitimate records to speak of, but then lays the blame for the lack of available literature on the recently deceased Sir Christopher Wren!

Whether the stories of Tubalcain, Nimrod, Athelstan and the others are correct or not is of no real consequence. There is, in fact, a measure of historical substance in some aspects – but these are all accounts of operative artificers, craftsmen and builders. Chronologically, the last account in the series of tales is that of King Athelstan and his stonemasons. Then, quite suddenly, around 800 years later there emerges a charitably based group of nobles and businessmen who support boys' and girls' educational foundations and meet in taverns. Nothing, it seems, happened in between, except that the latter fraternity was said to have inherited its secret signs and passwords from the former.

Something is drastically wrong here. There would be small likelihood of high-ranking nobility becoming involved in a tavern club with such little substance or pedigree. Nor indeed would Prince Edward, Duke of Kent, and Prince Augustus, Duke of Sussex, (the sons of King George III) have taken positions as Grand Masters of the Antients and Moderns respectively if Freemasonry were just an everyday fraternity of moralists and benefactors.

James Anderson said at the outset that the meaningful records had been lost when the Stuarts were exiled. So that is the key to understanding the real course of events. King George I was the son of Electress Sophia of Hanover. She was the daughter of Frederick V, Elector Palatine of the Rhine, whose wife was Elizabeth Stuart, a daughter of King James I (VI). John Wilkins, chaplain to the Palatinate in the middle 1600s had been the man who had founded the masonic group that became the Royal Society of King Charles II, for which Isaac Newton later became president in 1703. Another original founder of that Society was its professor of astronomy, Sir Christopher Wren.

Being the grandson of Frederick and Elizabeth, Britain's King George I was well aware that there were masonic traditions in the maternal branch of his family, but they had not formed part of his Hanoverian education. His successors were also conscious of the heritage, but they were similarly unaware of the detail. Their only hope of discovery rested with Christopher Wren, who did not die until 1723 – the year of the first Anderson *Constitutions*.

What Anderson really meant when he blamed Christopher

Wren for the chaotic state of English Freemasonry was not that
Wren had been responsible for losing anything – but that Wren's
loyalties were not with the new Hanoverian establishment. They
were with the Stuarts and the Palatinate. Anderson was convinced
that Wren, a founder member of the Royal Society, was fully aware
of secrets that the Hanoverian fraternity wanted to know – but he
died without revealing anything.

Royal Society

The Transition

It is on record that the first mason to be installed south of the Scottish Border was the statesman Sir Robert Moray. Knighted by King Charles I, this eventual close friend of Charles II was made a Freemason at Newcastle in 1641.[1] Freemasonry was very much a part of the Stuart tradition and, in 1601, King James VI of Scots had been initiated at the Lodge of Scone two years before his arrival in London as James I of England. His son and grandson, Charles I and Charles II, were also both patrons of Freemasonry.

Moray's initiation does not strictly qualify as an English installation because the lodge concerned was a travelling branch of the Lodge of Edinburgh, and Moray was himself a Scot. But Elias Ashmole, the antiquarian and founder of Oxford's Ashmolean Museum, was subsequently initiated into Freemasonry at Warrington, Lancashire, in October 1646. Hence, he is officially regarded as being England's first home-grown Freemason. His diary, however, gives the names of those present at his induction and, as pointed out by the Curator of the United Grand Lodge of England some years ago, the seven men who formed this lodge must have been Freemasons before Ashmole.[2] It is, therefore, clearly incorrect to claim that Freemasonry in England began when four gentlemen's tavern clubs amalgamated to form a Grand Lodge in 1717.

Ashmole's keen interest and involvement in hermetic magic is not generally mentioned in masonic works concerning him, since a practising alchemist is not the desired image of England's first Freemason. In contrast, however, the Ashmolean Museum has no problem with the subject, and makes the point that Ashmole used the pseudonym James Hasolle for his first book on alchemy, *Fasciculus chemicus.*[3] The fact that Ashmole was also Windsor Herald and Treasurer of the College of Arms holds a far greater appeal for idealized masonic society, but in Restoration times these two seemingly diverse facets would have been unremarkable. His *Theatrum chemichum Britannicum*, published in 1652, was of primary importance to the Rosicrucian movement (*see* page 45) in that it was a collated synthesis of English alchemical texts, and became a valuable reference source for manuscripts otherwise hard to access.

It is beyond dispute that Freemasonry of a 'speculative' style came into England from Scotland when the two Crowns were united in 1603. But it is also apparent that in 'operative' terms the London Company of Freemasons was granted a coat of arms as far back as 1472. Equally interesting is the fact that in 1655 the name was changed to the London Company of Masons. This appears to indicate that the word Freemason had taken on a new connotation – relating now more to a speculative craft, rather than to a particular form of operative stonemasonry. This still does not explain why the word Freemason is not found in etymological dictionaries of the early 1700s, but it does suggest that a key operative guild wished to draw a distinction between its own membership and that of the speculative lodges.

It appears that Freemasonry has been portrayed very strangely since 1723 – a hotchpotch of disconnected legends and a general lack of cohesion, with the reason given that the truly enigmatic secrets had been lost. The actual reason for the vagueness of otherwise intellectual men was not so much that everything had gone missing after the 1688 Revolution. It was more a question of their obstinacy in not acknowledging the facts of the matter. Information was there to find if Anderson and his allies had cared to look, but the political situation was such that they preferred not to do so.

This attitude arose after 1715, when James Francis Edward Stuart, the son of the exiled King James II (VII) made a bid to regain the crowns of his ancestral heritage. Soon after the coronation of George I, James Francis was proclaimed as the rightful King James VIII of Scots by Stuart adherents in Aberdeen, Brechin, Dundee, Montrose, Perth, St Andrews and Edinburgh. He then sailed to Scotland from Dunkirk, and in September that year his standard was raised at Braemar. His supporters seized Inverness and Perth from the Hanoverian guard, but they failed to take Edinburgh and Stirling castles, and their advance was halted at Sherriffmuir. South of the Border their penetration was feeble, and within a few weeks the 1715 Rising was terminated by a surrender at Preston, Lancashire, on 14 November. Soon afterwards, the deflated James Francis returned to France.

Despite its initial enthusiasm, the 1715 rebellion was one of the worst campaigns ever organized. But it was not destined to be the last Stuart attempt at restoration, and the people of Britain began to question their personal loyalties and sympathies: Were they Stuart or Hanover supporters?

In Latin, the name James is rendered as *Jacobus* – and from the time of the Stuart exile, their supporters had become known as Jacobites. Pre-1688 Freemasonry in Scotland and England had ostensibly been a Jacobite institution. But the post-1717 English variety of Anderson and his friends was essentially Hanoverian – a newly devised pseudo-masonry with no real provenance of its own. Whatever information might have been available from previous sources, it would have been unacceptable to the hard-line Hanoverians because it was of Scottish origin. Consequently, much of the new-style English Freemasonry has since bewildered masons and non-masons alike because its weak, often incomprehensible, tradition leaves so much to be desired. Only the introduction of charitable objectives and precepts of moral idealism appear to give it any meaningful substance, but we should not judge too hastily in this regard since there is a good deal more to uncover. Meanwhile, back in 1738, since Christopher Wren was a deceased mason of the old school it was convenient to blame him for spoiling everything!

Heresy

So, what was Christopher Wren's 'old school' of masonry? The picture comes together easily by looking at those few men of his acquaintance whom we have met already: King Charles II, Sir Robert Moray and Elias Ashmole – Freemasons all, but what was their communal meeting ground? It was the Royal Society at Gresham College in London. The Royal Society was, and is, a scientific academy for the purpose of studying natural philosophies. Freemasonry had the very same objectives and, even today, the ritual makes it clear that members are encouraged to 'devote time to the study of such liberal arts and sciences as may be within the compass of your attainments'.

Although Freemasonry is a secretive society, this does not mean that the secrets held amount to anything that would benefit any outsider to discover. All lodge ceremonies and rituals are scripted and rigorously repetitive. Nearly everything in those rituals is publicly available. The secrets are nothing more than the signs, tokens and passwords of recognition by way of which one mason knows the degree status of another. These words and definitions are left as blanks in the published rituals – and that is the full extent of it.

The Liberal Arts (*see* page 21) are not taught as subjects within the lodge environment, they are only alluded to. Neither are the sciences (as cited in the lodge dialogue), nor any natural philosophies taught or discussed. There are allegorical, illustrated lectures which point members towards an awareness of spiritual and philosophical enlightenment, but there is no practical instruction given. The lectures are delivered by way of rote, not by way of any qualified professional experience, and the lectures for each grade are not based on any ongoing research. They are fixed, rigid and the same, word-for-word, time after time. Thus, what it all amounts to these days is a 'role play', a costumed re-enactment of operating procedures that were followed in lodges at a time when new material was introduced and debated at each meeting. Freemasonry today exists as a framework for something that used to be a cumulative and progressive work experience. But the only 'work' necessary for lodge performance these days is that of learning scripted text off by heart.

Outside the formal lodge environment, in what are styled the 'private assemblies' (such as around the dinner table, or 'festive board' as it is called), it is stated in lodge instruction that a member may 'offer opinions on such subjects as are regularly introduced in our lectures'. The claim is that this 'privilege' enables one to 'strive through researching the more hidden paths of nature and science'. But in my own experience of some 20 years of lodge attendance, I never heard anyone discussing nature or science. Moreover, if one were to make a headline discovery that rocked the world of science and changed the course of history, it would not make one iota of difference to the lodge workings. The basic precepts in such matters have been fixed (albeit loosely) since the revisions of United Grand Lodge were introduced in 1816. The most up-to-date scientific statement in modern Craft ritual is that the Earth revolves, on its own axis, around the Sun, which is at the centre!

Although such a statement (which the 2nd-degree candidate is obliged to announce to the lodge as the required answer to an explicit question) is wholly naive by today's standards, it does pose an interesting scenario. It is the Copernican heliocentric principle as put forward by Galileo in 1632, and for which he was summoned before the Inquisition and imprisoned for 10 years until he died. In this respect, if we think in terms of the same question and answer in 1641, when Sir Robert Moray was installed, it would have held tremendous significance. To gain Fellow Craft masonic status on those terms meant that one was risking life and limb by admitting to such an heretical concept! This also demonstrates that progression through the degrees would have been impossible unless one was a scientific heretic. That is why Freemasonry was secretive and relied on brotherly support and loyalty. Outside the lodge confines one would know to discuss such punishable matters only with those who knew the signs and passwords of the fraternity. In short, Freemasonry true and proper, in its original uncorrupted form, was about liberal arts, science and natural philosophy.

The Invisible College

Science in the 1600s was concerned, in the main, with natural philosophy. Chemistry fell within the scope of this, but was a lowly art since chemists worked as assistants to the more experienced alchemists, who were practitioners of the senior profession, although detested by the Church. Scotland had a strong tradition in hermetic alchemy, and its research was subsidized from the royal purse as far back as the days of King James IV (1488–1513). Since masonic lodges were concerned with scientific experimentation, alchemy had a powerful and permanent influence on lodge operations.[4] One of the foremost collectors of alchemical manuscripts was Lord Balcarres, whose daughter was married to Sir Robert Moray. In turn, Moray was the patron of England's most notable 17th-century alchemist, Eirenaeus Philalethes, the revered mentor of Robert Boyle and others of the masonic Royal Society.

Although the Renaissance had brought a great flourish to academic and creative interests, throwing off the superstitious shackles of the Church in favour of reviving classical philosophy and literature, in this respect Britain fell into a repressed doldrums during the Cromwellian era. Following Cromwell's military overthrow and the 1649 execution of King Charles I, this hitherto rural politician became so powerful that in 1653 he chose to rule by martial force alone. He dissolved Parliament and appointed himself Lord Protector, with greater dictatorial powers than any king had ever known. He then sought to demolish the activities of the Anglican Church. At his order, the *Book of Common Prayer* was forbidden, as were the celebrations of Christmas and Easter. His dictatorship was more severe than any previous regime, and his puritanical directives lasted throughout the 1650s. Games, sports and entertainment were restricted, dissenters were tortured and banished, houses were sequestrated, punitive taxes were levied, universities were constrained, theatres and inns were closed, freedom of speech was denied, adultery was made a capital offence and mothers of illegitimate children were imprisoned.

No one was safe even at home, and any unwitting group of family or friends could be charged with plotting against an establishment that empowered crushing fines to be imposed at will by the military.

This was the environment which brought enterprising university students such as Christopher Wren and Robert Boyle together as pioneers of an undercover society of subversive academics, which grew to become the foremost scientific academy. It began at Oxford University during the 1650s, at a time when Oxford was in a state of restlessness. Having been the capital of Royalist England during the Civil War, Cromwell had appointed himself Chancellor of the University and the once lively streets were subdued and an air of general oppression prevailed.

Within the University, subjects such as astronomy and mathematics were considered demonic and were expressly forbidden by the Puritan commissioners. In fact, learning in general was frowned upon, for scholars were the greatest of all threats to the regime. There was, however, one man who stood apart from his colleagues on the University staff – an unusually free-thinking churchman, Dr John Wilkins. He was the maverick Warden of Wadham College, a future bishop who studied the wisdoms of the ancient world. At Oxford, Wilkins ran a philosophical group who met secretly by night in a local apothecary's house to discuss prohibited subjects. In fact, he was a positive enigma since he was married to Oliver Cromwell's sister, Robina, but fronted a secret society in blatant opposition to his brother-in-law's dictatorship. The Cromwell family was very mixed in outlook, however, and Elizabeth, another of the sisters, was a Stuart-supporting Royalist.[5]

The old city of Oxford

Immediately before coming to Wadham in 1648, Wilkins had published his controversial book *Mathematicall Magick*, which the Puritans considered wholly satanic. For a churchman even to acknowledge the notion of magic was inconceivable, especially when allied to numerology, the most diabolical of all occult aberrations!

Members of Wilkins' clandestine group, which became known as the *Invisible College*, included the young Christopher Wren, along with Robert Boyle (son of the Earl of Cork), the anatomist William Petty, and a technically-minded student called Robert Hooke. Other participants were the noted theologian Seth Ward – an older man who encouraged Wren's interest in astronomy – along with the cryptologist John Wallis and the physician Thomas Willis. The term *Invisible*, as applied to the group, was first used in a letter written by Robert Boyle,[6] but it was common in covert Rosicrucian circles. Rosicrucianism was directly allied to Freemasonry in Scotland, and the two were shown as synonymous in a metrical account of Perth, published in Edinburgh in 1638:

For we be brethren of the Rosie Crosse;
We have the Mason Word and the second sight.[7]

In order to fulfil their overriding scientific objectives, the fraternity was in no doubt as to the key that would unlock the doors of enlightenment. They knew that in order to advance science and medicine beyond the bounds of academic constraint, they had to discover the alchemical secrets of the ancient and medieval masters.

Among the more prominent alchemists of the day was the inscrutable Thomas Vaughan (brother of the poet Henry Vaughan), who styled himself Eirenaeus Philalethes. His writings on the subject of chemical hermeticism were no less confusing than those of any alchemist through the ages, but he was rather more forthcoming to his friends. In contrast to the general presumption that alchemy was about making gold from base metals by use of the Philosophers' Stone, Philalethes made it clear that the Stone was itself made from gold, 'but not common gold'. He stated that it was called a Stone because of its fixed nature and its resistance to fire, but that 'its appearance is that of a very fine powder'.[8] The French chemist, Nicolas Flamel, had written much the same back in 1416, referring to 'a fine powder of gold, which is the Stone'.

What especially intrigued the Oxford fraternity was that the Philosophers' Stone was traditionally associated with the defiance of gravity, and this compelling subject was a primary focus of their study. It had been stated in an old Alexandrian document, the *Iter Alexandri ad Paradisium*, that the Stone gave youth to the old, and that although outweighing its own quantity of gold, even a feather could tip the scales against it![9]

The students could not imagine why the universities were not encouraged towards such research. Instead, their textbooks were substantially out of date, and the majority of schooling was vested in long outmoded principles. The 2nd-century Alexandrian work of Ptolemy was considered a good enough guide to the celestial system, expounding the notion that the Earth was the fixed centre of the Universe, while in matters of natural philosophy Aristotle prevailed.

They were taught nothing of atomic structure, only that everything existed in varying combinations of the four basic elements: earth, water, fire and air. It did not take them long, however, to recognize that true alchemy was far from being a foolish medieval cult. Moreover, it emerged that geometry and numerology were at the hub of all alchemical learning. They were not taught mathematics since it was not in the interests of their masters that they learn anything of real consequence.

John Wilkins knew that within his circle were some of the most inventive young minds in Britain – minds that should not be confined to shady backroom sessions. It was determined, therefore, that they must come out into the open with something to transform philosophy into an accredited science. Undoubtedly, what they needed were precedents – new scientific laws that would rock the establishment to its foundation. Christopher Wren and his friend Robert Hooke were especially fascinated by the stars and, in due course, the pair were destined to become the foremost masters of astronomy since Galileo. Indeed, eventually their pioneering approach was to demolish and overawe the restrictive teaching methods of all the major academies.

In 1657, wonderful news arrived from London, when Christopher Wren (still only 27) was offered the position as Professor of Astronomy at Gresham College in Bishopsgate. Astronomy, though regarded with suspicion at Oxford, was now officially recognized at Gresham despite the punitive regulations that applied. The college founder Sir Thomas Gresham (the Tudor royal agent in Antwerp) stated in the early 1600s that no more than 10 thinkers in Europe were prepared to accept the heliocentric principle of Nicolas Copernicus![10] Established in 1597, Gresham College was associated from the outset with cutting-edge research, and Sir Thomas's daughter Anne was married to Nathaniel, brother of the Rosicrucian Grand Master, Sir Francis Bacon.

After Wren's lecture, members of a London-based philosophical group explained to their Oxford counterparts that life had been tough for them in the City. Cromwell's soldiers had invaded and disrupted their meetings, filling them with trepidation and fear for their lives. They had moved the venue numerous times to settle at the *Bull's Head* tavern in Cheapside, but now the Gresham College door was opened by virtue of Wren's fortuitous appointment. The New Philosophy, declared Wren, had been constrained for long enough. It was now time to straddle the divide and put science firmly on the map of academia.

Through the use of books brought in from Europe, they discovered the existence of theorems from ancient times – general propositions which were not self-evident (as conventional science was supposed to be), but were proven by chains of reasoning. They learned too about problems which could be expressed as symbols or formulae and solved by algebraic application. They found that astronomers such as Copernicus and Galileo had made revelations concerning the sun and the solar system, without the help of official tutoring, along with a new celestial concept of the heavenly bodies which completely overturned what they had been taught by the university clerics. In the event, it was not long before Robert Hooke (by then Professor of Geometry at Gresham College) reinvented the telescope with his own uniquely manufactured lenses, discovering not only the secret of Orion's alignment, but emerging as the first to determine sun-spots, Jupiter's rings and to calculate the rotation of Mars.

In all this, a prevailing mystery was the anomalous nature of their founder John Wilkins, for he was a reverend gentleman quite unlike any other. He had taken Holy Orders before 1645, but his *Mathematicall Magick* had a strong alchemical flavour which flew in the face of Church doctrine. Even more baffling to the group (considering his family alliance with Cromwell) was that Wilkins was chaplain to Charles Louis, Prince Palatine of the Rhine – eldest son of the King and Queen of Bohemia,[11] and a sworn enemy of the Lord Protector. Moreover, the Palatinate was steeped in Rosicrucian alchemy.

Rosicrucians were, by Inquisitional definition, heretics and meddlers in the occult. Back in the days of Elizabeth I, the Queen's adviser John Dee was a noted Rosicrucian,[12] as was the hermetic philosopher Robert Fludd who aided the translation (from Greek into English) of the King James Bible. In practice, however,

Rosicrucians were student chevaliers of the *Rosi-crucis* – the enigmatic symbol of the grand enlightenment (*see* chapter 13).

An intriguing, but poignant, aspect of post-1723 Freemasonry is that, whilst Euclid is revered in the Charges (although wrongly dated) there is no mention of John Dee. He had written the famous preface to the English translation of *Euclid* – the most remarkable monument to sacred geometry in which he urged the revival of the Euclidian art. James Anderson clearly knew of this work since he almost quotes from it on occasions. For example, concerning the 1st-century reign of Augustus Caesar, Dee wrote: '… in whose days our heavenly Archmaster was born'. On the same subject of Emperor Augustus, Anderson wrote: '… when the great Architect of the Church was born'. Just as Hanoverian Freemasonry ignored Elias Ashmole's hermetic interests, it also paid no heed to the work of John Dee, even though the 47th Proposition of the 1st *Book of Euclid* (the Pythagoras Theorem) is pictorially demonstrated (bottom centre) in Anderson's 1723 frontispiece (*see* plate 5), and is a traditional symbol of masonic perfection. The reason once again is that Dee's Rosicrucian connection was anathema to the newly devised strait-laced Freemasonry of Georgian times.

Wilkins' *Mathematicall Magick* specifically referenced the sepulchre of Frater Rosicrosse, as detailed in the 1614–15 *Fama Fraternitatis* of the Rosicrucian Manifestos. (Also incorporating the *Confessio Fraternitatis*, the Manifestos were German works that announced an impending age of new enlightenment and hermetic liberation in which certain universal secrets would be unlocked and made known.) Wilkins' work was also substantially based upon the mechanics section of Robert Fludd's *Utriusque Geomi Historia* (published in the Palatinate in 1619). Additionally, Wilkins frequently cited the late Stuart Chancellor, Sir Francis Bacon, who had been a master craftsman of the Rosicrucian Order. Indeed, it was Bacon's one-time vision of a fraternal scientific institute which led Wilkins to envisage the Oxford fraternity at a time when the Bohemian research of the Palitinate had been curtailed by the Thirty Years' War in Europe (1618–48).

Sir Francis Bacon (1561–1626), Grand Master of Rosicrucians

The apparent dichotomy of Dr Wilkins was a mystery to all. But for his group to thrive and survive, he made a strict masonic ruling from the outset: Whatever else might be discussed, the subjects of religion and politics were prohibited. Notwithstanding this, the Bible became a subject of continued study from the time of Wren's Gresham College lecture in 1657, particularly in respect of chronology and astronomical time frames. In fact, this lecture was a manifesto of things to come from the group, since it referred to the tyranny of the Greek and Roman cultures upon which all 17th-century academic society was based.

Despite his scientific genius, the Eton-educated Robert Boyle was short-sighted and not particularly adept at mathematics, so Robert Hooke helped him a good deal with calculations and experiments. Both were fascinated by the power of exerted pressures, so Boyle concentrated on air pumps, while Hooke investigated springs. In the course of their collaborative work, important mathematical formulae relating to compressed air and compressed springs were discovered. They become known respectively as *Boyle's Law* and *Hooke's Law* – two of the most crucial precedents in the world of emergent science, and equally important today.

A Royal Charter

In time, and specifically from 1660, the Rosicrucian aims of the group emerged into the open with the Restoration of the flamboyant King Charles II. Quite suddenly, and irrespective of clerical opinion, they gained approval and recognition by way of a Stuart charter in 1662, to become known henceforth as the Royal Society. Their motto was established as *Nullis in verba*, which translates roughly to 'Take no one's word for it' – a motto which had been used previously by Sir Francis Bacon.

The Society's new status was achieved by two influential members, namely the Scottish statesman Sir Robert Moray and the Gresham College president William, Viscount Brouncker – both of whom had direct access to the king. In the event, it was Moray who approached King Charles on behalf of the fraternity, securing his patronage and encouragement. Having been Attaché to Cardinal Richelieu in France during the Protectorate, Moray was a man of enormous influence in court and government circles, and was greatly respected by the royal household. By that time, other subsequently famous characters, such as Elias Ashmole and the diarist John Evelyn, had joined the group. Viscount Brouncker (though not a scientist) became the Society's first

President, with Robert Hooke appointed as the first Curator and, on 20 May 1663, some 150 Fellows were elected from the fast-growing overall membership.

The House of Stuart progenitor, Robert the Bruce had inaugurated the Elder Brethren of the Rosy Cross in 1317 – a Knight Templar institution[13] which was inherited 11 generations later by King Charles II. It is no coincidence that the first two known prominent masonic initiates in England, Sir Robert Moray and Elias Ashmole, were both foundation Fellows of the Royal Society and members of the Rosicrucian movement. The Royal Society's *New Philosophy* (as Wren had dubbed it) was therefore largely Rosicrucian and, as such, was immediately concerned with matters of hermetic alchemy.

King Charles's paternal aunt, Princess Elizabeth – the daughter of King James I (VI) – had married Frederick V, Elector Palatine, in 1613. Hence, it comes as no surprise that the House of Stuart, with its link to the Bohemian Palatinate, accompanied by John Wilkins' own Rosicrucian chaplainship, was eager to acknowledge the enthusiastic brotherhood of the Royal Society. In so doing, King Charles effectively reconstituted the Brethren of the Rosy Cross, taking on the Grand Mastership of his family's traditional Order.

To leave no doubt in anyone's mind that the Royal Society was a Rosicrucian establishment, the Society's historian Thomas Sprat included a descriptive frontispiece illustration in his 1667 *History of the Royal Society* (*see* plate 12). Designed by John Evelyn and engraved by Wenceslas Hollar, the Society's inaugural picture depicts a bust of King Charles, along with Viscount Brouncker and Sir Francis Bacon who had died many years before in 1626. Also featured in the engraving is the trumpet-bearing Angel of Fame from the *Fama Fraternitatis* of the 1614 Rosicrucian Manifestos, along with a number of books and masonic devices.[14]

Having moved to join their colleague Christopher Wren at Gresham College, the founding Fellows soon became a threat to all sectors of the establishment, whether governmental, educational or clerical. But, despite this, they appeared like a breath of fresh air to the people at large – and best of all, they had the popular King Charles as their patron, with his personal access to the masonic archive of the Kings of Scots.

4

Legacy of Invention

The Georgian Movement

Prior to James Anderson's mention that key masonic documents had been lost and destroyed, this was also stated to have been the case in 1718. George Payne, an early Grand Master of the premier Grand Lodge asked his members to bring whatever old literature they could find, so as 'to shew the usages of antient times'. But it was subsequently recorded that the more valuable manuscripts were 'tragically lost'. Anderson noted particular examples in his revised 1738 *Constitutions*, stating that papers 'writ by Mr Nicholas Stone, the Warden of Inigo Jones, were too hastily burnt by some scrupulous Brothers, that those papers might not fall into strange hands'. The question has recently been posed in the journal *Freemasonry Today*: 'Could it be that there was a ritualistic form of Accepted Freemasonry prior to 1717 that was unpalatable to those who wished to review the movement in the 1720s?'[1]

The answer to this would appear to be 'yes'. Everything points to the fact that speculative Freemasonry in England prior to Hanoverian intervention was not a role-playing organization as evolved from the dining clubs in 1717. It was concerned with matters that required scientific or technical qualification or experience. Such things would have been foreign to many, and generally unpalatable to the emergent Grand Lodge masons of the London group. It is impossible to discover precisely what these new members did as a cohesive unit outside of performing rituals in their tavern rooms. But in view of the benevolent reputation that evolved, it is likely that they established a Box Club to cement the aspect of mutual support. This was a custom of the old trade guilds, whereby contributions were made into a central pool for the benefit of less fortunate members. The welfare of 'poor and distressed Freemasons' and the support of their immediate relatives, including widows and orphans, is still a major concern today.

'Henceforth the House of Saxe Coburg-Gotha will be known as Windsor' – the 1917 proclamation of King George V

Irrespective of the new-style Freemasonry, the Royal Society prevailed into Hanoverian times, and thence after Queen Victoria's death into the Edwardian reign of Saxe Coburg-Gotha – the Germanic house of Victoria's consort, Prince Albert, that was obliged to change its name in 1917. After the accession of Victoria's grandson King George V in 1910, World War I was looming, and people began to believe there was a German fifth column in Britain. Notwithstanding the immediate royal family with its roots in Hanover, shopkeepers and business people of German extraction – even the Lord of the Admiralty, Louis Battenberg – found themselves at the wrong end of public opinion. By 1917, with the war well under way, the situation was so bad that King George changed his Saxe Coburg-Gotha family name to Windsor (in allusion to the royal castle in Berkshire). At the same time, Lord Louis changed his Battenberg of Hesse name to the more English-sounding Mountbatten.

Through all this, the Royal Society pressed on regardless, and today remains one of the world's foremost scientific institutions. But things did change after 1688, and more especially after 1714 when the enthusiastic flair of the early pioneers was subsumed by a more austere Georgian regime.

The Gresham Days

The life and times of England during the early years of the Royal Society were recorded by two of Britain's best-known diarists: John Evelyn, a cultivated man of means and lawyer of the Middle Temple who became Commissioner of the Privy Seal,[2] and Samuel Pepys, who became Secretary to the Admiralty.[3] In fact, Evelyn and Pepys joined forces to plan the Naval Hospital at Greenwich – one of the supreme achievements of Restoration architecture. Although not so well known as the others, Robert Hooke's diary is equally informative.[4]

Pepys recalled in his journal how, on 15 February 1665, he first visited Gresham College where he met with Robert Boyle,

Christopher Wren and others of the Royal Society who were not content to view the world through the eyes of Ptolemy and Aristotle. By 1664, Pepys was a regular visitor, and although he lacked personal training and experience in matters of mathematics and science, he found the meetings enthralling. What he loved most were the laboratory gadgets and gizmos, soon acquiring his own telescope, microscope, thermometer, scales and geometric instruments, which he said were a great help to his work at the Navy Board.

At a professional level, Pepys found his greatest ally to be the tenacious Robert Hooke, whose work with springs, pulleys and the like led him to invent a depth-sounding device, a diving bell and the marine barometer – all of which were of great significance to the Navy. However, not everything was straightforward for Hooke, especially when it came to giving unpractised public demonstrations. In one experiment concerning respiration, he was sealed in a large cask from which the air was gradually extracted, but things went badly wrong. By virtue of the cask's inner environmental change towards a vacuum state, his colleagues could not undo the seal quickly enough, and the near frantic curator finally emerged, gasping, with permanent damage to his ears and nose![5]

Nevertheless, mishaps or otherwise, London was bustling again in the 1660s after its 11 years of puritanical suppression. Charles II was skilful, well-liked and perfectly suited to the mood of the era. His primary concern was to allow the nation considerable freedom. In this regard, he allowed an abandoned gaiety to prevail, reopening the inns and theatres, while at the same time a new romantic spirit of learning and enquiry was born.

The group's interest in hermetic subjects was notably encouraged by the Cambridge Platonist Henry More and his pupil Anne, Viscountess Conway of Ragley Hall, who nurtured a group of intellectuals called the Hartlib Circle,[6] to which Robert Boyle and the physician William Petty belonged. They recognized that medieval alchemy, in the way it was generally portrayed (ie, the manufacture of gold from base metal), was a delusion conveyed to the outside world by propagandists and failed adepts. Alchemy, they knew, was a combination of practical and spiritual arts which had its root in metallurgy as practised by the ancient artificers.

Robert Boyle (who refused to take Holy Orders as scientists were expected to do) was as much a mystery to his friends as was John Wilkins. His father was the richest man in Britain and he wanted for nothing, yet few young men worked so hard and long without the need for personal gain. Being such a high-profile figure, Boyle suffered more than the others from clerical harassment, and he was viewed as being highly suspicious by the Church because of his determined research into matters of the occult. The bishops were aware that he had his own specially equipped alchemical workshop, and they watched him closely.

Ostensibly a scrupulous man, it is evident that Robert Boyle confronted a real dilemma in his work. He stated that so much alchemical writing was too obscure to be of any real value, but nevertheless he studied all that he could in order to pursue his research. Whether Boyle actually succeeded in making the Philosophers' Stone is unclear, but it seems that he did see it in operation after a Viennese friar found a quantity of the mysterious powder secreted in a small casket at his monastery.[7] In a related report to the Royal Society, Boyle made particular mention of the powder's ability to manipulate specific gravity – an attribute which has now been demonstrated in today's laboratory research.

The Vienna discovery is somewhat reminiscent of a similar box of alchemical powder which John Dee obtained from the Dissolution remnants of Glastonbury Abbey.[8] Boyle also managed to find an Eastern source for the Stone in its natural state, without having to go to the trouble of manufacturing it. This, once again, is something which has recently been shown to be possible. In his subsequent Royal Society *Philosophical Transactions* paper, Boyle noted that his objective was not to make gold but to 'produce good medicines for general use'. Given the reoccurring importance of this powder in the continuing story of Rosicrucian research (a powder of gold classified by physicists today as 'exotic matter'), it might prove to be the missing link to the otherwise ambiguous

King Athelstan legend in the masonic Charges. By virtue of some writing found with the powder, John Dee associated it with St Dunstan, the 10th-century Abbot of Glastonbury, who was attached to King Athelstan's court. It is also clear that it was an important substance at the Temple court of King Solomon (*see* page 325).

By virtue of a later programme to sanitize the early Royal Society's image in the Hanoverian era, Robert Boyle's alchemical pursuits were strategically lost to academia until modern times. Although he is best remembered for *Boyle's Law* concerning the volume of gases, along with his research into the elasticity of air, few have recognized that the tireless work and findings of this wealthy nobleman's son were fuelled by his overwhelming desire to understand the nature and functions of the great alchemical secret.

In those early days, the Royal Society welcomed members of various philosophical disciplines in the knowledge that all creative pursuits were as much science as those things which were most obviously so. Music was based upon mathematics, as was fine art, architecture and the metre of poetic writing. They were all aspects of the time-honoured Liberal Arts. It was decided, therefore, that men of such creative talents had much to offer the fraternity, which expanded to include the poets Abraham Cowley and Edmund Waller, along with the poetic dramatist John Dryden and the antiquary John Aubrey.

This practice was severely criticized by the French philosopher Voltaire (1694–1778) who, in making a comparison with the Academie Français, wrote that the Royal Society was badly governed and in need of laws. What he failed to realize was that this was precisely what made the Society work so well and achieve so much. It existed outside the constraints of formal academia and thereby afforded a freedom of research and expression that was not apparent in the strictly regulated French institution.

Fraternal Disputes

Not just confined to the dusty backrooms of Gresham College or to fume-laden laboratory workshops, the world of the founding fraternity was one of committed enthusiasts who took their working debates into every corner of their lives. It was a constant whirl of frock-coated, bewigged gentlemen, embroiled in the fevered conversation of inns and coffee houses. The City of London presented a more colourful stage than they had found in Oxford. It was a world of doctors and merchants, financiers, fine ladies and costermongers – all amid a bustle of carriages in narrow, rutted streets where flower girls cried, paupers begged, and the women of the night plied their trade.

Working colleagues though the Fellows were, it cannot be said that all was friendship and harmony within the group. In fact, there were many disputes – some heated but short-lived, while others rumbled on over the years. At one meeting, the botanist Sir Hans Sloane (whose manuscripts eventually formed the core of the British Museum collection in 1753) was rebuked by the President for making faces at his dissenters, and the medical professor John Woodward even fought a duel on the College steps after a row had disrupted the proceedings.

Within the Sloane collection was *Manuscript 3848*. Now at the British Library (dated October 1646) it is a constitutional document of old Masonic Charges from 77 years before James Anderson compiled his *Constitutions*,[9] and is one of the pre-1688 documents that Anderson accused Christopher Wren of losing. Also, *Sloane Manuscript 3323* is of a similar masonic nature, as is *SM 3329* – and both are from the latter 1600s. The important document in this group is *3848* – the others appear to stem from it. Unlike the *Regius* and *Cooke* manuscripts (*see* page 21), the content of *Sloane 3848* is mainly of Scottish origin[10] and discusses, among other things, the secret words of Freemasonry and rituals of identification.

In the course of occasional Society arguments, certain important discoveries were shelved and ultimately forgotten – a good example being Robert Hooke's 1662 marine chronometer for determining longitude. Consequently, a century later, the research was begun again from scratch by the Yorkshire joiner John Harrison. He achieved his result knowing nothing of Hooke's original design, which was not rediscovered until 1950 in the library of Trinity College, Cambridge.[11]

In contrast, however, there were times when the Fellows would leap to each other's aid. On one occasion, Christopher Wren was specifically asked to submit the result of an experiment concerning the incubation of chickens' eggs but, owing to more pressing commitments, he failed to comply. Nevertheless, Hooke told the President that he had indeed received Wren's submission in part, and he covered for his friend by verbally concocting a most plausible temporary report.

The worst disputes arose by virtue of Robert Hooke's salaried employment as the Society's Curator, whereas the other Fellows were all fee-paying members. Because of his specifically defined occupation, it was Hooke's role to conceive and progress all manner of experiments, passing them over to others for completion, and then helping them when necessary. The problem was that it often became a matter of debate as to who could actually claim credit for any resultant discovery or invention.

In February 1665, Samuel Pepys described in his diary a particular Society meeting at which Hooke (then aged 30) lectured on the nature of comets, proving with dates and examples that comets are periodic. At that time there was a nine-year-old boy living nearby in Shoreditch. His name was Edmund Halley, and he grew to become one of the most famous astronomers of all time – the Astronomer Royal no less. However, for all his great accomplishments and deserved status, Halley is most popularly remembered for announcing in 1704 that comets are periodic, long after Hooke was recorded by Pepys as pronouncing the very same.

In his 1665 book of microscopic studies entitled *Micrographia*, Robert Hooke commented on the concentric bands of coloured light which appear around the central area of a tight air-space between two sheets of transparent mica pressed together. From his studies in light waves, he determined that the rings were the result of interference, and that they occur when the separation between the surfaces is of the same order as the wavelength of light. Meanwhile, there was a young fellow studying for his bachelor's degree at Cambridge named Isaac Newton. Many years later, Newton commented on these very same light bands, and today they are known as *Newton's Rings*.[12]

Long before Isaac Newton came into the group's philosophical arena, Robert Hooke began the first specifically defined research into gravity. Setting a pendulum swinging, he noted that the wider the commencing arc, the longer it took to come to a halt. But why should it come to a halt at all and what force was it that drew the pendulum gradually, through decreasing arcs, to an eventual standstill? The answer was, of course, gravity – a subject which Robert was destined to pursue, for it baffled him that everything pulled or fell downwards, except for the stars which remained in their suspended positions. There had to be scientific laws which determine the nature and function of earthly weight, or the apparent lack of it in the heavens.

Hooke's *Micrographia* is one of the greatest scientific volumes ever published, and without doubt the foremost of all works concerning microscopy and biological research. But it was not limited to views through a microscope; there were telescopic observations of the moon and stars, descriptions of his newly invented thermometer, his barometer, his wind gauge and a hygrometer for measuring atmospheric humidity. He distinguished heat from burning, citing that burning ceases when oxygen expires no matter how much heat is applied, and put forward an abundance of revelatory material which brought proven science firmly out of the vague philosophical arena in which it had existed for so long.

This then was the operative scientific world of the Rosicrucian brotherhood in England. In terms of ultimate achievement, however, the Society's heyday was far from over, and the greatest of all scientists, Isaac Newton, was yet to appear on the scene, 16 years before the 1688 Revolution.

Fire and Pestilence

While Samuel Pepys battled to resurrect a Navy that had fallen into decline during the Cromwellian era, John Evelyn and King Charles prepared a paper concerning plans to improve the environment. Both were troubled by the amount of grime and smoke which enveloped the narrow streets of London, and they called their scheme *Fumifugium*. But the politicians, with their out-of-town estates, were not remotely interested in the welfare of the city dwellers – only in the revenue derived from them – and so the scheme came to nothing. As it transpired, a little time and thought applied by the reluctant authorities at that stage might have prevented the great disasters which followed soon afterwards.

The poverty ensuing from the harsh Protectorate remained evident in the 1660s, with the towns and cities in a state of filth and decay, while the Whig aristocracy had built themselves fine country mansions with public money. Then came the long, hot summer of 1665, bringing with it the worst of all dreaded diseases: bubonic plague. Pepys recorded that it began in the June when he saw some houses in London's Drury Lane marked with red crosses and the plea written on their doors, 'Lord have mercy upon us'. By August, thousands were dying each week. Eventually, the Black Death (carried by rats and fleas) killed nearly 70,000 people in the capital alone – about 15 per cent of the population – as a result of which King Charles made another attempt to save the city. He sensed that another such summer, with severe electric storms, could so easily bring fire to the crowded timber structures that lined the streets and lanes of the capital. He approached the city authorities and gave them express permission to pull down strategically located buildings to create fire breaks, but nothing was done and the consequence was a major calamity.

Again it was Samuel Pepys who gave the news to the King and his brother James, Duke of York, after he had seen a fire spreading on 1 September 1666. He recommended, just as Charles had already suggested, that buildings must be demolished around the fire without delay. But it was too late and the blaze was already moving at an incredible rate. Subsequently, Pepys found the Lord Mayor skulking in Canning Street, knowing the disaster was his fault. With smoke and flames pouring through the alleys and billowing to the sky, King Charles became the director of operations. Hose-in-hand, he laboured among the soldiers and firemen, while his brother James organized the clearing of crucial areas to prevent an outward spread of the conflagration. In the event, however, it was a lost cause and 100,000 residents were made homeless.[13]

Through some fluke of circumstance, Gresham College and its precious library were spared, but its facilities were temporarily lost to the Royal Society. In order that the merchants and businessmen could maintain the trading economy of London, the College became an interim Royal Exchange. Hence, the Fellows' research activities were curtailed for a time and the alchemical crucibles were placed on the back burner.

To mark the Great Fire of London as a constant reminder for the generations to come, Robert Hooke designed and built the 202-ft Doric-style Monument (the tallest of its kind in the world) in Fish Hill Street, close to where the fire started, and where the edifice remains a popular visitor attracton (*see* plate 25). Given the nature of the Royal Society's cause, however, Hooke also contrived a practical purpose for the Monument, designing it with an internal spiral staircase to double as an astronomical viewing station.[14]

Gone was the city of Chaucer and Shakespeare; gone was the beautiful old St Paul's, the Royal Exchange, the Guildhall, the Custom House and the Post Office, along with 87 city churches and the halls of 44 livery companies. Indeed, four-fifths of the city was destroyed, and this accounted for one-tenth of the nation's wealth production. Quite suddenly it was an age of architects and designers, and none was more prominent than the Royal Society's Christopher Wren, who entered the fray together with his colleague Robert Hooke. With the clearing of the debris completed by early December, Wren and Hooke began to measure the streets and sites, marking them up for restoration as great piles were driven into the ground.

The Act for Rebuilding was given royal assent in February 1667, stipulating new wider streets; also that buildings were to be of brick or stone, with slate or tiled roofs and no overhanging jetties or exterior woodwork. While Wren considered the more complex architectural work, Hooke was appointed Chief Surveyor, also gaining architectural commissions for the Royal College of Physicians, Montague House and the Bethlehem Hospital. Additionally, he worked on plans for various city companies: Grocers, Merchant Taylors and Mercers, along with Christ's Hospital School and Bridewell. In preparing the design for the physicians' college, Hooke made good use of his previous work with pulley-wheels and counterweights for wheel barometers, inventing the first ever sash windows.

Meanwhile, the 34-year-old Surveyor General, Christopher Wren, was faced with the seemingly insurmountable task of replacing innumerable buildings of the greatest magnitude and complexity – so many of which (though he built them to last for ever) were to be lost in the 1940 German air-raid blitz of World War II. Prized as the best known of his city masterworks is St Paul's Cathedral, but he also rebuilt 51 other churches of the 87 that were lost in the fire. While thousands of new houses and business premises were rising like a phoenix from the ashes, another Wren masterwork was the new Royal Exchange. When this opened for business, the Royal Society moved once more to Gresham College. At the same time, Wren was working on other London buildings outside the central city, including the Chelsea Hospital, St Clement Danes, the Strand, and the area of St James's where the Royal Society Club was subsequently installed.

If Freemasonry is about geometry, architecture, building, stone-masonry and all such things as are supposedly at its core (via Hiram Abiff, Prince Edwin, King Athelstan and the rest), then no one in the course of masonic history – not even King Solomon – has done so much as Sir Christopher Wren to further the masonic cause. And yet, for all that, James Anderson – the very man who compiled the *Constitutions* on which modern Freemasonry rests –

wrote in those *Constitutions* that Wren had allowed Freemasonry to fall into 'decay'. Even the librarian and curator of the United Grand Lodge of England expressed his bewilderment at this some years ago.[15]

Gravity on a Plate

The greatest of all misfortunes to settle upon the Royal Society followed Isaac Newton's arrival on the scene in 1672. From the very beginning, Newton and Hooke were on a wrong footing, which began with a disagreement over light refraction; also because Newton lodged a formal objection to Hooke's fee-exempt status as Curator. After only a few months, Newton threatened to leave the Society, but the Secretary, intelligence agent Henry Oldenburg, pleaded for him to stay, waiving his dues too, much to the annoyance of the other Fellows.

A major argument ensued in 1675 when Newton gave a lecture entitled *Discourse on Colour*, claiming originality when, as Robert Hooke stated, 'The main of it was contained in *Micrographia*.' This set Oldenburg firmly against Hooke, leading to regular disputes. In 1678, Oldenburg died and Robert Hooke was elected to become the new Secretary, which upset Newton even further.

Isaac Newton was a man of incredible talent and, like Boyle, Wilkins, Ashmole and others, he was an ardent alchemist. He was, however, a curious character and the others could not fathom him at all. Having embarked on a translation of the *Emerald Text* of Hermes, Newton recalled from his youth that *phoenix* was an old Graeco-Phoenician word for 'crimson', and his quest for the great enlightenment led to a new decoration of his quarters – crimson furniture, carpets, curtains, quilts, cushions and hangings. At his eventual death, no other colour was mentioned in the inventory of his furnishings.[16]

Newton's religious leaning was distinctly Arian, a form of early Christianity which rejected any concept of the Holy Trinity.[17] One of

his foremost studies concerned the structure of the ancient kingdoms, and he claimed the pre-eminence of the Judaic heritage as an
archive of divine knowledge and numerology. Although he was a
deeply spiritual man and a true authority on early religion, he
refused (like Boyle) to take Holy Orders, and constantly maintained
that the New Testament had been strategically distorted by the
Church before its publication.

In January 1684, Robert Hooke was in London at *Garaway's* coffee
house, off Cornhill, with Newton, Wren and the debonair Edmund
Halley who (as an honorary Oxford graduate) had become a Society
Fellow four years after Newton. They were discussing celestial harmony – the relationship between heavenly bodies and ratios in accordance with Pythagoras' *Music of the Spheres*. In the course of this, the
questions were posed: What kept the planets suspended in their
orbital positions around the sun? Why do they not fall down?

Letters written by Hooke to Newton between 1677 and 1680
make it clear that in his earlier research Hooke had discovered gravitational law to be based upon the principle of an Inverse Square (the
force of the attraction is proportionate to the inverse square of the
distance), but Newton had responded stating that he was not interested because he was working on other things. Nevertheless, at
Garaway's the matter was raised again, with Wren and Halley agree-
ing with Hooke's Inverse Square principle, while Newton apparently did not – and so the matter rested.

Then, in 1685, Hooke's long-standing ally King Charles II died,
and within two years Newton produced his *Principia Mathematica* in
which he stated the very same Inverse Square principle that Robert
Hooke had handed to him on a plate. It became known as the *Law of
Gravity* and, with no acknowledgement of Hooke's research, it
gained Newton a primary place in scientific history. Since no one
knew how he had come to his discovery, the antiquarian William
Stukeley explained in 1752 (25 years after Isaac Newton's death) that
Newton was inspired by an apple falling from a tree – the same
dubious tale that students are taught to this day.[18]

In practice, the big difference between Hooke and Newton (and

Hooke and Halley) was that so many aspects of research begun by Robert Hooke were never properly concluded. He made some amazing discoveries, and his *Micrographia* is acknowledged as one of the greatest scientific works ever written. But comet periodicity and gravity fell into the same pending tray as his marine chronometer. It is perfectly true that Hooke theorized the Inverse Square principle – but it was Newton who proved it.

Genius of the Few

The rebuilding of London continued through 42 years, during the course of which Isaac Newton became President of the Royal Society in 1703. Christopher Wren had been knighted by King Charles II in 1673, and Isaac Newton was knighted by Queen Anne in 1705. It is in English masonic records that, on 18 May 1691, a great meeting of accepted masons took place at St Paul's to adopt Sir Christopher Wren as a brother. The lodge to which this refers is uncertain, but it is presumed to be the *Goose and Gridiron* lodge, which actually dates from that year, and later became known as the Lodge of Antiquity. Wren is now listed as having been Master of that lodge, but this is fanciful myth.[19] Wren was a staunch Tory supporter, a well-known Jacobite, and already a long-term mason who would certainly not have joined a Whig lodge to become its Master. There never was any such meeting at St Paul's. In fact, there was no St Paul's. The old building had been completely demolished; work was not begun on the new cathedral until 1675, and the scaffold and screens were not taken down until the winter of 1708. Meanwhile, no one but the workmen were allowed beyond the screens, and in May 1691 Christopher Wren was busy in Richmond, working at Hampton Court Palace for Queen Mary.[20]

St Paul's Cathedral was the last of London's reconstructions and, with the work finished, the once low-slung, shambling city displayed an elegant skyline of towers, domes, steeples and spires. It should have been the most wonderful culmination, but by that time Wren had few surviving friends or family with whom to share his triumph. Twice a widower and not marrying again, he had also lost his beloved daughter Jane. His dear friend Robert Hooke, with whom he rebuilt the City, had died in 1703, as had Samuel Pepys, while Robert Boyle had died earlier in 1691, and John Evelyn in 1706.

King Charles had been succeeded by his brother James, who was deposed by the Whigs, in favour of William and Mary in 1688, and the Royal House of Stuart – Europe's longest reigning dynasty – had reached its monarchical end. So too went the heritage of the Rosicrucian Order from Britain, and the philosophical mind-set which had inspired and fuelled the pioneers of the Gresham brotherhood, moved into France and Italy.

It was Christopher Wren's inaugural Gresham College lecture in 1657 which had cemented the original group into a formal Society. But now his visits to the coffee houses and theatres were over, for the old haunts had gone and the new ones were quite different without his friends. They had become business places for a new breed of financial marketeers. As the resurrected city became operative once again, so the fraternity of Wren's early years became a figment of history. The days of their pioneering collaboration were done, and irrespective of how the Royal Society might progress in the future, that magical half-century could never be repeated. Nevertheless, as Britain moved towards a new era of Industrial Revolution, everyone knew that none of it would have been possible were it not for the grand legacy of invention, design and discovery, unrivalled in all history, and the incomparable genius of those few.

Power and Politics

Builders and Bees

Freemasonry is described these days as being concerned with speculative rather than operative stonemasonry, but the word 'speculative' is an odd choice when used as an alternative to 'non-operative'. Freemasons use a system of signs, tokens and passwords in accordance with medieval masonic practice, and the Great Lights and working tools of lodges include various implements associated with architectural design and building: compasses (dividers), a set-square, a ruler (called a 24-inch gauge), a plumb line and so forth. But that really is about as far as lodge-working goes in symbolic stonemasonry terms, apart from allegorical representations to alignment, rectitude and perfection in life as they might be construed in practical building.

It is only since the 18th century that the term 'speculative' has fallen into common masonic use since its inclusion in a letter from the Deputy Grand Master of the premier Grand Lodge in London to a colleague at The Hague on 12 July 1757. Significantly, however, an earlier building trade publication in 1703 had used the term in a very specific way, explaining:

> Some ingenious workmen understand the speculative part of architecture or building. But of these knowing sort of artificers there are few because few workmen look any further than the mechanical, practick or working part of architecture; not regarding the mathematical or speculative part of building.[1]

In architectural terms, a building is speculative before it becomes a physical reality. That is to say, when it is the province of the speculator – the architect – rather than the builder. At that stage, when at the drawing board, the architect is *free* of the masonry, but must have knowledge of all the operative practicalities. This includes not just an awareness of stone and building materials, but also the scientific aspects of stresses, strains and other such matters. The true *free*mason is therefore the architect, just as Hiram was the architect for King Solomon's Temple, while in a broader sense the Supreme Being of Freemasonry is defined as the Great Architect of the Universe.

Historically, architects and surveyors have often been practical builders too, and have certainly operated as site overseers or masters of works. In this sense, speculative masons are not, therefore, a product of modern symbolic Freemasonry. Back in 1620, when operative members were 'admitted' into the Worshipful Company of Masons of the City of London, it was stated that speculative members were also 'accepted'.[2]

When considering the furniture and tools of Freemasonry, their scope moves from the compasses of the architect to the trowel of the artisan, with the compasses and square being two of the Three Great Lights along with the volume of Sacred Law. In the 18th-century, William Blake portrayed the Great Architect with his compasses in his depictions of the *Ancient of Days* (*see* plate 1), but this was not a newly contrived image. The French illuminated *Bible Moralisée* used the same theme back in 1245 (*see* page 216), as did the vernacular encyclopedia, *Li Livres dou Tresor*, by Dante Alighieri's mentor, Brunetto Latini, from the same era.

Greatly admired by Isaac Newton was the Rosicrucian alchemist Michael Mair (b. 1566), physician to the German Emperor Rudolph II and a colleague in England of Robert Fludd. His book *Atlanta Fugiens* became one of the earliest textual models for the Royal Society.[3] In this work, Mair introduced the image of a master mason using compasses to prepare the architecture of the Philosophers' Stone as described in the Rosary of the Philosophers[4] – the *Rosarium Philophorum*:

Make a round circle of the man and the woman, and draw out
of this a square, and out of the square a triangle. Make a round
circle, and you will have the stone of the philosophers.

The Geometry of the Philosophers' Stone

For his symbol of London's rebirth from the fire, Christopher Wren
selected the phoenix – the mythical bird which rose from the ashes
in a blaze of new enlightenment. The great phoenix effigy which
commands the south portico pediment of St Paul's Cathedral was
carved by the Danish sculptor Caius Cibber, who also produced the
distinctly masonic plaque at the base of the Monument. This image
shows London as a collapsed and grieving woman,[5] holding the
sword of the City (*see* plate 32). Accompanying her is the figure of
Expedition and some citizens, with the buildings aflame behind
them. To the right of the plaque, the masons construct the new city,

while Envy skulks in the gutter below. Peace and Plenty survey the scene from above, and King Charles II approaches (wearing Roman attire), along with Justice, Victory and Fortitude. Central to the scene is Natural Science, accompanied by Liberty and Architecture who carries the requisite square and compasses.[6] And between the figures of London and Natural Science there is a beehive.

Not only are bees the biblical creature most associated with King Solomon, the beehive is also a recognizable emblem of Freemasonry, and it denotes industry. Honeycomb, being constructed of hexagonal prisms, was considered by philosophers to be the manifestation of divine harmony in nature, and bees have always been associated with insight and wisdom, as defined in the Proverbs of Solomon 24:13–14:

> My son, eat thou honey, because it is good …
> So shall the knowledge of wisdom be unto thy soul.

The masonic beehive

The hexagon is formed by dividing the circumference of a circle by chords equivalent to its radius. This produces a figure of six equal straight sides, as found in the cells of some organic life. Consequently, bees were held to be endowed with geometrical forethought, employing strength with economy of space as their guiding principles. King Solomon's Seal (two interlaced equilateral triangles within a circle) incorporates a natural hexagon, and the resultant hexagram symbolically denotes the unity (if not the harmony) of opposites: male and female, fire and water, hot and cold, earth and air, and so on. The bee was also a traditional device of the Royal House of Stuart, and is often seen engraved as a distinguishing mark of Jacobite glassware.

To the early Merovingian Kings of the Franks (AD 451–751),[7] King Solomon was the model of earthly kingship, and the bee was a most hallowed creature. When the grave of the 5th-century King Childeric I was unearthed in 1653, some 300 small golden bees were found stitched to his cloak. Emperor Napoleon I Bonaparte had these attached to his own coronation robe in 1804 – claiming his right by virtue of a family descent from James de Rohan-Stuardo, the natural son (legitimized 1677) of Charles II Stuart of Britain by Marguerite, Duchesse de Rohan. In modern Freemasonry, the beehive is used as an emblem of industry, bonding and mutual service.

The New Foundation

Following the death of Sir Christopher Wren in 1723, those at the forefront of Hanoverian Freemasonry began to formulate an historical backdrop for their evolving, non-operative Craft. Such things as tolerance and benevolence were cemented as objectives, while signs and tokens were established, along with the aim of building a socially aware community. There was little similarity between this and the more scientific or architecturally based movements whose format they endeavoured to emulate, but a convenient biblical metaphor was to hand – the building of Solomon's Temple. By way of allegory and symbolism, the methods of the Hiramic masons of Jerusalem could be used as emblematic models for building an exemplary Craft culture – and within such a framework it was logical enough to adopt the guise of a stonemasons' guild. That apart, there does appear to have been some friction at the outset between the premier Grand Lodge and the operative trade guilds with which they sought alignment, but this was soon overcome.[8] This seems to have been effected by enticing high-ranking nobility into the fold, with John, 2nd Duke of Montagu accepting the Grand Mastership in 1721, followed by Philip, Duke of Wharton on 17 January 1723.

Only from that date were any Minutes kept of the meetings. Anderson's first *Constitutions* were officially sanctioned, and it was determined that new lodges could only be considered 'Regular' (legitimate) if they were constituted by the Grand Master or an appointed deputy. So, in spite of the initial socially-minded objec- tives, the first real moves in the process of establishing an institute of fraternal 'equality' were actually the denial of freedom in the field, and the creation of a dictatorial hierarchy! In parallel, much the same was happening within the confines of the Royal Society as it became more bureaucratic and exacting in the Georgian style.

Although installed as King of Britain in 1714, George I openly mis- trusted the English since they had already rid themselves of two kings in the previous 65 years, and had executed the Queen of Scots prior to that. He preferred to rely on his German ministers and, since he could not speak a word of English, George ran his kingly affairs from Hanover with his prime minister Robert Walpole holding the reins at Westminster from 1721.

George II succeeded his father in 1727, only to display a similar lack of empathy with the populace. Ten years later, however, King George's eldest son Frederick, Prince of Wales, was initiated into Freemasonry at Kew, and Grand Lodge thereby gained its first royal member.[9] His membership was of little consequence though – and in opposition to his father, Frederick joined the Stuart cause after the 1745 Jacobite Rising of Bonnie Prince Charlie. During the course of this civil war and the simultaneous War of Austrian Succession (1740–48), there was very little lodge activity recorded, and it is claimed that, because of these campaigns, English Freemasonry fell into a severe decline. That is the official story – in practice quite the reverse was the case; the lodges were never so lively as they were during that era.

Divided Loyalties

So much has been written about Charles Edward Stuart and his attempt to regain the crowns of his grandfather, King James II (VII), that it is not possible to retell the whole story here, except for those parts of it that directly concern Freemasonry.

Despite an encouraging start in September 1745, and some Scots victories against the troops of King George's son William, Duke of Cumberland, the campaign met a disastrous end at Culloden Moor on 16 April 1746. There followed the Prince's dramatic flight to Skye with Flora Macdonald – the rest is romantic history. In the course of all this, masonic lodges (by virtue of their secrecy) became the perfect centres for intelligence operations on both sides. Notwithstanding the regulations imposed by Grand Lodge for the licensed constitution of all other lodges, there were many lodges in London and the provinces that ignored this directive. Just because the Whig aristocracy had established their presence within the premier Grand Lodge, this did not mean there were no Tory lodges classified as 'Irregular' by the tavern-club movement. Such lodges were especially prevalent in Wales and the West of England, and the Whig and Tory opposition lodges became nests of spies and secret agents, each endeavouring to infiltrate the other to gain inside information.

Although many of the aristocratic families created after 1688 were inclined to be Whigs, many of the older landed families retained their Tory position and their traditional Stuart support – which did not end with the Battle of Culloden. Even after the Rising, Jacobitism was rife in Northumbria, through the Midlands, down to the south of the country. Across the land there was an active net-work of Jacobite societies and Tory lodges in major centres such as London, Liverpool, Preston, Norwich, Bristol and Manchester.

Wherever Charles Edward travelled south of the Border, there were prestigious safe houses at his disposal. They included Stoneleigh Abbey (baronial seat of the Leighs of Warwick), Marbury Hall, Cheshire (the home of James, Earl of Barrymore – Member of Parliament for Wigan and leader of the English Jacobites),[10] Malpas Hall, Cheshire (belonging to the Stuart envoy Richard Minshull) and Blythefield Hall, Staffordshire (seat of the noble Bagot family). In London, Charles stayed at the Essex Street home of Lady Anne Primrose, the widow of Hugh, 3rd Viscount Primrose (ancestor of Lord Rosebery). Anne had been involved with the Jacobite cause during the 1745 Rising and, following Flora Macdonald's imprison-ment in England, it was Lady Anne who secured her release and gave her financial aid. A particularly significant visit by the Prince to Lady Anne's London house is recorded in the *Stuart Papers at Windsor* as having occurred on 16–22 September 1750, some years after the Rising.[11]

In 1752, Charles stayed at Westbrook House in Godalming, Surrey, with Eleanor Oglethorpe,[12] sister of the Crown agent James Oglethorpe, who founded Georgia, USA, and built Savannah. Eleanor worked for the Stuarts with the famed Jacobite agent Dr Samuel Johnson, and with Dr William King, Principal of St Mary Hall, Oxford. Other English supporters of the Prince included the Earls of Cornbury and Derwentwater, the Lords of Chesterfield, Bath, Sandwich and Pultney, along with the Dukes of Somerset, Westmorland, Beaufort[13] and, perhaps most surprisingly, King George II's own son Frederick, Prince of Wales, who was instrumen-tal in helping Lady Anne to secure the release of Flora Macdonald.

In the Welsh sector (which included the Shropshire and Cheshire border country) there were three prominent Jacobite lodges to which many of the nobility and gentry belonged. In the south were the Sea Serjeants of Carmarthen, whose headquarters was the Masonic Lodge at the *Red Lion* in Market Street.[15] In mid-Wales was the Tory

gentlemen's Montgomeryshire Club of Twenty-Seven, while the
north operated through another Tory lodge called the Cycle of the
White Rose.[16] This was headed by Sir Watkin Williams Wynn, Lord
Lieutenant and Member of Parliament for Denbighshire. The Cycle
was headquartered at Sir Watkin's house at Winnstay; then (following his death in 1749) at his widow's property, Llangedwyn Hall
near Oswestry.

In 1747, the estate house of Berse Drelincourt was built near
Wrexham for Mary, the widow of Peter Drelincourt, Dean of
Armagh, to become a masonic charity school for the residential education of children born to exiled Jacobite nobility. Technically, the
school was registered as an orphanage and, for reasons of strict security, access was forbidden to outsiders. Lady Anne Primrose (Mary's
daughter) eventually became director of operations.

The style of Freemasonry worked within Tory lodges (such as the
Sea Serjeants and the Cycle of the White Rose in the Welsh regions)
was somewhat akin to that which led to the Antients' Grand Lodge
foundation in 1751, thereafter referring to the premier Grand Lodge
as the Moderns. In 1760, Robert Jones of Glamorgan became Grand
Master of the Welsh Freemasons, and was also a member of the *One
Ton* lodge in Noble Street, London, along with the *Black Lion* lodge in
Jockey Field.[17] A close friend of the political activist John Wilkes, he
also attended other Tory lodges in London at the *Antwerp Tavern*, the
Turk's Head and *The Shakespeare*. Prior to Jones' appointment, the
Carmarthen Grand Masters of the 1750s were Sir Edward Mansell of
Trimsaran and David Gwynne of Talaris from 1754. (Plate 10 illus-
trates a summons of *The Globe* Lodge, Fleet Street, during this era.)

The following example of the scale of the inter-lodge hostility that
prevailed at this time comes from the *Transactions of the Antiquarian
Society* and from London's *Gentleman's Magazine and Historical Review,
1755*. Unable to infiltrate the Tory's *Red Lion* lodge in Market Street,
Carmarthen, at a time when borough elections were taking place, the
Whigs instituted their own new lodge at the nearby *Greyhound* in
Bridge Street. Arguments led to scuffles which, in turn, led to several
injuries and the killing of the *Red Lion* barber, whereupon wholesale

warfare erupted in the streets as reinforcements came in from out of town. The Tories occupied the castle, and the Whigs took the town hall. 'In short', wrote one correspondent, 'the town is full of fire, smoke and tumult.'[18] Another report stated that people were 'armed with guns, swords and other offensive weapons – threatening, assaulting, beating, knocking-down, wounding, maiming, shooting at and killing several'.[19] After the disturbances had died down, the rival masonic lodges each began legal proceedings against the other.

This was the state of Britain's Freemasonry in the 1740s and 1750s, at a time when the premier Grand Lodge lost 72 of its 271 member branches, yet the official records are remarkably quiet. William, 5th Lord Byron (great-uncle of the poet), was elected as Grand Master in 1747, and was never seen again in a masonic lodge until he nominated a successor in 1752.[20] Subsequently, he caused public feeling to well up against Freemasonry when he killed his neighbour, William Chatworth, in a sword fight at the *Star and Garter* in London's Pall Mall.

Even the individual member Freemasons whose lodges were tied to premier Grand Lodge were unhappy at this time, and they were especially angered when a *Bill of Incorporation* was presented to Parliament by their masters in 1768. By virtue of its terms, the feeling against the concept was intense, and members complained that it would constitute a legal way for the hierarchy to misappropriate their charity contributions for other purposes. At the outset, Horace Walpole, Earl of Oxford and son of Robert (the late Prime Minister), had written to a colleague, 'The Free Masons are in such low repute now in England ... I believe that nothing but a persecution could bring them into vogue again.'

In masonic circles, the most frequently given reason for the hostile 18th-century conflict between the Ancients and the Moderns is that the Ancients must have been Irish and unable to gain access to the English lodges – so they started their own! But the truth is far more straightforward than that. Whether English, Scots, Irish or Welsh, it was a party-political feud. The Ancients were essentially Jacobite Tories, whereas the Moderns were mostly Hanoverian Whigs.

The Dunkerley Episode

Prince Frederick predeceased his father in 1751 and, when George II died in 1760, he was succeeded by Frederick's eldest son as King George III. Soon afterwards, following an induction meeting at the *Horn Tavern* in London, three of the new King's brothers – the Dukes of Gloucester, York and Cumberland – were each given the spurious title of Past Grand Master by premier Grand Lodge.[21] This ensured that the Royal Family was wholly attached to their branch of the Craft, while also giving the impression to outsiders that Grand Lodge had a more solid foundation than in reality. From that point, the scene was set for a masonic institution headed by Hanoverian royalty, as it remains today.

The American War of Independence (1775–83) was a major world event in masonic terms since George Washington, John Hancock, Benjamin Franklin and other Founding Fathers of the emergent new Republic were Freemasons. But how could these eminent men be attached to a fraternity that was so heavily influenced by the very royal house whose colonial authority they challenged?

This fascinating aspect of transatlantic history is more than worthy of its own section in this book, and it shall be examined in detail in chapter 17. Meanwhile, the point to hold in mind is that the Tory Ancients and the Whig Moderns were competitive, antagonistic, and supported wholly conflicting political viewpoints. There were two distinct and opposing forms of Freemasonry in the latter 1700s, and the relationship between America and the Tory faction was far stronger than any academic history book is ever likely to reveal.

In 1782, Prince Henry, Duke of Cumberland, was installed as overall Grand Master in London and, with this formal royal patronage, the masonic cause of the Moderns was considerably strengthened. Another prominent character of the moment, known as Thomas Dunkerley, was an illegitimate son of George II. Born in 1724, he served (from the age of 10) in the Royal Navy, and his royal birthright was not announced until he was over 40. Having been initiated into Freemasonry in 1754, Dunkerley formed lodges in many of the ships in which he served, and when his parentage was recognized he was granted a personal income and rooms at Hampton Court Palace. Subsequently, he became Provincial Grand Master in numerous regions.[22]

The Duke of Cumberland died in 1790, whereupon his nephew, the Prince of Wales (later King George IV), took up the reins as Grand Master – at least nominally. In practice, he appointed a deputy to carry out the functions of the post.

In 1791, Dunkerley decided to introduce high degrees of a presumed Knight Templar style into English Freemasonry. He formed the Supreme Grand and Royal Conclave, inviting George III's young son, Prince Edward (the later Duke of Kent), to be overall Patron of an Order that would assume control of the said high degrees. But Dunkerley died in 1795, and no one really knew what the Supreme Grand and Royal Conclave was. It seems to have been little more than Dunkerley himself, possibly with the aid of a friend's sister, whom he referred to in correspondence as the Lady Patroness. There were, however, a number of regionally affiliated 'encampments' (lodges) whose members appointed Thomas Parkins, Lord Rancliffe, to succeed Dunkerley. But in all the 11 years of his appointment, Rancliffe only attended one meeting,[23] which was one more than the Duke of Kent attended!

Legal Exemption

During this period, and following the French Revolution (1789–99), an innovatory concept of voting was put forward by the British author Thomas Paine in his *The Rights of Man*. He suggested that people should have the right to appoint and change their own governments. This was too much for the Georgian politicians – Paine was indicted for treason and fled to Calais in 1792. By that time, almost every town in Britain had a Constitutional Information Club, or a Society of Friends. In 1793, the British Convention of

People's Delegates was held in Edinburgh and, in response to their plea for better workers' representation, the Government duly transported the leaders to the colonies. Hostilities were then commenced against the French who, along with the Americans, were said to have fuelled a widespread anti-Hanover mood in Britain.

Subsequently, the long-standing *Habeas Corpus Act* was suspended by prime minister William Pitt (the Younger) in 1794, so that citizens could be kept in prison indefinitely without need for trial. Following Pitt's *Unlawful Oaths Act* of 1797, Government spies roamed the country, bringing in anyone who belonged to a workers' group that Westminster deemed seditious, and they were duly sentenced without a hearing. (It was under the terms of this Act that the Tolpuddle Martyrs of Dorset were arrested long afterwards in 1834, and charged at the Dorchester Assizes with 'administering unlawful pledges of loyalty'.) Even the Royal Navy did not escape the harsh judgements in 1797. Most sailors were press-ganged into service, only to be treated abominably with miserable pay and conditions. But when seamen of the Fleet at Nore (near Sheerness) demonstrated for a revised ship-board policy and a grant of two meals a day instead of one, their leaders were hanged.[24] At this time, Britain was in a desperate position; France had conquered the Netherlands, and controlled the Dutch Fleet. France had also made an alliance with Spain, and practically controlled the Spanish Fleet.

Then, within a general stirring of public unrest, Pitt made it unlawful to speak, write or to have any opinion against the Government. He sent German troops into Ireland in 1797, prompting an Irish rebellion in the following year, which led to the arrest and death of the prominent leader Lord Edward Fitzgerald. Pitt then introduced the *Unlawful Societies Act* in 1799, whereupon workers' groups and unlicensed public meetings of any kind were forbidden anywhere in Britain. The coming together of men into any form of club or society for negotiation of improved working conditions or wages was henceforth defined as a punishable conspiracy. In fact, any organization which held secretive meetings came under the wrap of this Act which, potentially, could have closed all the masonic lodges. Given the royal patronage that applied, however, Pitt was pressured and obliged to relent in favour of Grand Lodge so that Freemasonry was made uniquely exempt from the law.[25]

The Sussex Years

One of the Duke of Kent's brothers was Prince Augustus, Duke of Sussex, who (despite his Hanoverian status) married twice into Jacobite families. He was first married in Rome to Lady Augusta Murray, daughter of the 4th Earl of Dunmore, on 4 April 1793. But this marriage was formally annulled in the following year because it had not been sanctioned by King George III, and therefore contravened the *Royal Marriages Act* of 1772. Much later, Augustus married Lady Celia Saunders, daughter of the 2nd Earl of Arran, on 2 May 1831. She was granted the style Duchess of Inverness, but the marriage was similarly deemed to be in breach of the Act.[26] However, in 1793 (the year of his first marriage) Augustus had resigned his right of succession to the British Crown, and pursued his own course irrespective of the restrictive Hanoverian statute.

In 1812, Sussex was installed as Grand Master of the Supreme Grand and Royal Conclave, but in the following year, with the Antients and Moderns finally amalgamated, he was also invited to become Grand Master of the new United Grand Lodge, which did not condone the higher degrees of the Conclave. This placed the Duke in a difficult situation, but he decided to accept the office and ride out the storm. In addition to that (and following some heated disputes about who had rights of supreme authority over the masons in France), Augustus was afforded another position in 1819, when selected to head the French Supreme Council in Britain.[27] This greatly appealed to him because, in contrast to Dunkerley's pseudo-Grand Conclave, it was a Templar-style institution with its roots in the exiled Stuart Rite, and would grant him the high-degree patent in Britain.

By virtue of his family ruining his first marriage, Augustus was rather more inclined towards Stuart than Hanoverian sympathy, and so he accepted the nomination. The trouble was that he could not tell his masonic colleagues in England about the plan, and therefore had his masonic secretary make the arrangements. This man was Joseph Hippolyte da Costa, the Portuguese mason who had been extricated by his English friends from papal custody, and who wrote about the Dionysian Artificers (*see* page 31). In the event, the office proved to be a title without a function because there was nothing the Duke could do to further his appointment without making his French collaboration known.

From this somewhat egotistical masonic era of Grand Councils and Supreme Conclaves, comes an intriguing and very ordinary sounding name, listed among all the aristocrats and royalty. It appears in the 1845 *Statutes of the Temple* by authority of the Grand Conclave in Scotland which states that in 1808 a certain 'Mr Alexander Deuchar was elected Commander of the Edinburgh Templars'. These are the *Statutes* of a pseudo-Templar Conclave in Scotland that had a serious effect on the relationship between English and Irish Freemasons before and after the amalgamation of the Ancients and Moderns.

Alexander Deuchar was a seal-engraver who became aware of the possibility of a French Templar Council being instituted in Britain long before the offer to head such a body was made to Duke Augustus. The background negotiations had begun when the French Council was itself formed in 1804. Major Müller of the 1st Royal Foot had the ear of the Duke's brother, Prince Edward, Duke of Kent, and Deuchar conspired with Müller to approach Edward for a Charter of Dispensation to establish an anti-Jacobite Templar authority in Scotland.

Deuchar's brother, David, was an officer in the Peninsula War (Britain against France in Portugal, 1808–14) and, during the campaign at Leira in Portugal, he stole the altar cross from a Templar chapel in the Castle of Tomar in order to aid his brother's endeav-our. In the old days, the Deuchars had served Scotland well and, from the time of Bannockburn (24 June 1314) and beyond, the Great Sword of Deuchar, with its family coat-of-arms, was a wel-come sight on any battlefield. By 1745, however, the table had turned, and the Deuchar allegiance swayed, so that Lyon of East Ogil (a Jacobite supporter of Charles Edward Stuart) made it his business to carry off the prized heirloom. The sword was, never-theless, retrieved after Culloden, to be held by the Hanoverian supporter Alexander Deuchar when he began his discussions with the Duke of Kent.

Seeing his opportunity to get a firm Hanoverian foothold in Scotland, the Duke agreed to Deuchar's request, and the new estab-lishment became known as the Scottish Conclave, with Deuchar as its Grand Master. However, the Duke of Kent asserted that the English Masonic rules must be followed, and that he would himself be the Royal Grand Patron of the Conclave established 'in that part of Great Britain called Scotland'. Not surprisingly, within a few decades influential Whigs were allowed to buy their way into the Conclave. The Duke of Leeds, for example (who had no Templar training) was admitted in 1848, to become Steward of the Great Priory within just a few months, and the Episcopal Bishop of Edinburgh was similarly admitted.[28]

The Scottish Grand Conclave was formally constituted in 1811, and falling under Deuchar's banner of intended Scottish subjuga-tion were several traditional Templar lodges of the legitimate Irish Grand Encampment whose warrants were from Ireland. In 1826, the Grand Master of these lodges in Scotland was Robert Martin, who wanted nothing whatever to do with the Deuchar interlopers or the Duke of Kent. The Conclave was formally denounced by the Dublin Encampment on 28 December 1827. All Encampment Templars who had succumbed to the unethically created Hanoverian protectorate in Scotland were instructed to surrender their original Irish warrants to Robert Martin. In condemning the establishment of the Deuchar Conclave, the Irish document stated,

'Every ancient Sir Knight knows that the Duke of Kent had no more authority to do so than Deuchar himself.'[29]

This completes an overview of the first 100 years of the new-style English Freemasonry as it evolved during the Georgian era. There is little mention in the records of those symbolic or charitable ideas that were seemingly in the minds of the original tavern-club members of the early 1700s. Apart from internal wrangling and disputes between different factions, the century was mainly concerned with the establishment of power bases and grand titles. There are references, here and there, of an evolving lodge ritual, which was added to at various stages – the first mention of the Temple pillars *Jachin* and *Boaz*, for example, occurring in 1762.[30] Not until the 1800s did anything that might be recognized by today's masons begin to take shape. The basic ceremonial format was settled in around 1816, while the philosophical and moral concepts were very much a product of the latter Victorian era. Despite the fact that the newly initiated Entered Apprentice Freemason believes himself to be in a privileged realm of ancient mysteries, there is actually not that much in modern ritual that can claim to be especially ancient, except in theory. This is not a criticism of current masonic practice, it is simply a recognition that the historical provenance of certain aspects is not always correct in the way it is conveyed.

6

Imperial Conquest

The Celtic Realms

Although there was a Grand Master for Wales by the middle 1700s, there was no formally constituted Grand Lodge as such. In Ireland and Scotland, however, Grand Lodges were established as separate institutions to the Grand Lodge of England, and they remain independent today. The Grand Lodge of Ireland was founded in 1725, and the Grand Lodge of Antient, Free and Accepted Masons of Scotland in 1736.

Documentary evidence of Freemasonry in Ireland dates back to the 1600s, and the present headquarters is in Dublin. The journal *Dublin Weekly* of 26 June 1725 relates that two days earlier Richard, Earl of Rosse, was installed as Grand Master of Ireland, and the story of privately-run Irish lodges immediately prior to this is worth noting.[1]

Unlike in the English system, women were not necessarily precluded from becoming masons in Ireland. A well-documented lady Freemason of the era was the Hon Elizabeth St Leger (b. 1693), sister of the 4th Viscount of Doneraile, County Cork.[2] Initiated in about 1715, Elizabeth's later portrait depicts her in a masonic attitude and wearing her apron.[3] Following the Earl of Rosse, the Irish Grand Master from 1731 was James, Lord Kingston. His father had been a Jacobite exile with King James and, on returning to Ireland in 1693, he was charged with recruiting for the Stuart cause. The same happened with Grand Master James in 1722.

The Honourable Elizabeth St Leger

The first extant reference to Freemasonry in Ireland comes from a student graduation speech delivered at Trinity College, Dublin, in 1688. It was stated that a new college was to be established with a society of Freemasons.[4] The penal laws William of Orange (*Billy Windmills* to his Irish subjects) drew up against the people of Ireland, Protestants and Catholics alike, were extremely harsh, particularly his ruinous 1699 prohibition of Irish wool exports to England. Many have wondered why the Protestants of Ireland were shamefully treated by the monarch they had served so well at the Battle of the Boyne – especially when his wife, Queen Mary, was a convinced Protestant – but the answer is straightforward. The trade sanction was imposed in 1699, but Mary had died in 1694, leaving William as the sole ruler. His interests were not with Britain or Ireland, and they were certainly not with the Protestants. His mission throughout was to maximize Holland's trading position against that of France. In Scotland, where the masonic tradition dates back to much earlier times, King William was equally ruthless, even though Scotland was a Protestant nation with a National Kirk. In fact, the Scots had been subjected to a blanket excommunication in the days of Robert the Bruce for standing against the Catholic King Edward of England. In this light it is surprising that for all his blatantly anti-Protestant behaviour, William III is still considered by so many to have been a champion of the Protestant cause.

When King James was deposed in December 1688, the Scots in general were most displeased at the loss of their dynastic monarchy, and in the very next year came the first Jacobite Rising. On 27 July 1689, Viscount Graham of Claverhouse (known as Bonnie Dundee), led a force of Highlanders against King William's troops at Killiecrankie, near Perth. The Scots' charge was successful, but Dundee was mortally wounded and died without knowing he had been appointed King's General. A few weeks later the Highlanders were less fortunate when defeated at Dunkeld. A particularly intriguing fact, however, comes from the Benedictine abbot Dom Augustin Calmet (1672–1757). He recorded that when Viscount Dundee fell at Killiecrankie he was wearing the Grand Prior's cross and sash of the Knights Templars – a pre-masonic Order which, according to a majority of modern reference sources, ceased to exist in 1307.[5]

Early in his reign, King William instructed that all Highland Chiefs should swear an oath of allegiance to him, but the majority were reluctant to comply. Their kings had always sworn fealty to the nation, rather than the reverse. In order to force the issue, Sir John Dalrymple, Secretary of State for Scotland, was empowered to persecute one reluctant clan as an example to the others. He chose the Macdonalds of Glencoe, who had failed to meet the deadline of 1 January 1692. The ageing MacDonald chief, MacIain, had actually tried to swear his oath at Fort William on 30 December, but no Crown officer was present, and as a result he did not manage to comply until 6 January – almost a week late.

Unlike some other clans, the Macdonalds had no military strength and so were easy prey. Their settlement nestled between the towering mountains of Glencoe, which constituted more of a geographical trap than a natural fortress. On 1 February, Dalrymple sent two companies of Argyll's Regiment, under Robert Campbell of Glenlyon, to exterminate the unsuspecting clan. Arriving in the guise of a peaceful mission, the soldiers took lodging with the hospitable families for many days. Then, on the bitter morning of 13 February, they cut down every Macdonald they could find, sparing neither the women, the elderly, nor the young. Not surprisingly, the dreadful Glencoe Massacre had the opposite effect to that intended. Instead of intimidating the clans into supporting the new regime, it caused them to form a strong Jacobite confederacy against the ruthless Dutchman and his Government. (In the next chapter the long-standing history of Templarism and Freemasonry in Scotland is investigated.)

The masonic Grand Lodge of Scotland was founded some years after those of England and Ireland. The reason for this might have been the much wider scope of Scottish Freemasonry, which had many more independent lodges from which to obtain agreement. Of the 100 lodges invited to the foundation meeting, representatives from only 33 attended. The other two-thirds did not see the point of a central regulatory body. By virtue of this, the Edinburgh-based Grand Lodge could not exert its authority in the same way as the London group and so the lodges were permitted to retain their own procedures, regalia and ritual. Subsequently, as new lodges were formed after 1736, it was necessary to afford them the same privilege.[6] The situation remains the same today and, although lodges in Scotland are chartered by Grand Lodge, they retain their individual modes of operation, and there is no rigidly standard ritual.

The Grand Lodge of Scotland is keen to assert that theirs is the only nation capable of proving a direct documented connection between operative stonemasonry and speculative Freemasonry. Certainly, Scotland holds the oldest masonic records in the world and even in today's lodge workings a stonemason's maul is used by the Master and Wardens.

The dissident preacher, Dr James Anderson (1680–1739), who prepared the 1723 *Constitutions* for the Grand Lodge of England, had been born into a Scottish masonic family. His father was a lodge member in Aberdeen, although there is no record of James having been initiated there. Well-known Scottish Freemasons of the 1700s included the poet Robert Burns, the architect Robert Adam, the author Sir Walter Scott, and John Paul Jones of Kirkcudbright, who founded the American Navy.

Edict of Rome

Back in England, the Grand Master Augustus, Duke of Sussex, died in 1843. During the 1750s, the Welsh Grand Master frequented a London lodge at the *Turk's Head* in Greek Street, Soho (*see* page 75). This was a lodge of The Most Antient and Honourable Fraternity of Free and Accepted Masons (the Antients), who had formed their Grand Lodge in 1751. Their original Grand Secretary was the Irish artist and wine merchant Laurence Dermott, who had been initiated into a Dublin lodge 10 years earlier. When publishing the *Constitutions of the Antients* in 1756, Dermott stated that the premier Grand Lodge (the Moderns) had perverted masonic traditions, and he moulded the Antients into a far more democratic organization.[7]

Unlike the Moderns, the Grand Master of the Antients had no independent or final authority in respect of existing or newly appointed lodges. Everything had to be ratified by mutual consent of the officers. Travelling warrants were issued into the military regiments so that lodges could be established and convened wherever the troops were stationed at home or abroad. This enabled the Antients to grow at a much faster pace than the Moderns, and there was a good deal of friction between the two.

In line with the York-based Grand Lodge of All England, the Antients differed considerably from the Moderns because they did not limit their function to the three degrees of English Craft Freemasonry. They and York (whose foundation lodge dated back to 1705) had an additional Chapter for the working of Royal Arch ritual, along with a different structure for their Knight Templar units (*see* page 148). In the event, the York Grand Lodge wound up in 1792, while the Antients and Moderns subsequently amalgamated on 27 December 1813. Prior to that, Augustus of Sussex was Grand Master of the Moderns, and his brother Edward, Duke of Kent, was Grand Master of the Antients. At the time of amalgamation, Edward stepped down to leave Augustus as the overall Grand Master of the new United Grand Lodge of England.[8] Lodges from each branch were then renumbered, with the Grand Master's Lodge of the Ancients becoming No 1, and the Moderns' Lodge of Antiquity becoming No 2. The rest were numbered alternately. Provincial Grand Lodges were formalized to run the regions, and the *Constitutions* were restructured into a new format in 1819.

When Augustus died, Thomas Dundas, Earl of Zetland (Shetland), took the reins for 27 years, during which period Freemasons' Hall in Great Queen Street, London, was substantially rebuilt and extended. He was followed by George Robinson, Lord Ripon – son of Frederick, Earl Grey (Whig prime minister 1830–34). However, George resigned the Grand Mastership in 1874 in order to join the Catholic Church, subsequent to which he became Viceroy of India.[9]

The Catholic Church had formally opposed and denounced Freemasonry from the time that Anderson's revised *Constitutions* were published. There have been numerous significant Vatican pronouncements in this respect,[10] with over a dozen in the 19th century alone. The first, known as *In Eminenti*, was a Bull of Pope Clement XII in 1738. He classified Freemasons as 'depraved and perverted', and decreed that they 'are to be condemned and prohibited, and by our present constitution, valid for ever, we do hereby condemn and prohibit them'. He added that Freemasonry has contempt for ecclesiastical authority, and that its members plot 'the overthrow of the whole of religious, political, and social order based on Christian institutions'. Clement concluded:

> We desire and command that both bishops and prelates and other local ordinaries, as well as inquisitors for heresy, shall

investigate and proceed against transgressors of whatever
state, grade, condition, order dignity or pre-eminence they may
be; and they are to pursue and punish them with condign
penalties as being most suspect of heresy.

As a result of this edict, Catholics were placed under penalty of
excommunication, incurred *ipso facto*, and were strictly forbidden to
enter or promote masonic societies in any way.[11]

In 1864, after numerous other denouncements, it was the turn of
Pope Pius IX to condemn Freemasonry with his encyclical letter,
Quanta Cura. This censured societies which draw no distinction
between 'the true religion and false ones'. Coming from the Catholic
hierarchy, this was very much a repeat of the way in which the
Anglican Church had admonished King James II (VII) for tolerating
different religions whilst granting people the liberty of their conscience. In this context, Pope Pius wrote that such organizations dare
to assert that 'liberty of conscience and worship is each man's personal right ... They do not think and consider that they are teaching
the liberty of sedition'.

The strange thing about all this is that Freemasonry, just like all
manner of other clubs and societies, was not (and is not) a religion,
nor in any way a religious institution. Hence, it is open to all. The
problematical difference between Freemasonry and other private
associations, as far as the Catholic Church was concerned, was that
Freemasonry embodied a vow of secrecy. This was contrary to the
'confessional' tradition of the doctrine, and was solemn enough to
override the Church obligation to confide secrets to one's priest. In
short, Freemasonry was an environment within which the Church
lacked the power of authority as it had in other walks of life.

A later encyclical from Pope Leo XIII in 1884 pursued this viewpoint even further. Whereas the previous decrees had suggested that
Freemasonry was irreligious, Leo's *Humanum Genus* went further in
claiming that it was anti-religious. When discussing 'that strongly
organized and widespread association called the Freemasons',
he stated:

No longer making any secret of their purposes, they are now boldly rising up against God himself. They are planning the destruction of the Holy Church publicly and openly, and with this the set purpose of utterly despoiling the nations of Christendom … We pray and beseech you, venerable brethren, to join your efforts with Ours, and earnestly to strive for the extirpation of this foul plague.

In order to put the masonic view of religious tolerance into perspective, we can see that, from the very outset of the 1723 *Constitutions*, this item of concern was addressed in a manner which made the position very clear:

Concerning God and religion: A mason is obliged by his tenure to obey the moral law; and if he rightly understands the Art, he will never be a stupid atheist nor an irreligious libertine. But though in ancient times masons were charged in every country to be of the religion of that country or nation, whatever it was, yet 'tis now thought more expedient only to oblige them to that religion in which all men agree, leaving their particular opinions to themselves: that is to be good men and true, or men of honour and honesty, by whatever denominations or persuasions they may be distinguished.

Although the definitions, 'stupid atheist' and 'irreligious libertine' have been superseded, along with a generally better wording since that time, the basic premise still prevails in that Freemasonry is religiously tolerant even though not religiously based.

Missing Documents

At the departure of George, Lord Ripon, United Grand Lodge realized another splendid coup in December 1874 when, Albert Edward, Prince of Wales (later King Edward VII), accepted the nomination as

Grand Master. This added particular weight to the Masonic Charge after initiation:

> Ancient no doubt it is, having subsisted from time immemorial. In every age, monarchs have been promoters of the Art,[12] have not thought it derogatory to their dignity to exchange the sceptre for the trowel, have participated in our mysteries and joined in our assemblies.

Electing to resign his office on his accession to the throne in 1901, Edward remained Protector of the Order,[13] but during his 26-year term he took Freemasonry to a new level of international prominence. This was particularly the case on the occasion of his mother Queen Victoria's golden jubilee. To celebrate this event, and also to make the point to Grand Lodges abroad that Imperial Britain still held a form of masonic sovereignty, Edward convened a special Jubilee Grand Lodge in 1897, with his brother Arthur (Duke of Connaught) and his son Albert (Duke of Clarence) in attendance (*see* plate 14).

A few years earlier, steps had been taken to clear the field of any potential opposition from supporters of the Royal House of Stuart, which had been responsible for the dissemination of traditional Scots (*Ecossais*) Freemasonry in France and other parts of Europe from 1688. Even from as late as 1733, some while after the foundation of premier Grand Lodge, there are records of *Ecossais* high degrees and Scots Masters at the *Devil's Tavern* lodge, Temple Bar, in London.[14] And, perhaps surprisingly for the Victorian era, the Jacobite Cycle of the White Rose (*see* page 75) had been revived in 1886 by Bertram, 5th Earl of Ashburnham. His colleagues in this were Melville Henri Massue, 9th Marquis de Ruvigny, along with the Celtic language authority Henry Jenner FSA, the writer and press correspondent Herbert Vivian, and the Hon Stuart Erskine.

The *Jacobite Peerage*, compiled by Melville de Ruvigny, relates that in the autumn of 1886, a select number of prominent people were sent elaborately sealed pamphlets from the White Rose (a traditional emblem of James II, Duke of York) marked 'Private and Confidential'.[15]

The communication reads as follows:

> For a long time past, it has seemed desirable that some efforts
> should be made to bring together those who, by hereditary
> descent or community of sentiment, are in sympathetic accord
> on the subject of history and the misfortunes of the Royal House
> of Stuart. It is now close to two-hundred years since the
> Revolution of 1688 dispossessed that House from the Throne of
> Great Britain. The chivalrous devotion of so many Englishmen
> and Scotsmen to that House, which they regarded as their lawful
> Sovereign, has never received a fitting tribute of respect and
> honour from those who, with an affectionate intensity, admire
> and reverence the disinterested loyalty of the noble men and
> women who freely gave up life and fortune for a Sacred Cause.

This approach by mail gave rise to a number of supportive replies,
and plans were made for a grand Stuart Exhibition in London. Relics
and relevant documents arrived from all over Britain, and arrangements were made to hold the display at the New Gallery
in 1889 to mark the bicentenary of Stuart exile. By 1887, plans
were under way, and two years later the Exhibition took place – but it
was not sponsored by the White Rose as originally planned. Instead,
by way of a strategic manoeuvre of the Imperial court, the patronage
was taken over by Queen Victoria herself. Notwithstanding Lord
Ashburnham's leadership of the White Rose, the Queen appointed
him president of the display, but retained her own control by excluding Ruvigny, Erskine, Vivian and Jenner. This was particularly hard
on Henry Jenner who, as Keeper of Manuscripts at the British
Museum, had been responsible for the Exhibition's manuscript collection, much of which was never seen again by the respective owners.

Aided in France by Marie, dowager Countess of Caithness,
plans had been made by Anne, Duchess of Roxburghe (Mistress
of Robes for the Queen), and others to organize a coinciding event
in Scotland. Charles Benedict Stuart, 4th Count of Albany in descent
from Prince Charles Edward, was invited to attend from Italy, but was

found dead soon afterwards. The circumstances were suspicious, and there was a common belief that he had been murdered.[16] Charles had supposedly fallen from his horse, but Father Torquato Armellini (Postulator of the Jesuits in Rome) maintained that his demise was in no way consistent with the presumed fall. In fact, the *post-mortem* examination revealed that Charles had died from suffocation.[17]

Prince Charles Benedict James Stuart, 4th Count of Albany,
after a representation by Michele Cammarano, c. 1868

The 1904–21 *Jacobite Peerage* relates that the Stuart documents which disappeared after the Exhibition were not the only such papers to go missing in the Hanoverian era. In 1817 (during the reign of King George III), a Dr Robert Watson purchased a collection of manuscripts concerning the Stuart dynasty. He bought them in Rome, where they had been the property of Cardinal Henry Stuart, the younger brother of Bonnie Prince Charlie. Watson paid £23.00 sterling (equivalent to about £1,000 today), and prepared to publish the contents, but the files were seized and taken to London. Some time later, he received an *ex gratia* payment from Westminster for having been deprived of his property. Not content with this, he pursued his right to the collection – but he too was found mysteriously dead (supposedly having committed suicide) in 1838. The papers have never since appeared in the public domain, and their whereabouts remain a matter of conjecture.

Subsequent to the Exhibition fiasco, Ruvigny, Vivian and Erskine founded the Legitimist Jacobite League of Great Britain and Ireland. In 1892, they attempted to lay a wreath at the Charing Cross statue of King Charles I in London, but were again blocked by Queen Victoria, who sent 'a considerable detachment of police' to obstruct the ceremony. In the wake of this, Herbert Vivian spent much of his time abroad as foreign news correspondent for the *Morning Post*, the *Daily Telegraph* and the *Daily Express*. Henry Jenner, a constant protagonist of the Celtic realms, wrote his noted *Handbook of the Cornish Language*, and became a Bard of the Breton Gorsedd, promoting the culture and arts of Brittany. Lord Ashburnham and the Marquis de Ruvigny also departed from the political stage to direct their future interests towards chivalric endeavours. In 1908, Ruvigny became Grand Master of the Stuart Order of the Realm of Sion – a continuation of Scotland's Order of the Thistle (equivalent to England's Order of the Garter) whose title had been usurped by the English Crown. This international organization later merged with its allies, the Knights Protectors of the Sacred Sepulchre, and the Order of the Sangréal (Holy Grail) – a long-standing dynastic Order of the Royal House of Stuart, founded in 1689.[18]

The Great Divide

The reign of Queen Victoria, *Regina et Imperatrix*, saw an amazing boom in masonic interest. In London, the number of lodges increased from 100 to 382, and the provinces showed a commensurate increase. On a global scale, English lodges numbered 2,543 throughout the British Empire by the end of the 19th century.[19] Clubs and Societies multiplied considerably within Victorian middle-class society, and Freemasonry was by far the largest and most influential of these in a period when imposing masonic halls and opulent lodges were built in a number of major centres. Although not at the Jubilee Grand Lodge with Edward, Arthur and Albert in 1897, Prince Edward's younger brother Leopold (who had died shortly before) was also a Freemason, and the Craft had become a truly royal institution. Throughout the land, masons, by definition, achieved a celebrity status, opening churches, theatres and pavilions, and Freemasonry, with openly paraded regalia, became a focus of public ceremony. The foundation stone for the Shakespeare Memorial Theatre at Stratford-on-Avon was laid with full masonic honours by William, Lord Leigh, Provincial Grand Master of Warwickshire, in 1877.[20] Similar events were held to establish Truro Cathedral in 1880, and the York Institute in 1883.[21] Truro was the first cathedral to be consecrated in England since the 16th-century Protestant Reformation, and Prince Edward's laying of the foundation stone led to other masonic cathedral foundations at Rochester, Peterborough and Liverpool.

Regular masonic newspapers also emerged in this era: *The Freemason* in 1869 and *The Freemason's Chronicle* in 1875. There was nothing discreet about being a Freemason in those times – in fact, quite the opposite; it was truly a mark of social prestige. Even private groups that were in no way masonic made applications for warrants to become lodges. The Savage Club, for example – a fraternity of writers, artists and thespians of London's bohemian sect – was consecrated at Freemasons' Hall on 18 January 1887, with the actor Sir Henry Irving as its Treasurer.[22] When French masons came to Britain, they could hardly believe the pomp and pageantry of the English institution, nor indeed the personal cost of it to members. Since the French Revolution (1789–99), such displays of class and financial status had become unfamiliar to them, while as republicans they were baffled by the apparent preoccupation with monarchy.

The French masonic journal *Le Monde Maçonnique* went so far as to criticize English Freemasonry for its cathedral bequests, claiming that it should concentrate rather more on moral architecture. In line with this, the Grand Orient of France asserted that the United Grand Lodge of England was like 'a body without a soul'. In retaliation,

The Freemason expressed the view that the English system was more solid and grounded than that of the French, which it described as too mystical and esoteric. There had always been differences because the Franco-Scottish system was founded on far more ancient traditions, whereas the more lately contrived English system had spent nearly two centuries endeavouring to find its feet. And it found them in what was a regeneration of medieval feudal benevolence – a realm of aristocratic and wealthy benefactors, adherents of the Empire who aspired to a popular Robin Hood image without having to steal from the rich. They were the rich.

This might not have been Freemasonry in its true sense, but it was an admirable enough concept. However, the French made the point that while there were visible displays of apparent altruism, cathedrals and pavilions did little to address the basic everyday needs of people at large. In respect of such matters as education and medical care, those who received the main benefit were the families of the lodge members. Again, there was nothing especially wrong with this. It is precisely the way that insurance companies, educational trusts and health-care institutions work today: those who pay the premiums receive the mutually sponsored benefits. But it was anathema to the French, who regarded themselves as 'citizens' first and masons second.

As far as the English masons were concerned, they had simply perpetuated the small-time Box Club tradition of the early trade guilds, and the fact that it had grown to big-league status was a sign of its operational success, not a mark of any fault in the system. In any event, since French masonry could not compete on equal-benefit terms for its members, and was certainly not a public welfare organization either, England's fraternity was consoled. Even if there might be areas for improvement, they still had a great deal of which to be proud.

The down-side of this was that Victorian Britain supported a great social divide. It was the hub of a wealthy and all-powerful Empire, but the poverty-stricken lifestyle of much of the population was among the worst in Europe. People were poorly rewarded for working incredibly long hours in unsafe conditions, and their lodgings were generally squalid and insanitary. The Poor Houses flourished, and

child labour was key to the financial success of the burgeoning entre-
preneurs. The death rate from disease, hypothermia and despair was
high and, unless one was in some form of public, financial or industrial employment, there was little chance to survive far beyond middle
age. This then was the great problem of Victorian Freemasonry since,
for all its apparent charity, it was run from the top by the very same
Hanoverian royal family who ran the country. If there was a social
divide in the nation, then Freemasonry was bound to find its place at
the better end of that divide and, as such, it became a greatly envied
institution. People did not necessarily want to be Freemasons – they
just aspired to be in the ranks of those who *could* become Freemasons.

The Latter Years

On the accession of Edward VII in 1901, his brother, the Duke of
Connaught, took the reins as Grand Master for 38 years. But as King
Edward's reign drew to a close in 1910, trouble was brewing in the
provinces, where the lodge officers complained that they had too little say in the working of Grand Lodge or the Board of General
Purposes in London. In short, their government was too centralized.
A committee of enquiry was established to look into this, but in 1914
the First World War erupted and the project was shelved. It was
agreed in 1916, however, that there would be a change in electoral
procedure in future, with equal representation from London and
the provinces – a situation which prevails today.[23]

After the War, in 1919, plans were laid to build a new Freemasons'
Hall, and this was facilitated by purchasing land adjacent to the original site. The Duke of Connaught's building work began in 1927, and
took six years to complete. The formal dedication was jointly
conducted by the Prince of Wales (later King Edward VIII and Duke
of Windsor), the Duke of York (later King George VI) and Prince
George (later Duke of Kent). In 1939, Connaught resigned his Grand
Mastership to the Duke of Kent, who was soon killed on active service

for the Royal Air Force in the Second World War (1939–45). He was succeeded by Henry, Earl of Harewood, who saw Grand Lodge through the London Blitz, followed by Edward, Duke of Devonshire, in 1947, and Lawrence, Earl of Scarborough, in 1952.

After two great wars and a succession of short-term Grand Masters, things began to stabilize at Grand Lodge, but it was not long before the subject of religion came to the fore again. It was a time when all the respect and public appeal of Victorian Freemasonry had fallen into obscurity, and followed the 1951 publication of *Darkness Visible* by Walton Hannah, an Anglican minister, who converted shortly afterwards to the Catholic priesthood. The book, subtitled *A Revelation and Interpretation of Freemasonry*, was a concoction of speculation and religious hearsay, but it led Grand Lodge to make an official public statement in 1962. Once more it was announced that Freemasonry is not a religion, it is not a substitute for religion, neither is it in any way anti-religious. It embodies a belief in a Supreme Being, but provides no religious system of its own, granting individual liberty in matters of belief and conscience. Nor is there any Masonic God: a Freemason worships according to his religion of choice. The Great Architect of the Universe is emblematic and symbolic of Creation, and can be envisioned in accordance with individual beliefs. Freemasonry does not seek to separate religions, nor to conjoin religions.

In operative practice, Freemasonry has no more to do with religion than a school assembly, which might have an opening prayer. Such things are traditional practices of ritual etiquette, but they have little or nothing to do with the main business of the classroom or, for that matter, the ceremonial working of a lodge.

Two years later, another debate arose concerning the physical penalties alluded to in the obligations of the Craft. This was a little more difficult to confront since the nature of these penalties for revealing masonic secrets to outsiders is indeed verbally expressed in a sort of 'cross my heart, and hope to die' fashion.[24] But Bishop Herbert decided that the said penalties of obligation were barbaric, as well as being quite illogical in their contexts. Grand Lodge asserted that they were simply historical and traditional references to penalties (real or symbolic) of the distant past and, to ease the situation, issued a 'permissive variation' which gave individual lodges the right to refer to them as such if desired. Subsequent to that, the debate subsided.[25]

Lord Scarborough's retirement in 1967 coincided with the 250th anniversary of the premier Grand Lodge of England – and in June of that year, Edward, Duke of Kent (grandson of King George V and cousin to Queen Elizabeth II), succeeded him at the Royal Albert Hall in London. Once more, English Freemasonry had another royal Grand Master. Edward still holds the office today, and it seems unlikely now that the familiar aspect of having royalty at the helm for so long a period will change at the next installation, whenever that might be. Meanwhile, the Duke's contributions to the Craft have been many and varied. It was largely at his instigation that the once customary position of 'no comment' when Freemasonry was challenged or criticized, became a position of 'limited comment'. But it remains that the very nature of masonic practice and closed-door ritual will always give rise to questions by virtue of the pledge of non-disclosure. There is, nevertheless, nothing secret about Freemasonry which is of any real consequence.

Masonic halls have their signs displayed all over the country, and are used for many additional community purposes. Freemasons' Hall in London is open to outside visitors, while books and items concerning Freemasonry are readily available in the shop. The problem is that many of us are attracted by mystery – especially sinister or conspiratorial mystery – and it is so easy to imagine this where it does not exist. Freemasonry provides an air of mystery – and no matter how much information is made available, we might always presume there is more to know. In this respect, there are many who are equally willing to relate their speculative theories on the matter. Board meetings of companies and corporations are conducted behind closed doors worldwide. Does that make them secret cabals? Maybe in some cases, but more generally it simply means that they are private. Masonic ritual is published and available. It is not secret. Nor indeed are the lodge workings secret in the strict sense. They are simply 'private'.

PART II

7

Knights of the Temple

The Children of Solomon

The brief history of the development of modern Freemasonry so far presented provides a necessary background against which we can explore certain aspects of Freemasonry to gain a deeper understanding of its origins and true nature. In the process, the subject begins to take on a rather more colourful and intriguing aspect.

Let us first look at the term *Freemason* itself. As we have seen, the masonic institution does not really know from where it originated, although a number of suggestions have been put forward. In chapter 2 it was suggested that the word might be: an abbreviated form of 'freestone mason'; related to stonemasons who were free to travel in seeking employment; or, perhaps, related to the Seven Liberal Arts – with the word *liber* meaning 'free'. Also, from a physical building perspective, the architect is (at the design stage) 'free' of the masonry, and in the 1st degree of Craft Freemasonry allusion is made to the fact that an Entered Apprentice must be 'free born', whatever that means in these modern times. There is also a much cited concept which suggests that it could refer to stonemasons who were 'freemen' of their respective towns or cities. But none of these explanations is wholly convincing and it is clear that before the 18th century the term was more commonly expressed as two words: *free mason*. Under the circumstances, it is worth looking at other masonic words with similarly vague origins to see if they might offer a clue.

The outer guard of a masonic lodge is called a Tyler. This is sometimes thought to relate to a roof tiler, but this is a spurious association and has no bearing on the Tyler's office. Armed with a sword,
the Tyler is one who cuts, and the description emanates from the
French word *tailleur*, from which also comes the English word 'tailor'.[1] Spelling adjustments such as this, based on the phonetic ren-
dering of another language are common. For example, in English
tennis the term for a nil or 'goose-egg' score is 'love', which makes
little sense until recognized as stemming from the French *l'oeuf*
(egg). Even some personal and family names have followed the
same route, with Sinclair (*see* page 159) – a particularly relevant name
in masonic terms – originating from *St Clair* (Holy Light). In masonic
terminology, the Tyler's sentinal presence signifies that the lodge is
'properly tyled', which is to say, secured.

In a similar vein, the masonic term 'due guard' – a sign of identification – comes from the French protective gesture, a *geste du garde*,
abbreviated to *du garde*. In a similar fashion, the Nimes-produced
fabric *serge de Nimes* becomes 'denim' in English[2] as a contraction of
de Nimes. Following this theme, we also discover that the masonic
term 'cowan' (relating to unskilled) comes from the French *couenne*
(ignoramus), and that the very definition 'freemason' (free mason)
itself derives from the same form of phonetic interpretation, being
originally *frère maçon* (brother mason), as detailed in Hugenot-dedi-
cated training literature.[3] Even in the modern language, the terminology is still to be found where French is concerned – as, for
example, in the 1991 book about the masonic symbolism in Mozart's
opera, *The Magic Flute*, entitled *Mozart Frère Maçon*.[4]

Since the English term 'free mason' first appeared in the 14th century, it is clear that its usage came in from France at that time.
Although Freemasonry was Scottish before it was English, it now
becomes clear that it was French before it was Scottish – or at least
that the concept was based on a French model. Given that there were
no stonemasons' guilds in Britain before that era, the question arises
whether there were such fraternal guilds in France. In fact, the
answer is 'yes', and among the best documented was that known

as the Children of Solomon, who built the *Notre Dame* cathedral at Chartres. Other masonic brotherhoods of medieval France included the Children of Father Soubise and the Children of Master Jacques.[5] In the course of their building work, the masonic guilds of Chartres donated their own windows to the cathedral project. These stained-glass portrayals incorporate symbols of the lodges in their cusps (such as levels, squares and compasses) which became the Great Lights and Working Tools of Freemasonry in later times (*see* plate 28).

Nothing could relate better to King Solomon's Temple – the root subject matter of modern Craft Freemasonry – than an original guild of master craftsmen called the Children of Solomon dating back to the 12th century in France. It becomes more fascinating, however, when we discover that this particular fraternity, who assisted in many Gothic cathedral projects, was under the leadership of St Bernard (1090–53), the Cistercian Abbot of Clairvaux. From 1128 he was the Patron and Protector of the Poor Knights of Christ and the Temple of Solomon, otherwise known as the Knights Templars. There is even a 14th-century illuminated manuscript which depicts St Bernard addressing the Chapter House Lodge of Clairvaux (*see* plate 17).

The Scottish Connection

Following the Templars' return from Jerusalem with a collection of ancient documents in 1127, St Bernard is said to have translated the geometry of King Solomon's masons who, under their master mason Hiram, were denoted by degrees of knowledge and proficiency. In modern masonic ritual, Hiram (an architect sent to Solomon by the Phoenician King of Tyre) is called Hiram Abiff, although the Bible mentions no such surname (1 Kings 5). The 3rd-degree lodge working relates that Hiram was murdered by junior workmen because he would not reveal the secrets of his degree, and it is in this respect that we find yet another item of French terminology. Hiram Abiff stems from *Hiram à biffe*, which means 'Hiram who was eliminated'.[6]

During the Crusades of the Middle Ages, a number of knightly orders emerged, including the Ordré de Sion (Order of Sion), founded by the First Crusade commander Godefroi de Bouillon in 1099. Others were the Knights Protectors of the Sacred Sepulchre and the Knights Templars. Having wrested Judaea from the Seljuk Turks, who had moved in and demolished the Caliphate tradition, Godefroi was proclaimed King of Jerusalem and Defender of the Holy Sepulchre. But he died in 1100 soon after his triumph, to be succeeded by his younger brother, Baudoin of Boulogne. After 18 years, Baudoin was followed by his cousin, Baudoin II du Bourg. According to the orthodox accounts, the Templars were founded in that year (1118), and were said to have been a group of nine Frenchmen who took vows of poverty, chastity and obedience, swearing to protect the Holy Land.

The Frankish historian, Guillaume de Tyre, wrote at the height of the Crusades (in around 1180) that the function of the Templars was to safeguard the highways for pilgrims. But, given the enormity of such an obligation, it is inconceivable that nine poor men succeeded without enlisting new recruits before their return to Europe in 1127. In truth, there was a good deal more to the Order than is conveyed in Guillaume's account. The Knights were in existence for some years before they were said to have been founded by Hugues de Payens, a cousin and vassal of the Count of Champagne. Their function was certainly not highway patrol and the King's chronicler Fulk de Chartres did not portray them in that light at all. They were the King's front-line diplomats in a Muslim environment, and the Bishop of Chartres wrote about the Knights as early as 1114, calling them the *Milice du Christi* (Soldiers of Christ).

At that time, the Templars were already installed at Baudoin's Jerusalem palace, which was located within the El-Aqsa Mosque on the site of King Solomon's Temple. When Baudoin moved to the nearby domed citadel on the Tower of David, the Temple quarters were left entirely to the Order of Templars. Deep beneath the mosque was the original vault complex, which had remained sealed and untouched since biblical times, and it was known by St Bernard to contain the wealth of Old Testament Jerusalem.

A Knight Templar Initiation

Hugues de Payens' second in command was the Flemish knight Godefroi Saint Omer, while another recruit was André de Montbard, a kinsman of the Count of Burgundy. In 1120, Fulk, Comte d'Anjou (father of Geoffrey Plantagenet), joined the Order, and was followed in 1124 by the Count of Champagne. The Knights were evidently far from poor, and there is no record of these illustrious noblemen policing the Bedouin-infested highways for the benefit of pilgrims. The task of ministering to travellers was actually performed by the separate Order of the Hospitallers of St John of Jerusalem. The Knights Templars were a very select and special unit, and had sworn a particular oath of obedience – not to the King or to their leader, but to St Bernard.

It was in this era that the Templar link was first made with Scotland. Both King David I of Scots (1124–53) and his sister Mary were attached by marriage to Godefroi's Flemish House of Boulogne.[7] There were direct family ties by way of these marriages between David, Hugues de Payens, and the Crusader Kings of Jerusalem. When David I acceded to the throne, the traditional Celtic Church of Scotland was ailing financially, and the elders felt it could best survive within the wrap of St Bernard's influential Cistercian Order. In general terms, Western Christianity outside Scotland had become highly Catholicized, and even Scotland had not escaped this influence, although it was not to be a permanent feature of the nation.

Catholicism had been introduced by the Saxon heiress, Margaret Atheling, who had fled to Scotland after William of Normandy's conquest of England in 1066. She had been raised at the court of her grandfather King Stephen of Hungary, and had spent some time with her great-uncle Edward the Confessor. On marrying King Malcolm Canmore (1058–93), Margaret became Queen of Scotland, but then set out to undermine everything that was foreign to her – bankrupting the nation in the process. Although sainted by Rome 150 years after her death, Margaret was a Scottish disaster, and she left the Celtic Church in ruins.

St Bernard's wealthy Cistercian Order was not attached to the Church of Rome, and consequently was able to assist. Today, the old Templar Church of Dull stands on Cistercian land inherited from the Celtic Order. In 1203, a new Cistercian monastery was founded on Iona (where St Columba's original Irish mission had been demolished by Norsemen in 807), and at length all the Celtic abbacies in Scotland became Cistercian.[8] It was, therefore, in the reign of King David that the Templar association with Scotland began, and in 1128 Hugues de Payens established a seat for the Order on the South Esk.[9] It was to be nearly two centuries later, however, that a movement of Templars into Scotland took place, shortly after which the term 'free mason' (*frère maçon*) entered the language.

A Sovereign Order

By 1127, the Templars' search beneath the Jerusalem Temple was over, and they returned to France with a wealth of treasure that has since become legendary. Fearing that the Vatican authorities would be intent on sequestrating what they had found, St Bernard wrote:

> The work has been accomplished with our help, and the Knights have been sent on a journey through France and Burgundy, under the protection of the Count of Champagne, where all precautions can be taken against all interference by public or ecclesiastical authority.[10]

In more recent times, the British explorer Sir Charles Warren conducted extensive excavations beneath the Temple Mount for the Palestine Exploration Fund in the 1860s.[11] Warren's team dug a number of vertical shafts down to the bedrock, and then opened lateral tunnels between them to identify the walls of the foundation and its subsequent extensions. Moving even deeper into the limestone rock, they discovered a subterranean labyrinth of winding corridors and passages. Branching off these were large storage facilities and a virtual fairyland of cleverly engineered caves and water cisterns.[12]

During the course of these excavations, the foundations of King Solomon's original Temple were found. The lower retaining walls were still intact, and their ancient masonry techniques were quite distinct from those of Prince Zerubabbel's second Temple and the later buildings of the Hasmonaean and Herodian eras on the same site. A mapping survey was conducted by British military engineers shortly afterwards in 1894, since when the underground complex has become inaccessible because of Muslim political and religious sensibilities. A reward from the 1894 project, however, was the discovery of a 12th-century Templar cross, a broken Templar sword and other related items.[13]

In the light of the Templars' overwhelming 12th-century success, a Grand Council was convened at Troyes in January 1128, chaired by the Cardinal Legate of France. At this event, international status as a Sovereign Order was conferred upon the Knights, while their Jerusalem headquarters became the governing office of the capital city. Under St Bernard's protectorate, the Templars were duly established as a Cistercian Order and Hugues de Payens formally installed as Grand Master.

The Templars' subsequent rise to prominence was remarkably swift as they became engaged in high-level politics and diplomacy in Europe and the Middle East, and were granted vast territories and estates across the map from Britain to Palestine. *The Anglo-Saxon Chronicle* states that when Hugues de Payens visited England's Henry I in Normandy: 'the King received him with great honour, and gave him great treasures in gold and silver'.[14] The Spanish King, Alfonso of Aragon, passed a third of his kingdom to the Order, and the whole of Christendom was at their feet.

When formally appointed Patron and Protector of the Templars at the Council of Troyes, St Bernard drew up the Order's Constitution (commonly known as *The Latin Rule*).[15] This was followed by his letter of exhortation to Hugues, entitled *In Praise of the New Knighthood*, which firmly established the Order as one of armed warrior monks,[16] and his subsequent translation of the geometry of King Solomon's masons was lodged with the Order of the Temple.

In 1128, garden land and a small church were granted to the Order near Holborn in London, and in 1161 the Knights built their own round temple off Fleet Street (*see* plate 8). This was subsequently extended and is still in use today, known as Temple Church. Since the 14th-century, the site of the London Templar headquarters near Temple Bar has been occupied by two Inns of Court – the Inner Temple and Middle Temple.

In 1139, Pope Innocent II (also a Cistercian) granted the Knights international independence from obligation to any authority save himself. Under the terms of his Bull *Omne Datum Optimum*, they were henceforth not beholden to kings, cardinals or governments, and were freed from all liability to tithes and taxes. This was followed in 1144 by Pope Celestine II's *Milites Templi* and Eugenius II's *Militia Dei* in 1145, which further cemented the extraordinary rights and privileges by allowing the Knights to consecrate their own ground and to collect taxes on Templar properties.

In time, the Templars' original *Latin Rule* proved inadequate in terms of encompassing the activities of a military Order when in field action. Moreover, a good many Knights did not understand Latin. Consequently, aspects of the old *Rule* were amended and updated, to be published as a new *French Rule* in 1165.[17]

The Royal Secret

Among the documentary artefacts which Hugues and the Knights brought out of Jerusalem were documents hidden during the Jewish Revolt against Roman dominion in AD 66–70. These included manuscripts which enabled them to challenge certain Roman Church doctrines and New Testament interpretation. For this reason, they refused to bear the upright Latin Cross, and wore a centred red cross with splayed arms (the *Cross Patee*) as their emblem after 1146. This was soon amended to become a Maltese Cross with 8 points. In both cases the object was that the emblem would sit octagonally within a circle so that emphasis was drawn towards the centre – a point within a circle ⊙.

Among their other discoveries from locations outside the Temple were numerous books from the East, some of which had been salvaged from the burned library of Alexandria in AD 391. There were ancient Essene works predating Jesus Christ, and volumes from Arabian and Greek philosophers – all of which were destined to be condemned by the Church. Additionally, there were items concerning numerology, geometry, architecture and music, along with manuscripts pertaining to metals and alloys.[18] In all, the Templars returned to Europe with the combined knowledge of thousands of years of study, recorded for posterity. But, for all that, it was the wealth of treasure found in the Jerusalem Temple vaults that formed their bullion reserve. This enabled them to issue promissory notes and implement a wide-scale banking system based on paper money instead of coinage with its own intrinsic value. By virtue of this, and the substantial grants and donations received after their return, the Order became the most powerful financial organization the world has ever known. Indeed, within a short space of time, they were bankers to monarchies and parliaments throughout Europe and the Levant.

By the time that Robert the Bruce was crowned King of Scots in 1306, the international influence of the Templars was truly feared by Pope Clement V, and in the following year he endeavoured to eliminate the Order. In this he was aiding King Philippe IV of France, who owed a fortune to the Templars – and Philippe's son-in-law was none other than Bruce's enemy, King Edward II Plantagenet of England (1307–27).

When the Dead Sea Scrolls of Essene record were discovered in 1947 at Qumrân, Judaea, and subsequently translated, the *Copper Scroll* (which gives details of the Jerusalem fortune) revealed in 1956 that, along with a vast stockpile of bullion and valuables, was buried an 'indeterminable treasure'. French masonic ritual stemming from the Middle Ages states that this treasure was the specific responsibility of the Templar Grand Knights of St Andrew, instituted by King

Baudoin II of Jerusalem who succeeded in 1118. These elite Knights were called the Guardian Princes of the Royal Secret. This is the first mention of there actually being a 'secret' worthy of a royally appointed Order.[19]

According to this same *Ecossais* tradition, the Knights of St Andrew were the inheritors of the Samaritan Magi who were the true ancestors of speculative masonry. The history dates back to the Temple Guard of Jerusalem in 586 BC. At the behest of King Josiah, they were summoned by the High Priest, Hilkiah, before the Temple of Solomon was destroyed by Prince Nebuchadnezzar of Babylon. Hilkiah, a priest of the goddess Anath, was renowned for discovering the Mosaic *Book of the Law*.[20] The captain of the Guard was Hilkiah's son Jeremiah, generally known in religiously motivated terms as a prophet (Jeremiah 1:1), and his task was to secrete the Ark of the Covenant and other valuable treasures from the Babylonian invader.

Persecution

The persecution of the Knights Templars has been covered in earlier books but, for the benefit of new readers, the subject is worth reiterating. By 1306, the Jerusalem Order was so powerful that Philippe IV of France viewed them with the utmost trepidation. He owed a great deal of money to the Knights and was practically bankrupt – and he also feared their political and esoteric might, which he knew to be far greater than his own.

Until that time the Templars had operated without papal interference, but King Philippe managed to change this. Following a Vatican edict forbidding him to tax the clergy, the French king arranged for the capture and murder of Pope Boniface VIII. His successor, Benedict XI, was also poisoned by Philippe's lawyer William de Nogaret,[21] and was replaced in 1305 by Philippe's own candidate, Bertrand de Got, Archbishop of Bordeaux, who duly became Pope

Clement V. With this new French Pope under his control, Philippe drew up his list of accusations against the Knights Templars. The easiest charge to lay was that of heresy,[22] for it was well-known that the Knights did not hold with the established doctrines of the Virgin Birth and the Resurrection. It was also known that their diplomatic and business affairs involved them with Jews, Gnostics and Muslims. With contrived papal support, therefore, King Philippe then persecuted the Templars in France and endeavoured to eliminate the Order in other countries.

On Friday 13 October 1307, Philippe's henchmen struck with a vengeance, and Templars were seized throughout France. Captured Knights were imprisoned, interrogated, tortured and burned. Paid witnesses were called to give evidence against the Order and some truly bizarre statements were obtained. The Templars were accused of a variety of practices deemed unsavoury, including necromancy, abortion, blasphemy and the black arts. Once they had given their evidence, under whatever circumstances of bribery or duress, the witnesses then disappeared without trace. But, despite all this, the King did not achieve his primary objective, for the Templar treasure remained beyond his grasp. His minions had scoured the length and breadth of Champagne and Languedoc but, all the while, a majority of the hoard was hidden away in the Treasury vaults of the Order's Chapter House in Paris. A painting in the Palace of Versailles depicts the Templars of the Paris Chapter with the Ark of the Covenant in 1147 (see plate 34).

In 14th-century France and Flanders, most aristocratic families had sons within the Church – if not as bishops, then as abbots of allied Orders. The Chaplain of the Manor of La Buzadière was one of these noblemen and, shortly before the papal edict against the Templars, there were seven Templar guests at the Lord of the Manor's castle. At this gathering, the Knights were alerted to the impending Inquisition and duly raced to Paris, where they informed their hierarchy of King Philippe's plan. Then, with an auxiliary contingent, they travelled to St Malo, spreading the word. The seven Knights were Gaston de la Pièrre Phoebus, Guidon de Montanor,

Gentilis de Foligno, Henri de Montfort, Louis de Grimoard, Pièrre Yorick de Rivault, and Cesare Minvielle.[23]

At that time, the Grand Master of the Order was Jacques de Molay. Knowing that Pope Clement V was a pawn of King Philippe, Molay arranged for the Paris hoard to be removed in a fleet of 18 galleys from La Rochelle. Most of these ships sailed to Scotland, and some to Portugal, but Philippe was unaware of this and arranged for the Templars to be pursued throughout Europe. With most of the treasure safely dispatched, Molay and some key officers remained in France to continue their work – a primary aspect of which was to get word to those Knights who were not aware of the impending onslaught. Couriers sped far and wide with their message of warning, but in many cases they were too late and their colleagues had already been seized.

Knights were arrested in England, but north of the Border in Scotland the papal Bulls were ineffective. This was because King Robert the Bruce and the whole Scottish nation had already been excommunicated for taking up arms against the Catholic King Edward II of England.[24] Edward was initially reluctant to turn against the Knights but, as King Philippe's son-in-law, he was in a difficult position and was obliged to comply with the rule of the Inquisition. Many Templars were arrested in England, while their lands and preceptories were confiscated and subsequently passed to the Knights Hospitallers of St John. In Scotland, however, the story was very different since an alliance with the Templars had been struck long before, when King David had granted Hugues and his Knights the lands of Ballantradoch by the Firth of Forth (now the village of Temple).

It is important to recognize that there was no Franco–Scots language barrier in those times. France and Scotland had been formally linked for trading and military purposes for many hundreds of years by way of the *Auld Alliance*.[25] This treaty (formally styled the League Offensive and Defensive) had been struck between Emperor Charlemagne of the Franks and King Eochaid IV of Scots in 807. It was by virtue of this that the Scots Guard (the *Garde Ecossais*) became the official household bodyguard of the French Royal House of Valois in the days after Philippe IV's Capetian dynasty. In this respect, the Scots Guard was prominent in Joan of Arc's cavalry at the Siege of Orléans against the English in 1429. Princess Mary Stuart, daughter of James V and subsequently Queen of Scots, married the Dauphin, François, to become Queen of France in 1559.

The Rosy Cross

Following the Templar Fleet's voyage from France, 50 or so French Knights settled in Scotland's Mull of Kintyre. Later, on 24 June 1313, realizing that their Grand Master, Jacques de Molay, could soon be executed in Europe, they applied the provisions of the Order's revised *Constitution* of 1307 and appointed a Knight named Pièrre d'Aumont as their Scottish Grand Master.[26] On the nearby island of Islay, and at Kilmartin on the mainland, there are numerous Templar graves still to be found, and some of their distinctive tombstone slabs depict the occupants as Knight Officers of the original Templar Fleet.

Under the auspices of King Robert the Bruce and his excommunicated clergy, the Order was restructured into a Church, with a hierarchy quite independent of Rome. The Templar Church had abbots, priests and even bishops – but no cardinals, and certainly no Pope. In preparation for a war against the English, they began to train the Scottish troops in the hit-and-run warfare tactics established in the Crusades. Templar gold was then used for arms to be manufactured in Ireland.[27]

At an Inquisition hearing in 1309, Bishop William Lamberton of St Andrews was under edict of Pope Clement V and King Edward II of England to expose all the Templars in Scotland, but the bishop struck a contrary deal at Holyrood House in the December of that year. By way of this arrangement, the Templars would receive sanctuary in Scotland, in return for arms and military expertise. The input of arms was substantial, for King Edward complained about the extent of weaponry imported from Ireland at this time, and the

Templars were formally outlawed by the Pope in 1312. It is on record that the Papal Legate, John de Soleure, judicially examined two English Knights at Holyrood in 1309. They were Walter de Clifton, Preceptor of Ballantradoch, and William de Middleton, both of whom were sentenced to house arrest for the duration of the Legate's visit. The reason that these were the only two is because the rest were on active service in Bruce's army.[28]

If ever England's House of Plantagenet had designs on the Scottish realm, these were dramatically heightened by the arrival of the Templars, and the eventual result was the 1314 Battle of Bannockburn. This battle was fought only three months after the Templar Grand Master, Jacques de Molay, was burned at the stake in France for refusing to reveal the Order's secrets to the Inquisitors of King Philippe IV.[29] Subsequent to Bannockburn, the Knights were appointed as the Royal Bodyguard, and established as official Guardians of the Palace. The Order was then promoted and encouraged by the succeeding Kings of Scots. Considerable tracts of land were passed to the Order (especially around the Lothians and Aberdeen) and the Knights also took possession of properties in the Western regions of Ayr, Lorn and Argyll.

The year 1317, however, saw a change in the administration of the Templars. Many had died at Bannockburn and, with their ranks depleted, it was thought advisable to invite Scottish Companions into the Order. The King of Scots was installed as the hereditary Sovereign Grand Master – and from that time, whichever descendant king held the office, he was to be known as Prince (Count) St Germain. Bruce then constituted a new Order called the Elder Brethren of the Rosy Cross.[30] The papal edict of Scots excommunication did not last indefinitely, being lifted in 1323 when Pope John XXII recognized Robert the Bruce as the rightful King of Scots. By virtue of this recognition, many historians have presumed that the Knights Templars must have disbanded in Scotland, but this was not the case. It was simply that Bruce had contrived to manage the Order under a new title. His Brethren of the Rosy Cross were seen to have been those who were valiant at Bannockburn, and this was a successful cover.

It was during subsequent Templar-influenced times that the Scottish national banking system evolved from the Order's financial experience in Europe and the Middle East. Scotland's soil held significant gold reserves and the Knights were quick to put these resources to use. This underground wealth was another of the reasons why the Plantagenet English were so keen to gain dominion in Scotland.[31] At a Paris banquet, hosted by King James V of Scots (1513–42) and his wife, Madeleine de France, more than 300 French guests were each presented with a goblet filled to the brim with Scottish gold. The Crown of Scotland (with its magnificent gems, including pearls from the River Tay) is made from Scottish gold and even today there are two gold mines currently being worked in Perthshire.[32]

In early masonic terms, the prevailing Royal Order associated with the Rosy Cross in Scotland was that of the Heredom (Holy Mount) of Kilwinning, Ayrshire – possibly founded by King David I – for which James Stewart, 5th High Steward (d. 1309), had been a Grand Master. It is for this reason that Freemasonry's current side degree, Knight of the Rosy Cross, is said to stem from that constitution – although it does so only in theory. The legitimate Rosicrucian Grand Mastership of St Germain was inherent in the 1688 exile of Stuart Household Orders to France. King James II (VII) subsequently constituted the Noble Order of the Guard of St Germain in Paris on 18 June 1692.

The Heredom of Kilwinning and Knight of the Rosy Cross degrees exist today within the Royal Order of Scotland. Inconsistent with its title, this Order made its first appearance at the *Thistle and Crown* ale-house in Chandos Street, London in 1730,[33] with a subsequently formalized establishment on 22 July 1750. Shortly afterwards, a charter was granted for an affiliated lodge at The Hague, but this was implemented instead in Edinburgh in 1753, subsequently to become the Grand Lodge of the Order in July 1776. The King of Scots was henceforth deemed to be the hereditary Grand Master, and his seat (draped in a purple robe, and bearing a replica of the open-topped crown of James IV) has since been held vacant at all meetings.

The Cathedral Builders

We cannot leave the early part of the Templars' story without look-ing at that aspect of their operation which was strictly geared to stonemasonry in the operative sense. This is one of their greatest surviving achievements in that it incorporated the sacred geometry of King Solomon's masons as transcribed by St Bernard, along with other facets of arcane and hermetic lore, which the Knights had brought out of Jerusalem. This is the design and building of the fab-ulous *Notre Dame* cathedrals of France.

These mammoth undertakings were managed with guilds of fraternal masons, the *frères maçons* of groups such as the Children of Solomon. When the 14th-century Inquisition against the Templars was at its height, these guilds were equally at risk. They were practi-tioners of the masonic crafts based on privileged information in accor-dance with the members' individually attained degrees. There were three such degrees: Apprentice Companion, Attained Companion and Master Companion – just as there are now three degrees in the main-stream of modern Craft Freemasonry. Jointly, the various guilds were known as the *Compagnons de Devoirs* (with the word *devoirs* signifying a duty of work).[34] In just the same way that the Templars were forced to flee the papal onslaught fronted by Philippe IV of France, so too did the cathedral guild brethren. It was from the Inquisition of these Companions that a severe interrogation to extract the most vital or secret information is still referred to as giving the 'third degree'.

Strategically placed around France in a mirror of the Virgo con-stellation[35] these magnificent cathedrals continue to baffle architects and builders today. The architecture is phenomenal and, despite the thousands of tons of richly decorated stone, the overall impression is one of magical weightlessness. The cathedrals were all built at much the same time, even though some took more than a century to com-plete. *Notre Dame* in Paris was begun in 1163, Chartres in 1194, Reims in 1211 and Amiens in 1221. Others of the same era were at Bayeux, Abbeville, Rouen, Laon, Evreux and Etampes. But of all these, *Notre Dame de Chartres* is said to stand on the most sacred ground.

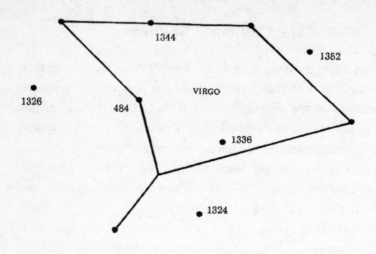

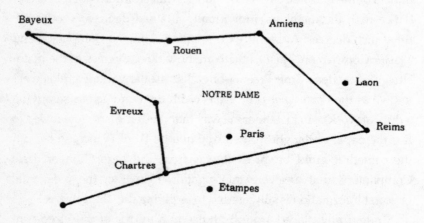

The Virgo Constellation and the *Notre Dame* Cathedrals of France

At this place, the telluric earth currents are at their highest, and the site was recognized for its divine atmosphere even in druidic times. (Induced by changes in the Earth's magnetic field, telluric currents are very low-frequency electric currents that occur naturally underground.) So venerated is the location of Chartres that it is the only cathedral not to have a single king, bishop, cardinal, canon or anyone else interred in the soil of its mound. It was a pagan site, dedicated to the traditional Mother Goddess – a site to which pilgrims travelled long before the time of Jesus. The original altar was built above the *Grotte des Druides*, which housed a sacred dolmen,[36] and was identified with the womb of the Earth.

The style of *Notre Dame* architecture is unique in that the vaulting – on an independent system of ribs – is sustained by piers and buttresses whose equilibrium is maintained by the opposing action of thrust and counter thrust. Adorned with motifs and shapes drawn from organic nature, the whole became known as 'Gothic' – a term derived from *Langue Argotique*, explained by the 19th-century French hermeticist Fulcanelli to be the guardian language of trans-mutation alchemy.[37]

The 17th-century Royal Society of King Charles II evolved directly from Robert the Bruce's 14th-century Knights of the Rosy Cross, which evolved in turn from the 12th-century Knights Templars and the Children of Solomon. However, a common factor emerges from all this. The lodge structure of Rosicrucian Freemasonry was indeed based on the working model of medieval stonemasons' guilds, but the reason for signs, passwords and fraternal secrecy had nothing to do with mortar and trowels, nor with levels of building proficiency. Instead, they had to do with protecting the underlying science of that proficiency, from the undertakings of St Bernard de Clairvaiux to Sir Christopher Wren. As we shall discover, the lost secret of Freemasonry is based on the arcane lore of Solomon's Temple, which presents itself as a sophisticated form of hermetic alchemy. Fulcanelli referred to it as the ancient wisdom of the Golden Fleece.

8

Hiramic Legend

The Masonic Apron

The Golden Fleece is actually mentioned in the 1st degree of Craft Freemasonry, but in a chivalric context – not as described by Fulcanelli. When presenting a white lambskin apron to the Entered Apprentice initiate, the Worshipful Master of the lodge states:

> It is more ancient than the Golden Fleece or the Roman Eagle, more honourable than the Star and Garter, or any other order that can be conferred upon you at this time, or any future period by king, prince, potentate, or any other person, except he be a mason.

In the first place, this information is wholly incorrect, and in the second it is acutely naive. It is precisely the sort of statement that leaves modern Freemasonry open to attack by outsiders. According to the *Transactions* of the Quatuor Coronati Lodge of Research: 'the earliest representations of the Freemason's apron are seen on the engraved portrait of Antony Sayer, the first Grand Master of the modern Craft (1717)'.[1] The *Transactions* further state that the masonic apron derives from the leather aprons worn by workmen in the Middle Ages and, in the frontispiece illustration of James Anderson's first *Book of Constitutions* (1723), a Tyler is seen on the left, bringing a number of aprons into the hall (*see* plate 5). These are large workmen's aprons, however, not the small badges of identification as worn today.

The masonic *Transactions* state that from 1731 the long apron became knee-length in a triangular shape with the point downwards. Then, from 1764, masons began wearing them upside down with the pointed flap folded over the rectangular portion so as to 'convince spectators that there was not a working mason amongst them'. The report continues with the explanation that 'by 1784 the apron was greatly reduced in size' – a style which Irish masons had worn from a little earlier.

If the said 'nobility' of the apron (as described in 1st-degree ritual) is meant to relate that work is a noble occupation, then it appears that in the latter 1700s this notion was sidelined because Freemasons of the era did not like this working-class association. They began to decorate their aprons with masonic symbols and insignia of office, together with lacework, gold fringes, rosettes, tassels and such. No longer anything to do with work, the apron became an in-house status symbol that was also paraded in public to gain esteem and social recognition. But recognition for what? Recognition for being of the wealthy middle and upper classes that could, in those days, become Freemasons.

The masonic apron is, at best, less than 300 years old, and in practice little more than 200 years old. To claim that it is 'more ancient than the Golden Fleece' is therefore ludicrous. The Most Illustrious Order of the Golden Fleece – the highest ranking Order of the Crown of Spain – was constituted on 10 January 1429 by Philip the Good, Duke of Burgundy. To claim that the apron is 'more honourable than the Star and Garter', England's most prestigious and sovereign knightly Order, founded by Edward III in 1348 as The Most Noble Order of the Garter, is equally ridiculous.

Like a good deal else upon which modern Freemasonry hangs, the apron is a latter-day introduction. It was a product of post-1717 Georgian invention in an attempt to emulate an institution which eluded them by virtue of its exile – an institution whose precepts and purposes had (as Anderson stated in 1723) been lost to the incoming Hanoverian establishment. In real terms, the apron is the recognizable badge of a Freemason, but it is certainly not more ancient or honourable than those chivalric foundations which are cited in lodge ritual.

Notwithstanding this, there is a legitimate way to attach an ancient and relevant symbolism to the masonic apron, although the ritual writers appear not to have considered it. In Old Testament times, a particular garment worn by the High Priest was a bibbed and girdled item called an *ephod*.[2] It was specifically the badge of the Levite guardians of the Ark of the Covenant, and with its bib folded down over the girdle it formed a small linen apron.[3] In 2 Samuel 6:13–15, King David (the father of King Solomon) is said to have been 'girded with a linen *ephod*' when he danced before the Ark.

The Widow's Son

No part of masonic Craft ritual is better known beyond the fraternity than the legend of Hiram Abiff, even if the details are vague to outsiders. The Hiramic account is conveyed to 3rd-degree masons as a staged re-enactment on entering their Master status. With the candidate taking part (under direction) in the role of Hiram, the story itself is unfamiliar, although it does concern a biblically documented character.

Hiram is given in the Old Testament book of 1 Kings 7:13–14 as 'a widow's son of the tribe of Napthali, and his father was a man of Tyre'. Hiram became the chief artificer of King Solomon's Temple in Jerusalem, and was described as 'a worker in brass; and he was filled with wisdom, and understanding, and cunning to work all works in brass. And he came to King Solomon, and wrought all his work'. (The word 'cunning' stems from *kenning*, which relates to 'knowing'.)

Throughout the balance of 1 Kings 7, Hiram's work on this project is detailed – two pillars of brass, with chapiters (pillar capitals) of brass; a cast molten sea (like a large laver); oxen, lions, cherubim, and various creatures of brass; pomegranate, lily and palm decorations of brass; ten wagons of brass, along with various bowls, shovels and basins, all 'of bright brass'. Over and above these, there are descriptions in the same context of an altar, a table for shew-bread, candlesticks, censers, snuffers and all manner of items made from gold.

In 2 Chronicles 2:14, Hiram is further discussed in a letter from Huram, King of Tyre, who introduces Hiram to King Solomon. In doing this, he gives more information concerning Hiram's exper-tise. He is said to be 'skilful to work in gold, and in silver, in brass, in iron, in stone, and in timber, in purple, in blue, and in fine linen, and in crimson; also to grave any manner of graving, and to find out every device which shall be put to him, with thy cunning men of my lord David, thy father.' (The importance of purple, blue and crimson relates to Hiram's mastery of specific dyes that were unique to the Canaanite region. The main source was the *murex* shellfish, which produced the most famous purple dye in the ancient world.)[4]

Hiram emerges as an all-round craftsman, who can work in just about any decorative material, and it is clear that he is Solomon's principal master in this regard. An error can be pin-pointed, how-ever, in the use of the term 'brass'. The English translation is not good in this respect and, since brass (an alloy of copper and zinc) is a comparatively modern substance, the translations would be more correctly rendered as bronze.[5]

The *Antiquities of the Jews* does not expand greatly on Hiram's abilities, except to say that he 'was skilful in all sorts of work; but his chief skill lay in working with gold, and silver, and brass; by whom were made all the mechanical works about the temple'.[6] In describing these works, it is related that Hiram made two hollow pillars for the Temple porch, calling the right-hand pillar *Jachin* and the other *Boaz*. The rest follows as in the Bible – a great brazen laver, an altar and the other items as previously listed. But it is quite clear from both accounts that Solomon, not Hiram, was the chief architect of the Temple.

King Solomon, architect of the Temple (woodcut by
Julius Schnoor von Carolsfeld, 1794–1872)

As with much that is inaccurate in biblical translation, Albert
Mackey's *Encyclopedia of Freemasonry*[7] asserts that 2 Chronicles was
badly mistranslated in the Authorized Old Testament. In addition to
describing Hiram's expertise in metalwork, the original Hebrew
does not state that he was a 'skilful worker in stone and timber'. The
words used actually identify 'stones' (as in gemstones) and 'woods'
(as in carving).[8] Hence, there is nothing on record to suggest that
Hiram was a master stonemason, and there is nothing to determine
that he was involved in the main building construction as is promulgated in Freemasonry. In fact, a fuller study of 1 Kings reveals quite
the opposite. It is explained that Solomon spent 13 years building
the Temple – verses 1–12 describe the main buildings, the porch and
the courtyard, and it is not until after all this has been completed
that verse 13 relates that Solomon brought Hiram out of Tyre.

Hiram was, therefore, neither the architect nor the master mason; he emerges only as a master artificer: the chief decorator and fittings manufacturer.

Hiram's death is not mentioned in the Bible, nor in the 1st or 2nd degree of Freemasonry, but it moves to centre-stage in the 3rd degree. He is named in Anderson's 1723 *Constitutions*, but the masonic legend of his death is not stated. Additionally, Hiram was mentioned (although only in passing) in an obscure masonic catechism known as the *Graham Manuscript* in 1726,[9] and in Samuel Pritchard's *Masonry Dissected* in 1730. But that is the extent of it until the Hiramic legend makes its first appearance in Anderson's revised *Constitutions* of 1738. The 3rd degree of Craft Freemasonry was introduced not long before in 1724, although Hiram did not personally feature in the lodge ritual of that decade. This suggests that the story of Hiram's murder that constitutes the climax of the Craft as it stands today has only existed for a maximum of 267 years.

The Death of the Builder

The man who introduced Hiram to the front line of Freemasonry was the French clergyman, Rev Jean Theophilus Desaguliers, Grand Master of the Grand Lodge of England 1719–22, and author of the General Regulations in the 1723 *Constitutions*. A member of the Georgian Royal Society, Desaguliers was a prominent philosophical scientist and inventor of the planetarium. He was also an inventor of mythology. Before he brought Hiram onto the scene, the principal character to represent the construction industry in masonic tradition was Noah.

The earlier Noah story concerned his three sons Shem, Ham and Japheth. It told of how they went to their father's grave in an attempt to discover a secret that had been buried with him, but found only Noah's body.[10] In trying to lift him by pulling at a finger, it came away. The same happened when pulling at Noah's wrist and his elbow – but eventually they succeeded in raising him by way of a five-point hold, subsequently known in Freemasonry as the Five Points of Fellowship – a form of embrace: foot to foot, knee to knee, breast to breast, cheek to cheek and hand to back. The bizarre tale relates that one brother said, 'Here is marrow in the bone.' The other said, 'But a dry bone', at which they dubbed the event with the non-sensical word *Mahabyn*.

Whatever the original purpose of this strange story, it lacked the key elements of a 'good' story, and so further elements were added – those of betrayal, murder, martyrdom and revenge. With these additions, Desaguliers had a more exciting plot, but felt it necessary to change the central character in order to associate the tale with stone-masonry instead of Noah's woodworking. Thus, the legend of Noah became the legend of Hiram Abiff against a backdrop of the building of Solomon's Temple.

In brief, the Hiramic legend tells of two Fellow Craft masons called Jubela and Jubelo, who insist that, with the Temple completed, they must now be told the secrets of a Master Mason. Hiram refuses to tell them, and Jubela strikes him with a 24-inch rule. Jubelo then strikes him with a square, but Hiram cannot escape from the courtyard because the gates are blocked. He is then confronted by a third antagonist, Jubelum, who persists with the same question. On getting the same refusal, Jubelum strikes Hiram on the forehead with a maul and kills him. The three then carry his body to a remote corner and dump it with the Temple rubbish. Subsequently filled with remorse, they move Hiram's corpse to a hill and bury it more suitably, placing a sprig of acacia at the head of the grave.

On the following day, Hiram's unexplained absence causes concern back at the Temple. King Solomon is approached by twelve Fellow Craft masons, who relate what they think has occurred. When the roll is called, Jubela, Jubelo and Jubelum are found to be missing – and so the hunt begins, with the twelve forming four parties of three to search north, south, east and west. Eventually, one of the three who travelled westward pulls on a sprig of acacia while resting, and discovers it to be loose, whereupon the assassins appear and surrender themselves into custody. Solomon has them executed, and sends the others back to retrieve Hiram's body.

It is at this point that the Noah account comes into play, for Solomon instructs the men to search Hiram's grave for the Master's secret. It is reckoned that the secret can be unlocked by knowing a particular word, which it is hoped might be written down and buried with Hiram. Going back to where the acacia sprig was found, they uncover the body and remove Hiram's badge of office for iden-tification. But on handing this to Solomon, they report that no secret word could be found. At this, it is decreed that Hiram's body should be disinterred, and that the first word uttered by any of the group after this will become the new Mason Word in place of that which was lost. (Although it is common these days to refer to the Mason's Word or Masons' Word, it was not originally stated as possessive or plural in pre-1700 literature. It was the Mason Word, as one might refer to a village hall or clock tower.)

A grand procession is then made to the grave, where attempts to raise Hiram are made with the grips (handshakes) of the 1st and 2nd degrees – but they each prove ineffective. In unison, the masons exclaim, 'Oh Lord, my God, is there no help for the widow's son?' At this, the Worshipful Master (in the role of Solomon) takes Hiram's hand with the Master Mason's grip (called the 'lion's paw') and raises the body on the Five Points of Fellowship. With Hiram's body then close upon his, he utters the substitute Mason Word, *Mahabyn*, as given in the earlier Noah account.[11] The word is whispered into the ear of the 3rd-degree candidate who, throughout the enactment of the story, has played the role of Hiram. (*See* chapter 13 for more on the Mason Word.)

Time and the Virgin

The Five Points of Fellowship relate to aspects in which masons should serve, pray for, keep the secrets of, support and counsel their brothers. They are worthy precepts, but they have no practical relevance in the way they are presented. It is not as if Hiram was somehow resurrected to life; he was dead and he stayed dead. The continuing story explains that he was buried back at the Temple where a monument was erected to his memory – a beautiful virgin, weeping over a broken column to represent the unfinished Temple (even though the Temple was finished). With a book of Hiram's virtuous accomplishments before her, she holds in her left hand an urn containing his ashes (in contrast to the earlier premise that his body was buried), and in her right hand a sprig of acacia, while the figure of Time stands behind, unfolding the ringlets of her hair. Notwithstanding the errors of design, it presents a suitably evocative image, and (known as the *Freemason's Rest*) it has often been used in cemeteries to identify masonic burials.

Time and the Virgin (The Freemason's Rest)

Although Freemasonry is not a secret society, merely a society with secrets, the unfathomable Mason Word *Mahabyn* (though well enough publicized and known these days), has been a high-point of those secrets since the middle 1700s. Hiram Abiff is undoubtedly the most celebrated mason of all time, and yet he was not a mason, neither was he named Abiff. His masonic work and ethics are revered by Freemasons worldwide, but they have no historical foundation.

Over the years, numerous attempts have been made to justify the Hiramic legend by linking it with something more historically or religiously solid. It has been aligned with the mythology of Osiris, the expulsion of Adam, the death and resurrection of Jesus, the murder of Thomas Becket, the burning of Jacques de Molay, and the execution of King Charles I. If one looks hard enough, there are limited similarities in each case, but they are all equally unconvincing with regard to having any Hiramic base.[12] Moreover, with the exception of Jesus, these characters, real or otherwise, are not venerated internationally by worshipful movements or fraternal societies. Like Jacques de Molay, the legendary Hiram Abiff was killed for not revealing his secret to the uninitiated. He is said to have preferred to lose his life rather than betray his trust – 'an instance of fortitude and integrity seldom equalled' – but unlike Jacques de Molay's execution, the story of Hiram's demise is a fabrication, so it actually proves nothing in real-life terms.

In the final event, the point of the story is conveyed by the explanation that Hiram's friends sought to assist him with their fellowship even after his death, thereby teaching the candidate to:

> ... look forward to blessed immortality ... that we may welcome the grim tyrant Death, and receive him as a kind messenger sent from our Supreme Grand Master to translate us from this imperfect to that perfect, glorious and celestial Lodge above, where the Supreme Architect of the Universe presides.

Freemasonry is not a religion in that it does not have a denominational aspect of its own. But, with sentiments such as this, it cannot be said that Freemasonry is not based on religious precepts. St Paul would have been more than pleased to have contrived this pronouncement when preaching his message of immortality.

The Master Craftsman

Extraordinary amounts of time and ingenuity have been expended by masonic scholars endeavouring to trace the probable, or even possible, origin of the Hiramic myth, but these efforts all fall short.[13] The only certain fact is that the account of Hiram's burial is an adapted version of an earlier story about the sons of Noah, but the story of Noah's disinterment was itself fictional. In reality, it seems likely that both stories are symbolic representations of another event – the unearthing of someone or something which sits at the heart of an older masonic tradition.

On looking again at the pre-Hiramic manuscript which contains the grave of Noah account, things become rather more interesting. Also contained in this document is the story of Bezaleel, who built the Ark of the Covenant for Moses at Mount Horeb in Sinai, and it is significant that Bezaleel is described in the Old Testament with the very same distinctions that are later afforded to Hiram. In discussing Bezaleel, Exodus 31:1–5 states:

> And the Lord spake unto Moses, saying, See I have called by name Bezaleel the son of Uri, the son of Hur, of the tribe of Judah. And I have filled him with the spirit of God in wisdom and in understanding, and in knowledge, and in all manner of workmanship, to devise cunning works, to work in gold, and in silver, and in brass. And in the cutting of stones, to set them, and in carving of timber, to work all manner of workmanship.

In addition to making the Ark of the Covenant (Exodus 37:1–9), Bezaleel made all the accoutrements for the wilderness Tabernacle –

items that are identical to those listed in the 1 Kings story of Hiram, including the altar, the laver, the candlesticks, the shewbread table, the bowls and shovels. The Tabernacle, moreover, had the same dimensional ratios, including the square Holy of Holies for residence of the Ark, that were later replicated in Solomon's Temple. It is in this same Exodus sequence about the Taberbacle that we also discover Bezaleel's involvement with the vestment of the Mosaic High Priest and his *ephod* (apron).[14]

It seems clear that the model for Hiram was not Noah, but the earlier master craftsman Bezaleel. Having ascertained this, however, a striking anomaly becomes apparent. The Tabernacle (Hebrew *Mishkan*: Dwelling Place) was enormous. Its walls were constructed of upright boards 13.5 ft high and 27 ins wide (*c.* 4 m x 69 cms). There were more than four dozen wide planks, with additional corner pieces, in an overall 3:1 ground ratio of 45 ft x 15 ft (*c.* 13.7 x 4.6 m) and 15 ft in height.[15] This was all covered and draped in heavy linen and goat skins, while curtained within was the Sanctuary of the Ark, contrived as a 15-ft cubic space.[16] This construction (a covered timber building rather than a tent) was set within a 150 ft by 75 ft enclosure called the Court of the Dwelling (*c.* 45.6 x 22.8 m) – about the size of an Olympic swimming pool. It was boundaried by 60 pegged wooden poles with bronze bases, and some 450 ft (137 m) of weighty curtaining, to a height of 7.5 feet (*c.* 2.28 m). For transportation, the dimensions, volume, and weight of all this would have been formidable, but the Israelites somehow took it with them from Sinai. It is further mentioned in Joshua 18:1 as being erected at Shiloh after the battle of Jericho and, according to 1 Kings 8:4, it was eventually in Jerusalem when Solomon dedicated the Temple.

The question that arises is this: The Tabernacle was taken to Jerusalem, and the Ark was taken to Jerusalem – but what about all the other valuable items? The golden altar, the shewbread table, the candlestick and all the other furnishings and equipment were integral to the Tabernacle and were not left sitting in the Sinai Desert. 1 Kings 8:4 even specifies that King Solomon had 'all the holy vessels that were in the Tabernacle'. Why then would he have needed to employ Hiram of Tyre to make them all again? Hiram most likely made the *Jachin* and *Boaz* pillars, along with the great brazen laver, the Temple's cherubim and the wagons, but not the other portable items with which he is credited.

Reverting to the *Graham Manuscript*, we see that it includes an extra-biblical element concerning Bezaleel. It discusses two young princes who sought instruction from him, whereupon the craftsman agreed so long as they promised not to impart the secrets to anyone else. They swore an oath to this effect, and were duly instructed by the master. After Bezaleel's death, it was thought by many that his secrets had died with him, but in fact they were safe with the princes that he taught.[17]

Around 1730 the reverend gentlemen, Jean Desaguliers and James Anderson, amalgamated the biblical account of Hiram of Tyre with the manuscript stories of Bezaleel and Noah. In doing this, they created a combined legend, which focused on their newly conceived figure of Hiram Abiff. But why did they feel it necessary to do this? The individual stories were fine as they were. Why purposely fabricate a new story which, almost from the outset, caused consternation among Freemasons who had never heard of the spurious master builder? And why sideline a legitimate figure such as Bezaleel – unless of course that was the express purpose of the exercise? If this was the reason, it is unlikely that researchers would set their sights in his direction while they were busy (as they have been for 267 years) struggling with the incomprehensible mystery of Hiram Abiff.

The fact that Anderson and Desaguliers were both resolute Protestant churchmen (Presbyterian and Calvinist respectively) might have had something to do with their 3rd-degree strategy in the days when the Grand Lodge of the Moderns was at odds with their opponents, the Antients. Maybe there was something pertinent to the story of Moses and Bezaleel that was more akin to the Antients' tradition, and from which they wanted to divert the attention of the Moderns. As we shall discover in chapter 20, this certainly appears to have been the case.

Tracing Boards

Having looked at the 3rd degree of Craft Freemsonry (The Master Mason's degree), it is now helpful to establish how this follows from the 1st and 2nd degrees of the Entered Apprentice and Fellow Craft masons.

Apart from the ceremonial rituals which deal with the opening and closing of lodges, together with initiation and raisings, each of the three degrees incorporates a descriptive lecture, which is explained with the aid of an illustrated collage called a Tracing Board. (Coloured examples of 1st, 2nd and 3rd-degree Tracing Boards are shown in plates 18, 19, 20.) There are a variety of designs used by different lodges, and some are more ornate than others but, in essence, they all follow the same individual themes. Tracing Boards first appeared in the late 18th century, and were further developed in the early 19th century. They are teaching devices, which are also used to decorate the lodges.

On entering a masonic lodge for the first time, the Entered Apprentice is likened to a rough-hewn stone (the Rough Ashlar), which will eventually become smoothed and perfected. It is at this stage that the prospect of being admitted to the 'mysteries and privileges of ancient Freemasonry' is potentially very exciting. Progressing through the three Craft degrees, however, concludes with the immensely disappointing Hiramic legend, and it is not until one joins the Royal Arch Chapter that the excitement builds again – but this time with a better purpose.

The aim of the 1st degree is that the candidate is introduced to his own psyche, while also gaining introduction to the format of a masonic lodge. The seven officers are likened to seven levels of consciousness – the Worshipful Master, the Senior and Junior Wardens, the Senior and Junior Deacons, the Tyler and the Inner Guard. The three columns depicted on the Tracing Board represent three principal agencies that operate through those levels. The first (Corinthian) concerns activity, exuberance and creativity. The second (Doric) relates to the passive, reflective and traditional nature. And the third (Ionic) denotes equilibrium.[18] The chequered pavement (as used in the lodge itself) is the ground-level contact with the physical world, while the columns reflect the psyche or soul as a mid-way dimension – a gateway to the heavens. A fourth dimension on the Board is the high central Glory, signifying the divinity of spirit.

The 1st-degree Tracing Board also contains other symbols, especially the cardinal points of the compass, which denote the Board's east–west directioning of consciousness. Also depicted is Jacob's Ladder – a route to higher levels, with its three principal rungs being Faith, Hope and Charity. In turn, each of these is associated with a progression through the three degrees. Incorporated within the ladder symbolism is a volume of the Sacred Law and a point within a circle ⊙. The Working Tools of an apprentice are also depicted: a common gavel, a 24-inch gauge (a ruler) and a chisel.

The candidate is kept in a state of darkness (hoodwinked) for a part of the ceremony, and divested of all metallic substances to signify poverty and a defenceless state. His right arm, left breast (to distinguish gender) and knee are bared, and only his right heel is slip-shod – together signifying a state of being 'neither naked nor clothed; neither barefoot nor shod' – and the point of all this is humility. Before gaining full admittance, a sharp implement is placed to the candidate's breast by the Guard, and he proceeds with a short cable-tow (noose) around his neck. Each of these is pertinent to the solemnity of the occasion, to his fraternal obligation, and to the symbolic penalties for any violation of the trust placed in him.

On being restored to the light, with his blindfold removed, the candidate is introduced to the Three Great Lights: the Volume of the Sacred Law (VSL), the square and compasses, along with the Lesser Lights, the sun, moon and the Master of the Lodge. Also described are the Jewels of the lodge: the level and plumb-rule, together with the square. Much else transpires in the course of all this, with descriptions of advancing through the lodge by means of straight and right-angular steps, and the whole is geared to an understanding of squares, uprightness, perfection and discipline. The initiate is taught about brotherly love, relief and truth, and about temperance, fortitude, prudence and justice, culminating with the signs, tokens and password of the degree.

First and Second Degree Tracing Boards

Being deemed a 'progressive science', the 2nd-degree Tracing Board of the Fellow Craft mason expands upon the former. Jacob's Ladder becomes a winding (or curved) staircase, while the candidate is likened to a newly ripened ear of corn. He is now deemed to be in control of his mundane persona, and ready to begin his rise to the upper levels of consciousness.[19] The staircase still proceeds in an east to west direction, but now conveys a more complex structure, moving from the physical body, through the spirit, towards divinity in seven levels of consciousness. It is also associated with the Seven Liberal Arts. The Working Tools of this degree are the level (justice), the plumb-rule (mercy), and the square (truth). Concentrating on matters of morality, these tools are each concerned with testing one's self against some absolute criterion.

The degree conveys that, during the building of Solomon's Temple, Fellow Craft masons ascended to the middle chamber in order to receive their wages. This is likened to the receipt of one's dues in life, but that one will only be entitled to what one deserves. The middle chamber symbol is given pictorially either as a letter 'G' (the initial of the Deity) or as an All-seeing Eye. Also shown on the Tracing Board are the Temple pillars of *Boaz* ('in strength') and *Jachin* ('to establish'), supporting the terrestrial and celestial globes to denote Masonry Universal. Together, the pillars are said to represent 'stability'.

During the 2nd-degree ritual, the candidate is reminded that the Temple pillars were made hollow so as to serve as repositories for masonic secrets, and a new form of advancement through the lodge is learned, along with some information concerning Euclidian geometry. Once again, the ceremony is geared throughout towards teaching the Fellow Craft mason the new signs, tokens and passwords of the degree.

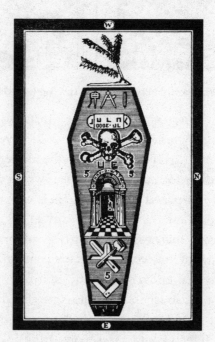

Third Degree Tracing Board

At this stage of masonic progression, a good deal of ground has been covered. Much of it has concerned the workings and protocols of the lodge, while other aspects relate to spiritual awareness and an aspiration towards certain moral and charitable virtues. Along with these, there have been lectures and instructional sequences – often Old Testament based, or concerned with the Liberal Arts. In many respects, these aspects appear decidedly naive and superficial, and the biblical sections are generally interpretations of a somewhat dubious nature. However, a level of high anticipation persists because the 3rd degree is yet to come. Everything has been building towards this, and it is in this Master's degree that the ultimate and wonderful secrets of Freemasonry must be revealed. But this, of all unexpected things, is the 'let-down' degree, and what one is subjected to is the fabricated legend of the death of Hiram Abiff.

If there is any big and overwhelming secret inherent in this degree, then it is beyond the bounds of any normal comprehension. It has been said that 'The Master Mason's degree is difficult to interpret because the ritual describes a psychological process which occurs only rarely in our society.'[20] But if the mason who has been prepared for this degree by virtue of calculated training and conditioning through its predecessors cannot interpret it, then something is dramatically wrong.

The reason for the incomprehensible nature of the Hiramic legend is actually quite easy to understand. It was summed up long before it came into being by Sir Isaac Newton, who wrote during his own quest for the great philosophical secret:

> A man may imagine things that are false,
> but he can only understand things that are true.

The Transition

Early Guilds

Given that there is little of any substance in the Hiramic culmination of the Craft degrees, it might be wondered what on earth Freemasonry was about prior to its introduction in the 1730s. What, for example, was its fascination for educated scholars such as Elias Ashmole and Sir Christopher Wren? It is for this reason that we must separate the Hanoverian masonic establishment from anything that went before. James Anderson had alluded to Wren as if he were a Freemason of the Grand Lodge Craft because it had suited him to do so. But for all the possible linguistic derivations of the term, a line must be drawn at this stage between what *is* Freemasonry and what it *was*.

In early times, the Knights Templars had referred to each other as 'brother masons' (*frères maçons*), and the term has continued in French masonic use to the present day. Alongside this, the style used for a French Freemason is *Franc Maçon*. The idea that speculative Freemasonry evolved from medieval guilds of stonemasons such as the Children of Solomon in France is true, but only to a point. There were no such guilds in Britain at that time and, although the lodge structure was introduced into Scotland by the Templars from 1307, that did not mean that the Knights were themselves operative, or even speculative, stonemasons.

Lodges of a masonic style began to appear in Scotland from the 15th century when workers' guilds were established under royal charter, but they were trade and craft institutions, and not necessarily to do with stonemasonry. Neither were they in any way philosophical. In 1474, King James III chartered guilds of weavers, cordwainers (leather-workers), wrights (metalworkers), masons (stoneworkers), glaziers, painters, bowyers (bow-makers), upholsterers, slaters, sievewrights (sieve and basket makers) and coopers (barrel makers). In 1483 were added hammermen (blacksmiths, cutlers and armourers), saddlers and fleshers (butchers). From 1500, James IV chartered guilds of surgeons and barbers, and from 1530 King James V added bakers, bonnet-makers and goldsmiths. Meanwhile, the Templar Chapters were running in parallel, but quite independently of all this.

Outlaws of the Privy Seal

Following the 1312 outlawry of the Knights Templars in Catholic England, their lands and preceptories were passed to the separate Knights Hospitallers of St John (*see* page 142). In Scotland, for all practical purposes, the Templars were represented from 1317 by the Brethren of the Rosy Cross, but there were still the Templar estates to consider. Pope Clement V had issued a Bull demanding that they should be passed into Hospitaller ownership and although the directive was not implemented in Scotland, the Scottish Hospitallers did provide a suitable cover for the Templars' property interests.

North of the border, the administrative association of the two Orders continued in an informal fashion for a long period, but James IV of Scots formalized it by way of a royal charter on 19 October 1488. The Scottish estates remained under Templar ownership, but were henceforth seen to be managed by William Knollis, Preceptor of the Scottish Hospitallers at Torphichen in West Lothian. Knollis was appointed Treasurer by James IV on 18 June 1488, and was installed as Governor of Blackness Castle, near Bowness on the Firth of Forth. Then, on 19 October, all Templar properties were settled under Hospitaller administration. Three years later, on 10 January

1491 – and in recognition of his services – Knollis was granted a permanent Scottish parliamentary seat as Lord St John.

The Knights Hospitallers had been founded in the Holy Land shortly before the Templars and, under their Grand Master, Raimond Dupuy, they provided welfare and medical aid for pilgrims and victims of the Crusades. In fact, their Jerusalem hospital existed some while before the First Crusade of 1096, having been established in about 1050 by a Frenchman known as Gerhard the Holy. From 1530, the Knights Hospitallers of St John were re-established as the Knights of Malta, having left the Holy Land after the Crusades ended in 1291.

As distinct from the Templars' familiar eight-pointed red cross, the Knights of Malta bore a similar device in white. (A later offshoot of the Maltese Order, chartered in 1888, created Britain's St John Ambulance Association.) As well as having insignia of different colours, the Knights Templars and Knights Hospitallers also wore the robe colours of their respective monastic Orders, with the Templar mantle emulating the white cassock of the Cistercians, and the Hospitaller mantle emulating the black cassock of the Benedictines.

Irrespective of the property arrangements, the Scottish *Three Estates* Parliament[1] decreed in 1560 that any chivalric Order which paid lip-service to the Pope had to be disbanded. The Knights Hospitallers fell to the edict, and in recompense their Preceptor, James Sandilands, Lord St John, was granted the estates and hereditary barony of Torphichen by Mary, Queen of Scots.

Prior to this, Henry VIII Tudor of England had also assaulted the Catholic establishment, desecrating churches throughout the land. Even though the monks and friars of their respective Orders were not part of the Church's ecclesiastical structure, Henry demolished their abbeys and monasteries, burning the libraries and art collections to cause the greatest cultural loss in British history. In the course of this, he also set his sights against chivalric bodies that were attached to the monastic Orders, banishing many knights from his realm. The Templars retaliated by scuttling Henry's flagship, the *Mary Rose,* and she sank off Spithead on her maiden voyage.[2]

From 1560, the Templars came under the leadership of David Seton. He was a kinsman of Lord George Seton and his sister Mary – one of the *Four Maries* who had accompanied Mary Stuart to France in 1548, and returned with her to Scotland in 1561. In order to safeguard Templar interests from the Hospitaller confiscations by the State, David Seton reconstituted the Scottish Templars under a new identity: the Order of the Knights Templars of St Anthony.[3]

The *Privy Seal Register of Scotland* details that from 1590 there were two land grants made by King James VI to the Templars of St Anthony, each requiring that the Knights should found an operative hospital. The second of these land grants, awarded in 1593, was for a chapel, monastery and hospital at Leith. Completed in 1614, the hospital for the poor and infirm was called the King James Hospital, and bore the royal arms. At that stage, the Edinburgh lands of the Order of St Anthony were transferred by King James to the Kirk Session of South Leith in order to support the hospital which bore his name.

Despite a popular perception that the Templars ceased to exist in the early 1300s, the *Privy Seal* entries at the Edinburgh Register House[4] prove otherwise. The original 17th-century Seal of the monastic preceptory of the Knights Templars and Canons of St Anthony is preserved in the library of the Faculty of Advocates in Edinburgh.[5] It bears the figure of St Anthony (*c.* AD 300) in a hermit's mantle, with a book in one hand and a short staff in the other. At his feet is a sow with a bell around her neck. Above the saint's head is the letter 'T' – the *Tau* emblem of the St Anthony Order, which the Knights wore in blue upon black gowns.[6] The extensive monastery – 325 ft (*c.* 99 m) from east to west – was erected in South Leith on the left side of St Anthony's Wynd, off Kirkgate, where the Knights also had a chapel, a cemetery and gardens. These, and all the lands of the preceptory, were vested by James VI in the Kirk Session of Leith, 1614. The Wynd and hospital were eventually demolished in 1822, and the site was recorded as 'that place and piece of ground whreon the Church and Preceptory of St Anthony of the Knights Templars once stood'.

Seal of the Knights Templars and Canons of St Anthony of Leith

Eleven years before dedicating the hospital, James VI of Scots had also become James I of England in 1603. The Templar tradition of the Kings of Scots came with him to London, along with the St Germain heritable Grand Mastership of the Knights of the Rosy Cross. In 1613, his daughter Elizabeth married Frederick V, Elector Palatine of the Rhine, thereby cementing a family link with the Rosicrucian fraternity of Heidelberg. Everything was then in place for James's grandson, King Charles II, to connect with Christopher Wren's College for the Promoting of Physico-Mathematical Experimental Learning at Gresham College in November 1660. Subsequently, in 1662 and 1663, royal charters were granted by Charles, and the Royal Society of London for Improving Natural Knowledge was formally inaugurated.[7] The initial purpose of the group was to study the work and ideas of the Rosicrucian Master, Sir Francis Bacon. It is for this reason that Bacon was depicted in the Society's inaugural engraving, published in 1667 (see plate 12).[8]

The Riches of Salomon

We have learned that Hanoverian records were contrived to show that Sir Christopher Wren was initiated into Freemasonry on 18 May 1691 at a great meeting of accepted masons in St Paul's Cathedral (*see* page 65), but there was no St Paul's at that time, just the demolished ruin of the Fire of London, and a new building under construction. From 1660, Christopher Wren's informal lodge had been the Royal Society itself – a Rosicrucian establishment based on a Scottish masonic model long before the Stuart deposition of 1688. There was no connection between the physico-mathematical and natural philosophical nature of this institution and the gentlemen's dining-club type of Freemasonry that was born without any satisfactory provenance in 1717. Everything about the new form of Georgian Freemasonry had to be adapted from an earlier concept – or invented from scratch – and it was by virtue of this that the Hiramic legend came into being.

In the course of this inventive phase, there were vestiges of information that had been collected from the Stuart tradition of Wren and his colleagues, and one of these concerned the importance of King Solomon's Temple. Hence, it claimed a centre-stage position in the new masonic structure, but not in the way that it had once been important to Sir Christopher Wren and Sir Isaac Newton. The new organization understood little or nothing about the scientific aspects and alchemical principles of the Temple. Instead, what the Grand Lodge officers invented was mythology.

The Royal Society president Isaac Newton went to extraordinary lengths in constructing his floor-plan of Solomon's Temple from the biblical dimensions given in 1 Kings, and insisted that Solomon had designed the Temple with privileged eyes and divine guidance (*see* page 17). Newton believed that the geometry was not only a building blueprint, but a time-frame chronology, and strove earnestly to emulate the Old Testament king who was his greatest inspiration.[9]

Along with Robert Boyle and other members of the Royal Society, Newton knew that the great secret of King Solomon and the artificers of biblical times, such as Tubalcain, Bezaleel and Hiram, was a powerful and unique form of alchemical science based on the time-honoured, but elusive, Philosophers' Stone. He wrote extensively concerning the present sanctuary of the Ark of the Covenant, maintaining that it was not a terrestrial realm as was the Holy of Holies in the Jerusalem Temple, and that its linear dimensions were different. He made the point that 'with the force of inevitability, the quantitative expression of superiority was taking possession of the holiest of holies'.[10] Quite what he meant by this is not easy to determine, but while the Holy of Holies was the Temple's cubic residence of the Ark of the Covenant, the 'holiest' of holies was the Ark itself, which Revelation 11:19 indicates would dwell in the Temple of Heaven.[11]

In his related studies, Newton was especially interested in an anonymous alchemical treatise passed to him by Ezekiel Foxcroft, a Fellow of King's College, Cambridge. Foxcroft was the English translator of Johann Valentin Andreae's *Chemical Wedding* (1690) – a Rosicrucian document allied to the 1614 *Fama Fraternitatis* and the 1615 *Confessio Fraternitatis* – German tractates jointly known as the *Rosicrucian Manifestos*. The treatise which Foxcroft handed to Newton was entitled, *Manna – a disquisition on the nature of alchemy.*[12] In 1675, Newton added his own notes to this manuscript, including the statement:

> This philosophy, both speculative and active, is not only to be
> found in the volume of nature, but also in the sacred scriptures,
> as in Genesis, Job, Psalms, Isaiah and others. In the knowledge
> of this philosophy, God made Solomon the greatest philoso-
> pher in the world.[13]

In Sir Francis Bacon's famous work, *The New Atlantis* (written *c*. 1623 and published in 1627), he refers to the 'House of Salomon', within his concept of an ideal State. In this context – well over a century before the Industrial Revolution – Bacon's visions of future techno-logical advancement were extraordinary. He discussed air travel, submarines, propulsion engines and advanced ballistics, while setting down so many ideas for scientific discovery that the Fellows of the Royal Society had a ready-made check-list of things to research, discover and invent. Bacon called these visionary ideas the Riches of Salomon, and described them almost as if they had once existed, but were in need of rediscovery. In Rosicrucian circles, the House of Salomon (Solomon) was referred to as the Temple of the Rosie Cross.[14]

It is worth making the point that there never was, in the course of all history, any form of secret society called 'The Rosicrucians'.[15] Rosicrucianism was a wide and undefined philosophical tradition. There were individual Rosicrucians (as indeed were many of those in the Royal Society), and it might be said there was a Rosicrucian movement, but there was no formal organization as such. In real terms, Rosicrucianism was a utopian myth, but in pursuance of that ideal, many of the greatest discoveries in the world of science and medicine were made. Without this ideal, as supported by those such as Sir Francis Bacon, scientists would not have known what they were seeking to discover, and, consequently would have been far less likely to have made their discoveries. From this viewpoint, the *Rosicrucian Manifestos* were like proclamations of enlightenment to come.

However, it would be incorrect to suggest, as many have done, that post-1717 Georgian Freemasonry evolved from Rosicrucianism. What it did was endeavour to emulate it – and in some limited ways it succeeded. Modern Freemasonry combines an esoteric approach to religion with ethical teaching, and has an emphasis on philanthropy – and much the same can be said of certain aspects of Rosicrucianism – but that is where the similarity ends. Unlike Rosicrucian philosophy, English Freemasonry has never been concerned with the reform or advancement of the arts and sciences, nor with any practical form of scientific or natural philosophical research. These were the streams which flowed within the early Royal Society, and with which the likes of Christopher Wren were involved. Whether or not Wren was ever an initiated Freemason is entirely irrelevant. It was what Wren personified that the Anderson masons aspired to become.

Christopher Wren was as enthusiastic as Isaac Newton about the extraordinary mathematical magic of King Solomon's Temple. It was, therefore, no wonder that the Hanoverian Freemasons latched onto this when Desaguliers became the Grand Master of the Moderns in 1719. As a Fellow of the Royal Society, he would have been fully aware of ongoing research from the Society's published *Transactions*. It was worth creating a whole new degree just to cement the new-style Freemasonry to this Solomon tradition – and that is precisely what happened after 1724, when the 3rd degree was formulated. Unfortunately, instead of extending the thrust of the previous two degrees by incorporating Newtonian or other Temple philosophy into the new degree, the fictitious legend of Hiram Abiff became the focus and the whole impetus was lost.

Meanwhile, a rather more adequate 3rd degree already existed. It was much older, and had evolved quite separately from Craft Freemasonry, with records of a Scottish working as far back as 1590 in Stirling. Laurence Dermott, Grand Secretary of the Antients, explained to the Moderns that he knew of this degree, which existed quite independently of the Craft, and that he firmly believed it to be 'the root, heart, and marrow of Freemasonry', but he was ignored. Much later, the Antients included it as a formal aspect of their ritual in 1772. But it was not until December 1813, when the Antients and Moderns were amalgamated, that the Modern faction was finally obliged to relent, due to pressure from the members for something better than Hiram Abiff.

The additional working was called the Royal Arch, and Dermott had been correct; it was indeed far more substantial than the established 3rd degree. But it was too late to make a substitution, and it was determined that there could be no more than three degrees because that would, in effect, demote all the existing Master Masons. The Holy Royal Arch was therefore added as a Chapter extension of the 3rd degree, finally giving the Craft brethren something of culminating consequence. We shall return to the Royal Arch later, at which stage the great significance of Bezaleel, as against Hiram, will become apparent, as will the related term *Manna* in accordance with the title of the treatise acquired by Isaac Newton.

Statutes and Charters

The fact that Sir Robert Moray had been initiated into a masonic lodge in 1641, followed by Elias Ashmole in 1646 (*see* chapter 3) serves to prove that, alongside Templar and Rosicrucian activities, there was a form of Freemasonry operating in England in Stuart times. Ashmole's own diary entry is quite specific in this regard, stating:

> 1646 October 16th, 4H.30pm. I was made a Free-Mason at Warrington in Lancashire with Col Henry Mainwaring of Karincham in Cheshire.

It is somewhat strange that Moray is always cited as being the first Freemason to be initiated in England, followed by Ashmole, but Col Mainwaring rarely gets mentioned, although he was in fact Ashmole's father-in law, and was initiated on the same day.[16] It transpires that the lodge at Warrington was specially convened for the purpose of these initiations, being what is termed an 'occasional lodge' which might only have existed for that one particular day. No other references to it have ever been discovered. Five years earlier, Sir Robert Moray's initiation in Newcastle was conducted by a military lodge stationed from Edinburgh when he was General Quartermaster to the Scots Army – so in practice, his was a Scottish initiation even though taking place in England. Something similar might have been the case for Ashmole since there is no record in England of initiations for any of the seven named men who formed the October 1646 lodge at Warrington.

Clearly, the soldiers of the military lodges of the mid-1600s were not operative stonemasons. But it seems that masonic lodges prior to the 1590s were operative stonemasons' guilds, although there is evidence of a few non-operatives gaining admission. The edges of transition from operative to speculative masonry are blurred, but there is no doubt that it took place in Scotland.

Among the most prominent families in Scotland at that time was the old Norman family of St Clair. They arrived in the 11th century before the 1066 Norman conquest of England and in 1057 they received the Barony of Rosslyn (a few miles south of Edinburgh) from Malcolm III Canmore. A later Sir William de St Clair, Sheriff of Edinburgh, was a close colleague of King Alexander III (1249–86). By the time of King James II of Scots (1437–60), the St Clair name had become Sinclair, and William Sinclair, Earl of Caithness, Grand Admiral of Scotland, was appointed hereditary Patron and Protector of the Scottish Masons by King James in 1441. The document of appointment, signed by James, is held by the Grand Lodge of Scotland, along with details of the hereditary appointment as recorded by Grand Lodge Secretary, Alex Lawrie, in 1804.[17] William Sinclair was a Knight of the Golden Fleece and a Knight of the Coquille St Jacques (the Order of Santiago di Compostela), a 12th-century foundation with strong Templar connections.[18]

In 1583, the Aberdeenshire laird William Schaw was appointed by King James IV to reorganize the stonemasons of Aberdeen and the surrounding area. And, in 1598, as the King's Master of Works, he issued the first of the now famous *Schaw Statutes*, which set out the duties of masons to their lodges and to the public. (Schaw and his assistant, James Boswell of Auchinlek, were initiated in 1598, and are among the first non-operative masons on record.) From that time, lodge Minutes begin to appear, commencing with those of Aitchinson's Haven and Edinburgh, followed by Haddington. In 1599, the *Second Schaw Statutes* were issued, and these identified the lodges of Kilwinning, Edinburgh, Stirling and St Andrews.[19] It is with these *Statutes* that the earliest veiled reference is made to some form of esoteric knowledge within the craft of stonemasonry, and members were instructed to 'practice the Art of Memory'.

Kilwinning is regarded as the Mother Lodge of Scotland, although the oldest extant records held by the Grand Lodge of

Scotland are the Minutes of Aitchinson's Haven in Midlothian, dated 9 January 1598. The Minutes for the Lodge of Edinburgh (St Mary's Chapel) No 1, dated 31 July 1599, are the oldest for a lodge which is still in existence, and Schaw designated Kilwinning as Lodge No 2. The Kilwinning members were not happy about this second ranking, and consequently ignored the second *Schaw Statutes* in their Minutes.[20] Outside of Templar circles, use of the term 'free mason' was uncommon in Scotland, but appears occasionally in 17th-century Minutes. The Lodge of Melrose, for example, recorded the attendance of a *frie mason* in 1674. By about 1600, lodge working had a distinctive format in Scotland, and incorporated an elaborate system of signs and rituals. Also, as a result of the *Schaw Statutes*, the masonic terminology of today's lodges had begun to develop: there were master masons, fellows of the craft, and entered apprentices, along with rules concerning how many masters had to be present to convene a lodge.

William Schaw fully expected to gain royal assent for his legislations, but King James's approval was not forthcoming. This was probably because Schaw sought to grant masonic lodges a peculiar status that ignored the planning permission rights of burgh and other local authorities. It was also plain that James was not about to undermine the hereditary patronage of the Sinclairs of Rosslyn, who were still the guardians of Scottish masonry. The prevailing William Sinclair had his position confirmed and was further empowered to superintend judicial procedures – at which time, in 1602, William Schaw died, and in the following year King James moved to London when the Scottish and English crowns were united.

In 1617, William Sinclair went to Ireland, transferring the baronies of Rosslyn and Pentland to his magistrate son – another William – who was knighted in that year and subsequently became Sheriff of Edinburgh. A Sinclair Charter of 1628 proves an interesting document because, as well as applying to stonemasons, it was also relevant to hammermen, which included wrights, smiths and others of the metalworking trades. It is at this stage that the singular importance of 'stone' moves out of the picture, with 'geometry' and the use of geometric instruments becoming the deciding factor in what constitutes a mason. Also brought beneath the same banner were slaters, glaziers and various other craftsmen 'that wirkis be square reule, lyne or compass under the art of geometrie'.[21] The transition towards speculative masonry had begun, and by virtue of a document to this effect issued by James VI concerning Dundee craftsmen in 1592, Sir William Sinclair created a realm of masons who were involved with geometry, but not necessarily with stone.

Although the craftsmen of Fife, the Lothians, Stirling, Dundee and elsewhere were happy to sign the Sinclair Charter, the stoneworking lodge members of Kilwinning were not convinced about the new concept. Also they continued to be unhappy about being designated Lodge No 2. In 1628, James Murray (Shaw's successor as Master of Works) met with William Sinclair at Rosslyn to discuss the issue, but little was resolved. The two factions remained in opposition, albeit Sinclair obtained royal sanction for his charter from King Charles I in 1631. Murray then approached the King to have his own position confirmed in relation to that of Sinclair, and the debate rumbled on. In essence, it was no more than an argument about the relative powers of the Masters of Works as against the Patrons of Masonry, each of which position was a royal appointment without clearly defined parameters of operation. The result was that it became a matter based on which of the two men could wield the greatest individual influence in the field.

In 1634, Anthony Alexander succeeded Murray as Master of Works, and was astute enough to join the Lodge of St Mary's, thereby gaining some masonic support and a distinct advantage over Sir William Sinclair. And so it progressed – to the extent that King Charles ended up in a dispute with his own Chancellor, and no one could agree who had final authority in respect of masonic lodges in Scotland. In the course of all this, Alexander and Sinclair both died, with their successors continuing the feud until (with nothing resolved) the Civil War erupted and the warring masons were the last thing on the mind of King Charles I.

Throughout the Cromwellian era, silence descended on the masonic dispute as a matter of front-line interest. However, with the Restoration of Charles II in 1660, the King took matters into his own hands. The new masters of geometry were not the workmen, but the young academics of the *Invisible College*, who had emerged from the Protectorate with a keen interest in all matters relating to mathematics, architecture, science, alchemy and astronomy. It was the time of Christopher Wren, Robert Boyle and Robert Hooke – and the Royal Society was born.

Sir Robert Moray had initially persuaded King Charles to charter the Society as a royal institution and, alongside this, Charles appointed Robert's brother, Sir William Moray of Dreghorn as his Overseer of Works north of the Scottish Border, to be aided by Sir John Veitch of Dawyck. They were jointly given full responsibility as wardens over all trades, crafts and building works. If ever there was a conclusion to the earlier conflict in Scotland, it did not occur until a wholly new style of operation evolved nearly a century after Anthony Alexander and William Sinclair. Somewhere during this period, with no definitive records to explain how it happened, speculative Freemasonry had emerged, just as it had done in London. In 1736, the Grand Lodge of Scotland came into being, and its first Grand Master was the descendant William Sinclair.

The Art of Memory

What had happened during that 100 years of apparent masonic silence was that a great wave of Neoplatonist thought had swept through Britain and Europe. (Neoplatonism first emerged in about AD 250 as a combination of Platonic philosophy and the oriental mysticism of Plotonius. It claimed that the human intellect was not related to the material world, and that individual spirituality would increase in relation to one's contempt for earthly values.) The preceding Renaissance was not just a revival of classical interests in matters of architecture, art and literature, but had also given rise to a new fascination with ancient wisdom philosophies, esoterica, and subjects such as magic, alchemy and astrology. At the same time, religion was being viewed rather more circumspectly, and new branches of investigative theology emerged. It had become an age of research, experiment and thought. If the Renaissance was (as its name determines) a 'rebirth' of artistic values, the subsequent era was one which sought a rebirth of moral and spiritual virtues, along with a hankering to understand more about nature and natural phenomena.

It is in this context that the secrecy associated with masonic lodges began to emerge. Esoteric studies were about secret things – the hidden (*occult*) forces of nature and the mysterious secrets of the universe. People studied privately, or formed disussion groups which became competitive – keeping their thought processes and their conclusions private as if they were the guardians of great untold secrets. If they came to no conclusions, then equally this was kept secret. Many such groups arose from clubs and societies that already existed, among which were the trade and craft guilds – the masonic lodges. If some aspect of knowledge was deemed unique or special (in the same way as a particular craft skill), then it was kept secret as exclusive in-house information. What distinguished the Royal Society was that its doors of knowledge were never closed; the members published everything.

In the course of keeping their secrets (whatever, if anything, they might have been worth), members began to use codes and symbols of expression and mutual recognition. The greater their exclusivity, the greater the secret – and the greater its potential value. Popular favourites in symbolic terms were ancient Egyptian hieroglyphs; they were ready made for such a purpose – simple, yet mystical and intriguing. Before the 1799 Rosetta Stone discovery made their translation possible, hieroglyphs were not understood, making them the perfect magical symbols, and consequently they were used extensively. It is partly for this reason that Freemasonry is often reckoned to trace back to ancient Egypt, but in practice there was no direct masonic significance to the old inscriptions. Latter-day secret societies did not inherit these signs from their predecessors in Egypt; they simply copied them because they were available and suited the new purpose. The same applied to numerous other signs and symbols from other cultures, and the pagan marks of the old Celtic realms provided other common favourites – such as star pentacles and the like.

What did come largely from Egypt (especially out of Grecian Alexandria), and gave specific purpose to many of the ancient symbols, was hermetic thought. The very word 'alchemy' stems from the Arabic *al* (the) and *khame* (blackness). *Al-khame* was defined as the science which overcomes the blackness, or that which enlightens through intuitive perception. The All-seeing Eye, which eventually became a masonic symbol, was originally attributed to blackness (or nothingness) by alchemists – the ability to see light out of darkness, to perceive order out of chaos. This particular symbol has many variations, including the Egyptian Eye of Horus (the *Wedjat*), and the eye in the triangle, sometimes called the Eye of God, used in Christian artwork (*see* plate 4).

The *Wedjat* Eye of Horus

William Schaw had instructed that Scottish masons should practice the Art of Memory. In *The Origins of Freemasonry*, David Stevenson, Professor of Scottish History at the University of St Andrews, relates that many prominent Scots of Schaw's era were deeply interested in hermeticism, and that King James VI had personally sponsored the Italian alchemist John Damian.[22] This interest was greatly enhanced after James's daughter Elizabeth married the Elector Palatine, and brought Rosicrucian thought into an academic mainstream of Scottish consciousness.

The Art of Memory was a particular technique that had evolved and developed in ancient Greece. It was used by lawyers and other public orators as a means of remembering lengthy speeches, and had been used by Shakespearian and other actors of the Tudor period. It works in much the same way that a modern lecturer might use slides and projected images, with each one in sequence being brought on screen in time to remind the speaker of what comes next. The man who brought this old memory system to light in Tudor times was the Italian philosopher Giulio Camillo (1479–1544). His *Memory Theatre* became a model for *The Globe* in London, which was built in such a way that its layout of tiers, supports, gangways and entrances was a memory-jogging mechanism for actors of the Elizabethan court. A copy of Camillo's book, *L'Idea del Theatro*, was held in the library of the Queen's astrological advisor, John Dee (*see* page 45).[23] It was said that, with selected images and ornaments strategically placed in sequence through *The Globe* auditorium, anyone 'will be able to discourse on any subject no less fluently than Cicero'.[24] Another noted Art of Memory exponent was the Italian philosopher Giordano Bruno, who lived in England 1583–5, and who exerted a strong influence on William Schaw.

The Art of Memory was relevant to Schaw's stonemasons because it specifically concerned buildings, and would come naturally to those who were experienced in construction. Even today, as a consequence of this, one of the primary aspects of lodge ritual in Freemasonry is the ability to learn and memorize lengthy (often multi-page) sequences and Tracing Board lectures off by heart.

Good, word-perfect renditions of such passages are, in many ways, as important to lodge working as understanding the content of the passages themselves.

The way that the memory system works is to become wholly familiar with the internal layout of a suitably complex building. Visual images of its rooms, corridors and stairways must become second nature, and a method of mentally walking through the building, from one room to another, must be devised. Only one building has to be used, because once memorized it is a constant. When learning individual aspects of a trade, or individual sections of text for an oratory, each separate aspect is allocated a room in the building in the same progressive sequence as the walkthrough that has been confined to memory. Hospitals and other such buildings with named departments are particularly good, since one can assign departments of the building to departments (subject sections) of memorized text. When the time comes to relate the information, whether verbally or literally, one simply imagines a walk through the building's predetermined route, and the mind is jogged, a room at a time, through the memorized sequence. The same principle has been successfully used by those who regularly take a certain walk through a town – maybe a walk to school or work. The street corners, buildings and various landmarks become familiar in their sequence and, in the same way, aspects of sequential learning can be assigned to each.

Prominent in the Neoplatonist fever of the early 1600s was the work of the 1st-century Roman architect Vitruvius,[25] who had been so admired by Leonardo da Vinci. It was Vitruvius who had the greatest influence on the way that masonic thought changed in the 17th century, and his concept of the architect led directly to the philosophical progression from 'operative' stonemasonry to 'operative' Freemasonry. In this original context, the Freemason was still an operative worker – an architect. It was the later era of 18th-century dining-club fraternities which led to the 'speculative' Freemason, who was neither a mason nor an architect. Even back in the time of Julius Caesar, Vitruvius had recognized (as stated in the first book of his *De Architectura*) that: '… the architect should be equipped with the knowledge of many branches of study and varied kinds of learning, for it is by his judgement that all work done by the other arts is put to the test.' He made the point that the true architect must be as familiar with the stone as with the pencil. He must know the theory and the practicalities, and by virtue of his expertise (not the builder's) will a building stand or fall. He wrote:

> Let the architect be educated, skilful with the pencil, instructed
> in geometry, know much history, have followed the philoso-
> phers with attention, understand music, have some knowledge
> of medicine, know the opinions of the jurists, and be
> acquainted with astronomy and the theory of the heavens.

What Vitruvius had described 1,600 years before was to be achieved by Christopher Wren, professor of astronomy and the greatest archi-tect of the Stuart era. Wren emerged from the mid-1600s through to the 1720s as the epitome of the masonic ideal. He was the ultimate 'operative' Freemason. Desaguliers, Anderson and their colleagues were well aware of this, but Wren died without joining their frater-nity, and for this they never forgave him. Wren would have been the first Grand Master of England, but he chose to keep his distance from a 'speculative' club that was simply shadowing masonic reality. Consequently, following Wren's demise, James Anderson accused him of hindering masonic progress by withholding his secrets. In truth, Wren's greatest secret was not a secret at all. He was quite simply the decisive Vitruvian Man, and that was not some-thing he could have imparted to anyone.

10

Rosslyn

Heritage of St Clair

During the 12th and 13th-century reigns of David I, Malcolm IV and William the Lion, a policy of bringing Flemish settlers to Scotland was implemented. The nation was in a progressive mood, and the Flemings were traditionally experienced in trade, agriculture and urban development. Many of the Scottish families often credited with Norman descent are actually of Flemish origin, and Flemish heraldry can be traced for the families of Balliol, Bruce, Comyn, Douglas, Lindsay, Fleming, Hay, Graham and others.[1]

The common inference that such families were Norman results from an English rewriting of Scottish registers from Victorian times. The Normans (Norsemen) were Vikings who had acquired Neustria in Northern France, and then invaded England in 1066. On marrying Giselle, daughter of the French King Charles III (893–922), Rollo the Viking gave Neustria the new name of Normandy. His descendant, William the Conqueror, led the invasion of England against the House of Wessex, but at no time did this incursion move into Scotland. The Normans who subsequently entered Scotland went there peacefully, with Scots royal consent.

Among the few notable Norman families in medieval Scotland was that of St Clair who held the royal patronage of Scottish masons, with William Sinclair becoming the first Grand Master of Scottish Freemasonry in 1736 (*see* page 153). Back in the 11th century, Henri de St Clair (from St Clair-sur-Elle in La Manche)[2] was a crusader with Godefroi de Bouillon, and more than two centuries later his descendant – also Henri de St Clair – was a commander of the Knights Templars at the Battle of Bannockburn (1314). The St Clairs (who eventually became the Sinclair Earls of Caithness) were of dual Viking heritage through the Dukes of Normandy and the Jarls (Earls) of Orkney. Following the Inquisition of the Templars, the St Clairs became Scots Ambassadors to both England and France. Henry de St Clair (son of Henri the Crusader) was a Privy Councillor, and his sister Richilde married into the family of Chaumont, who were kin to Hugues de Payens, the original Grand Master of the Templars.[3]

The Templar legacy of the St Clairs is particularly evident at Roslin, near to the Order's original centre at Ballantradoch. There, a little south of Edinburgh, stands the fascinating 15th-century Rosslyn Chapel. At first glance it resembles a miniature Gothic cathedral, with its pointed-arch windows, and climbing buttresses topped with elaborate pinnacles. Closer inspection reveals that it is actually a strange combination of Nordic, Celtic and Gothic styles. These days the Midlothian town of the Saint-Clairs is spelled Roslin, although the chapel retains the traditional Rosslyn spelling. In Celtic

Rosslyn Chapel

times, the place was called Ross Lyn, relating to the rock promon-
tory (*ross*) of a waterfall (*lyn*). Equally, according to the Royal Celtic
Society in 1916, it could mean the wood (*ross*) of the lake (*lyn*),
depending on the extent of Irish or Welsh influence on the Scots
Gaelic interpretation of the era.[4]

The principal authority on Rosslyn and the St Clairs was Father
Richard Augustine Hay, Canon of St Genevieve in Paris and Prior
of St Piermont. In 1690, he compiled a 3-volume study entitled *A
Genealogie of the Sainteclairs of Rosslyn*.[5] It was eventually published
in 1835 and, being extracted from archives and charters of the family,
is regarded as the primary work on the subject.

The St Clairs received the barony of Rosslyn from Malcolm III
Canmore in 1057, and in the following century they built their castle
in the vicinity. Subsequently, in 1304, a new castle was built in a
more strategic location nearby. Deep beneath this fortress, it is said
that the sealed vaults still contain some of the Templar treasure
brought from France during the Catholic Inquisition.[6] Now mostly a
ruin with one habitable section, the castle was set on a rock promon-
tory by the precipitous banks of the West Esk River, and was subjected to frequent attack by the English since it guarded a natural
gateway to Edinburgh. With the Sinclairs being staunch supporters
of the Stuart (Stewart) kings, its destruction came in 1650 from the
cannon of the Cromwellian General Monk during the Civil War.

When the Templar Fleet left the coast of Brittany in 1307, the
majority of ships and their valuable cargo went to Scotland via
Ireland and the Western Isles, but some went to Portugal, where the
Templars became reincorporated as the Knights of Christ. The
Portuguese navigator Vasco da Gama, who pioneered the Cape
route to India in 1497, was a Knight of Christ. Earlier, Prince Henry
the Navigator (1394–1460) was the Order's Grand Master. The historian and biographer Andrew Sinclair has written at length about the
history of the Sinclairs' own navigational exploits, imparting a
detailed account of the Sinclair fleet's transatlantic voyage in 1398,
long before the supposed discovery of America by Christopher
Columbus.[7]

From the time that Rosslyn came into St Clair possession, prominent family members were buried there, with the exception of
Rosabelle, the wife of Baron Henri the Crusader. She was drowned off
the coast to leave a haunting memory, as recalled by Sir Walter Scott
during the 19th century. In his *The Lay of the Last Minstrel*, he wrote:

> And each Sinclair was buried there,
> With candle, book and knell;
> But the sea-caves rung,
> And the wild winds sung
> The dirge of lovely Rosabelle.

Throughout their early years, the St Clair Barons of Rosslyn were of
the highest ranking Scots nobility, and they were numbered among
the closest confederates of the kings. The 13th-century Sir William
de St Clair, Sheriff of Edinburgh and Justiciar for Galloway, was also
Sheriff of Lothian, Linlithgow and Dumfries. He was so closely
attached to the Royal House that King Alexander III selected him as
foster father to the Crown Prince of Scotland.

Following the death of Robert the Bruce in 1329, a later Sir
William St Clair, Bishop of Dunkeld, set out for the Holy Land with
Bruce's heart in a silver casket.[8] Along with Sir James Douglas and
two other knights, he was to bury the casket in Jerusalem. On reach-
ing Andalusia in southern Spain, however, the party was confronted
by the Moorish cavalry. Seeing no way out, the four men charged the
invincible foe and were duly slain. The Moors were nonetheless so
impressed with the knights' courage that they returned the casket to
Scotland. Bruce's heart was later buried at Melrose Abbey, which is
itself steeped in Templar and Cistercian tradition.

It was a descendant William Sinclair, Earl of Caithness, Grand
Admiral and Chancellor of Scotland, who founded Rosslyn Chapel
in 1446 on the site of the family's original castle. The St Clairs
(having adapted their name to Sinclair in the late 1300s) were by
then the eminent guardians of the Kings of Scots. Given that James II
had appointed William to the post of Hereditary Patron and

Protector of Scottish Masons, he was able to call upon the finest builders in the country, along with the most expert craftsmen in Europe. Once the Rosslyn foundations were laid, building work started in 1450, and the chapel was completed in 1486 by William's son Oliver. It was meant to be part of a larger collegiate church but this was never built, although the foundations are still discernible.

The Mystery of the Chapel

In spite of its age, Rosslyn Chapel is still in regular use, although it has undergone extensive conservation procedures in recent years. The building is 35 ft x 69 ft (c. 10.7 m x 21 m), with a roof height of 44 ft (13.4 m). Many hundreds of stone carvings adorn the walls and ceilings. They relate to biblical culture and display a wealth of masonic symbols and iconography. There are swords, compasses, trowels, squares and mauls in abundance, along with various allusions to King Solomon's Temple. Rosslyn Chapel provides an unusually stimulating visual and spiritual experience.

Apart from the Judaic and esoteric carvings, the Christian influence is evident in an assortment of related depictions in stone. Amid all this there are recurring traces of Islam, and the whole is strangely bound within a pagan framework of winding serpents, dragons and woodland trees. Everywhere, the wild face of the Green Man peers from the stone foliage of the pillars and arches, symbolizing elemental life forces and the cycle of life. All this is enveloped in a vast array of fruits, herbs, leaves, spices, flowers, vines and the emblematic plants of the garden paradise. Inch for inch, Rosslyn is undoubtedly the most extravagantly decorated church in Britain, although not one crafted image can be construed as being art for art's sake. Each carving has a purpose, and each purpose relates to the next; despite the seeming ambiguity of the scene, an almost magical harmony reigns throughout. The Rosslyn archivist, Robert Brydon, has described the chapel as an 'allegorical book in stone'.[9]

Rosslyn does not have any familiar style of church imagery. Although clearly a holy shrine, it was never about religion in any recognized sense. It was built by Christians as a sacred domain on a site long since dedicated to St Matthew (near St Matthew's Well), but there is no Mary Madonna, no figure of Jesus, and no apostles in the decorations. Strangely, however, there is a non-biblical Christian item by the south door in the shape of Veronica's Veil – the cloth with which the legendary Veronica is said to have mopped the face of Jesus in the Via Dolorosa, and which became imprinted with his image (*Vera icon* meaning True image). From the Old Testament, the figure of Moses is identifiable, carved into a window recess – but this Moses has horns, just as depicted by Michelangelo (1475–1564) in his marble statue of the prophet at the tomb of Pope Julius II.[10] From the earliest of recorded times in ancient Mesopotamia, horns were pictorially associated with godly communication. Later, horns or small wings became objects of kingly or warrior adornment, being attached to helmets such as those of the Vikings[11] and the 5th-century Merovingian King Clovis of the Franks.[12]

Another Old Testament character is depicted in a nearby window recess – the figure of Melchizedek, Priest-King of Salem. It was he who offered Abraham the first Grail communion when he presented the bread and wine after Abraham's army had defeated the troops of some troublesome kings (Genesis 14:18–20). It was into the priestly Order of Melchizedek that the New Testament records Jesus' own initiation six months after his Resurrection (Hebrews 3:1 and 5:6). Fragments of the *Prince Melchizedek Document* found among the Dead Sea Scrolls indicate that Melchizedek and the Archangel Michael were one and the same, and he is called the Heavenly One and the Prince of Light.[13]

In his carved portrayal at Rosslyn, Melchizedek holds a chalice, while in his earlier statue representation at Chartres Cathedral (built by the masonic Children of Solomon – *see* page 161) his chalice contains a stone, said to be the Philosophers' Stone or the *Manna*.[14] The two characters, Moses and Melchizedek, are brought together by this very symbolism since it was within a golden bowl that Moses was said to have placed the *manna* in the Ark of the Covenant

(Exodus 16:33). In a 1744 masonic ritual of the Holy Royal Arch, Moses is given as the first biblical Grand Master,[15] and his Ark of Testimony (built by the craftsman Bezaleel) is still found at the crest of the Grand Lodge arms today.

Arms of the United Grand Lodge of England,
(Ark of the Covenant at the crest)

The steps to Rosslyn's small crypt carried the excessive wear of early times, and they have been replaced for the sake of safety. And there was a fireplace, but no explanation for its requirement has been found. Pilgrims apparently visited the crypt in droves – but what did they journey to see? It has been suggested that it might have been a builder's office rather than a sacristy for relics,[16] but it is damp, dingy and inconveniently situated. Even if this was so, it would not account for its centuries of hard use after the construction was finished. Sealed with stone beyond the crypt is a vault which also lies beneath the chapel, and it is here that the ultimate relic of Rosslyn is said to reside along with the armoured Barons of Rosslyn.

They were interred during the building work before the vault was sealed on completion. Sir Walter Scott's *Lay* refers to them:

> Seemed all on fire that chapel proud,
> Where Roslin's chiefs uncoffined lie;
> Each baron, for a sable shroud,
> Sheathed in his iron panoply.

Rosslyn Chapel has been likened to the Temple of Solomon and is often called the Chapel of the Holy Grail. There is a long-standing tradition that the place holds a great and wonderful secret, but what it is nobody knows. What is known is that when Marie de Guise (the wife of King James V) was made privy to the secret by William Sinclair's grandson, she promised to remain his 'true mistress' and to keep it silent all the days of her life.

Some have suggested that the Holy Grail or the Ark of the Covenant resides at Rosslyn, while others prefer the idea of a scroll written by Jesus or, more realistically, manuscripts brought back from Jerusalem by the Knights Templars.[17] These speculations have led to Rosslyn becoming the site of a competitive treasure hunt, although more in literary theory than in practice. For some years now the chapel has been strategically protected so that searches and excavations have not been possible during its drying-out and renovation. The quality of the latter, however, leaves much to be desired, and reports of appalling workmanship have been submitted by the Friends of Rosslyn to the Historic Scotland authority.

Notwithstanding this, in 1992, Andrew Sinclair, a Founding Fellow of Churchill College, Cambridge, wrote of a drilling investigation that he gained permission to undertake some time earlier.[18] To begin, he used archaeological groundscan equipment to survey the whole chapel. This revealed large cavities beneath, while the radar pulses also detected the metal of the armour of the buried knights, and what appeared to be some sort of metallic shrine. Also, beneath the churchyard, were found the remnants of the foundations of a large cruciform church, which had never been completed. Inside, there were hidden stairways to secret vaults, but on lifting the slabs, access proved impossible without major excavation. It was decided to check beneath with the use of endoscopic cameras passed through holes bored with fine core drills. The attempt was abortive however – drill bits jammed, rubble infilled the bores, and dust veiled the camera lenses. At every stage, the investigation was thwarted and eventually had to be abandoned.

Among the mysterious legends of Rosslyn is the tale of a murdered apprentice and it is noticeably similar to the mythical killing of Hiram Abiff. The story relates that a master mason was given a model of a beautiful pillar that his patron wanted him to replicate. Rather than work from a model, the mason went abroad to see the original for himself. But, on his return, he discovered that an apprentice had carved a marvellous pillar that he had envisioned in a dream. The master was so envious and filled with rage that he struck the apprentice with his maul and killed him. The Apprentice Pillar remains within Rosslyn Chapel to this day, and is the best-known feature of its interior workmanship.

Though unlikely to be true, the account was important enough for someone to deface the carving that is reckoned to be the apprentice in question. Apprentices were not allowed to wear beards, but there was a beard on the carved head until someone chiselled it off, presumably to add weight to the story. Clearly, it did not originally depict an apprentice, but its identity (if indeed a real person) remains unknown. Meanwhile the pillar, with entwined dragons at its base and the exquisite spiralling of its design, has been likened to the Yggdrasil tree of Norse mythology: the world ash tree which binds Heaven, Earth and Hell into the Tree of Life.[19]

Truth and the Temple

A secret that Rosslyn does hold is contained in an inscription made by William Sinclair, the chapel's founder and architect. Niven

Sinclair, another of the family name, has recently written at length about this. While the chapel is considered to be a story in stone – yet despite all of the carvings, from fallen angels to a veritable menagerie of animals, from the Green Man to Solomon's Temple, and from a cornucopia of plants to the dragons of the pillar, there is only one original inscription in the whole building. It is written in the Latin lettering of Lombardy on a lintel of the south aisle, and reads:

> *Forte est vinu; fortior est Rex; fortiores*
> *sunt mulieres' sup on vincit veritas.*
> Wine is strong; the king is stronger; women
> are stronger, but above all truth conquers.

What is known about William Sinclair is that, like Isaac Newton in later times, he had an in-depth knowledge of biblical history and was fascinated by scriptural lore. He was a Christian, or so it would seem, but his views (like those of the Templars) were not of the standard doctrine. In filling his chapel with plants and animals, instead of saints and apostles, William brought God and Nature into alignment. In the Judaeo-Christian doctrine, which sprang from an original Hebrew perception, Nature (including the sun and the heavens) was seen to be a servant of Jehovah, who was said to have created everything:[20] 'The heavens declare the glory of God, and the firmament sheweth his handiwork' (Psalm 19:1).

Within this religiously-minded culture, God was reckoned to transcend even Nature herself and, as a consequence of this evolving thought process, the true harmony of humankind and Nature was forfeit. In Mesopotamian, Canaanite and Egyptian thought, the inexplicable divine was seen to be manifest within Nature, and Nature enveloped both the gods and society. This belief, however, was shattered for all time by those who forsook harmony in favour of subservience. Hence the balance of the relationship between humankind and the phenomenal world was destroyed, and what was ultimately lost was integrity.

Nature (which is still referred to in the female sense) had long been venerated as the great beneficial Mother, but the Mother was shunned by a society which held the male godhead supreme – an unapproachable, unseen, solitary godhead, whose name could not even be uttered out loud. In Solomon's day, the High Priest of the Jerusalem Temple was the only one permitted to say the divine name – and that only once a year on the Day of Atonement. In fact, he could only say the ineffable word within the Holy of Holies (the inner sanctum of the Temple), and even then it had to be under his breath, beyond the earshot of others.[21]

As far as the biblical descendants of Abraham were concerned, the power of Jehovah was to be feared beyond measure, and the concept of this power became so awesome that it was said to transcend all things, material and immaterial. No longer was God seen to exist within Nature; it was held that God had created Nature. When writing for Chicago University in the 1940s, the oriental scholar Henri Frankfort summarized the situation by making the point that:

> ... the ancient bond between man and Nature was destroyed. Those who served Jehovah must forego the richness, the fulfilment, and the consolation of a life which moves in tune with the great rhythms of the Earth and sky.[22]

William Sinclair was plainly not of this Judaeo-Christian persuasion. He believed that God (the Father) and Nature (the Mother) were coexistent. In fact, more than that – they were One, and we (along with all his plants and animals) are a part of that One. Druidic veneration of Nature was no different to the Judaeo-Christian veneration of God. They became separated because, although the female role of Nature was understood by all as symbolic, the male role of God within the union had been manipulated to give the impression that God was somehow like a person – a divine character in his own right, who could make things.

How then does William's inscription about Truth conquering tie in with this and the building that he called his 'Chapel in the

Woods'? In the first place, it is a reminder to religious stalwarts that even the Bible places Truth above doctrines and interpretations – for the inscription has a biblical origin. Secondly, it is an inscription with express masonic significance.

Books and writings considered to be heretical were often burned in the Inquisitional era of William Sinclair, but an inscription in a chapel – that was different. His Church accusers were not likely to deface a holy shrine. His judgement concerning orthodox clerical opinion was not far wrong. The Presbytery records of Dalkeith reveal that Rev William Knox of Cockpen (brother of the Presbyterian reformer John Knox) was censured 'for baptising the Laird of Rosling's bairne' in Rosslyn Chapel. The official opinion of the Kirk was that Rosslyn was a 'house of idolatrie, and not ane place appointit for teiching the word and ministratioun of ye sacrements'!

After that, the all-powerful Kirk repeatedly warned Oliver St Clair that his house was idolatrous, and that he had until 17 August 1572 to demolish the altars of Rosslyn. On 31 August of that year it was reported by the local minister George Ramsay that 'the altars of Roslene were haille demolishit'. So, in a way, Lord William had misjudged the Church authorities. They were certainly not reluctant to destroy a holy shrine; but somehow his inscription survived – probably because its meaning and purpose were not recognized.

William's inscription consists of edited high-points from chapters 3 and 4 of the Old Testament book of 1 Esdras. This book has not been in Authorized English Bibles since the 1611 translation, but it was in the Bible of William's day, and is found in the Greek *Septuagint* from which the Authorized Edition was translated.[23] The aspect to which the Sinclair inscription relates is concerned with the 6th century BC and with Prince Zerubbabel of Judah, who rebuilt the Temple of Jerusalem after the Israelites returned home from 70 years of Babylonian captivity. Royal Arch masonic ritual deals with precisely this aspect of Israelite history. Based on 1 Esdras and Ezra 5–6, it contemplates the destruction of King

Solomon's original Temple by Nebuchadnezzar, and tells of how Zerubbabel (given as an ancestor of Jesus in Matthew 1:12–14) sought permission from the Persian King Darius to build another. Leading to this request was a competition between Zerubbabel and two others to see who was the wisest, and they each wrote for the King what they perceived to be the strongest and most influential of things.

The first man wrote that wine was the strongest because it can lead the mind astray. The second believed that a king was the strongest because he reigned over other men. The third participant, Zerubbabel, reckoned that women were stronger than either because they give birth to the kings who plant the vineyards to make the wine. But, he added that even women cannot compete with the Truth, which 'conquereth for evermore' (1 Esdras 4:41). The judges agreed, exclaiming 'Great is Truth', whereupon Darius asked Zerubbabel to confide his greatest wish. He reminded Darius that, on being enthroned, he had promised to rebuild the Temple of Jerusalem, and that his greatest wish was that this should be done.

The Zerubbabel inscription of Sir William Sinclair

On 11 December 1688, after William of Orange had landed with intent to usurp the Stuart throne, his supporters caused a good deal of damage within Rosslyn Chapel. It then remained unused until 1736, when its windows were glazed for the first time by James Sinclair, who also laid a new flagstone floor. But it was not until 1861 that services recommenced, and on Tuesday 22 April 1862 Rosslyn Chapel was rededicated by the Bishop of Edinburgh.

Despite the damage already sustained, it was not until 1954 that the most serious desecration took place. In May of that year, the

Ancient Monuments branch of the Ministry of Works announced that the whole place would be cleaned with ammonia, flushed with water, scrubbed and sealed inside with magnesium silica fluoride. It was this which led to the presently unfortunate eroded look of the internal carvings, which are now rounded instead of sharp; rough instead of smooth, and shallow instead of deep. The 1950s was an era of plastics experimentation, and magnesium silica fluoride was a platicized cement slurry. The coating was brushed throughout the interior, and dried to an impermeable waterproof, airproof layer. The result was that the chapel's stone construction soaked up rain water, but could not breathe to dry out before the next rainfall. Inside the humidity rose and the condensation build-up was high. William's Chapel in the Woods had been ruined.

Eventually, in 1995, plans were made for whatever remedial measures were possible, and, in 1997, free-standing scaffolding was erected around the whole building, with draped tarpaulins to keep further rain at bay. Since then, external repairs of a sort have been made to the walls, pinnacles and buttresses, along with roof and gulley renovations. But despite all debate and discussion, the problem of the internal coating still remains. No one knows how to remove it, and as soon as the building is subjected once more to the full rigour of the elements, the saturation process will begin again

Sinclair in America

Rosslyn Chapel's visitor literature[24] makes the point that within the building 'There are carvings of plants [maize, agaves and cacti] from the New World which pre-date the discovery of America by Columbus by one hundred years.' Norse ancestors of the Sinclairs had certainly explored the Atlantic as far back as the 10th century, and in Hauk's Book of The Icelandic Saga (extant copy dated 1320), Leif Ericsson is described as having crossed the Atlantic to Vineland the Good in 999. Indeed, the Orkney sailors had reached land to the West within Henry Sinclair's own 14th-century lifetime. Their reports claimed that the natives of a faraway place called Estotilands sowed corn and exported furs and sulphur to Greenland.

Estotilands was the place eventually called Nova Scotia (New Scotland) in Canada. The Orkney sailors also told of a southern country called Drogio. The natives of Drogio ran naked in the hot winds but, across the sea, the people were very refined. Their land was rich in gold, and they had cities and great temples to their gods. These accounts were all confirmed when voyagers travelled to the Caribbean Islands, and onwards to Florida and Mexico, the home of the Aztec Indians. In disregard of these early discoveries, however, academic tradition has it that the Aztec empire was not explored until the Spanish conquistador Hernán Cortéz arrived there in 1519.

From 1391, the master of Henry Sinclair's fleet was the Venetian sea captain, Antonio Zeno.[25] The Zenos were among the oldest families of Venice, and had been noted admirals and ambassadors from the 8th century. Before Sinclair and Zeno made their own passage across the Atlantic Ocean, Henry drew up a contract with his daughter Elizabeth and her husband, Sir John Drummond. The deed was sealed at Rosslyn on 13 May 1396, and empowered Sir John and Elizabeth to claim Henry's Norwegian lands if he and his sons should perish in the expedition.[26]

In May 1398, the Sinclair fleet set sail. There were 12 warships and 100 men, some of whom had made the voyage before. Their first port of call was Nova Scotia, where they landed at Cape Blomidon in the Bay of Fundy. Even today, the Micmac Indians tell of the incoming ships of the great god who they call Glooscap, and that he taught them about the stars and how to fish with nets. On his return home to Venice, Antonio Zeno wrote that, at this place, he had seen streams of pitch running into the sea, and a mountain that issued smoke from its base. Nova Scotia is certainly very rich in coal, and there are exposed coastal seams of pitch where the coal brooks run at Asphalt. Nearby, the greasy underground residues often smoulder beneath the hills of Cape Smokey. At Louisburg on

Cape Breton, a primitive canon found in 1849 is of the Venetian type used by Zeno, and of a style that was quite obsolete by the time of Christopher Columbus.

From Nova Scotia, Sinclair continued southwards. Evidence of the journey can be seen at Massachusetts and Rhode Island. At Westford, Massachusetts, where one of Henry's knights died, the grave is still discernible. Punched into a rock ledge is the 7-ft effigy of a 14th-century knight wearing a basinet, chain-mail and a sur-coat. The figure bears a sword of the 1300s and a shield with Pentland heraldry. The knight's sword is broken below the hilt, indicative of the customary broken sword that would have been buried with the knight.

At Newport, Rhode Island, is a well-preserved medieval tower. Its construction (an octagon within a circle, and eight arches around) is based on the circular model of the Templar churches. Similar remains are to be found at the 12th-century Orphir Chapel on Orkney. The Newport architecture is Scottish, and its design is repli-cated at the St Clair Church, Corstorphine, where Henry Sinclair's daughter has her memorial. Rhode Island was not officially founded until 1636, but its founding was no chance event. At the Public Records Office in London, a text dated four years earlier describes the 'rounde stone towre' at Newport. It proposed that the tower be used as a garrison for the soldiers of Sir Edmund Plouden, who col-onized the area.

More than 50 years after the Sinclair expedition, Christopher Columbus was born into the Age of Discovery in Europe. In Portugal, he became a Knight of Christ in the revised Templar Order, as did his contemporaries Vasco da Gama, Bartolomeu Dias and Ferdinand Magellan. Additionally, he belonged to the Order of the Crescent (founded by King René d'Anjou) – also known as the Order of the Ship. The Crescent knights were particularly concerned with matters of navigation, but had been condemned by the Church for insisting that the world was round!

Through John Drummond and others, Columbus knew precisely where he was heading, and it was not to Asia as the history books tell. Maps of the transatlantic New World were already in existence within his Templar circle. In particular, he had access to the new Globe of the World, which was completed in 1492 – precisely the year that he set sail. This was produced by the Nuremberg cartographer, Martin Behaim – a navigational business partner of a certain John Affonso Escorcio – an alias of John Drummond, whose grandfather had been on the Sinclair voyage in 1398.[27]

John Drummond was related to the Drummond Earls of Perth, where the records confirm that he was with King Ferdinand and Queen Isabella of Spain when Columbus sought their royal patronage in 1492. Both Columbus and Drummond had lived on the Island of Madeira, where Drummond's father, John the Scot, had settled in 1419 along with Columbus' father-in-law, Bartholomew Perestrello.

John the Scot's father was Sir John Drummond of Stobhall, Justiciar of Scotland. Sir John's sister, Anabella, was the wife of King Robert III of Scots. Sir John's own wife was Elizabeth Sinclair, whose nephew, William Sinclair, was the founder of Rosslyn Chapel. The route of navigational knowledge from Henry Sinclair of Rosslyn, Earl of Orkney, down to Christopher Columbus is therefore a matter of clearly defined record, and the latter's famous American 'discovery' would never have taken place were it not for the Sinclair voyage of nearly a century before.

Mysterious Science

The Portable Lodge

The masonic tradition of the Sinclairs of Rosslyn has embraced the individually recognizable, yet distinctly connected cultures of both stonemasonry and Freemasonry. The structural workmanship of Rosslyn Chapel is the epitome of the former, while its decorative features are wholly emblematic of the latter. The 15th-century Chapel abounds with carved images of so many tools and symbols that became icons of the masonic lodge tradition, and these are now artistically depicted on Tracing Boards to aid the instructional process of the Craft (*see* page 135).

It is often stated that the precursors of Tracing Boards were cloths that were unrolled onto the floor of the lodge. To some extent they were, but it is not strictly true to say that boards took the place of Floor Cloths since boards were also laid on the floor, and each can be used for different ritual purposes. So their histories are, in some respects, parallel as well as evolutionary.

Although the term 'lodge' is used to define a convened masonic meeting, it is also used to define the temple quality of the room where that meeting is held. Hence, while a lodge may be convened in a lodge, that was not always the case, neither is it mandatory today. Masonic meetings are often held in rooms that are not designed specifically for the purpose and lodges were often formed in the back rooms or upper rooms of taverns, hired for the occasion. Any such room had to be decorated and fitted with the appropriate trappings and furniture, and it all had to go back to its non-masonic normality after the meeting, so everything that related to creating a lodge environment was portable.

One of the Tyler's functions was to chalk, or otherwise mark out, the form of the lodge on the floor. Its shape was ambiguously called an 'oblong square'. Sometimes that would be the extent of it, while on other occasions the 'oblong square' (a rectangle also strangely known as a *parallelopipedon*) would include various masonic symbols. At the end of a meeting there was the job of mopping up.

In time, this practice became better organized and instead of marking out and mopping up the lodge was painted onto a cloth that could simply be unrolled. As the concept became more popular, masonic symbols were added to the designs, followed by individual cloths that were attributed to the different degrees of working. But then the artists became more ambitious and, instead of bearing mere basic outlines, they transformed the cloths into artworks in their own right. This led to a situation where some Floor Cloths were so heavily worked and expensive that no one wanted to walk on them. Instead, they were hung on display like conventional paintings, which gave rise to a practical dilemma. Where was the lodge? It was on the wall.

Since one could not then stand within the lodge, it became the practice to deem a lodge operatively formed so long as its cloth was displayed. However, since different cloths related to different degrees, they could not be hung permanently. Also, the matter of portability was still a consideration despite many lodges acquiring their own meeting halls – and most of all there was the matter of size. Floor Cloths were necessarily large. The most common practice, therefore, was to get them off the floor, but not to hang them. Instead, they were draped over planks that were raised on trestles, giving rise to the term Trestle Board. Having then contrived a table as one might at a bazaar or occasional fair, relevant objects were placed on top of the cloth in addition to its painted images. But this soon led to a practice which defeated the original objective in that plain cloths became adequate, so long as the variously important objects were placed on them. A good example is shown in the frontispiece of Anderson's 1784 *Constitutions* (*see* plate 7).

This was inconvenient in the smaller lodges, and added once again to the problems of transportation and setting-up. Hence, there was a return to the original idea, but this time the images of certain objects and key aspects of the degrees were painted on panels. These were smaller than the Trestle Board drapes, and easier to use in the upright position – sometimes on easels – thereby leading to the panel style of Tracing Board that is common today.

The parallel situation of cloths and boards occurred because, as the former evolved into the latter, there remained a requirement for floor cloths in many instances. Even now, some lodges do not have permanent venues. Church halls and the like have to be used, and carpets constituting the chequered masonic pavement are laid. This is even the case in many permanent lodges, where it makes practical sense for the pavement to be in the form of a movable carpet. Also, a black floor cloth is a necessary item in the 3rd Craft degree – laid down as a coffin-shaped grave for the enactment of Hiram Abiff's burial.

Set rules were never established for the design of Floor Cloths or Tracing Boards; they simply had to perform their respective functions as determined by the degrees. There are, therefore, many variations on the themes, as can be seen for example on page 137 and in plates 18, 19 and 20. Sometimes the boards are complete as they stand, while in other instances they allow for lines and additions to be drawn on them in the course of the related lectures. This is a throw-back to the design boards (generally waxed panels) used by operative master stonemasons, who would mark out the day's plans for their workmen. In Victorian times, when artistry was important to the extent that masons even began hand-painting their aprons, some Tracing Boards were cleverly devised in the form of a hinged book. On the front panel (as might be the front cover) is the 1st degree. When turned around, the back cover is the 2nd degree and, when opened up, the 3rd degree is revealed.

In 1813, when the Ancients and Moderns were amalgamated to form the United Grand Lodge of England, a Lodge of Reconciliation was set up to produce a more standard form of ritual. This was ratified and adopted three years later. Subsequently, an Emulation Lodge of Improvement was formed in 1823 so that Master Masons could prepare for office and succession to the Worshipful Master's chair. The Lodge meets at Freemasons' Hall in London, and a Brother who works a ceremony in accordance with Emulation ritual, without any prompt or correction, is awarded a silver matchbox. The test is severe enough that only 340 have been awarded since 1897. Some of the better-known and more attractive Tracing Boards are those used by the Lodge of Emulation.[1]

The Kirkwall Scroll

Among the most famous Floor Cloths is that which has become known as the Kirkwall Scroll. In fact, although it is presumed by some to be a Floor Cloth, others consider it to have been made as a decorative wall hanging. Either way, it might be the oldest such item in existence – and if not the oldest, then it is certainly unique in its presentation.

At 18 ft 6 in long, and 5 ft 6 in wide (c. 5.6 x 1.7 m), the linen cloth hangs in the Kirkwall Kilwinning Lodge No 38 at Kirkwall on the Isle of Orkney – the one-time Earldom of the Sinclairs. In a way, it is the masonic equivalent of the Shroud of Turin; its provenance is debated and contested, its origin is unknown, and its presumed age is often a matter of what the opposing schools of opinion *want* it to be. And as with the Shroud, scientific analysis leans one way, while in contrast there are those who doubt the validity of the analysis.

There is no record yet discovered which explains how, why or when the Scroll came to be at the Kirkwall Lodge, but there is reason to suspect that it was perhaps transfered from Kirkwall Castle. Built in the 14th century by Lord Henry Sinclair, Kirkwall had been severely damaged and little used since the 1600s, but was not finally demolished until 1865. The first report on the Scroll was published a little after this in 1897 by George W Speth, a founder of the Quatuor Coronati Lodge of Research in London. There is also evidence from a century earlier that a Floor Cloth, gifted by a William Graeme, was being used in lodge rituals by 1786, but it is not clear if this was the same cloth. Even the lodge book poses the question: Was this the Kirkwall Scroll?

It was reported in 2001 by Andrew Sinclair that, in liaison with a CID Inspector from the Northern Constabulary, samples of the Kirkwall Scroll were submitted by him for analysis at the Accelerator Mass Spectrometry Department of Oxford University.[2] The Scroll consists of a wide central strip, with narrower borders sewn down each side, and samples were taken from the bottom edges of each. Analyses of the side-panel samples were inconclusive, but the central panel revealed a radiocarbon date of the 15th century and was of the same era as the building of Rosslyn Chapel.

No sooner was this announcement made than a number of masonic antiquarians claimed that it could not be so. This assumption was based essentially on the fact that a design similar to the arms of the Ancients is painted on one of the sections and, since the Ancients were not formally constituted until 1751, it meant that the Scroll could be no older. However, this is the equivalent of saying that because the Moderns were not formally operative until 1717, everything masonic was designed after that. Such arguments are indicative of a persistent reluctance to concede that the roots of Freemasonry date back long before the *Goose and Gridiron*, and that it was a Stuart institution (as even James Anderson admitted) way before it was restructured in Georgian times. In romantic terms, it is almost as if the 18th-century Jacobite war between Stuart and Hanover is still being played out today with a masonic Floor Cloth as its battleground.

Another point of debate is the suggestion that the side panels, with their painted lines of separation, are not sewn to the central strip, but simply show the marks of heavy creasing from storage. This appears to be a feasible notion, but there are no equivalently heavy crease marks horizontally in the cloth, so it presupposes that the cloth was twice folded lengthways, and then stored full-length in some convenient place. This is unlikely, but possible, and the argument would be easily resolved by studying the reverse of the cloth. The outer strips appear to be of the same material, but even this is a point of contention, and they could well have been added at a later date than the original centrepiece.

The naive artwork on the linen is presumed to be painted in oils, but no one really knows whether this is the case, or whether tempera or some other medium has been used. The cloth itself has been dated to the 15th century, but if the painting was not done until the 18th century, this necessarily presupposes that someone just happened to have a 19-ft piece of 300-year-old cloth tucked away in readiness. Again, this is most unlikely, but possible – so the answer to the Kirkwall Scroll's age must lie in treating it like any other painted work of art. What has to be scientifically dated is not the cloth, but the paint, whose binding structure and organic pigments would react very precisely to analysis. As it stands, it seems the contentions and the mysteries of the Scroll are somehow preferred to any action regarding the panels or the paint that would finally solve the mystery.

In George Speth's description of 1897,[3] he explains that the border on the spectator's left appears to represent the Hebrew wanderings from Mesopotamia, via Canaan into Egypt, with the Tigris and Euphrates rivers within the lower design, and the Nile running uppermost. The right border conveys the Israelites' later journey out of Egypt, through Sinai with Moses and Joshua, and into the Promised Land. This panel incorporates the Ark of the Covenant, along with the manna and golden calf episodes at the foot of Mount Horeb.

The side panels are interpreted from bottom to top, but the central section is designed in panels moving from top to bottom. They begin with Eve in the Garden of Eden, and end at the base with panels of masonic symbolism. In between are representations of the

Tabernacle including the Holy of Holies, and images relating to the Ark of the Covenant (*see* plate 16). There are many similarities to aspects of the Scottish tradition, and some inscriptions are written in a masonic cipher known as the Enochian Alphabet. Such things are intriguing and worthy of closer scrutiny, including a more positive age analysis, but the present, and seemingly reluctant, official line is that the Scroll is kept high on a wall out of direct sunlight, and it is 'best to leave well alone'.

A Golden Philosophy

The pictorial imagery of the Kirkwall Scroll leads us back again to the Sinai realm of Moses and Bezaleel, along with the manna, the golden calf and the Ark of the Covenant. Although this aspect of Exodus study is beyond the bounds of modern Craft Freemasonry, it was clearly of great importance when the Scroll was made, and had been expressly significant to Isaac Newton, Robert Boyle and their Royal Society colleagues (*see* page 18). Moreover, their research was directly linked to their interests in Melchizedek, the Philosophers' Stone and the alchemical tradition that was so much a part of Rosicrucian culture prior to the 1688 Revolution and the subsequent reorganization of Freemasonry from 1717.

As we pursue a course towards the lost secrets of Freemasonry, this is an appropriate point at which to pull some strands together. This is best done by way of a series of questions:

✠ From what was the Ark of the Covenant made?[4]
✠ From what was the golden calf made?[5]
✠ With what was the Philosophers' Stone associated?
✠ What is the primary subject matter of hermetic alchemy?
✠ What did the Queen of Sheba bring to King Solomon?[6]
✠ What was Solomon said to have had in abundance?[7]
✠ What was the subject of Newton's treatise entitled *Manna*?

And the answer to all these questions is the same – gold! This begins to set a far more intriguing scene than anything at the forefront of modern Freemasonry. It is difficult to see at present how gold might fit into the masonic scenario, but let us look at another set of questions:

✠ What did Melchizedek present to Abraham?[8]
✠ How is *manna* described in the Old Testament?[9]
✠ What was King Solomon's dynasty called?[10]
✠ What was placed on the sacred table of Solomon's Temple?[11]
✠ With what did Solomon pay King Huram for sending him gold?[12]
✠ To what did Jesus liken the divinity of his body?[13]

Again, the answer to these questions is the same – bread! (King Solomon's dynasty was called the 'house of bread'). In these respects, bread seems to be as significant as gold, even to the extent that Solomon received gold from the Phoenician king, and paid him for it with bread. In the Old Testament book of Job 28:5–6, it is stated:

> As for the earth, out of it cometh bread; and under it is turned
> up as it were fire. The stones of it are the place of sapphires;
> and it hath dust of gold.

The dust of gold (along with fire, as in the quote from Job) appears in Exodus 32:20, when Moses took the golden calf that his brother Aaron had made, and 'burnt it with fire, and ground it to a powder'.

Both Nicolas Flamel and Eirenaeus Philalethes (a mentor of the Royal Society) described the Philosophers' Stone as being a 'powder of gold' (*see* page 43). Robert Boyle recorded how this strangely exotic substance had very unusual qualities, and ancient Alexandrian texts confirmed the same. The powdery substance (ie, the bread) that the Israelites ate at Mount Horeb was called *manna* and in the treatise that so fascinated Isaac Newton *manna* was directly associated with gold and the Philosophers' Stone. Indeed, *manna* was so important to the ancient culture that Moses placed a golden cup of it in the Ark of the Covenant.[14]

This seems to suggest that one of the lost secrets of ancient Freemasonry may somehow be connected with the science of this unique and highly venerated substance – a science that was known to the Knights Templars, but that then fell into obscurity. In this connection, from an era before Moses, a relief carving of the riches of Pharaoh Tuthmoses III (c. 1450 BC) at the Temple of Karnak should be taken into account. In the metals section of the treasures of Egypt there are a number of cone-shaped items labelled as 'cunning work' (as the Bible classifies the work of Bezaleel and Hiram).[15] They are explained as being made 'one of silver, and thirty of gold', but they carry the inscribed description, 'white bread'.[16]

Noah and the Ark

Another Old Testament character who features in masonic ritual, although not in the Craft degrees, is Noah. He appears in a degree known as Royal Ark Mariners, the first records of which come from a 1790 lodge meeting in Bath. In 1816, the Ark Mariners were taken under the wing of the Mark Masons, a popular side degree that also resides beyond the Craft and is available to Master Masons. Mark Masonry grew from the concept that the medieval stonemasons selected for themselves private marks of recognition with which they could personalize their work. The essence of Mark teaching is that education is the reward of labour, and that fraud can never succeed.[17] The qualification for candidates to the Royal Ark Mariners is that they must first be Mark Masons.[18]

The Ark Mariner degree relates to the story of Noah and the Deluge from the Old Testament book of Genesis 6–9. The quaint ceremony develops the themes of making new beginnings and adopting new outlooks in life. By virtue of Noah and his sons constructing the Ark to save life from the Flood, the subject of building (as with Solomon's Temple) is a feature of the ritual, but not the primary one. The main thrust is that human endeavour is not comparable with

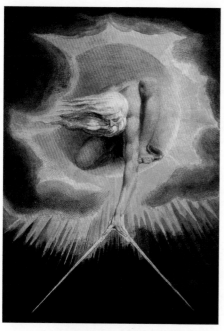

1 *The Ancient of Days*
William Blake, 1794

2 *Jacob's Ladder*
William Blake (1757–1827)

3 *Allegory of the Liberal Arts*
Biagio d'Antonio da Firenze (1445–1510)

4 *Supper at Emmaus*
Jacapo Pontormo, 1525

5 Frontispiece of James Anderson's
Constitutions of the Free-Masons, 1723

6 Obelisk in Alexandria that was taken to New York (*left*),
and its partner (both originally from Heliopolis) erected in London (*right*)

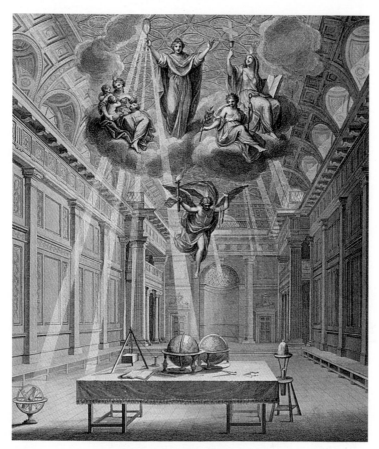

7 Frontispiece of James Anderson's revised
Constitutions of the Free-Masons, 1784

8 The 12th-century Round Church of the Knights Templars in London

9 Rosicrucian image depicting the *Boaz* and *Jachin* pillars, and other masonic similarities

10 Masonic summons of the 18th-century Globe Lodge in Fleet Street, London

11 Rosicrucian image with the Point within a Circle, and other masonic similarities

12 Foundation frontispiece of Thomas Sprat's *History of the Royal Society of London*, 1667

13 *Freemasonry Instructing the People*
(The Masonic Marianne) Charles Mercereau, 1875

14 Edward, Prince of Wales, and the Victoria
Jubilee Grand Lodge of 1897

15 *King Solomon of Judah*
Simeon Solomon, 1854

16 The Kirkwall Scroll
(Ark of the Covenant section)

17 St Bernard and the 12th-century Chapter House Lodge of Clairvaux Abbey

18 First Degree Tracing Board

19 Second Degree Tracing Board

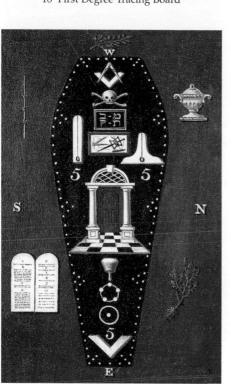

20 Third Degree Tracing Board
(The legend of Hiram Abiff)

21 *King Solomon and the Temple*
Sir Edward Burne-Jones (window), 1890

22 Egyptian obelisk at Luxor

23 Irish Round Tower at Glendalough

24 *The Ark of the Covenant in Jerusalem*
Blaise Nicolas Le Sueur, 1747

25 The 17th-century Fire of London
Monument in Fish Hill Street

26 Site of the *Goose and Gridiron* tavern
in 1870 before its demolition

27 *Sir Francis Dashwood – The Conversation*
Bartolommeo Nazari (1699–1758)

28 Level and Compasses in the 12th-century
Masons' Window at Chartres Cathedral

29 *Viennese Masonic Lodge Initiation* (Mozart seated on the extreme left)
Ignaz Unterberger, 1784

30 Frontispiece of *Ars Magna Lucis et Umbrae* (The Great
Art of Light and Darkness) by Athanasius Kircher, 1646

31 Prince Charles Edward Stuart and the Count of St Germain present the Charter
of Arras to the Companions of the Chapitre Primordian de Rose-Croix in 1747

32 Fire of London plaque on the Fish Hill Street Monument

33 *Benn's Club* – The Jacobite Aldermen of London
Thomas Hudson (1701–79)

34 *Knights Templars at the Paris Chapter House on 22 April 1147*
François-Marius Granet, 1844, Château de Versailles

35 *Prince Charles Edward Stuart in Edinburgh, 1745*
William Brassey Hole (1846–1917)

36 Ark of the Covenant – Royal Arch Room at the George Washington Masonic National Memorial in Alexandria, Virginia

37 *Drafting the Declaration of Independence, 1776* (Benjamin Franklin, John Adams, Thomas Jefferson) Jean Leon Jerome Ferris (1863–1930)

38 *Benjamin Franklin at the Court of Louis XVI and Marie Antoinette* (*The Crown of Laurel*) Robert Edge Pine (1730–88)

39 *George Washington as a Freemason*
American School, 19th century

40 *The Boston Tea Party*
18th-century anonymous print

41 *Allegory of Masonic Support*
English School, 1810

42 *Liberty Displaying the Arts and Sciences*
Samuel Jennings for the Library Company of Philadelphia, 1792

divine justice unless one is in tune with the divine. It was in this regard that the sons of Noah were said to have searched their father's grave for his secret (*see* page 8).

Noah and his sons building the Ark (woodcut by
Julius Schnoor von Carolsfeld, 1794–1872)

The term 'Ark' is a little confusing since it is used in the Old Testament in respect of Noah's Ark (a boat), the Ark of the Covenant (a coffer) and Moses' basket-like ark of bulrushes. As defined by the Oxford Word Library, however, *ark* is an obsolete Greek form of the modern word 'arc', and was equivalent to the Latin *arca*: a chest or box. Something hidden or secreted in such a box is called 'arcane', while a profound mystery is an *arcanum* (plural *arcana*) as in alchemy and the Tarot. A repository for preserving documents is an 'archive', and an item of great antiquity is 'archaic' or 'archaean'. Hence, the study of such items through excavation and analysis becomes 'archaeology'. The biblical word 'ark' is rendered from the old Greek of the *Septuagint* (3rd century BC)[19] and had its Hebrew parallel in *āron* – a box or container, as used to describe a coffin in Genesis 50:26 and a cash box in 2 Kings 12:10.[20] Arks have also been identified with floating vessels, such as Noah's Ark and the ark of Moses, while even today Britain's flagship aircraft carrier (and the fifth of that name) is called *HMS Ark Royal*.

Many of the key stories in Genesis, including those of Adam and Eve, Noah's Ark and the Tower of Babel, stem from original accounts that were written long before Genesis was compiled in the 6th century BC. Dating from the 3rd millennium BC, these texts were held in the great libraries of Nineveh and Babylon, to be discovered and reinterpreted by the Israelite priests during their decades of Babylonian captivity from 586 BC.

One of the most intriguing Old Testament and Mesopotamian parallels is the story of the great Flood, and there is a remarkable amount of ancient information about this. This is perhaps why so much attention is paid to the event in Genesis, where it occupies no fewer than 80 verses. When making comparisons between the biblical and Mesopotamian texts, the similarities are very striking, but the most obvious difference is the biblical change of time frame so that Noah could become the revised hero of the piece. The Genesis tale is no more than an adapted version of the Mesopotamian accounts, which feature the same forewarning of a single man with a view to safeguarding the seeds of life.

The most complete and comprehensive version of the Flood saga comes from the 12 Babylonian texts of the *Epic of Gilgamesh*.[21] These were among some 20,000 preserved clay tablets found in the mid-19th century among the Nineveh ruins of Assyria, and since then numerous other tablets in the series have come to light. They relate the mythical adventures of Gilgamesh (King of Uruk in about 2650 BC), who travelled to meet with the long dead Uta-napishtim of Shuruppak who reigned when the Flood struck the region.[22] Hence, the Babylonian epic enabled a literal retelling of Uta-napishtim's account of the Flood based on ancient Sumerian records. The main

Gilgamesh tablets date from about 2000 BC, but the information was from even earlier texts, some of which have been found in part, dating from beyond 3000 BC.[23]

There is a Genesis similarity in the report that the boat of Uta-napishtim was said to have come to rest on a mountain, but this is specifically called Mount Nisir, as against the Bible's wider description of the mountains of Ararat (Genesis 8:4). The range of Ararat (meaning 'high peaks')[24] was to the north of Mesopotamia, and the Hebrew book of Jubilees 5:26 explains that the Ark landed on the Ararat mountain of Lubar.[25]

Among the additionally discovered material, a poem entitled *The Deluge* was unearthed at Nippur.[26] Quite unrelated to the more general adventures of Gilgamesh (written in Akkadian), this Sumerian poem is solely concerned with the Flood and refers to Uta-napishtim as Zi-u-sudra. It is the oldest known version of the story, and has one particular feature which is immensely significant and quite different to the Genesis adaptation – a feature which distinguishes it from the 'animals two-by-two' imagery of the Noah's Ark story. The original account does not portray Zi-u-sudra as the saviour of a menagerie, but as the preserver of the seeds of life.[27]

The text relates that Zi-u-sudra did indeed take some animals into his boat, but it specifies only an ox and some sheep, along with some other beasts and fowl. These were taken aboard as provisions, not to preserve the species. The matter of preservation is more fully covered in a Babylonian account, which explains that King Zi-u-sudra built an enclosed ship in which he would convey 'the seed of all living creatures'.[28] Once again (as in the *Epic of Gilgamesh*), the operative word is 'seed', and from the conjoined accounts we learn that the vessel of Zi-u-sudra (the original Noah) was not a floating zoo for the salvation of living creatures, but a clinical container ship for the seeds of human and animal life in storage.

It is of particular significance that Ark Mariner Freemasonry should settle on the subject of Noah, while at the same time claiming to be based on an old masonic tradition that is quite separate to the mainstream of lodge teaching. In the same way as Moses and

Bezaleel, Noah commands a position on the edge of Freemasonry, but appears to hold the key to something far more important than has ever been related in any post-1717 ritual.

The fact is that figures such as Moses and Noah, along with Nimrod, who is briefly introduced as a Master in the Old Charges (*see* chapter 2), and Tubalcain the great artificer of Genesis, held primary positions in the more scientifically philosophical Freemasonry of the pre-Hanoverian era. These characters have managed to cling on to the very fringes of the new Order, but without anybody knowing quite why. Stories of the Flood and the Tower of Babel (as cited in the 15th-century *Matthew Cooke Manuscript*) plainly have relevance to the ancient mysteries and lost secrets, but have been sidelined to accommodate imaginary tales of Temple builders in the days of King Solomon.

Many people (masons and non-masons alike) are aware that Freemasonry was once founded upon something of substance to the extent that its Rosicrucian arm was fronted by the greatest scientific minds of the Stuart era. It was certainly not about Hiram Abiff, who was never once mentioned until the reign of King George II (1727–60). It was about aspects of ancient wisdom that had been preserved through the ages, and were brought to light in the West when the Knights Templars returned from Jerusalem in 1127. We know that one of these scientific aspects concerned gold – a Mosaic science with a determinable root in Egypt. And we know from the book of Exodus that Moses came out of Egypt with the Israelites.

From another perspective, the story of Noah now moves into a similar scientific framework – not one of chemistry and physics as with the *manna* of the Philosophers' Stone, but one of clinical biology based on nothing less than genetic engineering. In this regard, it is worth posing another question. Within the context of the Kirkwall Scroll (which is indisputably masonic whatever its age), why is Eve the topmost figure of the central panel? Eve has nothing to do with Freemasonry! Or, does she?

Seeds of Life

Mesopotamia (the land encompassed by present-day Iraq), along with Canaan (Palestine/Israel) and Egypt was not a sand-covered region in early times. The overall territory (with the Mediterranean Sea bordering Egypt and Canaan) includes three great rivers: in the west is the north-flowing Nile, while in the east the Tigris and Euphrates run south into the Persian Gulf. From about 10,000 BC, towards the end of the last Ice Age, this Near Eastern land mass was especially suited to irrigation, particularly in its river plateau and delta regions. In consequence, it was the earliest cradle of civilization and, for reasons of both culture and agriculture, it has been dubbed the Fertile Crescent. When the English explorer, Sir Charles Leonard Woolley undertook excavations in the Mesopotamian desert in the 1920s, he was surprised to find rich virgin soil beneath an 8-ft layer of flood clay under the sand.[37]

In the Old Testament, the Flood is portrayed as an act of God's vengeance. The original Mesopotamian tablets (from which the Genesis account was extracted) tell a very similar story, although relating to 'gods' in the plural. But the texts additionally state that when the great flood swept through the land, a store of human and animal seeds were preserved in clinical storage.

From around 1640 BC, an Akkadian text called the *Atra-hasis Epic* gives lengthy details of *in vitro* fertilization techniques and, in one instance, seven surrogate mothers are referred to as the 'creatresses of destiny'.[29] The lady scientist in charge of such projects is referred to as Nîn-kharsag, and her 'creation chamber' at the *E-Gal* (Great House) was called the House of Shimtî, from the Sumerian *sh-im-tî*, meaning 'breath-wind-life'. It is explained that, alongside her work with human life forms, Nîn-kharsag also researched matters of cross-fertilization in the animal world, and was especially concerned with crops.

Nîn-kharsag was the designated Lady of Life and her emblem (which is to be found on tablet and cylinder-seal representations) was a symbolic womb, shaped rather like the Greek letter omega (Ω).[30] She was also called the Lady Fashioner, the Lady of Form-giving, and

Lady of the Embryo, while a text entitled *Enki and the World Order* calls her the Midwife of the Country.

> Nîn-kharsag, being uniquely great,
> Makes the womb contract.
> Nîn-kharsag, being a great mother,
> Sets the birth-giving going.[31]

After the Flood, which covered the land with silt and clay, the grain crops had to be reinstated, along with the herds of cattle and flocks of sheep which were given priority at the House of Shimtî. According to one tablet (pieced together from 17 fragments),[32] the matters of farming and agriculture were placed in the hands of Ashnan and her brother Lahar, who were themselves products of the 'creation chamber'.[33] They were given the task of preparing the ground, and of farming grain and cattle respectively, with sheep a joint responsibility.[34]

In the days of Isaac Newton and Christopher Wren, Professor Charles Rollin (1661–1741), Principal of the Collège de Beauvais, wrote his multi-volume history of the ancient world, *Histoire Ancienne*, in which he discussed 'the manner in which arts and sciences were invented, cultivated and improved'. This sheds a good deal of light on the fact that philosophical academics of his era had a better understanding of ancient cultures than they are credited with by modern academia. Rollin stated:

> The nearer we approach those countries which were once
> inhabited by the sons of Noah, in the greater perfection we find
> the arts and sciences ... When men attempted to revive those
> arts and sciences, they were obliged to go back to the source
> from whence they originally flowed.

Recently, the journal *Scientific American* concurred with the tablet texts of old Mesopotamia in a study of crop genetics. Discussing ancient intervention by those such as Nîn-kharsag, the article states: 'Comparing the genomes of major cereal crop species shows their close interrelationships and reveals the hand of humans in directing their evolution.' The report continues:

> As our ancestors domesticated these plants, they were creating the crops we know now through a process very much like modern plant breeding. From the wild varieties, they selectively propagated and crossbred individual plants possessing desirable traits, such as bigger grains or larger numbers of grains ... The human modification of cereal plants through selective propagation and crossbreeding began in prehistoric times.[35]

Modern science has now proved this; Charles Rollin knew it intuitively, and the ancient texts recorded it over 4,000 years ago. Genetic modification is not a product of the modern age; it is one of the oldest sciences on record. Some 99 per cent of all today's agricultural production stems from a base of just 24 plant species developed from those early times. In line with the research of Professor Daniel Zohary of the Hebrew University in Jerusalem, independent research by the Patrick Foundation has recently confirmed that DNA data reveals domestication and cross-fertilization to have begun precisely as the Kharsag tablets of Eden explain.[36] This applies to crops, domesticated animals and humans.

Eve is in prime position at the top of the Kirkwall Scroll because she was very much a part of this same genetic research, and the pre-Hanoverian philosophers knew this to be the case. The very name Eve is said to mean 'life', and Nîn-kharsag was called the Lady of Life.

Early in her research, Nîn-kharsag was recorded to have borne an experimental surrogate child from an implanted, cultured embryo. This was created with the ovum of another woman, fertilized by Nîn-kharsag's husband, the regional overlord Enki. The male outcome of the successful experiment was called the *Adâma* (the Earthling),[38] who grew to become the appointed delegate of the gods.[39] At Eridu in Southern Mesopotamia, he was given charge of the temple, to become the world's first recorded priest. Tablets relating the story of Adâma (alternatively Adâpa) were first discovered, along with the *Enûma elish* Creation epic in the library ruins of King Ashur-banipal (668–31 BC);[40] then also in the Egyptian archives of Pharaoh Amenhotep III, who reigned in about 1400 BC. They explain that Adâma, was a 'mighty man' (a *hu-mannan*), who was granted extraordinary powers of control and was anointed into kingship.

Nîn-kharsag and Enki at the House of Shimtî,
from a Sumerian cylinder-seal relief

Following an initial expedition to Nineveh by Britain's foremost Assyriologist, Sir Henry Creswicke Rawlinson, who discovered Ashur-banipal's library in 1845, the first *Enûma elish* tablets were unearthed in the 1848–76 excavations of Sir Austen Henry Layard. They were subsequently published by George Smith of the British Museum in 1876 under the title, *The Chaldean Account of Genesis*. Other tablets and fragments containing versions of the same epic were found at Ashur, Kish and Uruk (all in modern-day Iraq), and it was ascertained from colophons (publishers' imprints) that an even older text existed in a more ancient language.

The *Adâpa Tablet*[41] relates that, being of divine origin, the Adâma was of the Royal Seed.[42] This means that the great importance of the biblical Adam was not that he was the first man on Earth, but that he was the first genetically engineered man to be granted the priest-kingly status of Eden. Khâwa (the biblical Eve) was created in precisely the same manner by Nîn-kharsag, but since deiform and kingly lines were reckoned to transcend through the matrilineal bloodline (ie, by way of mitochondrial DNA), then Eve became the designated Queen of Life – the *Nîn Khâwa*.

The name Eve is said in Genesis (3:20) to signify the 'mother of all living', and this is repeated in the 1st-century *Antiquities of the Jews*, wherein Flavius Josephus explains: 'Now a woman is called in the Hebrew tongue *Issa* (she-man); but the name of this woman was Eve, which signifies the mother of all living.'[43] In Hebrew, the name Eve was Hawah (as against the Sumerian Khâwa, although pronounced the same), but the verbal root which gave rise to this was *hayah* ('to live').[44] Hence, Eve was the *Nîn-tî* (Lady of Life) – a style previously held by Nîn-kharsag.

The Sumerian word *tî* (as in *Nîn-tî*) meant 'to make live', but another Sumerian word, *ti* (pronounced tee), meant 'rib'.[45] Thus, when Nîn-kharsag's title, *Nîn-tî*, was applied to her daughter and transposed to the name Eve, it was correctly interpreted by the Old Testament compilers. But in translating from Sumerian they misidentified *tî* for *ti* in Genesis 2:21–23, and assumed that Eve must have emanated from Adam's rib – a biblical concept that had nothing whatever to do with the original accounts.

Knowledge of this ancient, but technically advanced, form of genetic engineering emerges as one of the lost, but lately rediscovered aspects of science – and, by virtue of this, doubtless one of the lost secrets of ancient Freemasonry. But there is much more to come when we return to the biblically-related Rosicrucian mystery of gold.

The Temple of Light

Pillars and Obelisks

In line with the Egyptian practice of placing free-standing pillars at temple entrances, Hiram of Tyre introduced the same theme at the Jerusalem porch of King Solomon's Temple. The bronze pillars sit at the heart of modern Freemasonry, and were called *Boaz* and *Jachin* (1 Kings 7:21 and 2 Chronicles 3:17). Boaz was the great-grandfather of Solomon's father King David, and the Hebrew word *boaz* means 'in strength'. *Jachin* stems from a Phoenician verbal root meaning 'he will be'[1] and in masonic tradition they are jointly (but incorrectly) said to convey: 'In strength, I will establish [this mine house that it may stand forever].' In this instance, the said 'house' represents the Royal House of David, rather than the Temple as such.

2 Kings 25:13 relates that in 586 BC Nebuchadnezzar smashed the pillars and removed the bronze scrap to Babylon. When the Romans eventually gained control of Jerusalem in the pre-Gospel era, they also took Egypt from the Greeks, with Cleopatra VII and her son being the last of the Ptolemaic pharaohs. From 27 BC Emperor Augustus (Octavian) made Egypt his personal estate,[2] and immediately set his sights on the free-standing pillars of the realm – the obelisks.[3] Removing them from Heliopolis and Karnak, he erected some at his palace in Alexandria, and shipped others to Rome. Emperor Caligula subsequently moved part of the Alexandrian collection to Rome in AD 37.

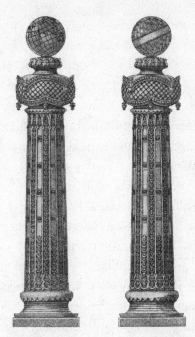

The masonic pillars of *Boaz* and *Jachin*

Emperors from Domitian (AD 81–96) to Hadrian (AD 117–138) continued the practice, as did others down to Constantius (son of Constantine the Great) who brought another to Lateran in about AD 355. In all, 50 obelisks are on record as having been removed from Egypt during this period – from Heliopolis, Thebes (Luxor), Karnak, Memphis, Sais, Tanis and Aswan. Today, 13 of these remain in Rome, along with one in Florence, another in Urbino, and one moved by Emperor Theodosius to Constantinople in AD 390. A further movement of obelisks occurred much later in history, to the extent that of the 30 which now exist in various countries, only 4 of the 6 left in Egypt are where the pharaohs erected them.

Over and above those mentioned, Egyptian obelisks can also be found at Caesaria in Israel, Catania in Sicily, and in New York. France has two – in Paris and Arles – and England has two – in London, and in Wimborne, Dorset. There are also some latter-day stylized obelisks such as the Washington DC monument, the Brandywine Memorial monument, PA, and the Duke of Wellington monuments in Dublin and Wellington, Somerset. If there is any consolation for Egypt after all this plundering, the oldest of all the obelisks – erected by Senusret I in about 1950 BC (1,000 years before King Solomon) – remains at Heliopolis. By far the tallest, however, is that which stands at Lateran in Rome.[4] It was so large that 12 ft (c. 4 m) was cut from it for transportation, but it is still much higher than the Needles in London and New York, which are about two-thirds of its size.[5] By far the smallest is the Kingston Lacy monument, inscribed with Cleopatra's name, at Wimborne.[6]

But what has all this to do with Freemasonry? There are three answers to this. The first is the obvious one: obelisks are the work of stonemasons. The second answer is 'hieroglyphics'.[7] Apart from a few obelisks which are uninscribed, the majority display a wealth of signs and symbols that were ready-made for codes and ciphers before their true meanings were understood. Unlike artefacts that eventually found their way into museums, obelisks were on view in the piazzas of Rome for hundreds of years. By the late 16th century, so many occult and philosophical groups were using hieroglyphic symbols that Pope Sixtus V became embarrassed that his city was the main source of supply. He decided to sanctify the obelisks of Rome, topping them all with crosses and other Christian devices, as they remain today. When having the Vatican obelisk moved to the front of St Peter's Church in 1587 (a risky job which Michelangelo declined to accept), Sixtus even had an exorcism performed, just in case there were demons lurking.

Awareness of hieroglyphs did not blossom in Britain because everyone concerned with esoterica had visited Rome, but by way of a publication that became popular at the time. Written in 1643 by the Jesuit polymath, Athanasius Kircher, it was entitled *Lingua Ægyptiaca Restituta*.[8] Kircher was professor of mathematics at the College of Rome, and had aided the St Peter's architect, Bernini, with the installation of an Egyptian obelisk.[9] Gian Lorenzo Bernini (1598–1680) gained the patronage of popes Paul V and Urban VIII, and is revered by many as the greatest sculptor of the 17th century.

Athanasius Kircher based his linguistic conclusions on a dubious Greek work entitled *Hieroglyphica*, by the 5th-century magus Horapollo Nilacus.[10] The problem was that neither Horapollo nor Kircher had the faintest idea what they were writing about. They did not translate the hieroglyphs, they interpreted them in accordance with the mystical cultures of their own times.

It was not until 1822 that the hieroglyphic code was broken by the French Egyptologist, Jean François Champollion. This decipher- ing was achieved by way of the now famous Rosetta Stone, found near Alexandria in 1799 by Lieutenant Bouchard of the Napoleonic expedition into Egypt.[11] The black basalt stone from 196 BC carries the same content in three different scripts: Egyptian hieroglyphics, Egyptian demotic (everyday cursive writing) and scribal Greek. It came to Britain in 1801, where Champollion and the physicist Thomas Young compared its Ptolemy V cartouche[12] with that of Cleopatra VII at Kingston Lacy. On identifying their corresponding symbols, the structure of hieroglyphs became clear. A comparative analysis of the Rosetta Stone's three texts (with the Greek language being readily familiar), then revealed the hieroglyphic code. The 45- in (114.5 cm) slab has been at the British Museum since 1802.

Following Napoleon's Egyptian campaign, many Europeans had become fascinated with the ancient civilization, and the three obelisks which had the greatest impact on Western thought patterns associated with Freemasonry soon made their way across the map. The first – one of a pair erected by Rameses II (*c.* 1279–12 BC) – arrived in Paris from Luxor in 1833. The man behind this transfer was Champollion himself, and on 22 October 1836 the monument was raised in La Place de la Concorde.[13]

Another was set up on the Thames Embankment in London on 12 September 1878. It was romantically styled *Cleopatra's Needle*, although it pre-dates the famous queen (51–30 BC) by more than 1,000 years. Erected by Pharaoh Tuthmoses III *c.* 1468 BC, it came from the Temple of the Sun at Heliopolis, and was one of a pair which had been moved to Alexandria by Emperor Augustus in 12 BC. At 68 ft 6 in high (20.88 m), and weighing 186 tons, the obelisk

The barge *Cleopatra* in London (left), and the erection of
the New York obelisk (right)

left Alexandria in a specially made tube-shaped iron barge named
Cleopatra (which is how the Needle got its name). Disaster struck in
the Bay of Biscay, however, when a gale separated the barge from
her mother ship, and *Cleopatra* was lost at sea until found by a
Glasgow steamer crew, who towed her to safety.

The masonic connection with Tuthmoses III was that he was the
very pharaoh whose relief carving cites the 'white bread of gold' at
Karnak. This was not known about in the 1800s, but it was clear
that certain inscriptions on the Needle were akin to Rosicrucian
symbols used in the days of Sir Francis Bacon. It was not until
1878, however, that the London Freemasons of Victorian times got
their first glimpse of the Tuthmoses originals – and they dated
back 3,000 years.

The second obelisk of the Tuthmoses pair found its way to New
York three years later. It too was dubbed *Cleopatra's Needle*, and
was erected in Central Park, with a commemorative ceremony on
22 February 1881. Although now badly eroded by harsh weather,
this obelisk's hieroglyphs were equally intriguing, and some have
been likened to masonic symbols.[14]

Moses of Egypt

The late Victorian era was a time of particular enquiry in Britain when, in the wake of the Industrial Revolution, many were hankering for an imagined lost Golden Age. Romance and legend were high on the agenda, and the people were supplied with requisite portrayals from writers such as Alfred, Lord Tennyson, and artists such as the members of the Pre-Raphaelite Brotherhood. Ancient Greek and Roman mythology became extremely popular and, above all, at a time when archaeology was emerging as a profession, so was ancient history – especially Bible history and the history of Egypt. To answer the call on this front, Milner & Sowerby of London published English translations of the *Antiquities of the Jews* and *Wars of the Jews* by the 1st-century Galilean chronicler, Flavius Josephus, along with another of his works entitled *Against Apion*.

The last proved to be particularly revealing since it brought to light the writings of Manetho, a Graeco-Egyptian priest of Heliopolis who was adviser to Pharaoh Ptolemy I (*c.* 305–282 BC). Until the 1870s, all most people knew about the biblical Moses was what they had learned from the Old Testament. Exodus 11:3 states that 'Moses was very great in the land of Egypt, in the sight of Pharaoh's servants, and in the sight of the people.' But Manetho's History of Egypt (*The Ægyptiaca*) now gave them more, stating that Moses had been an Egyptian priest at Heliopolis.[15] To this, Josephus added that Moses was a commander of the Egyptian army in the war against Ethiopia.[16] Moreover, in support of Manetho's chronicle, Moses is cited in Exodus 2:19 as 'an Egyptian'.

So, was there a nominal link of some sort between Moses and Tuthmoses? The final answers to this emerged in the 1930s from Sigmund Freud and the Egyptologist, James Henry Breasted of the University of Chicago. Researching the name Moses in 1934, Breasted wrote that it derives from the Egyptian word *mose* (Greek: *mosis*), which relates to an 'offspring' or 'heir'.[17] Hence, Tuthmoses (Tuthmosis or Thothmose) means 'Heir of Thoth', and Amenmose (Amenmosis) 'Heir of Amen'. Subsequently, pursuing the same etymology, Freud showed that the name Moses was in no way Israelite and is, in any event, written in Hebrew as *Mosheh* (stemming from the verb 'to draw').[18] In full accord with Manetho, and with Georg Steindorff, Professor of Egyptology at the University of Leipsig,[19] all agreed that the name Moses denoted a royal heir of Egypt – a descendant in the line of Tuthmoses.

Turning to Tuthmoses III, we find that Heliopolis (originally called *On*, relating to the light of the sun god – as in Genesis 41:45)[20] was a centre of the White Brotherhood – the master craftsmen of Tuthmoses III. There were 39 members on the High Council of Karnak,[21] where the pharaoh erected nine obelisks, and the Brotherhood's name derived from its preoccupation with an enigmatic white powder. This mysterious priestly society eventually became known as the Therapeutate (cognate with the English word 'therapeutic'), and it was they who most influenced the community of Qumrân, near Jerusalem, where the *Dead Sea Scrolls* were found in 1947.[22] From the days of Cleopatra, the sect at Qumrân were called the Essenes – from the Greek *essenoi*, meaning 'physician'. Josephus confirmed this in his *Wars of the Jews*, adding that the Essenes were very practised in the art of healing.[23]

The Bible explains (as latter-day archaeology now confirms) that the Jewish patriarchs and early Hebrews had used simple outside stone altars as places of reverence and sacrifice. Examples are those erected by Noah (Genesis 8:20) and Abraham (Genesis 22:9). It was Moses who brought the more refined concept of temple ritual out of Egypt when he and Bezaleel erected the Tabernacle for the Israelites in Sinai.

The Power of Tchãm

The third reason why obelisks have a unique quality is that they relate to an ancient philosophical science. This was discovered as a result of 1950s US Army Air Force installations of low-frequency radio navigation systems in the South Pacific.

All the obelisks removed from Egypt have been raised on plinths and podiums – some are very large and ornate with statues and fountains. But this is not the way they would have looked originally. Although some were erected as commemorative monuments, the basic principle of the Egyptian obelisk as a working object was that it should rise from the ground with direct earth contact. For stability, they were lowered onto buried foundation blocks. We should not be deceived by the 7-ft stone plinth that sits beneath the Senusret obelisk in Heliopolis today. Labib Habachi, former Chief Inspector of Egyptian Antiquities, explains that the obelisk was lifted and then lowered onto this block in 1950 by the German engineers, Krupp of Essen, so as to bring its eroding base above the rising Nile flood level.[24] Where part of the foundation block was visible, like a slab or low pedestal, it was of the same stone as the obelisk, and the earth contact was not affected. Victorian artwork from explorers such as Amelia Edwards identifies the way in which obelisks were encountered in the 19th century. The photographs in plate 6 show the American Cleopatra's Needle as it was in Alexandria, compared with its partner's plinth erection in London.

Looking in some ways similar to the Egyptian obelisks are the stone Round Towers of Ireland; they are equally tall and have pointed tops. Their main differences are that they are round instead of four-sided, and are block-built rather than hewn. There are 64 of these towers, and they are unique to Ireland, with good examples at Cashel, Kilmacduagh, Clondalkin, Devenish, Kells and Glendalough (*see* plate 23).

The individual towers were built near monasteries, where the monks practised a form of eco-agriculture dependent on crop rotation, and each tower was aligned with a particular star at the winter solstice. They are mostly constructed of sandstone or limestone and they display uncanny paramagnetic properties – ie, they are non-metallic, but are attracted to powerful magnetism. Precisely the same is the case with the Egyptian obelisks, which are of red granite and were directly linked to the agriculture of the temple gardens. As discussed in the last chapter, Egypt was a pioneer nation in crop engineering in the Fertile Crescent and, notwithstanding all other sciences, food production ranked with medicine (then as today) as the most essential requirement.

Philip Callahan, the designer of Japan's air navigation system, explains that the secret of the obelisks and towers can be demonstrated by making a scale model with sandpaper. Experiments show that it acts as a highly efficient magnetic antenna.[25] In this respect, it works very much like a superconductor which, unlike a conductor, does not allow any voltage potential or magnetic field to exist within itself. It is a perfect insulator, while at the same time being sensitive to magnetic fields of infinitely minute proportions, and it will respond to incalculably small magnetic forces. This has the effect of attracting cosmic radiation, thereby heightening the Earth's own magnetism and enriching the surrounding soil for plant growth. Tests have revealed that plants with model sandpaper round towers (or obelisks) in their soil flourish far better than those without.[26]

The reason that the Round Towers appear to emulate the obelisks of Egypt is because they stem from precisely the same culture. Ireland in the Dark Ages was greatly influenced by Egypt. The old Gaelic histories of Eire relate that the High Kings of Ireland emerged in two stages from the 18th and 26th dynasties of Egypt, as did the agricultural methods which were developed by the priests in Eireland from around 570 BC.

It was by virtue of two Scythian-Egyptian royal marriages that the Scots Gaels of Ireland evolved. The first occurred in about 1360 BC, when Niul, Prince of Scythia[27] and Governor of Capacyront by the Red Sea, married the daughter of Pharaoh Smenkhkare,[28] whom Manetho's *Egyptian King List* records as Achencheres.[29] By virtue of this, the daughter became a Princess of Scythia, and was nominally styled Princess Scota, meaning 'ruler of people'.

Correctly stated, this pharaoh's name was Smenkh-ka-ra (Vigorous is the Soul of Ra).[30] Alternatively, since Ra was the sun god of the Heliopolis House of Light, called On,[31] Smenkh-ka-ra was also Smenkh-ka-ra-on – from the phonetic ending of which derives

A sandpaper Round Tower

the Israelite name Aaron. The Irish chronicles state that by virtue of the royal marriage 'Niul and Aaron entered into an alliance of friendship with one another.'[32] The Irish text further relates that Gaedheal (Gael), the son of Niul and Scota, was born in Egypt 'at the time when Moses began to act as leader of the children of Israel'.[33] Given that the prevailing *Moses* (royal heir) was Aaron's brother, as documented in the Old Testament book of Exodus 4:14, it has been accepted by many, since the 1930s investigations of Freud and Breasted, that Moses can be identified with Pharaoh Akhenaton[34] in descent from Tuthmoses III.

The second Princess Scota with an Irish-Egyptian connection was the daughter of Pharaoh Nekau (Nechonibus, *c.* 610–595 BC). She married Prince Galamh of Scythia (a descendant of the earlier marriage), and their son Eire-ahmon was the ancestral forbear of the Scots Kings of Ireland, a branch of which eventually founded Scotland.

Returning to the paramagnetic obelisks, it appears that, in the more ancient times of Tuthmoses III (*c.* 1450 BC), Egypt had another related aspect of technology that was not known by the Irish or Egyptians in the 6th century BC. It had, in fact, been curtailed around 750 years earlier. Originally, the apex pyramidions of the obelisks were capped with a substance called *tchām*. In the 4th century, St Ephraim of Antioch described this as looking like 'white copper'.[35] When writing about *tchām* in 1924, Sir Ernest A Wallis Budge, curator of Egyptian Antiquities at the British Museum, confirmed that none has ever been found, and that the valuable *tchām* was removed after the 18th dynasty of Tuthmoses and Akhenaton when many aspects of traditional culture were forsaken by a less enlightened regime.[36]

Although long known to have been a gold or electrum composite,[37] research into the nature of *tchām* has recently led to the discovery that it was a bright form of gold in a glass-like state. It has proved to be highly superconductive, and was also used on the pyramid capstones. We shall be further discussing this gold-glass in due course (*see* page 336), but at this stage it can be said that it retains its own luminescence by virtue of containing energized light waves. This Transition Group elemental substance (especially when in a conical or apex shape) has the ability to respond to radio waves, just as a lens will collect and focus light, making it brighter. In combination with the obelisk structure as a paramagnetic antenna, cosmic waves can be detected and enhanced by *tchām*, then stored as electromagnetic energy. Hence, just as superconductive devices are being researched today for the purpose of collecting, storing and distributing energy in the form of light waves, it would seem that the ancients used a similar technology at their obelisk sites for the purposes of crop enhancement.

House of Gold

A 1744 masonic ritual of the Holy Royal Arch cites Moses as the first biblical Grand Master (*see* page 165). From the earliest times, Moses was considered to have been a primary guardian (an *argus*) of the hermetic wisdom, which came out of Egypt. The Roman writer and scientist, Pliny the Elder (AD 23–79), wrote of Moses as a great magician, and the Hebrew *Midrash* recalls Moses as an arch-wizard. He is recorded as a master of the Royal Art in a 3rd-century treatise entitled *The Domestic Chemistry of Moses*, and was revered as such by the 4th-century Greek monk Zosimus. In the 8th century, the Arabic scholar, Jābir ibn Hayyān, claimed that Moses possessed the Divine Science, and in 987 he was similarly extolled in the famous *Kitāb al-fihrist* (Index Book) of Ibn al-Nadîm. He was likewise recorded as a student of Hermes in the *Turba Philosophorum* (Assembly of the Philosophers) – a 12th-century Latin work translated from early Hebrew and Arabic sources.[38]

Scholars throughout Europe and Asia wrote reams of literature questioning how it was that Moses could burn the Golden Calf with fire to produce a magical powder, when gold does not burn, it melts. The matter was raised in the 12th-century *Mirqraot G'dolot* Bible commentaries of the Spanish Jew Abraham Ibn Esra,[39] and the trans-mutation of gold became known as the Mosaico-hermetic Art. Later, in his *Alchymica*, the 17th-century German philosopher Johann Kunckel of the Académie Royale continued the Golden Calf debate, as did Olars Borrichius in two works of 1668 and 1675. Also in 1668, Johannes Helviticus declared the Golden Calf transmutation to be 'the most rare and incomparable wonder', with Georges Wolfgang Wedel (1645–71) declaring much the same in his *De Moses Chemico* (Moses the Chemist). Then, in 1742, Abbé Lenglet de Fresnoy summed up the only conclusion that had been reached after so much speculation in his *Histoire de la philosophie hermetique*:

> Moses was trained in all the sciences of the Egyptians, of which
> the most secret, and at the same time the most essential, was
> the transmutation of metals ... It was called by the Egyptians
> the Sacred Art, the Divine Science.

Most people do not dwell too much on the Golden Calf episode of Exodus because its science is not an aspect of the religious establishment. Judaeo-Christian doctrine is more concerned with the fact that Moses destroyed a graven image, a golden idol of worship that was anathema to the evolving faith of the Israelites. But the fact is that Moses did not destroy the idol; he transformed it into something else – and in a manner which, as centuries of scholars have pondered upon, is seemingly impossible. He began with gold and, through the use of fire, ended up with a powder – just as Flamel, Philalethes, Fludd, Boyle and the Newtonian school explained was the nature of the Philosophers' Stone. But why would the Israelites ingest it? Maybe it was the same 'white bread of gold' as detailed on the Karnak temple relief of Tuthmoses III, whose White Brotherhood founded the college of physicians known as the Therapeutate.

Moses burns the Golden Calf at Mount Horeb
(woodcut by Julius Schnoor von Carolsfeld, 1794–1872)

We can now rejoin the enthusiasts of the late Victorian and early Edwardian eras in the intermediate stage of solving the Golden Calf puzzle, thereby cementing the philosophical link between Moses, Tuthmoses and the pharaonic culture in general. What follows are details of an archaeological discovery made in the early 1900s which I have discussed at greater length in a previous book,[40] but its relevance has a new masonic focus in this investigation. In any case, it is worth repeating because it is, without doubt, the greatest biblical revelation of all time.

To set the masonic scene, we should look again at the 1st-degree Tracing Board, and the ritual which establishes at the outset what the masonic quest entails. In plate 18, at the base of the ladder – in front of the Three Great Lights of Freemasonry (the Square, Compasses and the Volume of the Sacred Law) – can be seen a diagram of a point within a circle ⊙. The same is more obvious in the 3rd-degree Tracing Board, near the base of the image (plate 20). In each of the three degrees there are references to a requirement for Light, as in a quest for enlightenment or illumination. It is pertinent, therefore, that the Ashmolean Museum's library of hieroglyphs and ancient symbols defines a point within a circle as an Egyptian ideogram for Light,[41] and it is a symbol that is discovered in a more original context.

Soon after the Egyptian obelisks were erected in London and New York, archaeology was subject to a number of regulatory guidelines, and funding bodies were established. One of these was the London-based Egypt Exploration Fund, and an early pioneer was the English archaeologist Sir WM Flinders Petrie (1853–1942). It was mainly as a result of his discoveries that the Department of Ancient Egypt and Sudan was founded at the British Museum and, in 1892, the nearby Petrie Museum was established as a teaching resource at London's University College.

The Sinai peninsula was largely unexplored at that time – a seemingly individual part of Egypt which sits above the Red Sea between the Nile Delta and Jordan. This was the land crossed by the Israelites on their journey out of Egypt to the Promised Land

under the leaderships of Moses and Joshua, as described in the Old
Testament books of Exodus, Leviticus and Numbers. Obtaining the
necessary sponsorship from the Egypt Exploration Fund, Petrie
and his team set out to investigate and map the peninsula in
January 1904.

Back in the 4th century, an order of Greek Christian monks had
founded the mission of St Catherine's Monastery on a mountain in
southern Sinai, and had dubbed the place *Gebel Musa* (Mount of
Moses). It was clear, however, that this was an inaccurate conclusion
since it did not comply with the Bible's geographical references for
Mount Horeb. The book of Exodus explains the route taken by
Moses and the Israelites, when they departed from the Egyptian Delta
region of Goshen, travelling beyond the Red Sea towards the land of
Midian. Following this line of direction across the wilderness region
of Shur, the holy mountain of Moses is found soaring to over 2,600 ft
within a high sandstone plateau above the Plain of Paran. Today it is
known as Serâbît el Khâdim (the Prominence of the Guardians), and it
was to this rugged outcrop that the Petrie expedition came in March
1904. They had no particular expectation of the place, but it was part
of the survey and they made their way to the summit where, to their
astonishment, they made a monumental discovery.

Built over an expanse of some 230 ft (*c.* 70 m), extending from a
great man-made cave, they found the ruin of an old temple, with
inscriptions dating back to the 4th-dynasty Pharaoh Sneferu, who
reigned about 2600 BC.[42] Subsequently, Petrie wrote, 'The whole of
it was buried, and no one had any knowledge of it until we cleared
the site.'[43] It would perhaps not have surprised them to find a
Semitic altar stone, or some other ritualistic landmark at the Horeb
mountain, but this was a vast Egyptian temple and clearly of some
importance.

Dedicated to the goddess Hathor throughout its operative life,
the Serâbît temple appears to have ceased all function during the
12th century BC, when Egypt fell into financial decline and to outside influence, leading eventually to the Greek rule of the Ptolemies.
It was, however, fully operational before the Giza pyramids were

THE TEMPLE OF LIGHT

built, and continued in service beyond the eras of Tutankhamun and Rameses the Great. But why would there have been such an important Egyptian temple hundreds of miles away from the pharaonic centres at the top of a desolate mountain?

The temple had been constructed from sandstone quarried from the mountain cave. Its structure was a series of adjoining halls, shrines, courts, cubicles and chambers, all set within a surrounding enclosure. Of these, the main features uncovered were the Hall of Hathor, the Sanctuary, the Shrine of Kings and the Portico Court. All around were pillars and stelae denoting the Egyptian kings through the ages, while certain of them, such as Tuthmoses III were depicted many times on standing stones and wall reliefs. After clearing the site, Petrie wrote: 'There is no other such monument known which makes us regret the more that it is not in better preservation.'

The inner temple had been cut into the natural rock, with flat walls that were carefully smoothed. In the centre was a large upright pillar of Amenemhet III (c. 1841–1797 BC). Also portrayed was his chamberlain, Khenemsu, and his seal-bearer, Ameny-senb. Deep within the cave Petrie found a limestone stela of Rameses I – a slab upon which Rameses (traditionally reckoned by Egyptologists to be an opposer of the monotheistic Aten god cult of Pharaoh Akhenaten) had surprisingly described himself as 'The ruler of all that Aten embraces'.[44] Also found was an Amarna statue-head of Akhenaten's mother, Queen Tiye, with her cartouche set in the crown.

In the courts and halls of the outer temple were numerous stone-carved rectangular tanks and circular basins, along with a variety of curiously shaped bench-altars with recessed fronts and split-level surfaces. There were also round tables, trays and saucers, together with alabaster vases and cups, many of which were shaped like lotus flowers. In addition, the rooms housed a good collection of glazed plaques, cartouches, scarabs and sacred ornaments, designed with spirals, diagonal-squares and basketwork. There were wands of an unidentified hard material, and in the Portico Court were two conical stones of about 6 in (15 cm) and 9 in (22.5 cm) in height respectively. The explorers were baffled enough by these, but they

were further confounded by the discovery of a metallurgist's crucible and a curiously preserved supply of fine powder, an impalpa-
ble white ash. Unlike the more conventional ashes outside the
temple, it was perfectly clean and unadulterated. Petrie recorded
that he sieved it and winnowed it in a breeze, but stated 'I never
found a fragment of bone or anything else.'[45]

In the course of this, a baffling hieroglyph was discovered which
appeared to relate to the powder. It was subsequently ascertained
that it had been seen before in Egypt by the German philologist Karl
Richard Lepsius in 1845, and had been mentioned earlier by Jean
François Champollion. Even he could not translate it – despite the
fact that he pioneered the art of understanding Egyptian hieroglyphics. By a series of cross-references with other symbols (a process
which continued until the 1950s) all that could be discovered was a
list of the things which it was not, and there appeared to be nothing
left that it might be. It was ascertained, however, that the glyph signified some form of 'stone' which was extremely precious, and the
best that the debating Egyptologists could determine in 1955 was
that the mysterious substance was 'a valuable mineral product'.[46]

During the investigations, other causes of wonderment for the
scientists were the innumerable inscribed references to 'bread'
found at the temple. Why on earth would a powder be described as
a 'stone' and what could it possibly have to do with bread? At this
stage, another valuable substance associated with the Serâbît sanctuary came into the equation – gold.

On one of the rock tablets near the cave entrance was a representation of Tuthmoses IV in the presence of Hathor. Before him were
two offering stands topped with lotus flowers, and behind him a
man bearing a conical object described as 'white bread' – precisely as
in the Tuthmoses treasure relief at Karnak. Another stela detailed the
mason Ankhib offering two bread-cakes to the king and there were
similar portrayals elsewhere in the temple complex. One of the most
significant representations was of Hathor and Amenhotep III. The
goddess, complete with her customary cow horns and solar disc,
holds a necklace in one hand, while offering the emblem of life and

dominion to the pharaoh with the other.[47] Behind her is the treasurer Sobekhotep, who holds in readiness a conical loaf of 'white bread'. Sobekhotep is described as the man who 'brought the noble Precious Stone to his majesty'.[48] Furthermore, he is said to be the 'true royal acquaintance' and the 'Great One over the secrets of the House of Gold'. But Petrie found no gold at the temple – not that he would have expected to, for no gold was ever mined in Sinai, only copper and turquoise, and he found no traces of these either.

According to Exodus, the gold-plated Ark of the Covenant was built at this place, which concurs with the numerous mentions of gold in the temple inscriptions. But the nearest gold mines were way across the Red Sea in Nubia and Kush. There is, however, another record of gold being worked in Sinai. In ancient times, the Egyptians called the Sinai peninsula by the name Bia, and at the British Museum is a related stela of the Middle Kingdom treasurer Si-Hathor. The inscription on this stone relates, in the treasurer's words, 'I visited Bia as a child; I compelled the Great Ones to wash gold.'[49] Again, this confirms the temple inscriptions in its use of the term Great Ones.

Unknown to Petrie or any of the scientists, the Royal Society mentor Eirenaeus Philalethes had already answered the question about the powder and the stone back in 1667. In his alchemical treatise *Secrets Revealed*, he revealed the nature of the Philosophers' Stone, making the point that the Stone was itself made of gold and that the alchemical art was in perfecting this process. He stated: 'Our Stone is nothing but gold digested to the highest degree of purity and subtle fixation ... Our gold, no longer vulgar, is the ultimate goal of Nature.'[50] In another work entitled *A Brief Guide to the Celestial Ruby*, Philalethes further pronounced:

> It is called a Stone by virtue of its fixed nature; it resists the action of fire as successfully as any stone. In species it is gold, more purer than the purest; it is fixed and incombustible like a stone, but its appearance is that of a very fine powder.[51]

Serâbît artefacts which may be of special importance in respect of the precious Stone are two round-topped stelae from the reigns of Tuthmoses III and Amenhotep III. The first, which depicts a presentation by Tuthmoses to the god Amun-re, is inscribed: 'The presenting of a white bread that he may be given life'. The second shows Amenhotep offering the Stone to the god Sopdu, and states: 'He gave the gold of reward; the mouths rejoiced.'

The ultimate symbol which governed the mysterious secret of the House of Gold was found inscribed in the Shrine of the Kings. It is the pharaonic cartouche emblem of Ra, the sun god of Heliopolis – the same as on the masonic Tracing Boards – the traditional ideogram for Light ☉ – a point within a circle.

13

The Lost Word

The Quest

If Freemasonry can be summed up in brief, it might be said to constitute a mystical quest, like those for the Holy Grail and the Golden Fleece. Its search, however, is not for a physical or legendary relic, but for a Lost Word that provides the key to unlock particular ancient secrets. Masonic tradition relates that Noah, Moses, Solomon, Hiram and other past masters knew the word and were guardians of the secrets.

We have learned how the meaningless word *Mahabyn* was introduced for the Craft in the 1720s by the Sloane MS catechism because the original word had itself been lost or forgotten (*see* chapter 8). Shortly afterwards, a revised catechism introduced the alternative word *Machbenah*. This was an attempted correction based on a phonetic recollection, but it still has no meaning in any language as it stands. In lodge ritual today, an element of uncertainty prevails as to which is the better word and, although referred to as a single Mason Word, they are given together as '*Mahabyn* or *Machbenah*'. For our purposes, however, these are both irrelevant and we need to ascertain what the original Mason Word might have been – or at least to what it related.

The concept of a secret Mason Word can be traced back to 1638, when it was referred to as if it had existed for a while before – but for how long is not clear. Its reference stems from a lengthy Scottish ode by the Perth schoolmaster Henry Adamson entitled *The Muses'*

Threnodie. In the form of an imaginary dialogue, one of the lament's characters assures the other that the bridge over the River Tay (lost in a flood in 1621) would be rebuilt, exclaiming as his assurance:

> For we be brethren of the Rosie Crosse;
> We have the Mason Word and the second sight.

In its context, Adamson's reference would seem to be to operative stonemasonry, rather than speculative Freemasonry, except for his mention of the Rosie Crosse. Other subsequent and equally innocuous references to the Word eventually led to its discussion at an assembly of the Church of Scotland in July 1649. The Presbyterians of the Kirk had become alarmed by the Word's association in the poem with 'second sight', which they regarded as highly sinister.[1] These were the days of puritanical doctrine and witchcraft trials, when anything not taught or upheld by the Kirk was regarded with great suspicion. If Adamson was suggesting that Freemasons and Rosicrucians could see the invisible it was a blasphemy indeed! Then, in 1652, it was discovered that James Ainslie, a candidate for the ministry, knew the Mason Word. The accusation against him was so serious that it passed beyond the jurisdiction of the Kirk Session to the General Synod.

An explanation of second sight was attempted a year or so later by Sir Thomas Urqhart of Cromarty who, in writing about the 'massone word', described it as a means of recognition – a way of identifying other masons as if by second sight. In 1663, a sacked minister compared the word to 'what passeth between Christ and his people'. But the general feeling of the Kirk was that anything kept so secret must be in some way heretical or harmful. In consequence, masons were accused of wizardry, and of communicating with spirits and familiars.

Through a period of more than 30 years, there are less than a dozen extant written references to the Mason Word, and they all emanate from Scotland. The first known mention by an Englishman comes from Andrew Marvell's satirical pamphlet *The Rehearsal*

Transposed in 1672. In this attack on Samuel Parker, Archdeacon of
Canterbury, Marvell stated that 'those who have the Mason Word
secretly discern one another'.[2] The next was in a treatise by folklore
enthusiast Robert Kirk. Dated 1691, it refers to a letter to Robert
Boyle of the Royal Society, stating that the Mason Word was like
a rabbinical tradition linked to the *Boaz* and *Jachin* pillars of King
Solomon's Temple.[3] He also commented on the secret sign of a hand-
shake passed between Brethren. Within the 53 years from 1638, the
Word had moved from the stonemasons' guilds into the realm
of speculative Freemasonry. Then, in 1697, an English visitor to
Scotland wrote: 'The Lairds of Roslin have been great architects of
buildings for these many generations; they are obliged to receive the
Mason Word.'

To understand the feeling generated by the Kirk ministers against
working stonemasons and Freemasons during that era, it is necessary to look at the overall environment in which this fear and antagonism took place.

Behind Closed Doors

The late Renaissance was a particularly spiritual era, when everyday
people became interested in astronomy and the natural forces of
existence. They were not necessarily scholars or academics, but
aspired in some way to be knowledgeable. Spiritual interests
included supernatural interests, and there was a passion for phenomena, especially magic and such things that were known to wise
astrologers and seers. Was this such a far cry from the workaday
builder and his box of tools? People at large were seeking a route to
the divine and a means of perfecting their lives. The Church had
its own agenda; it had become political and dogmatic, and was of little relevance to spiritual quest. But were not the square, the rule and
the plumb-line contained in the tool box themselves instruments of
perfection? Were they not emblematic of the quest?

Building was not just about bricks and mortar, it was about rectitude and artistic design – and about geometry. The masons learned
how Plato had written that God is expressed in geometry. In the
Middle Ages the *Bible Moralisée* had depicted God as an architect
and, in the 1630s, the philosophical author Sir Thomas Browne
called God the High Architect of the World.[4]

God the Architect, from the *Bible Moralisée*, 1245

In this context, the masons (and those of other artisan trades) were fortunate because they already had their guild lodges where they could meet and discuss subjects of mutual interest with friends. It is for this reason that the movement from operative to speculative lodges is so hard to define. It did not happen in a day or a year, nor was it a predetermined plan; it simply evolved through time as the emphases of the lodge meetings changed. At the same time, the Rosicrucian movement – a truly philosophical entity – was emerging, although not a formally organized institution distinct from the Knights of the Rosy Cross. As Puritanism pulled in one direction, so those with minds of their own pulled in the other.

For the most part, the artisan lodge members were Christians. They might have been Presbyterians, Anglicans or Catholics, but their desire was to pull together. Hence, it was necessary that the lodges were not in any way doctrinal, and the way to cope with this was to avoid religious discussion altogether. (This was exactly the same rule that Dr John Wilkins implemented for the *Invisible College* before it became the Royal Society.) However, those religions with histories far older than Christianity could not be avoided, and the members became fascinated with the ancient Egyptian and Judaic cultures. It was as if they somehow contained a secret element which had disappeared when the Romans intervened. What greater and wiser king had there ever been than Solomon? And what more magnificent civilization than that of Egypt?

It was not understood at the time that the true Egyptian culture had collapsed with the 18th dynasty of Tuthmoses in the 14th century BC. The subsequent Ramesside era created a break from traditional Egyptian royal descent, leading to conquest and control by Libyan, Nubian, Kushite and Persian kings, followed by the Greek Ptolemies and Cleopatra queens from 305 BC. It was during this latter era of the Greek pharaohs[5] that Hermes was identified with Thoth and their separate traditions became one. A good deal of ancient lore attributed to Thoth became incorporated under the Hermes banner, including the mystical art of *al-khame* (alchemy) as practised long before by the Egyptian priests of Karnak, Memphis and Heliopolis.

The new centre of hermetic operations became Alexandria, founded in 331 BC by Alexander the Great of Macedonia. This emerged as the most important cultural centre of the ancient world. It was an academic focus for the greatest scholars, scientists, doctors, mathematicians and philosophers, who travelled from far and wide to study the largest collection of arcane documents ever gathered together in one place. But then one day in AD 391, a fevered Christian mob, led by Bishop Theophilus, marched upon the Serapeum where the collection was held. The knowledge base of this library was the greatest threat to the newly established Church of Rome and, on instruction from Emperor Theodosius, it was burned to the ground. More than half a million irreplaceable documents, representing the finest minds and wisdom of ages, were lost for all time. The legacy of this archive was the fount of knowledge so earnestly sought by the early Freemasons and Rosicrucians. This was why those such as Robert Boyle and Isaac Newton spent their lives researching ancient cultures for clues as to the secrets they held. Now and again they found inspiration, resulting in some of the greatest discoveries in scientific history, but they were haunted by the possibility that these might only be rediscoveries, and that there was potentially much more as yet beyond their grasp.

Alongside this, the 16th-century Protestant Reformation (whatever its merits for some) had spoiled things for many by removing colour and spectacle from their lives. In Britain, the Presbyterian and Puritan movements were drab and austere in the 1600s compared with the pageantry of earlier times, and there was little to encourage people towards the new-style Protestant regime. The traditional days of celebration had been sidelined as frivolous and papist by the prevailing establishment, leaving the people with nothing to celebrate. Religion was no longer uplifting; it had become solemn and boring – it had no magic! Hence, people had to create their own magic, their own pageantry – especially after Oliver Cromwell closed all the Anglican churches, which at least maintained a remnant of some enchantment. And so clubs, societies, lodges and confraternities of friends were formed, badges, banners and livery were invented, and feast days were celebrated under the patronage of adopted saints.

In Scotland, the philosophically motivated craft guilds and masonic lodges were especially suited to this purpose. Thus it was that, irrespective of Protestant reform, the masons, wrights, coopers, hammermen and slaters paid no heed to the Kirk. Dressed in their respective uniforms, with pipes and drums, they held pageants and processions to celebrate Candlemass, Corpus Christi and whatever else presented an opportunity for festive pursuits.

Not surprisingly, just as in Cromwellian England, the Kirk stepped in with laws of suppression. Public ceremonies – even plays and drama – were banned. It was said that actors who pretended to be other people were violating God's choice in creation. But this did not curtail the need for celebration, just as it did not curtail the yearning for arcane knowledge. It simply forced the play-acting and the quest for enlightenment behind closed doors – and the secretive lodge was born.

The Secret of the Stone

One way or another, the Mason Word was plainly meaningful. Even within the shattered ritual and disembodied masonic remnant of modern times, it clearly related to some sort of divine inspiration. In 1605 (not long before the Adamson poem), the Rosicrucian master Sir Francis Bacon had written a treatise entitled *The Proficience and Advancement of Learning*. In this, he drew a distinction between knowledge and wisdom, thereby separating the human from the divine, and he referred to the latter as 'the light of nature'.[6] He identified the spirit of man as being the Lamp of God, and that universal knowledge as obtained from its light.[7] Moreover, it was held that the greatest wisdom and inspiration of the divine plan comes from the most ancient of anything that we can possibly access. It is that which happened 'at the beginning' (*b'rei-shêeth*), when 'the earth was without form, and void; and darkness was upon the face of the deep … and God said Let there be light, and there was light' (Genesis 1:1–2).

When a candidate is asked in 1st-degree ritual what he desires the most, the required answer is Light. Those things which are not in the light are in the dark – in the blackness – and alchemy is the science of overcoming 'the blackness' (*al-khame*). Just as the Dead Sea Scrolls tell of the great cosmic battle between the Children of Light and the Sons of Darkness, so the same conflict is played out on the chequered pavement of the masonic lodge. Interestingly, this pavement is reminiscent of the black-and-white *Beauceant* war banner of the Knights Templars. In a document known as the *Dundee Manuscript* from 1727, it is stated that, as in battle tactics, the square pavement of masonry 'is for a master mason to draw his ground draughts on'[8] – in essence, a draft board.

The first printing of Bacon's *Advancement of Learning* at the British Museum contains a quote from the Proverbs of Solomon concerning the divine plan: 'It is the glory of God to conceal a thing; but the glory of a king is to find it out' (a variation of Proverbs 25:2).[9] In the New Testament Gospel of John 8:12, Jesus is recorded as saying, 'He that followeth me shall not walk in darkness, but shall have the light of life.' In this regard, Albert Pike, the much revered Grand Master of the Southern Jurisdiction *Scottish Rite* in Arkansas from 1864, wrote that 'Masonry to the Masonic Brethren is a search after, and a journeying towards, Light.' All things considered, therefore, the Mason Word is undoubtedly related to Light, in perfect accord with the 'point within a circle' inscription ⊙ at the temple of Moses in Sinai. It was here that the Tabernacle was erected, the Golden Calf was transformed, and the Ark of the Covenant was made.

Given that the Mason Word continued to be so important for such a length of time, it seems impossible that it should have been forgotten. But there is no record of it ever being written down by those who truly knew it and its progression through time was a phonetic progression. For example, *Mahabyn* (as originally written in the 1720s for the first substitute word) is often written today as *Mahabone*. This is equally meaningless, but if the first rendition actually had been meaningful, then neither the correct word nor its meaning would be deduced from the way it is written today. On that basis, it might be helpful to consider phonetics in order to discover the original Mason Word. Since the word *Mahabyn* appeared only in the brief Noah legend, and was substituted by another phonetically recollected word very soon after, the more reliable key to the Mason Word is, in the first instance, not *Mahabyn*, but *Machbenah*.

In consideration of the way Freemasonry and the masonic quest are described in ritual, we are constantly led to the search for enlightenment. On being questioned about his direction of travel in the lodge, the 1st-degree candidate states that he comes 'from the west, travelling east'. On then being asked why he travels eastwards, he answers, 'In search of Light in Masonry' – an allusion to the illuminating light of the rising sun. This places us once again at the foot of Jacob's ladder on the Tracing Board, where the sun symbol, also the symbol of light, is delineated as a point within a circle ⊙. It was also the symbol of On (Heliopolis) – the Egyptian temple of the sun god – and was the symbol of Ra (or Re), the sun god himself. Interestingly, it later became an alchemical symbol for gold.

In addition to this, the twin pillar concept of King Solomon's Temple was based on the free-standing pillars of the Egyptian temples – the obelisks which, in turn, were specifically dedicated to Ra,[10] whose capital was at Heliopolis. The Heliopolis bird of enlightenment, the Phoenix, was known to the Egyptians as the *benu bird*, which came from the east as a physical manifestation of Ra. Associated with this culture, and dating back to the 1st dynasty (*c.* 3000 BC) was the pyramid-shaped *benben* stone (*ben* stemming from the verb *weben*: 'to rise up'). An inscription to the sun god at Heliopolis reads, *Ubenek em benben* ('You shine in the *benben*').[11] Another sun god dedication, from the 6th-dynasty *Pyramid Texts*, reads, 'You rose up as the *benben* stone in the mansion of the phoenix.'

The pillars of Tuthmoses at Heliopolis were symbols of unity and of a concept known as *Ma'at*, which defined 'a level and just foundation' – precisely as Freemasonry is itself described.[12] This ideal of righteous judgement was synonymous with divine kingship, and

A *benben* pyramidion with winged disc

not surprisingly *Ma'at*, the goddess of truth and law, was said to be the sister of Thoth. Her weighing of truth in the balance was conducted with a feather,[13] and her truth was identified with the most noble of metals: gold.

In the same way that the *Wisdom of Lamech* is said in the Old Charges of Freemasonry to have been preserved in the antediluvian pillars of Tubalcain, so too were the secrets of Heliopolis said to be held within the obelisks of the temple – most especially within their pyramidions. The stone of these monuments was called *Mat*,[14] while the Egyptian word for 'pillar' was *Meht*.[15] The great 'enlightenment of the stone' was the *Mat-benu*. In parallel (and equally associated with the Phoenix), the 'light of the pillars' was the *Meht-benu*, and the 'light of truth' was the *Ma'at-benu* – each phonetically very similar. Either way (as *Mat-benu*, *Meht-benu* or *Ma'at-benu*), we have a very persuasive root for what sounded perhaps in Scotland like *Machbenah*. With the inclusive syllables *Ma* and *ben*, there is also a close phonetic resemblance to *Mahabyn* (*Ma'at-ben*) – and the same ideogram prevailed throughout: a point within a circle ⊙.

The Light Bearer

In Egypt the obelisks were known as *tekhenu*, from which derives the Greek root of the English word 'technology'. The prefix 'techno-' relates specifically to a study of the Liberal Arts as described in Freemasonry, while a 'technology' is a written discourse or treatise concerning those Arts.[16]

For all practical purposes with regard to Light and the Liberal Arts – as akin to *Ma'at* (Truth) – Freemasonry would have been far better defined and understood if the Heliopolis Temple structure had been introduced into ritual instead of the Jerusalem Temple model. Maybe this might have prevented the Tuthmoses Needles being separated in London and New York, for the symbolic power of the *Mat* (the Stone) – just as with the *Boaz* and *Jachin* pillars of Solomon – resides in their togetherness. As it is, the pairs have all been separated, with individual obelisks set upon plinths, dispersed across the world. But modern physics can now make *tchām* from gold, and a matched pair of *tekhenu*, properly spaced and embedded, together with *tchām* pyramidion caps, would perhaps be revelatory in both masonic and scientific terms by virtue of their enhanced cosmic attraction (*see* page 202).

The word 'ritual' stems from *ritu* (truth or redness).[17] It is synonymous with *Ma'at*, and is said physically to reveal itself as the purest of all metals: gold, which is deemed to be ultimately noble. In line with this, *phoenix* is the ancient Graeco-Phoenician word for 'red-gold' (or 'crimson' – hence *phoenician* – the obsessively favourite colour of Isaac Newton).[18] The Greek historian Herodotus (*c.* 450 BC) claimed that the Phoenix (or *benu bird*) represented 'the red and gold of the setting and rising sun'.

Heliopolis was the sun centre of Egypt, but this is its Greek name. The Israelites called the place On, but to the Egyptians it was known as Annu,[19] from which the Latin-English word 'annum' (year) derives.[20] In Akkadian Mesopotamia, Annu or Anum had been the equivalent of Ra, whereas in Sumer (southern Mesopotamia) he was the great sky god Anu. It is for this reason that the winged disc of the Lord of the Sun is found in both Mesopotamia and Egypt.

The determination of the earthly calendar was said to be the pre-rogative of the great Anu.[21] An *annum* related to the Earth's solar orbit, and yet again was denoted by a point within a circle ☉. It was called a *sha* – an ideogram of 360° stemming from *sha-at-am*, which lit-erally means 'a passing', with a 360° passing defining an orbit. (Even then – around 3000 BC – it was understood that the Earth revolved around the Sun.) The Orbit of Light was deemed to be the realm of the sun god, and was thus defined as the *Sha-Ra-On* (Sharon).

The transmitter of light (the light bearer) was the Rose of Sharon: the carrier of the *Rosi Crucis*. *Rosi* represented the *ritu* (the redness of truth), and *crucis* related to a cup as in 'crucible'. This was equiva-lent to the sacred Vessel of Light in Kabbalah, and is why the mysti-cal technology of *The Zohar* has been likened to the Holy Grail.[22] The light bearer has been variously identified in different cultures, from Nîn-kharsag to Venus, and in that guise was the queen in the Old Testament Song of Solomon 2:1: 'I am the rose of Sharon …' (I am the truth of the Orbit of Light).

A problem which beset emergent Freemasonry in 1667, and which could not have been foreseen, was directly related to this particular *Sharon* aspect of the Craft. The Puritan faction in Britain was damag-ing to cultural pursuits in many ways, but most effectively and per-manently so by way of its own literary culture. As the Cromwellian movement set it sights fiercely against kingship and the Royal House of Stuart in military terms, so too did its writers, not the least of whom was the London-born poet John Milton (1608–1674). The powerful and dogmatic rhetoric of his *Paradise Lost* was a direct assault against the new philosophy of Christopher Wren and others of the Royal Society. Ignoring Copernicus, Galileo, and the scientific discoveries of his day, Milton's cosmic vision centred on the traditional Christian belief that the Earth (not the Sun) was at the centre of the Universe.

The story of *Paradise Lost* concerns the heavenly revolt of Satan, leading to his fall from grace and the establishment of Hell. At the time of publication, the heated debate over the Mason Word was in full swing, with the Puritans and the Kirk Presbytery claiming that masons were occultists with 'second sight' (likened to the evil eye), who could see the invisible. Worse than that, the Rosicrucian academics of the Royal Society actually believed that the Earth revolved around the Sun. Freemasons were, therefore, accused of being heretical sun cultists!

This was a difficult enough image with which to contend, but Milton added more fuel to the fire when referring to Venus the light bearer. There was a passage in the Old Testament book of Isaiah 14:12 which prophesied the overthrow of Babylon's king, stating: 'How are you fallen from heaven, day star, son of the dawn!' As is made clear by the term 'son of the dawn', the Isaiah reference was to the King of Babylon, but astronomically the 'day star' or 'morning star' is Venus, which appears in the sky before sunrise. In Latin, Venus 'the light-bringer' was referred to as the *lux-fer*, or as it was more commonly written, 'the *lucifer*'.[23] What Milton did was to treat this descriptive feminine term as a proper noun (in accordance with St Jerome's *Vulgate* translation, and as it appears in the Isaiah verse today). But more than that – Lucifer was aligned in *Paradise Lost* with Satan.[24]

> Of Lucifer, so by allusion called,
> Of that bright star to Satan paragon'd.[25]

Prior to 1667, the term *lucifer* (*lux-fer*: 'light-bringer') had never been associated with a male entity – and certainly not with an evil satan. Even after Milton's death, in 18th-century dictionaries, the correct reference is given. For instance, the 1721–94 *Nathan Bailey's Etymological Dictionary* states: '*Lucifer* – The morning or day star; the planet Venus, when it rises before the sun'. But, notwithstanding, following Milton's lead, Freemasons were now not only sun cultists – they were also satanists!

And so, from 1667, Lucifer became an alternative name for Satan, while its association with Venus, light bearer and goddess of love, was forgotten by way of clerical indoctrination. What is perhaps surprising is that, more than three centuries later, the Puritan view is still being expressed by a body of hard-line religious extremists. They pretend on the Internet, and in their books, to be investigators into a liberal conspiracy, but in reality they pursue a modern-day

witch hunt that accuses Freemasons of being satanists and devil-
worshippers. In reality, the 'conspiracy' is entirely on their side and
it is they (not the masons) who cling to a medieval belief in Satan,[26]
making them so fearful of those whom they accuse.

The clear dishonesty in the *Vulgate* Isaiah translation can be seen
from the word that was misrepresented as Lucifer. The direct Greek
equivalent to *lux-fer* (light-bringer) was *phos phoros* (from which the
Latin and English word *phosphorus* derives). Where this was used in
the New Testament (2 Peter 1:19), it was translated as 'day star'.
This is absoluely correct; *lux-fer* and *phos phoros* are identical in
referring to the light bringer (or light carrier), and the word 'phosphorus' is rightly given in today's *Oxford English Dictionary* as relating to the morning star. This was never a derogatory term, and was
even applied in relation to the Messiah (Revelation 22:16 – 'I am the
root and the offspring of David, and the bright and morning star.')

But the original term used in Isaiah was not *phos phoros* but the
Hebrew word *heylel*. This derives from the primitive *halal*, and is
used 165 times in the Old Testament. Examples can be found in 1
Kings 20:11, Psalms 10:3, and Proverbs 20:14, and in each case (along
with many others) *heylel* relates to boasting. Isaiah 14:12 should not
read as 'How are you fallen from heaven, day star, son of the dawn!'
but 'How are you fallen from heaven, boastful one, son of the dawn!'
As the writer of Isaiah intended, this was a direct reference to the
Babylonian king, and had no connection whatever to Venus or a
light bearer of any kind. Not only was John Milton's misuse of *lux-
fer* thoroughly ill-disposed, it was (as derived from the *Vulgate* translation) the wrong word in any event.

Divine Food

In the hermetic lore of the Egyptian mystery schools, the process of
achieving enlightened consciousness was of express importance. To
aid the process, the temple philosophers prepared a miraculous

'powder of projection' by which it was possible to transmute base human ignorance into an ingot of spiritual gold.[27] This exotic powder, as produced by the Karnak Brotherhood of Tuthmoses III, was directly related to the Great Ones at the Mosaic temple in Sinai, and is what became alchemically termed the Philosophers'. Stone, as defined by Flamel and Philalethes.

We have seen how Moses transformed the Golden Calf into an ingestible powder in Exodus, the second book of the Old Testament. In the last book of the New Testament, it appears that the sacred *manna* was still in use around 1,400 years later. The Revelation 2:17 states:

> To him that overcometh will I give to eat of the hidden manna,
> and will give him a white stone, and in the stone a new name
> written, which no man knoweth saving he that receiveth it.

In the New Testament book of 1 Corinthians 10:3, *manna* is referred to as a spiritual food, while also being established as the true bread of the Eucharist in the Gospel of John 6:31–41. It is to what the *Lord's Prayer* refers: 'Give us this day our daily bread', and the *Lord's Prayer* (as defined in Matthew 6:9–13 and Luke 11:2–4) was originally transposed from an Egyptian prayer to the state-god Amen. It began, 'Amen, Amen, who art in heaven'. Traditionally, the Christian rendition places the name of Amen at the end of this prayer – a practice that was also adopted for other prayers and hymns.

Much the same was the case with other biblical books and extracts. The Ten Commandments were drawn from the pharaonic confessions of Spell 125 in the Egyptian *Book of the Dead*,[28] while the Psalms of David were likewise drawn from hymns of Egyptian origin. This Egyptian relationship is particularly noticeable in the Bible's books of the prophets, and good examples are found in the Proverbs of Solomon – the 'words of the wise', which are customarily attributed to King Solomon himself. The Proverbs were translated almost verbatim into Hebrew from the writings of an Egyptian sage called Amenemope[29] (now held in the British Museum). Verse after verse of the book of Proverbs can be attributed to this Egyptian original, and it has been determined that the writings of Amenemope were extracted from a far older work entitled *The Wisdom of Ptah-hotep*,[30] which originates from more than 2,000 years before the time of King Solomon.[31]

A parallel to The Revelation account concerning the 'white stone' appears in the much later Holy Grail tradition of the Middle Ages. It is presented in the romance of *Parzival* by the Bavarian knight Wolfram von Eschenbach. In his Introduction to the work, Wolfram (*c.* 1200) stated that the information came from the Knight Templar attaché Kyôt le Provençale. It reads:

> Around the end of the stone, an inscription in letters tells the name and lineage of those, be they maids or boys, who are called to make the journey to the Grail. No one needs to read the inscription, for as soon as it has been read it vanishes.[32]

The stone being discussed here was said by Kyôt to be the 'perfection of earthly paradise', with remarkable healing and anti-ageing properties. It was called *Lapis Exillis*, a variant of *Lapis Elixir*, which again is the alchemical Philosophers' Stone. The text continues:

> By the power of that stone the Phoenix burns to ashes, but the ashes speedily restore him to life again. Thus doth the Phoenix moult and change its plumage, after which he is bright and shining as before.[33]

From the ancient Egyptian period to the Templar era, the Phoenix (or *benu bird*) was persistently associated with the science behind this alchemical lore. But more than that, the Phoenix was itself representative of the scientific process, for it was the Phoenix which, like the Golden Calf, was burned to ashes from which came the grand enlightenment. The Phoenix and the Philosophers' Stone are, in essence, the same thing.

In the Alexandrian legend *Iter Alexandri ad Paradisium* – a parable of Alexander the Great's journey to Paradise, the Stone appears again. Paradise, in its original portrayal, was the realm of *Pairi Daize* which, in the old Avestan language,[34] was the kingdom of Ahura Mazda, the Persian god of Light. The enchanted Paradise Stone is described as giving youth to the old,[35] and was said to outweigh its own quantity of gold, although even a feather could tip the scales against it! This, as will become evident in chapter 20, is precisely the case. Modern science now reveals that the 'powder of projection' – the *manna* or Philosophers' Stone – can indeed weigh a good deal more, or considerably less, than the gold from which it is produced. Moreover, precisely as described in Wolfram's account, it can be made to weigh absolutely nothing, and then to vanish entirely.

In respect of the Bible's first reference to *manna* (which the more ancient Sumerians of Mesopotamia referred to as *shem-man-na*, meaning 'highward fire-stone') Exodus 16:15 states that:

> When the children of Israel saw it, they said to one another, It is *manna*, for they wist not what it was, And Moses said unto them, This is the bread which the Lord hath given you to eat.

In the *Septuagint* Bible (the earliest extant Old Testament) it is referred to as 'bread of the presence'.[36] Flavius Josephus addressed this in his 1st-century *Antiquities of the Jews*, explaining that 'the Hebrews call this food *manna*, for the particle *man*, in our language, is the asking of a question: What is this?'[37] Hence, although *man-na* meant 'fire-stone' in Sumerian, its derivative *man-hu* (or *manna*) was a question in Hebrew.[38]

The same question also appears in the Egyptian *Book of the Dead* – the oldest complete book in the world. Also known as the *Papyrus of Ani* (a royal scribe), this 18th-dynasty scroll from Thebes (acquired by the British Museum in 1888) is extensively illustrated and around 76 ft (over 23 m) in length.[39] In this ancient ritualistic work, the 'bread of the presence' is called *tchefau food*, and the pharaoh seeking the terminal enlightenment asks, at every stage of his journey, the repetitive question, 'What is it?'

At the very opening of the *Book of the Dead*, a hymn to Osiris moves straight into the key subject of the text, while at the same time drawing a link between the culture of Heliopolis and that of ancient Sumer:

> Thou art the Lord in whom praises are ascribed in the name of Anti; thou art the Prince of divine food in Anu.

Anti was Antu, wife of the Sumerian sky god Anu. Further into the document, another enlightening reference is given:

> I know you, and I know your names, and I know also the name of the mighty god before whose face you set your celestial food. His name is Tekhem [*Tchām*].

In the Egyptian tradition, as inscribed at the Horeb temple in Sinai, the hermetic culture of the pharaohs was described as the House of Gold. In the subsequent but genealogically related culture of Jerusalem, the equivalent kingly tradition was referred to as the House of Bread (*Beth-le-hem*). The gold and the bread are the same thing, as indicated by the treasure relief of Tuthmoses III at Karnak (*see* chapter 11). In the context of the scientific realm of *al-khame*, everything conjoins: light, gold, bread, fire, the Phoenix, the obelisks, the Philosophers' Stone, the Golden Calf and, not least, the Ark of the Covenant which, it should be borne in mind, is the top-most crest of the arms of the United Grand Lodge of England.

PART III

14

Anti-Masonry

Reformation

To continue the historical story of Freemasonry, it is necessary to link up more firmly with the 17th-century Rosicrucian network, and to follow the Stuart Orders into France after the 1688 Whig Revolution in England. This will help bring about an understanding of the *Scottish Rite* and draw distinctions between it and the rather different 'exported' *Scottish Rite* that found its way across the Atlantic some while before America's own Revolution: the 1775–83 War of Independence against the Hanoverian monarchy. First, this is a good opportunity to address the subject of anti-masonry in the light of the puritanical witch-hunting era of the 1600s.

A quick glance at the Internet reveals that these days anti-masonry is predominantly an American-led institution. This stems from the enormous difference between the way that Christianity evolved in America, as against its history in Britain and the rest of Europe – a structural difference that began in the 1600s and persists to this day.

Back in the early 4th-century period of the Roman Church, there were a number of other Christian sects – Arians, Gnostics and Nestorians – and in one way or another their individual cultures survived, but not at any level of mainstream influence. In general terms, Europe became Catholic, while the Celtic Church prevailed in Britain until St Augustine was appointed Archbishop of Canterbury from Rome in 601. Thereafter, a majority of England was Catholic, with the Celtic Church remaining in Wales, the South West, Ireland and Scotland. Then, over a period of time, Catholicism partially infiltrated these regions as well.

The next major change occurred during a disagreement over the Vatican-approved sale of Indulgences (decrees of absolution), when an Augustinian monk and professor of theology at the University of Wittenberg in Germany nailed a written protest to the door of his local church in October 1517. His act of formal objection was destined to split the Western Church permanently in two. The monk's name was Martin Luther, and his fellow 'protesters' became known as Protestants.

It was not by chance that Martin Luther's protest gained support in some very influential circles, for Rome had many enemies in high places. Not the least of these were the Knights Templars, who had themselves been condemned by the Catholic Inquisition. The truth was not so much that Luther gained the support of others, but that he was a willing participant in an already active movement. Nevertheless, his stand against a particular Church practice gave rise to a much larger scale Reformation movement and the establishment of an alternative Christian society outside Vatican control. The Protestants then emerged under the unified banner of the Rosy Cross – an emblem that was incorporated into Martin Luther's own personal seal.

The Protestant split with Rome propagated an environment of democratic free thinking, and fuelled the cultural and intellectual ideals of the Renaissance. Indeed, the High Renaissance movement of 1500–20 had set the perfect scene for Luther's stand against episcopal subjugation. It was a dignified age of the individual – a time when Leonardo, Raphael and Michelangelo developed the harmony of classical art to its highest form. It was also an age in which the excitement of traditional scholarship re-emerged in a burst of colour, eventually to cross new frontiers of science, architecture and design.

In England, the most significant consequence of the Reformation was the formal rejection of the Pope's authority and his replacement as head of the English Catholic Church by King Henry VIII Tudor.

The Rose-Cross seal of Martin Luther

This was followed, in due course, by the establishment of the wholly independent Church of England (the Protestant Anglican Church) under Henry's daughter, Queen Elizabeth I, who was excommunicated by Rome in 1570. Meanwhile, Scotland's secession from a somewhat limited papal influence occurred in 1560 at the instigation of Protestant reformer John Knox, at which time the Church of Scotland (the Kirk) came into being. Eventually, the Scottish Episcopal Church (more akin to the Anglican model) became a popular alternative. In 1562, the French Protestants (Huguenots) rose against their own Catholic monarchy, and the resultant civil struggles (which lasted until 1598) became known as the Wars of Religion.

Throughout this period, the Bible was not generally available. Most people's knowledge of its contents had come from pulpits and preachers. Various attempts at biblical translation from Greek and Latin met with only limited success, and it was not until 1611 that the Authorized Edition of King James I of England (James VI of Scots) saw the light of day. Even then, it took many years for it to become an item of widespread ownership, and it was during this era that the Pilgrim Fathers set sail for America in 1620.

In Britain, a period of puritanical control occurred soon afterwards, but it did not last very long and by the 1660s matters had became more settled. Socially active movements such as the Quakers and Methodists emerged within the Protestant faction, but they were never in any way confrontational; nor are they today. In fact, they assist the maintenance of a generally healthy and tolerant environment. Individual Christian denominations are now of relatively small consequence in Britain and Western Europe, except where politically motivated policies perpetuate a division between Catholic and Protestant, especially in Northern Ireland. But other than this, no one cares or takes much interest in the religious beliefs (or lack of beliefs) of others.

In America, however, the past 400 years have seen a different evolution. It began in the days of the Pilgrim Fathers and a more widespread transatlantic movement by Protestants from Britain, Holland and Germany. The ships landed on the Eastern seaboard in Massachusetts, New York, Pennsylvania, Maryland and Virginia. Many of the voyagers had their Bibles with them – newly acquired and, as yet, unread. Consequently, as their local churches were established, doctrines were formulated on the scriptural interpretations devised in each region. In time, a plethora of individual church groups spread westwards, becoming competitive, one against the other. Their respective Bible interpretations became literal dogma, and the various ministries became prophetic and evangelical to an extent unheard of across the ocean. The situation is little different today, and it is from within these dogmatically opinionated groups that manifestations of anti-masonry arise. With their culture still firmly set in the puritanical witch-hunting framework of the 1600s, it is easy to accuse Freemasons and other non-conformists of being Satanists, for these people truly do believe in a satanic Antichrist figure.

The Biblical Satan

Satan, as the popularly conceived role of a fiendish demonic character, does not appear anywhere in the Bible's Old Testament. Even in other ancient scriptures he does not exist as certain sectors of

Christendom have come to know him.[1] This perception of Satan is
that of an evil imperialist whose despicable horde wages war upon
God and humankind. But this devilish figure was an invention of
the evangelical era, a fabulous myth with no more historic worth
than any figment of a Gothic novel.

Satans (plural), though rarely mentioned in the Old Testament, are
generally portrayed as obedient servants or sons of God who perform
specific duties of strategic obstruction.[2] The Hebrew root of the word
'satan' is *STN*, which defines an opposer, adversary or accuser,
whereas the Greek equivalent was *diabolos* (from which derive the
words diabolical and devil), again meaning no more than an obstruc-
tor or slanderer. Until the Roman Christian era, the term 'satan' had no
sinister connotation whatever and, in biblical times, members of a
political opposition party would customarily have been called 'satans'.

In the Old Testament, satans are seen as members of the heavenly
court – angels who carry out God's more aggressive dictates. In the
book of Job (1:6–12, 2:1–7), for example, a satan is sent twice by God to
tease and frustrate Job, but with the express instruction that he should
not harm the man – an instruction that is duly obeyed. In 1 Chronicles
21:1, a satan figure suggests that King David should count the number
of the Children of Israel, and also receives a passing mention in Psalm
109:6. A magistrate style of satan appears in Zechariah 3:1–2, siding
with the Israelites in their endeavour to re-establish their family sta-
tions in Jerusalem after the Babylonian captivity. These are the only
entries – there are just four in the whole of the Old Testament – and in
no instance is anything remotely dark or sinister implied.

In the New Testament, only one reference introduces a devil character. The other satanic entries are all symbolic – for example, at the
Last Supper, it is stated: 'Then entered Satan into Judas surnamed
Iscariot, being of the number of the twelve.'[3] Elsewhere, when the
scribes admonished Jesus for performing exorcisms when he was
not himself a priest: 'he called them unto him, and said unto them in
parables, How can Satan cast out Satan?'[4] A few other references in
the Acts and Epistles are of a similarly obscure nature.[5] The
Revelation then refers to blasphemers as being of the 'synagogue of

Satan',[6] while claiming that, having been dismissed from heaven, Satan would remain imprisoned for 1,000 years.[7]

In the midst of these, the most telling reference in terms of the obstructive nature of a satan arises in Matthew 16:23, when Jesus accuses the apostle Peter of being a satan. It occurs when Peter rebukes Jesus for being too complacent, whereupon Jesus 'turned and said unto Peter, Get thee behind me Satan; thou art an offence to me, for thou savourest not the things that be of God, but those that be of men'.[8]

Additionally, there is the best known satanic reference in the New Testament, and the only one which has a devil figure appearing as an actual character. Occurring in Matthew 4:5–11, it tells of how Satan took Jesus 'up into an exceedingly high mountain, and showeth him all the kingdoms of the world, and the glory of them; and saith unto him, All these things I will give thee if thou wilt fall down and worship me'. Jesus declined the offer, whereupon 'the devil leaveth him and, behold, angels came and ministered unto him'.[9]

Whoever the devilish tempter of this passage might have been (whether real or symbolic), he is not presented as being in any way persuasive or influential, and bears absolutely no similarity to the terrible demon of satanic mythology. There is nothing remotely fearsome about any of the biblical portrayals, and there is not even the vaguest reference to a physical description. So, from where did the diabolical horned Satan of the fire-and-brimstone preachers emanate?

Horns and Hooves

The menacing figure of Christian mythology emerged mainly through the onset of medieval Christian Dualism – the concept of two opposing and equally powerful gods.[10] According to different traditions, Satan was either the brother or the son of Jehovah, or was even the competitive and aggressive aspect of Jehovah himself. In essence, the said Jehovah–Satan conflict was representative of the ancient pre-Christian tradition of the symbolic battle between Light and Darkness as perceived by the Persian mystics, but this had nothing to do with an Antichrist figure. The eventual Christian image of Satan was a concept that emerged in Roman Imperial times.

The early Catholic faith was based on the subjugation of the masses to the dominion of the bishops, and to facilitate this an Antichrist (anti-Catholic) figure was necessary as a perceived enemy. This enemy was said to be Satan, the 'evil one' who would claim the souls of any who did not offer absolute obedience to the Church. Authority was then established on the back of a statement made by St Paul in the New Testament Epistle to the Romans (13:1–2):

> Let every soul be subject unto the higher powers. For there is no power but of God; the powers that be are ordained of God. Whosoever therefore resisteth the power, resisteth the ordinance of God; and they that resist shall receive to themselves damnation.

It then remained only for the Church to become the self-nominated bridge between God and the people. This was done by granting a vicarious office to the Pope, who became designated Vicar of Christ.

For this scheme of threat and trepidation to succeed, it was imperative to promote the notion that this diabolical Satan had existed from the beginning of time, and there was no earlier story with which he could be associated than that of Adam and Eve. The only problem was that Genesis made no mention whatever of Satan, but there was the inherent account of Eve and the serpent. It was, therefore, determined that this story should be rewritten to suit the desired purpose. The original text was a Jewish version after all, and Christianity had become divorced from Judaism, even from the liberal Judaism of Jesus.

In those days, there was no comprehensive translation of the Bible available to Christians at large. The Jews had their Hebrew, Aramaic and Greek versions of the Old Testament, while the primary Christian Bible (the *Vulgate*) existed in an obscure form of

Church Latin, translated from Greek by St Jerome in the 4th century. Outside the immediate Roman Church of the West, there were enthusiastic Eastern Christian branches in places such as Syria and Ethiopia, and it was mainly from these regions (where the Jewish competition was stronger) that the new Genesis accounts emerged for the Christian market. Among these was an Ethiopic work called *The Book of Adam and Eve* (subtitled *The Conflict of Adam and Eve with Satan*), which was produced sometime around the 6th century.[11] This lengthy book not only features Satan as a central character, but even goes so far as to say that the cross of Jesus was erected on the very spot where Adam was buried!

A Syriac work entitled *The Book of the Cave of Treasures* is a compendium of earthly history from the creation of the world to the crucifixion of Jesus. It appears to have been compiled in the 4th century, but the oldest extant text comes from the late 6th century.[12] Once again, the book introduces Satan as the constant protagonist of evil, setting the scene for the dark and sinister element that flourished in the Church-promoted Gothic tradition which evolved as a product of the brutal Catholic Inquisitions. In one instance, Adam and Eve are seen to be dwelling in a cave when Satan comes 14 times to tempt them, but each time an angel of God puts the demon to flight. The book even maintains that orthodox Christianity was in place before the time of Adam and Eve and the emergent Hebrews!

Another volume which upholds a similar notion is *The Book of the Bee*,[13] a Nestorian Syriac text from about 1222 compiled by Bishop Shelêmôn of Basra, Iraq. Its title is explained by virtue of the fact that it 'gathered the heavenly dew from the blossoms of the two Testaments, and the flowers of the holy books', thereby applying Christian doctrine to the traditional Jewish scriptures which it reinterpreted.

Since the biblical Satan carried no physical description, he was generally considered in early artwork to look like any other angel (albeit a fallen one according to emergent lore). It was not until the year 591 that Pope Gregory I made his announcement concerning the devil's characteristics, thereby establishing the base satanic personality which has been promulgated from that time. 'Satan has horns and hooves', said Gregory, 'and powers to control the weather.'[14] Henceforth, horned animals (in particular stags and goats) were considered to be devilish, while the pictorial imagery of Satan became ever more exaggerated by the addition of a tail, bat's wings and a variety of bodily characteristics based upon the satyrs of Greek mythology.

As for the Antichrist, so often preached to strike terror and sub-jugation, there is no such character in the New Testament. The word (with a small 'a') only appears in the Epistles of John, but not in relation to a specific figure. It is used simply as a term to define those opposed to the teachings of Jesus. 1 John 2:18 states that 'even now are there many antichrists'. 1 John 2:22 continues with 'he that denieth that Jesus is the Christ; he is antichrist'.[15] There is nothing here that relates to any satanic being, and the author of the John epistles plainly recognized that Christ had many opposers. In much the same way, the word 'satanist' was used right up until Puritan times. The pamphlet *An Harbour for Faithful and True Subjects*, issued by John Aylmer, Bishop of London in 1559, refers to all those other than Christians as 'satanists'. Like the terms antichrist, atheist and infidel, it was a commonly used description of unbelievers in general, and its complexion did not change until the onset of the witch-hunts.[16]

In short, the satanic myth is no more than a fictional fable. It was concocted long after Bible times, and was designed to under-mine historical record while intimidating Christians into compli-ance with the dogmatic and subjugative rule of the bishops. In the light of this, it makes little sense that the descendants of those who broke free from such restrictive dogma (in order to pursue their own courses of religious freedom in the New World) should end up so many centuries after the event being the only ones who remain convinced by it!

The Demons of Taxil

The truly unfortunate aspect of all this is that once an organized body such as the Freemasons begin to feel that they should retaliate against ludicrous accusations of satanism and the like, the whole scenario grows out of all proportion. The retaliation adds fuel to the fire of the accusers, and the back-and-forth debate leads to the Freemasons undermining their own credibility. It has been argued in masonic circles that allowing malicious assault to go unanswered can leave long-term debris to serve as a bridgehead for the next attackers.[17] This might well be true, but the debris remains in any event since the responses are ignored.

For the longest time, the official policy of Freemasonry was to ignore malicious and sensational assaults, but since 1984 it has become the practice to respond. The very nature of those who level unfounded and unwarranted accusations against others in any walk of life is that their express purpose is to draw attention back to themselves. The person or group that gives an initial response then becomes confused by the fact that their explanation was not sufficient, and thereafter tries again, placing even more wood on the fire. Ultimately, a type of panic can then ensue, to the extent that lies and fabrications emanate from both sides in an attempt to win an argument that cannot be won by either party because it has no basis for existence in the first place. On the way through, however, the malicious accuser achieves all the publicity sought in the first place.

In this regard, no one is more misquoted than the 19th-century Arkansas Grand Master and masonic scholar Albert Pike (*see* page 220). Such constant page-numbered references to his writings rely on the premise that few people, if any, will check them because they are not that easy to access. A good example of this is Pike's use on occasions of the term 'light bringer', which he correctly renders in Latin as *lucifer*, when referring to the masonic quest for Light as being *luciferian*.

The link between Albert Pike's *lucifer* terminology and satanism was first made in the late 1800s by a Frenchman named Gabriel Jorgand-Pages – better known by his pseudonym Léo Taxil. He became renowned as an ingenious hoaxer, managing to get beaches cleared on many occasions by fake reports of shark attacks, while fooling Swiss archaeologists about the existence of an entire Roman town at the bottom of a lake. He used contrived pornographic photography to discredit churchmen, and was prosecuted on charges ranging from plagiarism to fraud – but through much of this he was also a Freemason. Notwithstanding all the traditional tolerance and fraternal instincts of Freemasonry, the embarrassment became so great that Taxil was expelled in 1881. The consequence of this was his formulation of an elaborate hoax against Freemasons.

At that time, Gothic horror was popular in France, with many books and plays on the subject. Taxil decided to tap into this with the invention of a masonic rite that he called Palladism. He introduced it in an 1891 book entitled *Are There Women in Freemasonry?* claiming that Palladism was controlled from America by Albert Pike. Taxil's descriptions of this supposed satanic rite and its High Temple Mistress grade were graphically sexual and were said to have been imported into France by one Phileas Walder who, with the aid of an occult mystic known as Eliphas Levi, had founded the Lodge of the Lotus. The Catholic hierarchy reacted quickly to this, and the impetuous Bishop Fava of Grenoble published his own book on the subject, with its details extracted directly from Taxil. Other works soon followed from writers such as Adolphe Ricoux and Leon Meurin, a Jesuit bishop from Mauritius. Albert Pike was referred to as the High Priest of the Synagogue of Satan, and the scene was set for another treatise from Léo Taxil: *The Devil in the Nineteenth Century*.

Issued under the *nom de plume* Dr Bataille, this work was published in 240 episodes, and it further exaggerated the concept of masonic devil worship. It explained how Albert Pike met secretly on Friday afternoons with a demon who would bring a winged crocodile to play the piano at his lodge meetings, and thoroughly spurious texts were cited as being quoted extracts from Pike's rituals. Masonic documents were invented and forged in France, as were staged photographs and drawings of hideous goings-on in America. By that time, the Palladian Rite was reckoned to have bases established in

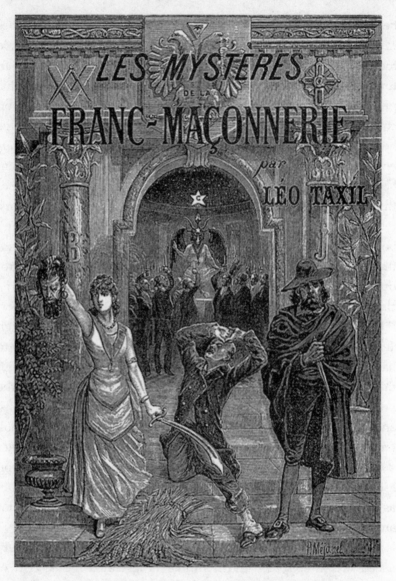

Frontispiece from Léo Taxil's *Les Mysteres de la
Franc-Maçonnerie* (*The Mysteries of the Freemasons*)

Charleston, Washington, Rome, Berlin, Naples and Calcutta. Then,
under his own name (as if to substantiate the work of Bataille), Taxil
published a complementary work entitled *The Mysteries of the
Freemasons Revealed*.

A female demon named Bitruand was credited with the senior position of influence in France, and she was said to be the chosen grandmother of the Antichrist. All that was needed to complete the hoax were the inside revelations of a reformed lodge member, and these appeared as the *Memoirs of an Ex-Palladist* by a certain Diana Vaughan. This 24-part work revealed how, on Albert Pike's death, his American Grand Mastership had been passed to another in Rome and, to give it weight and authenticity, the names of well-known masons in France, Italy and England were included as being part of the Palladian network.[18] It was all so successful and convincing that even the *New Illustrated Larousse Encyclopedia* carried a two-column entry concerning Palladism and the Palladian Rite. In 1896 (still writing as Diana Vaughan), Taxil announced his discovery that Satan had his earthly headquarters deep within a cave on the Rock of Gibraltar.

At that stage, consternation arose within the Catholic Church, and the bishops began to wonder if they had been hoodwinked. An in-depth investigation into the affair was conducted by Arthur E Waite of the Theosophical Society who, although not a lover of Freemasonry, produced a devastating exposé of what he termed the *Pala Dium* in his book *Devil Worship in France, or the Question of Lucifer*.[19] One by one, Léo Taxil's frauds, fabrications, forgeries, falsehoods and fictions were unmasked, to be classified thereafter as 'an extraordinary literary swindle'.

At an International Anti-Masonic Congress in Trent, Austria, on 26 September 1896, even the anti-masons became concerned. It was suggested that the said Diana Vaughan should be made to appear with proofs of her claims, at which point Taxil's collaborator, Charles Hacks, was forced to admit that she did not exist. The same demand came from the Catholic newspaper *Universe*, which met with the same response. The Vatican Council was enormously embarrassed since it was Taxil's original pronouncements about Albert Pike which had led to the 1884 encyclical *Humanum Genus* of Pope Leo XIII, which had claimed that Freemasons were 'rising up against God himself' and 'planning the destruction of the Holy Church' (*see* page 90).

Under extreme pressure, Taxil agreed to appear at the Paris Geographical Society on 19 April 1897, stating that he would bring Diana Vaughan with him, but he could not find a willing impersonator, so the days of his hoax were numbered. Ironically, a real Diana Vaughan did indeed exist, but she had nothing whatever to do with Freemasonry. Taxil had simply used her name after he met her once in Paris on a visit from the United States. She was actually a travelling sales representative for Remington Typewriters. Taxil arrived alone for the Geographical Society event, where he insisted (for the sake of his safety) that all sticks, umbrellas and the like should be left in the cloakroom. As his final joke, while seemingly awaiting Miss Vaughan's arrival, he collected cash from the attendees by raffling a portable Remington typewriter! In respect of Pope Leo's *Humanum Genus*, Taxil stated that he had earned a good deal of money from 'the unknown idiocy of Catholics' whereupon, before leaving the stage under an armed police escort, he announced publicly and for the press, 'The Palladium exists no more. I was its creator, and I have destroyed it.'[20]

Amusing as this might seem, the repercussions were great because out-of-print book publishers of esoterica continued to reprint facsimiles and translations of the pseudo-Diana Vaughan work without any mention of Taxil's confession on the matter. It is from this, along with Taxil's other writings and various spin-off books of the early 1900s, that modern anti-masons (knowingly or unwittingly) obtain their misguided information about Freemasonry and Albert Pike, whose 11-ft bronze statue by the Italian sculptor Gaetano Trentaove is located in downtown Washington, DC.

There are many things about Freemasonry which are perhaps naive and might be considered silly by modern standards – many Freemasons will themselves concede to that. Leading Freemasons have also acknowledged that criticism might be expected because of the inherent secrecy of lodge ritual. Similarly, this produces a naturally intriguing arena for investigative journalists and conspiracy theorists. Also, because Freemasonry is spiritual but not religious, the accusatory door is opened to those who judge that it *should* be a religious institution, and then condemn it because it is not.

Like any formal establishment, whether it is governmental, institutional, corporate or social (and masonic membership is bigger than most on a world scale), Freemasonry has had its share of internal malpractice and misuse of membership. But for all that, the condemnations of those of malicious intent or subversive practice are wholly unfounded. While there are plenty of powerful and influential men – world leaders, good and bad at their jobs – who are Freemasons, this does not determine that Freemasonry is about world leadership. It is, however, about personal advancement in spiritual, philosophical and educational terms – and if that leads to advancement in professional life, then it is no different to any other form of study and learning.

A pertinent note on which to conclude this subject is indicative of the situation that applies when teeth are biting to such a degree that they will not let go under any circumstances. It concerns an anti-masonic author called Stephen Knight, whose 1976 book, *Jack the Ripper*,[21] suggested a masonic involvement in the infamous London murders, and was produced as the cinema movie *Murder by Decree*. This was followed by Knight's 1983 bestselling work entitled *The Brotherhood*,[22] which promulgated other dark visions of Freemasonry. Stephen Knight died of a brain tumour in 1985, aged only 34. This led quickly to the tongue-in-cheek question, 'How did the masons organize that?' But this was followed by a more seriously intended response, given in a 1990 radio interview, that masons had used an ultra-sound death ray to induce the tumour! Regrettable though it might be, the anti-masonic playground is designed to remain a no-win circus for Freemasons as things currently stand.

The Tudor Stage

Secret Service

The foundation stone of the Shakespeare Memorial Theatre was laid in a masonic ceremony at Stratford-on-Avon in 1877 (*see* page 96). The proceedings were led by William, Lord Leigh, Provincial Grand Master of Warwickshire. Performances began there in the following year, but the building was destroyed by fire in 1926. Soon afterwards, the foundation stone was laid for a new theatre,[1] and this ceremony was also conducted with full masonic honours in July 1929. On this occasion, the event was hosted by Sir Arthur Olivier Villiers Russell, Lord Ampthill, Pro Grand Master[2] of the United Grand Lodge of England. He used a 4,000 year-old Egyptian maul from Saqqara for the occasion, and there were 600 Freemasons present, all dressed in full regalia. William Shakespeare (1564–1616) lived during England's Elizabethan and early Stuart eras, and died a full century before the Grand Lodge establishment. So what possibly could have been his connection to Hanoverian Freemasonry?

We know that James I Stuart of England (1603–25) – James VI of Scots from 1567 – was a Freemason long before the initiation of Sir Robert Moray in 1641. But, irrespective of the Scottish roots of the Craft, the earliest known illustration of a Freemason actually comes from England in 1598. This was during the Shakespearean era, and before the Scottish and English crowns were united under King James. The picture appeared in a work called *The Mirrour of Policie*, published in London by Adam Islip. With the scales of justice on its title page, the book carried the descriptive sub-title, *A work no less profitable than necessary for all magistrates and governors of estates and commonweals.*[3] The publication was about the legal aspects of land management and public usage; it had nothing to do with building or stonemasonry. So why the picture of a Freemason, complete with his square and compasses, and a crown at his feet to signify the Royal Art?

The Mirrour of Policie – an English Freemason, 1598

A closer inspection of this woodcut reveals that it is not actually a square that the mason holds over his shoulder. It is the base and hypotenuse section of a right-angled triangle. The perpendicular which forms the square is lying on the ground. This is in keeping with the 47th Proposition of Euclid,[4] which is so important to Freemasonry (*see* base image in plate 5). It is perhaps also representative of a 3rd degree that might have existed in Elizabethan times. This means that the Hiramic 3rd degree, as introduced in the 1730s, becomes an allegory in itself. This is an intriguing prospect because it suggests that it might not be such a naive working after all. In fact, it could mean that Craft ritual throughout is allegorical – no different to a Shakespearean play wherein superficial stories are used, much like New Testament parables, to convey a deeper meaning for those with ears to hear.[5]

Although the Copernican solar principle in lodge ritual may initially have appeared obsolete, it now seems that its inclusion is indeed significant. Far from denoting a limited extent of scientific knowledge, it is symbolic of the fact that, in the early days of the *Invisible College*, embryonic Freemasonry supported the science of Galileo (1564–1642) when it was deemed outrageous and heretical. It was introduced as a statement of principle – a stance against nonsensical dogma – and this could remain the same today.

A colleague and confederate of William Shakespeare in the Poetry and Magic Society of the Elizabethan Court was the Rosicrucian Grand Master, Sir Francis Bacon (1561–1626). Subsequently knighted by James I (VI), Bacon was created Viscount St Albans to become King's Advocate and Lord Chancellor of England. His circle of literary acquaintance also included Christopher Marlowe, Edmund Spenser, Ben Jonson, Edward de Vere, John Fletcher and Philip Sidney, all of whom were directly or indirectly attached to the national Intelligence Service which had been set up during the Elizabethan conflict with Spain.

Placed in charge of the Secret Service, as Ambassador to France from 1570, was Sir Francis Walsingham, a hitherto Protestant field agent.[6] His 1587 report concerning the impending Spanish Armada, entitled *The Plot for Intelligence out of Spain* (now held within the Sloane Manuscripts at the British Museum), is regarded as the formal inaugural document of the Secret Service Department.

Early in his Intelligence career, Walsingham established a team of espionage agents. One of the earliest was the noted astrologer and mathematician John Dee (1527–1608). He was placed in charge of affairs in Poland, being responsible for reporting on intrigue between the Vatican and Spain.[7] A few years earlier, in 1562, Dee had discovered a book entitled *Stenographia* by Johannes Trithemius, the Benedictine Abbot of Sponheim (1462–1516), and from this he learned a good deal about codes and ciphers, producing his own explanatory work on the subject for Walsingham's spy network.[8] Subsequently, numbers were used by the Secret Service to denote the agents themselves, along with other people and places. England was number 039, Holland 096, Germany 070, the Queen of Spain 055, and Mary, Queen of Scots 003. As for secret agent John Dee (the 'original James Bond'), he was 007.[9]

Apart from his Government activities, Dee was Queen Elizabeth's closest adviser, and a practising alchemist under royal licence. He was also famed for his *Liber Mystorium* which, because of its inherent 'angelic conversations', is often said to concern an ancient art (devised by the biblical Enoch and called Enochian magic) that allows the adept to command angels to fulfil personal desires. However, the work (now at the British Museum) had nothing to do with angels. It was actually compiled as a record of discussions relating to Vatican Intelligence, presented in a heavily coded form with the help of Dee's lawyer confederate Edward Kelly.[10] The Catholics, in their attempt to discredit Dee's reports, were quick to invent a body of propaganda suggesting that he was some kind of black magician who consorted with the angel Uriel in a strange alien language. Dee, in turn, used this to good advantage by playing on his supposed links to the spirit world. Eventually, some decades later, his encrypted writings were fully explained to the Royal Society by Dr Robert Hooke (inventor of the spirit level and marine barometer). Yet there are still plenty of books produced today which naively centre upon the Church-promoted counter-intelligence concerning the presumed supernatural abilities of John Dee.

On 30 May 1593, Christopher Marlowe was stabbed to death at a London meeting-house in Deptford, where Robert Poley, the espionage attaché and steward to Walsingham's daughter, was staying.[11] Also there, as given in the Coroner's report, were Poley's assistant Nicholas Skeres and the Walsingham secretary Ingram Fritzer. Precisely which of the men committed the murder is still a matter of debate. Fritzer was imprisoned after the event, but was conveniently released with a Queen's Pardon the following month. What is clear is that Marlowe had been arrested on the previous Sunday, 20 May, and charged with heresy, but had been released on bail pending trial by the Star Chamber – a bail which actually expired on the day of his murder.[12] It seems likely, therefore, that his killing was politically motivated in order to prevent him from giving away State secrets in court.

Shakespearean Masonry

Having entered the realm of Bacon and Shakespeare, we are in the arena of Rosicrucian theatre – an auditorium where *The Globe* (built in 1599) was itself a model for the Art of Memory (*see* page 153). The masonic environment – which is no less a playhouse than *The Globe* – is established on the same principles, with officers and furniture having designated positions and perambulations within the confines of the lodge. Hence, not only the Craft workings, but the lodge itself becomes an allegory of a wider stage. In this context, *Boaz* and *Jachin* (the pillars of Solomon) assume the grandeur of the Pillars of Hercules, as depicted in Sir Francis Bacon's *Advancement and Proficience of Learning – The Partitions of the Sciences* (1605). He used this pictorial theme again in his *Great Instauration – The Renewal of the Sciences* (1620) and in his *Sylva Sylvarum – A Natural History* (1626) which contains his unfinished *New Atlantis*.

Peter Dawkins of the Francis Bacon Research Trust explains that the left-hand pillar – as we view it – is the Sun pillar (Wisdom), and the other is the Moon pillar (Intelligence). The Sun pillar (in the light) is denoted by the word Science and is surmounted by the globe of the visible world (the *mundus visibilis*). This is equivalent to *Jachin* (Establishment). The Moon pillar (in the shade) is denoted by the word Philosophy and is surmounted by the intellectual world (the *mundus intellectualis*). It is equivalent to *Boaz* (Strength). In university terms, the Sun pillar carries the name of Oxford, while the

Baconian pillars and the ship *Argo*

Moon pillar is defined as Cambridge. Between them is the ship *Argo* in quest for the Golden Fleece, and beneath the *Argo* (between the pillars) is the motto, *Multi pertransibunt & augebitur scientia* (Many shall pass through and learning shall be increased).[13]

With regard to *The Mirrour of Policie* with its picture of a Freemason, it is perhaps no coincidence that its issue in 1598 coincided with the very first publication of a Shakespearean play: *Love's Labour's Lost*. When James Anderson's *Constitutions* were published in 1723, this coincided with the centenary of the first folio edition of Shakespeare's plays. In reference to William, Earl of Pembroke, and Philip, Earl of Montgomery, the original 1623 *Folio of Comedies, Histories and Tragedies* had been dedicated (in masonic terminology) 'To the Most Noble and incomparable pair of Brethren'. At the same time, in 1723, the Benson Medley edition of *Shakespeare's Sonnets* was also published, with a title-page headpiece depicting the square and compasses along with the higher degrees of Freemasonry.[14] It was with this edition (issued by Alexander Pope) that Freemasonry announced itself to the world. Soon afterwards, in 1733, masonic symbols including the square and compasses appeared again in the tailpiece of Dr Peter Shaw's compilation of *The Philosophical Works of Francis Bacon.*[15]

In the light of such apparent links between William Shakespeare and Freemasonry, it is not surprising to discover that there are distinct similarities between the Bard's writings and masonic ritual. In the Craft degrees, when references are made to a password, it is not rendered in full, but in parts. The Worshipful Master asks the candidate to name the Word, whereupon he claims that he cannot state the Word as a whole. He is then asked to 'letter or halve it'. In Act V, Scene II of *Love's Labour's Lost*, the scene is similarly played out by three couples conversing about a word. Biron says to the Princess, 'One word in secret'. Taking up the thread, Maria says to Dumain, 'Name it', and Longaville then says to Katherine, 'Let's part the word'.

Concerning the lost secrets of Freemasonry, the Worshipful Master asks his Warden, 'How do you hope to find them?' The correct answer to this is, 'By the centre'. In Act II, Scene II of *Hamlet*, Polonius states, 'I will find where truth is hid, though it were hid indeed – Within the centre.'

The 'apron-men' are referred to in Act IV, Scene VI of *Coriolanus*, and *The Tempest* is alive with masonic implication concerning Prospero, the master who rises through degrees within the play. He is introduced as being of good repute (1st degree); he is a student of the Liberal Arts (2nd degree), and in Act III, Scene II, is the object of assault by three ruffians, who plan to beat his brain with a log and steal his books (3rd degree).

A special performance of *The Tempest* was given at *The Globe* by Shakespeare's company, The King's Men, for Princess Elizabeth Stuart and Frederick V, Elector Palatine, before their marriage in February 1613.[16] They subsequently became King and Queen of Bohemia, but only for a few months in 1619–20, which led to Frederick being called the Winter King. Their Protestant reign was cut short by the Catholic League and the Holy Roman Empire, whose joint forces defeated the Bohemians at the Battle of White Mountain near Prague.[17] It was their son Charles Louis, Prince Palatine, to whom John Wilkins had been chaplain before his *Invisible College* activities at Oxford. Their younger son, Prince Rupert, was a general in the Royalist army of his uncle, King Charles I, and it was he who gave Oliver Cromwell's armoured troopers the nickname 'Ironsides'.

The Bohemian Connection

Prague had been a melting-pot of Rosicrucian activity from Elizabethan times when the renowned alchemist, Count Michael Maier (1566–1622), was appointed as physician to the court of Emperor Rudolph II. In 1612, Maier came to London with Frederick before the Elector's marriage to Princess Elizabeth Stuart. And in England, Maier and Shakespeare shared the same publisher, Thomas Creede. During that era, Robert Fludd, John Dee, Edward Kelly, Giordano Bruno and Johannes Kepler all spent time in Prague, while the University of Heidelberg (where the Palatinate had its primary castle) was the hub of affiliated European academia. It was from this fraternity that the term 'bohemian' derived for philosophically minded, socially unconventional people.

Giordano Bruno (1548–1600) was burned at the stake by the Catholic Inquisition for his belief in the Copernican astronomical system. In the 1580s, however, he spent over two years in England, where he had a significant influence on the Elizabethan court. He was an ardent scholar of the Egyptian mystery schools, and was noted for his socially-minded views concerning religious toleration and philanthropy. He associated the hermetic arts directly with his chivalric ideals, and in so many ways was the epitome of what emergent Freemasonry aspired to be.[18] It could perhaps be said that Bruno was the originator of the masonic concept in social terms, and his aptitude for the Art of Memory certainly inspired William Schaw, who produced the *Masonic Statutes* in Scotland. In Shakespearean terms, Bruno the benevolent magus is adequately painted in the character of Prospero, and might very well have been the inspirational model.[19]

Johannes Kepler, another of the 'bohemian' fraternity in Prague came from Württemberg, and in 1596 (at the age of 24) published his *Cosmographic Mystery* in which he postulated a model of the solar system and defended the Copernican principle. A keen Pythagorean, Kepler believed that the Universe was a harmonic entity, and that numbers and patterns governed all creation.[20] From studying observations of Mars collated over 20 years by his master, Tycho Brahe (mathematician to the royal court at Prague), Kepler concluded that there was a discrepancy between the observed positions and those of Copernican theory. This led to his discovery that planetary orbits were not circular but elliptical, and to the formulation of *Kepler's Laws*. These appeared in his books, *New Astronomy* and *Harmony of the World*, published in 1609 and 1619 respectively. In the course of this, the planets' distances from the sun and their periodical times were calculated and, despite continuing ecclesiastical opposition, the Heliocentric Principle was proved.

At the same time, the Italian natural philosopher Galileo was perfecting his telescope, which subsequently confirmed *Kepler's Laws*. Galileo was able to locate a smaller example of the system in action by revealing the orbits of the moons around Jupiter, thus paving the way for Christopher Wren, Robert Hooke, Edmund Halley and Isaac Newton. Meanwhile, in retribution for Kepler's heretical philosophy, his mother was seized, imprisoned and tortured for being a witch.

Those such as Bruno and Kepler were the front-line instigators of the 'bohemian' stream which fed into the Scottish traditions of the Stuart court to emerge jointly as the Royal Society. Following Frederick V's overthrow by the Catholic League, he and Elizabeth moved to Holland and set up a court of exile at The Hague.[21] It was here that Elizabeth's nephew, the forthcoming King Charles II, lived during the Cromwellian Protectorate before Samuel Pepys went to bring him home for the 1660 Restoration.[22] Hence it was that when Charles arrived in London, he was already embroiled in the great alchemical quest, and was delighted to find young men such as Wren, Hooke and Boyle continuing the work of Bruno and Kepler. At that time, Stuart Rosicrucianism and Elizabethan Freemasonry were much in the same mould, and they remained so in Britain until the Whig Revolution of 1688, when the Stuarts were exiled to Europe once again. When the new-style Georgian Freemasonry emerged from 1717, the best it could do was to endeavour to pick up some threads – but they were few. The scientific Rosicrucians continued their operations abroad, but it seems that some of their signs and symbols were preserved with the new Freemasonry just as they had been used in the days of Francis Bacon and William Shakespeare.

Plates 9 and 11 show the similarity between Rosicrucian emblems and the Masonic devices. The Rosicrucian pillars, marked *J* and *B*, are noticeable as *Jachin* and *Boaz*. Individually denoted by the sun and moon, they are also akin to the Herculean pillars of Francis Bacon's work. In the other plate, the All-seeing Eye is central, while the small left-hand pillar at the base is captioned as that of Zerubabbel in accordance with the William Sinclair inscription (*see* page 253). The pillar to the right (the Pillar of Beauty) is similar to the Apprentice Pillar at Rosslyn Chapel, and is identified as *Raphadon* (Place of Rest) – a word used in the 15th degree of *Scottish Rite* Freemasonry, known as Knight of the East or Sword.[23]

In respect of emblematic similarities, another relevant comparison is one that relates directly to the Mason Word and its relationship to Light. Plate 7 from Anderson's 1784 *Constitutions* depicts rays of light reflected within Grand Lodge from a mirror. This notion was developed from an earlier frontispiece in the book *Ars Magna Lucis et Umbrae* (The Great Art of Light and Darkness), published in 1646 by Athanasius Kircher (*see* plate 30). Kircher might not have been the greatest authority on Egyptian hieroglyphics (*see* page 196), but it was his concept of projected light by way of mirrors which led to the Sorcerer's Lamp, subsequently known as the *Laterna Magica* (Magic Lantern).

Kircher's work was greatly inspirational to Royal Society philosophers such as Christiaan Huygens and Isaac Newton but, like all science of the period, it was fully hermetic in nature. His illustration displays a number of themes akin to Freemasonry. The caduceus of Hermes, for example, is topped by the All-seeing Eye, above which is the Volume of the Sacred Law. This is pure masonic imagery from at least 92 years before it was seemingly introduced by James Anderson and his colleagues. An interesting reference given by Kircher in connection with the Eye is that Heliopolis was called *Ainschems* by the Arabs (meaning the Eye of the Sun). Thus, the point within a circle ⊙ was not just a symbol of light, as in a straightforward sun disc, but a symbol of its central focus.

The use of the All-seeing Eye atop the caduceus in this image (*see* plate 30) is especially significant. Its connection with *al-khame* was noted earlier (*see* page 155), along with its common association with the Eye of God, but the Eye also has a further implication in Rosicrucian philosophy.

The caduceus (two serpents spiralling around a central staff) has been a symbol of healing since the days of the Egyptian Therapeutate, and it is still used as an insignia by medical institutions worldwide. In the esoteric tradition, the staff and serpents represent the spinal cord and the sensory nervous system. Above the spinal column (where Kircher placed the Eye) is generally shown the central node of the pineal gland.[24] In the hermetic lore of the Egyptian mystery schools, the process of achieving enlightened consciousness was of express importance, with spiritual regeneration taking place by upward degrees through the 33 vertebrae of the spinal column.[25] It is for this reason that 'beyond the Craft' Freemasonry was founded upon 33 degrees.[26]

The pineal is a small cone-shaped gland, situated within the brain, although outside the ventricles and not forming a part of the brain matter as such. About the size of a grain of corn, it was thought by the French philosopher René Descartes (1596–1650)[27] to be the 'seat of the soul' – the point at which the mind and body are conjoined.[28] The ancient Greeks considered likewise, and in the 4th century BC, the Greek physician and anatomist Herophilus of Alexandria described the pineal as an organ which regulated the flow of thought. This gland has long intrigued anatomists because, while the brain consists of two halves, the pineal has no counter-part.[29] It has long been known as the Eye of Wisdom (or the Third Eye), the chakra of heightened self-awareness and inner vision,[30] representing the ability to see things clearly with intuitive know-ledge. In this respect, it is the All-seeing Eye, and Kircher identified it correctly as such.

Fine Devices

Returning now to *The Mirrour of Policie* (1589)[31] – a translation from Guillaume de la Perrière's *Le miroir politique* – another of the author's books, *The Theater of Fine Devices*, was registered at Stationer's Hall, London, on 9 May 1593. The registration was lodged by the book's publisher Richard Field, a friend of William Shakespeare, from Stratford-on-Avon. Shortly before this, an intriguing verse by Edward de Vere, Earl of Oxford, had emanated from within the court circle. Entitled *Labour and its Reward*, it alluded to the fact that learning is available to those of any social station:

> The mason poor that builds the lordly halls,
> Dwells not in them; they are for high degree.
> His cottage is compact in paper walls,
> And not with brick or stone, as others be.[32]

The Theater of Fine Devices had previously been registered in Paris in 1539 under the title *Le Théâtre des bons engins*, and was published in Lyon in 1545. It was translated into English by the poet Thomas Combe – another friend of Shakespeare, to whom the Bard bequeathed his sword. Dedicated to Marguerite de France, Queen of Navarre,[33] the book includes 100 small representative emblems of magic or moral qualities. They are illustrated by way of various gods, goddesses and figures such as Hermes and Pythagoras – all alchemical in flavour and intensely allegorical. In one instance (rather like the Egyptian truth scales of Ma'at), falsehood is weighed to be lighter than a feather. In others, men and women are seen holding gigantic keys.

What is unusual, however, when considering the quality of Richard Field's other publications, is that Guillaume's emblematic drawings (despite being called 'fine devices') are very crudely made. They have interesting content, but no artistry to commend them – and yet Field even published a further edition in 1614, as if there were some particular merit to the work. In fact, the best of all the book's images is that placed by Richard Field on the title page, which is quite different to that of the earlier French edition. Some 26 years before Sir Robert Moray's initiation, Field's imprint emblem for the book (set within some outer scroll-work) was a masonic wreath and anchor.

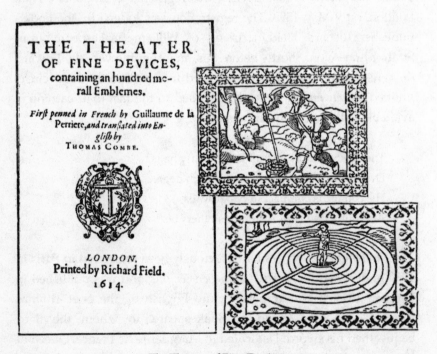

The Theater of Fine Devices

In his original Dedication of the work, Guillaume had likened his images to Egyptian hieroglyphs, referring to them as 'expositions'. But within the overall context, one particular image is quite unlike the rest because its pictorial location is based on reality. It depicts (well enough for immediate recognition) the labyrinth design from Chartres Cathedral. There is a man in the middle of the labyrinth but, oddly, his feet are unseen, and he stands within what resembles a hole at the centre. As stated in lodge ritual concerning the lost secret of Freemasonry, the man is 'at the centre'. As we will see, this image is connected to the point within a circle ⊙, along with the light, bread, gold, Philosophers' Stone and Ark of the Covenant (*see* page 292).

The House of Salomon

There appears little doubt that, although much of what underpinned original masonic thought was Egyptian and Tuthmosaic, the concept of linking post-1717 Freemasonry with King Solomon was developed from the writings of Sir Francis Bacon. Thus, the Temple of Light was moved literally from Heliopolis to Jerusalem. This was not altogether wrong in historical terms because Solomon was equally involved with the mystic arts – in particular that concerning the white 'bread of gold'. The most ancient biblical text of the *Septuagint* confirms (3 Kings 5:7, 10:11) that King Huram of Tyre supplied Solomon with alluvial gold from the mines of Ophir, near Sheba, while his requirement in return for this and all his favours was that Solomon should 'give bread to my household'.

The eventual masonic theme was largely inspired by Bacon's *New Atlantis*, which concerned the Isle of Bensalem, over which a King Salomon (Solomon) reigned in the days of yore. His establishment was called the House of Salomon, or the College of the Workmen of Six Days. There were deep grottoes and great towers for the observation of natural phenomena; large buildings in which

meteors, the wind, thunder and rain were imitated; extensive botan-
ical gardens and fields where all manner of animals and insects were
studied. The learned men of the College collated their experimental
results, and deliberated as to what should be published, and what
should be researched further. It was, in effect, a mythical island-
based Royal Society.

The 1667 *History of the Royal Society of London* was compiled by
the Society's historian Thomas Sprat, a friend of John Wilkins from
Wadham College, Oxford. The Introduction to a subsequent printing
of this work begins with the statement:

> Lord Bacon's Salomon's House in the *New Atlantis* was a
> prophetic scheme of the Royal Society ... Bacon forecast the tri-
> umph of the new empiricism; legions of propagandists urged its
> adoption in the universities or in scientific pseudo-monasteries
> throughout the forties and fifties; and the Royal Society gave it
> a focus and a symbol.[34]

Sprat emphasized the fact that 'Francis Bacon was the one great man
who had the true imagination of the whole extent of this enterprise.'
By the Georgian and Victorian eras, however, this had largely been forgotten. The English stage had become Germanic, austere and acutely
materialistic to the extent that Bacon was no longer regarded as an
inspired philosopher but as a 'vague visionary'. This attitude was evident in the critical essays of Lord Thomas Macaulay,[35] whose comments were based on a superficial scanning of Bacon's work and
shaped by the judgements of his own time.[36] Not only was the Royal
Society's true *raison d'être* lost to mind in the world of practical
science – and indeed to the world of history – it had also been forgotten
in the environment of the masonic lodge. Bacon's idea that although
knowledge might prevail, the wisdom of ages rests with the deceased,
had given way to the symbolism of this concept – in other words, that
for wisdom to be retrieved, one would need to resurrect the dead.
The legend of Hiram Abiff was thus superimposed as if it were itself
the very history on which the precepts of Freemasonry were based.

One of the great lost secrets of the Craft, therefore, is the secret of its very being – the reason for its existence based on the Art of Memory. Rituals, playlets and scripted recitals had been devised as ways of recalling the bigger pictures which they symbolized. But the symbols became the purpose in themselves, thereby denying Brethren the true reason for their membership. In this light, it is hardly surprising that the latter-day lodge workings of Freemasonry appear so naive and superficial, and that they leave so many in a state of puzzlement. The playlets do not exist for their own sake; they exist to be what Francis Bacon called the Idols of Theatre – representative, allegorical enactments – microcosms of those philosophies to which they allude.

William Shakespeare lived in London at a time when commerce, trade and crafts were divided among chartered City Corporations and Livery Companies which comprised the framework of London and contributed most of the Lord Mayors for about six centuries. In a Shakespearean manuscript for a play entitled *Sir Thomas More* there are three pages which have a peculiar interest for Freemasons.[37]

A particular rule of the Corporations gave qualified London workmen a monopoly over work in the City. Exceptions were rarely made in favour of outsiders or unskilled workmen (called 'cowans' in Freemasonry), but if an employer did make use of a cowan, the man was sworn to secrecy. If the members of a lodge then discovered such an employment, they would take steps to drive the man out by a process called 'mobbing'. This was not something known to people at large, and yet Shakespeare included just such an incident in the script for his *Thomas More* play. This has often been cited to 'prove' that Shakespeare was a Freemason, but it is not actually proof of this. What it proves is that, as a poet and playwright, Shakespeare was a good researcher. Notwithstanding this, his close link with Francis Bacon and the numerous insider references in his plays do indeed indicate his personal involvement with masonic aspects of the Rosicrucian movement. To what degree is uncertain, but clearly it was considered important enough for Grand Masters to officiate at the Shakespeare Memorial Theatre foundations in 1877 and 1929.

Guilds and Traditions

The Mysteries

The difficulty in identifying the birth of Freemasonry is that there was no specific moment of birth. There were dates on which certain aspects were ratified, but the institution (as it has existed for the past three centuries) evolved from different, but loosely related, movements. A consequence of this amalgam of concepts was that the individual ideals of each were diluted, if not bypassed altogether. For example, the two main routes to Freemasonry were through the trade and craft guilds on the one hand, and the scientific institutes on the other. But Freemasons do not have to be tradesmen, craftsmen or scientists. Each of these routes, whether artisan or academic, was in its own way philosophical. But Freemasons do not have to be philosophers either.

When an Entered Apprentice is initiated into Freemasonry, he is admitted to the 'mysteries and privileges' of the Craft. Privileges are easy to identify; they exist in every society, club, institute, association, corporation, company or whatever. They are simply those things which come with membership and employment – maybe access to a particular library or the use of specialist facilities. The term 'mysteries' is harder to define. It might be imagined that, in masonic terms, this refers to explanations of signs, symbols and allegories, and in some measure it does. But none of these would have been wondered about before joining a lodge because they are not a part of everyday life. Wanting these particular mysteries revealed is something that is unlikely to occur to a non-mason. They only become intriguing once the need to know about them has been established.

So, why is it so important to gain access to these mysteries? The short answer is that it is not. These things are not the mysteries, nor are the scientific or natural philosophical aspects that appear to sit within the masonic ideal. Such things might be mysterious, and they are indeed alluded to, but they are not taught. One can learn more about science and natural philosophy from reading a single issue of *New Scientist* than would be gleaned in a lifetime of lodge member-ship. The 'mysteries' are those aspects of Freemasonry that were embodied within its initial concept. The lodge itself constitutes the mystery by virtue of its own evolvement. Lodges were originally called Mysteries.

In the last chapter, William Shakespeare was discussed in connec-tion with the City Corporations and Livery Companies of London. These institutions were first established in the 1170s as craft and trade guilds. Just as in Scotland, they were initially designed as an early form of business directory. If one wanted builders, roofers or carpenters for a major project, the Guilds had members to recom-mend. They were also mutual protection societies and associations for the pursuit of common purpose, like early forms of trades unions. They had no mystery – at least not in the way that might be imagined.

The foremost of these Guilds as it exists today is the Drapers' Company. This was founded in 1180, chartered by royal decree of Edward III in 1364, and from whose membership came the first Lord Mayor of London, Henry fitz Alwyn, in 1209. The full title of the Company, which has a golden-fleeced ram at the crest of its arms is *The Master and Wardens and Brethren and Sisters of the Guild or Fraternity of the Blessed Virgin Mary of the Mystery of Drapers of the City of London.*[1]

To begin, it is pertinent to note the use of the terms Master and Wardens, precisely as they are used within Freemasonry, as are the terms Brethren and Fraternity. But here we have a mention of Sisters as well – a noticeable difference between the trade guilds and the emergent masonic lodges. Women were afforded membership as drapers, milliners, bookbinders and goldsmiths, but would not have been slaters, hammermen or masons. They were, nevertheless, obliged to give up their memberships if they married men who belonged to other guilds. However, it was not the outside members (men or women), but the senior officers of the Livery Companies who met after work at the *Apple Tree* or the *Goose and Gridiron*. They already knew who the Masters and Wardens were, for they were themselves the hierarchy of the City Guilds. The taverns were their mutual after-hours meeting places, just as the Lloyd's fraternity was associated with the coffee houses. After a while, the inter-guild meetings were organized on a more regular basis, and moved out of the bars into back rooms or upper rooms, where the players contrived a lodge format based on their formal Livery Company ceremonies. What we also see within the Drapers' title, however (as in that of other such Companies), is the word Mystery – the *Mystery of Drapers*.

Irrespective of the fact that England's kings from 1066 were Normans – culminating (via a marital link) with Stephen, Comte de Blois – a more decidedly French-influenced monarchy arose from Anjou with the House of Plantagenet from 1154. Along with this, a London headquarters for the Knights Templars was established in 1161 near Fleet Street (in the area still known as Temple), which greatly enhanced the French flavour of the City at that time.[2] French was widely used in the capital, and the English language changed considerably because of this, with a mixture of words being used as the French and English citizens developed their forms of communication.

The origin of the word 'mystery', in the way that we understand it, comes from ancient Greek references to private ceremonies.[3] But with regard to the Drapers, Mercers, Grocers, Vintners, Merchant Taylors and other Livery Companies, the word 'mystery' was a corruption of the Old French *mestier*, which referred to an 'occupational trade'.[4] *Mystery of Drapers* simply means 'Trade of Drapers'.

Masonic lodges are therefore 'mysteries' on two counts: 1) Lodge meetings are private ceremonies; 2) They are *mestiers* in that they follow the example of the London Livery Companies on which they were modelled, even to the extent of insignia, arms, badges, banners and regalia. These are the 'mysteries' to which a mason is admitted.

Along with Freemasonry, another offshoot of the London Mysteries is the City & Guilds Group. From 1858, the City & Guilds Institute has been Britain's leading provider of training and national vocational qualifications (NVQs) for the workplace. Granted a Royal Charter in 1900, City & Guilds International now has 8,500 centres worldwide, offering more than 500 qualifications.[5]

The Soul of the City

In London and Scotland, the Knights Templars were influential from the 12th century. They grew even more prominent in Scotland from the 14th century. From their experiences in the Middle East, they introduced new trade and banking systems into Britain, while funding and encouraging schools, hospitals, universities and a form of mutual contribution aid which eventually became the insurance industry. In Scotland, they were responsible for promoting the concept of medieval French craft guilds (such as the Children of Solomon), with lodge meetings organized on a model of chivalric Chapters. They had already established the same in London and, although these guilds did not become widespread in England, they grew to become the hub of the national economy with their centre of City Government at the Guildhall, which remains the headquarters of the Corporation of London today.

The philosophical implications of the Baconian era were powerful in the North and the South of Britain, as were the social effects of the Reformation, which transformed the united kingdoms into a nation of philosophers after 1603. Meanwhile, the Prague fraternity – and the 'bohemian' group in general – were forging ahead with natural philosophical research, which reached its zenith in 1662 with the foundation of the Royal Society under King Charles II. But just four years later came the Great Fire of London, and it took until 1708 to rebuild the City. In the course of this was the 1688 Whig Revolution, and the Stuarts were gone.

The City Guilds were fully occupied during the rebuilding programme. Many of them had lost their bases and, alongside Christopher Wren, they pulled together to repair and improve their environment. It was during this period that the Masters and Wardens began to meet in the mutual territory of the ale houses. First a major plague, then a catastrophic fire, followed by a Dutch invasion coupled with a royal deposition – all within 23 years. The City's streets might well have been intact again from 1708, but its soul had yet to be repaired.

Maybe Giordano Bruno and Francis Bacon had known the answer after all. Perhaps the Masters and Wardens *should* be looking back to Egypt, to King Solomon, and to the great wisdom cultures of the past. From 1703, Isaac Newton was President of the sorely shaken Royal Society, and that was precisely what he was doing. One thing was certain: the City community did not blame an accident in a Pudding Lane bakery for the London fire, as popular history has since suggested. Rightly or wrongly, they blamed the Catholics. Also (as later history fails to record), they were aware of the Vatican plot which, via William of Orange, had sent their dynasty into exile (*see* page 11). The inscription on the plaque added to the Hooke–Wren Monument in Fish Hill Street made the feelings of the London Aldermen quite clear. It reads:

> This Pillar was set up in Perpetual Remembrance of the dreadful Burning of this Ancient City, begun and carried on by Treachery and Malice of the Popish Faction in the beginning of September in the Year of our Lord 1666, in order to the carrying on of the horrid Plot for Extirpating the Protestant Religion, and the old English Liberty, and Introducing Popery and Slavery.

In April 1687, King James II (VII of Scots) wrote his thoughts concerning this in his *Declaration for Liberty of Conscience* – and its words rang in everyone's ears. Citing what he termed 'matters of mere religion', he wrote:

> It has ever been contrary to our inclination, as we think it is to the interests of governments, which it destroys by spoiling trade, depopulating countries and discouraging strangers. And finally, that it never obtained the end for which it was employed.[6]

The sentiment that religion had 'never obtained the end for which it was employed' applied not just to Catholic conspiracy against the Crown, but to the harsh Puritan movement of Oliver Cromwell which had executed James's father, King Charles I, and aided the Catholic Inquisition with its own witch-hunts and prosecution of so-called heretics. No group of people better understood James's sentiments than those who had felt the brunt of spoiled government and ruined commerce – the Masters and Wardens of the City Guilds. When their informal meetings became formalized by way of a Grand Lodge foundation in 1717, their lesson was put into practice: Freemasonry would not be a religious institution, nor would religious debate be permitted. It was to be a benevolent, socially-minded fraternity, and that was God enough. This is not to say that there were not aspects that could be deemed spiritual – many forms of ceremony and assembly contain a spiritual element – but that does not mean they are about religion.

Just as Lord Thomas Macaulay had endeavoured to ridicule Sir Francis Bacon from the mind-set of his Victorian era nearly 300 years later, it is easy now to scoff at Freemasonry nearly 300 years after its foundation from a modern perspective. Some of its traditions might appear quaint and naive; some actually are. Some of the pageantry might appear antiquated and bizarre, but all traditional pageantry is like that – from the wigs of Britain's judiciary to the coronation ceremonies of her monarchs. Without it, legacies would be lost and forgotten, to disappear like the Baconian wisdom philosophy, and only possible to retrieve by the Hiramic impossibility of resurrecting the dead.

A Parcel of Rogues

Following the Orange regime of William and Mary from 1689, Queen Anne (Mary's sister) reigned 1702–14. For want of knowing how else to classify her, history records hers as a Stuart monarchy. But Anne's politics bore no similarity to those of her family tradition, and the Scots refused to acknowledge her. Mary and Anne were the daughters of King James and his first wife, Anne Hyde of Clarendon, but following Anne Hyde's early death, James had married Mary Beatrix d'Este de Modena in 1673. She gave birth to the new royal heir, James Francis Edward Stuart, shortly before her husband's deposition, and it was he that the Scots claimed should be their rightful monarch, not Anne.

Initially, the Protestants of the Church of Ireland thought they would fare well enough under Queen Anne, but she made life very difficult for them by pursuing a course of antagonism against the Irish Catholics. In direct contradiction of her father and uncle's tolerant attitudes, Anne excluded Catholics from the electorate, and from every corporate or public office; they were debarred from universities and higher education; they were not allowed to be school teachers, and their terms of employment were generally constrained. Not surprisingly, these impositions affected everyone, Catholics and Protestants alike, especially since the Catholics of Ireland were in the majority as employers. Consequently, the unfortunate Protestants of the Irish Church laity found themselves denied jobs, services and provisions.

Having introduced her *Penal Laws* against the Catholics of Ireland, Anne then set her sights against the Protestants with her 1704 *Irish Test Act* against the Ulster dissenters. These Presbyterians and Reformists – the very same who oppose the Catholics in Ireland today – were ostracized from all forms of civil and military employment under the Crown. The only sacrament tolerated by Anne was that of the Anglican Communion, and next on her agenda of control was Scotland. She wrote to the Scottish Parliament declaring her intention to dissolve the ancient institution, whereupon the ministers cited a precedent to invalidate the Queen's intention (*see* page 27). It came from the 1320 *Declaration of Arbroath* – Scotland's Written Constitution as enacted by Robert the Bruce, which stated that if a monarch should:

> ... make us or our kingdom subject to the King of England
> or the English, we should exert ourselves at once to drive him
> out as our enemy and a subverter of his own rights and ours,
> and make some other man, who was well able to defend us,
> our king.

Since Anne's plan was to subject the kingdom to domination from Westminster, this meant that the Scots would have a legal right to elect a sovereign of their own choosing. Anne duly retaliated by making use of the large number of English nobles who had, by virtue of the 1603 Union of Crowns, been granted vast estates in Scotland, and who sat in the Scottish Parliament. Further estates were transferred, and many large bribes and land grants were dispensed to those who previously had lands and titles removed from them. This swayed things in Anne's favour and, by 1707, the scene was set. It was time for a new vote in Scotland and, to ensure the desired result, Edinburgh's Parliament House was placed under the armed guard of soldiers of the Queen's regiments. The outcome was a marginal victory for Anne and the implementation of the *Act of Union*. From 1 May 1707, the Scottish Parliament was active no longer.[7] The Crowns of Scotland and England were no longer merely conjoined, they became one as Westminster took control of the newly united kingdoms, henceforth known as Great Britain.[8] The greatest affront to the Scottish nation emerged in the dismissal of their individual status by virtue of the national term United Kingdom – thereby defining a singular impossibility. It is like calling America the United State!

The story of this unprecedented conspiracy was subsequently lamented by Scotland's Bard, Robert Burns – the most illustrious and revered of all Scottish Freemasons, initiated at St David's Lodge, Tarbolton, on 4 July 1781, and later Deputy Master of the St James's Lodge.[9] He wrote:

> Farewell to all our Scottish fame;
> Farewell our ancient glory.
> Farewell even to the Scottish name,
> So famed in martial story.
> But faith and power! To my last hour,
> I make this declaration:
> We're bought and sold for English gold.
> Such a parcel of rogues in a nation!

The Jacobite Scene

At that stage, neither the Grand Lodge of England, nor those of Scotland and Ireland, had been formed, but the first was not long in coming, soon to be followed by the introduction of Freemasonry into America. Opposing factions were already arising outside the masonic structure in terms of who supported whom in monarchical terms, and the rival figureheads in this contest were Queen Anne and her half-brother James Francis Edward Stuart. But, following the *Act of Union*, there was another aspect of the game yet to be played out, and this concerned the matter of who was to succeed Queen Anne. She actually conceived eighteen times, but only five children were born alive, of whom only one lived beyond infancy, eventually dying at the age of eleven. Thus, Anne had no surviving children by her husband Prince George of Denmark.

Although the Scots could not drive out the English Queen, by 1706 it had become likely that she would not have an heir, and would therefore have to choose a successor. In preparation for this, the Scots introduced a *Bill of Security*, which determined that they did not have to conform with Anne's nomination. In the event, the *Act of Union* put an end to that notion, but the future looked reasonably bright in that Anne elected Sophia, the daughter of Frederick V, Elector Palatine, and Elizabeth Stuart, to become the next Queen of Britain. Sophia was the sister of Charles Louis, Prince Palatine, and of Prince Rupert of the Rhine. The Rosicrucian community also was content enough with this, but a further problem arose because, by the time of Queen Anne's death in 1714, Sophia had also died. She had been married to Ernest Augustus, Elector of Hanover, who was also deceased, but they did have a son. He was Georg von Brunswick, the new Elector of Hanover. The Whig ministers at Westminster therefore installed Georg (first of the House of Hanover) as King George I of Great Britain in spite of loud protests from the Tory benches.

While Sophia was a granddaughter of King James I (VI) and a niece of Charles I, in direct male-line descent from Charles, the true successor was still James Francis Edward Stuart. The Scots and the English Tories knew that for a change of dynasty to prevail there had to be either an extinction of the previous dynasty or a formal abdication by that dynasty. But James II (VII) had not abdicated – he had been deposed and exiled by a foreign invader. His son, James Francis, was still the legal heir to the throne, and the Scots had proclaimed him as titular King James VIII in 1707.

The reason why the Whigs refused to acknowledge James Francis was that he declined to be tied to the Anglican Church as Westminster demanded. There was also the Scottish Kirk to consider, along with the Catholics and those of other denominations. But George of Hanover was totally compliant and much to the convenience of the Whig aristocracy, he spoke only German, and spent most of his time abroad. The reins of national administration were held by his Lord of the Treasury, Robert Walpole, who became the first effective Prime Minister and developed the undemocratic concept of the

Cabinet – an inner circle of ministers who meet privately outside the House of Commons to formulate and control Government policy. From that time, not only did the people have no say in matters of their own government, neither did the majority of MPs who were subsequently regulated by the Whips (so named after the deputies of Hunt Masters) in accordance with Cabinet requirements.

Scottish and English royalists made an attempt to gain the Crown for James Francis, but the 1715 Rising was unsuccessful and so James returned across the water to continue his French exile at St Germain-en-Laye, Paris. It was, however, only three years after George's coronation that the Masters and Wardens of the City Corporations and Livery Companies founded the Grand Lodge of England, and modern Freemasonry was officially defined. This foundation has been referred to as a Hanoverian establishment (*see* page 27) – and indeed it was by virtue of its time frame – but whether it was in terms of allegiance is another matter. It certainly seems to have become so from the time the Georgian Royal Family became involved in the 1760s, but a quick glance at *Burke's Peerage* reveals a different situation in the early days.

When James Anderson produced his *Constitutions* in 1723, the London Grand Master was Philip, 6th Baron and 1st Duke of Wharton (*see* plate 5, which depicts Philip receiving the Constitutional Roll and compasses from his predecessor John, Lord Montagu). But Philip was charged with high treason, and outlawed on 3 April 1729 after fighting for James Francis Edward Stuart.[10] Philip even established a distinctly Jacobite lodge in Spain.[11] Plainly, the Jacobite influence was strong among Freemasons of the era – not surprisingly so because of its connection with the London Guilds and the Royal Society.

Among the leading Jacobite protagonists of the mid-1700s in London were Henry Marshal, Master of the Drapers' Company, and William Benn, Master of the Fletchers' and Lord Mayor of London. They, along with fellow Aldermen of the City: Thomas Rawlinson of the Grocers', Robert Alsop of the Ironmongers' and Edward Ironside and John Blachford, both of the Goldsmiths', accompanied by Blachford's brother, were the seven officers of a lodge (with William

Benn as the Worshipful Master) that became known as *Benn's Club* (plate 33).

Stuart Masonry

Although George II's son Prince Frederick was a Freemason in the 1730s, it was not until 1766, when three of his sons were initiated, that there was any significant connection between Hanoverian royalty and Freemasonry. Not only were they admitted to the Craft, but the records were adjusted to give them each a spurious Past Master status, as if they had risen through the ranks. Brothers of King George III, they were the Princes Edward, William and Henry – respectively the Dukes of York, Gloucester and Cumberland.[12] The timing of this was such that it followed the death of King George II, and was after the lodge conflict between the Whigs and Tories that prevailed through the 1750s after the Battle of Culloden (*see* chapter 5).

Frederick's part in the masonic story is particularly interesting since he is generally held as having been inactive,[13] but this was not the case; he was simply inactive as far as Hanoverian records determine. Despite being Prince of Wales and heir to the throne, Frederick belonged to a secret Jacobite lodge at the *Cocoa Tree* coffee house in St James's, which was affiliated to the most influential of all Stuart undercover operations, the Hell Fire Club. As things transpired, Frederick predeceased his father in 1751, leaving his own eldest son to succeed as King George III in 1760. Had this not happened, there is reason to suspect that Frederick's Jacobite intrigue and intense hatred of his father might have led him to allow Charles Edward Stuart into Britain with a plan to share the kingdoms and the growing Empire.[14]

Not only did the English Grand Master, Philip, Duke of Wharton, set up a Jacobite lodge in Spain, but Patrick Gordon and James Keith (the Earl Marischal) established lodges in Russia. George Hamilton did likewise in Switzerland, and Lord Winton in Rome. Many of

James Stuart's closest advisers were masons, including the Duke of Ormonde and Ezekiel Hamilton (an Anglican clergyman at the Stuarts' Palazzo Muti in Rome).[15] Also prominent in the ranks of Jacobite Freemasonry were Pierre André O'Heguerty of the Franco-Irish shipowning fraternity, and Charles Radcliffe, Earl of Derwentwater.[16]

The main difficulty encountered by the 18th-century Jacobite Freemasons was that much of Europe was Catholic, and Pope Clement XII had condemned Freemasonry in 1738. European litera-ture explains that this was as a result of English lodges being brought under Hanoverian control but, whatever the reasons, Freemasons were excommunicated, although this had little or no effect outside the Papal States.[17] Around 30,000 masons were driven underground in Florence but, in France, King Louis XIV did not bother to publish the ordinance, stating that 'a law not promulgated has no force'.[18]

By the time that James's son, Charles Edward Stuart, took the family reins, most of the great names in France were members of affiliated lodges. Whether the 'Bonnie Prince' wanted the role or not, he was regarded as the hereditary sovereign head of Stuart Freemasonry in descent from King Charles II.[19] What he could not do, however, with the papal eye on him at all times, was to admit openly to his position. On 21 September 1777, Baron Watcher, an envoy of Karl Ferdinand, Duke of Brunswick (husband of King George III's sister, Augusta), specifically asked Charles Edward in Florence if he was the secret Grand Master. Quite truthfully, Charles denied that he was, since there were branches of Freemasonry that were not his prerogative, including a newly developed *Scottish Rite* in France. Charles Edward was the Grand Master of *Jacobite* lodges, which were quite distinct and separate. It was learned soon after, however, that the German objective was to gain the Prince's admit-tance so as to report him to the Vatican authorities.

Watcher pursued the matter for three years, claiming that he could secure Charles great acclaim from the German masonic com-munity, but King Gustav III of Sweden finally stepped in. Gustav was himself Grand Master of the Swedish Freemasons, and knew that Charles Edward's superiority was acknowledged in Stockholm. The King pronounced that the German endeavour was deviously motivated, thereby relieving the Prince's predicament, but in return he asked Charles for the sovereign Grand Mastership of the Order of the Knights Templars of Jerusalem if he were to pay an agreed sum for the privilege. Charles conceded to the request, but not immediately. The title, it was agreed, would pass to Gustav when the Stuart Prince died. Irrespective of the arrangement, however, the money was never paid, and there was no transference of the title.[20]

Charles Edward had been formally invested as Grand Master of the Order of the Temple of Jerusalem in the Audience Room of Holyrood Palace, Edinburgh, on Tuesday 24 September 1745. This was in the early stage of his Jacobite Rising against King George II, which ended in a Scots defeat on 16 April in the following year at Drummossie Moor, Culloden. During the Stuart absence from Britain, the Templar Grand Mastership had been held in trust for the exiled Kings of Scots by appointed Regents. The Regent in September 1745 was James Murray, Duke of Atholl, who had succeeded John Erskine, Earl of Mar. The Prince's father, James Francis Edward Stuart, had hitherto issued a *Royal Declaration and Regency Commission* passing his hereditary entitlements and regencies to Charles Edward on 23 December 1743. It is recorded in the *Statutes of the Order of the Temple* that, on taking his vow in the presence of ten Knights, Charles declared, 'You may be sure that, when I truly come into my own, I will raise the Order to what it was in the days of William the Lion' (King of Scots 1165–1214).[21]

One of the most debated issues in terms of Jacobite Freemasonry is that of the *Chapitre Primordian de Rose Croix*. This Chapter was founded in 1745, and formally constituted by the Charter of Arras in 1747 by Charles Edward Stuart and his cousin, the Marquis de Montferrat. Better known as the Comte de St Germain,[22] the Marquis was a confidant of Mme de Pompadour, a later ministerial adviser to the French Court,[23] and author of the alchemical treatise entitled *Holy Trinosophia*. The St Germain title (*see* chapter 3) comes by way of Chancellorship of the Elder Brethren of the Rosy Cross, as created by Robert the Bruce in 1317. The 18th-century engraving in plate 31 shows Prince Charlie and Count St Germain presenting the Charter of Arras to the Companions of the Order.

Seal of the *Chapitre Primordian de Rose Croix*

Despite the fact that the Chapter of Arras is detailed in Albert Mackey's *Encyclopedia of Freemasonry*, 1908, other writers (beginning with George Speth, a founder and Secretary of Quatuar Coronati Lodge, London, in 1886)[24] often decline to acknowledge the Charter of 15 April 1747 because it cites Charles Edward as 'King of England, France, Scotland and Ireland'. They ask, 'How can that be? His father was still alive in 1747. The document must be a hoax.' The answer to this is straightforward. James Francis formally transferred his royal prerogatives to Charles Edward in December 1743. In addition, two days before the Grand Mastership of the Templars was bestowed, Charles was figuratively granted the royal honours in Scotland.

On Sunday 22 September 1745, following Prince Charlie's victory at the Battle of Prestonpans, the clergy were wholly supportive when representatives of the Presbyterian, Catholic and Episcopal Churches were united to witness and approve his figurative crowning as King Charles III. The proceedings were conducted within the precincts of the Abbey of Holyrood House by the Episcopalian Rev William Harper of Old Saint Paul's, Edinburgh.[25] Since the Crown and Honours of Scotland were held by the Hanoverian Court, a substitute laurel wreath was placed on Charles's head by Laurence Oliphant of Gask. Oliphant's *Memoir* confirms that, earlier that day, a preparation for this event had been made at Charles Edward's State apartment, where the laurel crown lay in readiness.[26] As for the item in the Charter which relates to Charles also being King of France, the Stuarts were always regarded as titular monarchs of France, and Mary, Queen of Scots, had reigned as Queen of France in any event.

France and the Feminine

It is a common misconception that it was some form of masonic plot which led to the French Revolution (1789–99) but, in practice, quite the reverse was the case. French Freemasons, being generally of the middle and upper classes, including many of the aristocracy, were often at the receiving end of the terror. The mistake arises because the revolutionary citizens made use of a primary sentiment of masonic ritual: *Liberté, Egalité, Fraternité*. Also relevant is that Louis Philippe, Duc d'Orleans, Grand Master of the French Masons, was himself an opponent of King Louis XVI. He actually voted in favour of the King's execution, but only because he sought the crown for himself and, for his pains, soon became another victim of the guillotine.

Freemasons were torn both ways in the French Revolution, but their general mood was exemplified by the Marquis de Lafayette. A recent hero of the American Revolution, he rejected any part in the outrageous violence.[27] Being an internal civil struggle, he saw it as being quite different to the American effort against a foreign power. Later, however, he claimed that 'The Revolution' was not simply an event with a beginning and an end. It was a continual effort for 'the victory of right over privilege'.[28]

An attempt was made to set up a unified French Grand Lodge from 1733, but it was not until 1773 that the Grand Orient de France was formally established. Then in 1801 the regulatory codes, *Régulateur du maçon*, were issued to establish the *French Rite* of Freemasonry.[29] Since there were mixed feelings about the Revolution within masonic circles, it was generally the case that afterwards the movement supported Emperor Napoleon Bonaparte in his effort to stabilize the otherwise disunited nation.

An interesting aspect of the French masonic system was that, from 1750, women were also afforded the opportunity to participate in mixed lodges designed for the purpose. It was called Adoptive Masonry. The practice declined in 1860, but interest was renewed in the 20th century, and in 1952 the Grand Female Lodge of France was established.

The image of *Freemasonry*, like *Liberty* (Marianne), has long been characterized as a personality in France. But unlike the flag-bearing, warrior image of *Liberty* who personifies the Republic, the Masonic Marianne is a much softer figure of charity and benevolence (*see* plate 13). According to the Grand Orient, the name Marianne originated from the Marian culture of Languedoc in Southern France, and became popular in the late 1700s.[30] This is the Provençal region where the tradition of Mary Magdalene had long prevailed as a libertarian concept, and where the Cassianite monks of La Sainte-Baume had guarded her sepulchre from the 4th century.[31] As discussed in *The Magdalene Legacy*, the medieval records of Southern France cite Mary Magdalene as having been the wife of Jesus, and she was greatly venerated as such. She sailed to the region in AD 44, and died at Aix-en-Provence in AD 63. For the same reason, it was also to Mary Magdalene that the Knights Templars had originally consecrated the *Notre Dame de Lumière* (Our Lady of Light) cathedrals in France, and to whom St Bernard de Clairvaux required the Order's obedience.[32]

Outside France, there is the Feminine Grand Lodge of Belgium, and there are a few other women's masonic institutions, including the London based Honourable Fraternity of Ancient Freemasons, whose charitable activities focus on cancer care. In the United States there is Le Droit Humain, along with American Co-Masonry (under the auspices of the American Federation of Human Rights), and the Eastern Order of International Co-Freemasonry, each of which grant equal access to women. Headquartered in Washington DC, is the *Adoptive Rite* of the International Order of the Eastern Star for female relatives of Master Masons, while the Ladies Oriental Shrine of North America lends necessary help to the Shriners Hospitals for Children, and the International Order of Job's Daughters caters for girls and young women relatives. In general terms, however, Freemasonry remains a male prerogative, and many Grand Lodges do not recognize the female institutions.

Into America

Scottish Rite

Among the masonic associates of James Francis Edward Stuart in France was Chevalier Andrew Michael Ramsay (1686–1743), a political theorist and short-term tutor of the four-year-old Prince Charles Edward in 1724.[1] He was an eccentric character and, although ostensibly a Jacobite, was not much liked by James who found him irritating. Consequently, Ramsay's employment as tutor only lasted a year. A Scot by birth, he spent most of his life in France where, in 1737, he became Orator of the Grand Lodge of France and then Chancellor of the Paris Grand Lodge. He is especially remembered in Freemasonry because of an oration he wrote for a Grand Lodge presentation on 21 March 1737. There is no record that he ever delivered the address, but the document was circulated, and it was this which gave rise to what subsequently became known as the Ancient and Accepted Rite. It is perhaps better known (with its familiar 33-degree structure) as the *Scottish Rite*.

It must be emphasized that there was a distinct difference between the old-style Rosicrucian system of the Stuarts in France and this newly devised form of Scottish-tagged Freemasonry. The latter emanated directly from Chevalier Ramsay's oration and, although styled 'Ancient', there is no record of its inherent degrees in ceremonial use before 1760.[2] The definition Scottish (*Ecossais*) was simply to distinguish this Rite from English (*Anglais*) Freemasonry, which had been apparent in France from about 1725,[3] and the designation was made possible because Ramsay was himself Scottish.

An important aspect of the *Scottish Rite* is that the designated 33-degree structure is not actually comprised of degrees, but of individually constructed add-ons that give the impression of high-ranking status to outsiders. In practice, the highest authentic degree in Freemasonry remains the 3rd degree of the Master Mason, along with its Royal Arch Chapter. It is also important not to confuse the Ancient and Accepted Rite with those who were styled the 'Antients' in Britain and Ireland – ie, The Most Antient and Honourable Fraternity of Free and Accepted Masons. This was a quite distinct institution, as is that of the Ancient Free and Accepted Masons of Scotland. The *Scottish Rite* is also distinct from the Royal Order of Scotland (*see* chapter 7).

Ramsay created a myth that linked Freemasonry to the Crusades, in which era, he said, there were many lodges in Germany, Italy, Spain and France, from where the concept moved to Scotland in 1286.[4] This appealed greatly to the French because, apart from the Christian connotations, it gave Freemasonry a pseudo-knightly gloss that remains in the *Scottish Rite* workings today. Ramsay did not devise these degrees, but his oration inspired and encouraged their subsequent invention to suit the chivalric model that he put forward.

For all his masonic interest, Ramsay was a committed Catholic, although he came from a Presbyterian background. His views concerning women were to some extent coloured by this, and he claimed that women were excluded from Freemasonry because 'their presence might insensibly corrupt the purity of our maxims and manners'. In contrast to Ramsay, Charles Edward Stuart had been raised in Rome in a Catholic environment, but a letter written by him (held within the Stuart Papers at Windsor) records that, at the age of 30, he formally renounced any Catholic affiliation in 1750 at London's New Church in the Strand (later called St Mary-le-Strand). It reads:

> In order to make my renunciation of the errors of the Church of
> Rome the most authentic and the less liable afterwards to mali-
> cious interpretations, I went to London in the year 1750, and in
> that capital did then make a solemn abjuration of the Romish
> religion, and did embrace that of the Church of England, as by
> law established in the thirty-nine articles, in which I hope to
> live and die.[5]

Apart from flying in the face of his own Church by linking
Freemasonry with the Catholic Crusades, Ramsay's oration sought
to remove it from the Templar and predominantly Scottish-
based history of the trade guilds, and from the London Livery
Companies. He claimed that Freemasonry was the realm of 'religious and warrior princes who designed to enlighten, edify and
protect the living temples of the Most High'. It is not correct to give
Chevalier Ramsay credit or blame (depending on how one views
the matter) for the manufacture of the so-called *Scottish Rite* degrees
that ensued, but he certainly provided the arena for their largely
fictional content, and for their designation of being both Ancient
and Scottish, which they are not.

Although Freemasonry is not a religious institution, the associated *Scottish Rite* does have distinctly religious overtones, with an
emphasis on God throughout. Following the Master Mason's 3rd
degree, the 4th to 14th degrees of *Scottish Rite* and its Lodge of
Perfection are known as the Ineffable Degrees. In a quasi-kabbalistic
manner, their principal purpose is to contemplate the ineffable name
of God, with a primary focus on moral virtues. The 15th to 18th
degrees constitute the Chapter of the Rose Croix, which are mainly
concerned with matters of religion, philosophy and ethics. The 19th
to 30th degrees of the Council of Kadosh (relating to Holy) are of a
chivalric nature, and are again philosophical, dealing with such matters as justice and responsibility. The Consistory Degrees are the 31st
and 32nd, which are idealistic contemplations of self-examination
relating to spiritual and temporal harmony. (As with all forms of
Freemasonry, workings vary between Grand Lodges. The foregoing

descriptions are therefore general, rather than rigid explanations of the *Scottish Rite* structure.)

Organized throughout in a sequence of entertaining and colourful playlets, *Scottish Rite* ceremonies are much briefer than those of the Craft degrees (or Blue Lodge degrees as they are called in North America), and they do not require the memorizing of lengthy passages in the same way. The 33rd degree is different to the rest in that it is more in the nature of an award of merit for completing the others, or for having subsequently attained an officer status. It falls within the Court of Honour as a conferral by the Supreme Council, and it cannot be requested.

Some of the *Scottish Rite* degrees have interesting content, although many are brief and superficial. An uncomfortable element also exists in that, by virtue of the Ramsay ideal, some of them are presented as if they are chivalric Orders in their own right. The most unfortunate problem is that while a majority of the degrees are fairly universal in approach, it is impossible to progress through all the grades in an honest manner without a Christian affiliation. This is contrary to the basic liberal precepts of Craft Freemasonry, and therefore makes the 33-degree structure something else entirely. This is not stated as being in any way a criticism of *Scottish Rite* Freemasonry, but simply to distinguish it from the Craft, and to define why it is that many Craft Master Masons perceive the *Scottish Rite* as a separate entity.

This said, the true value of the Rite lies not within its badges and degrees, nor with its internal configuration, but with its objectives in the community. The USA Southern Jurisdiction, for example, centres its philanthropic endeavours on the plight of children with learning difficulties. It has 162 childhood language centres, with analytical and remedial programmes that are charitably available. Hence, although it can be said that the markedly Christian aspects of the *Scottish Rite* are in contrast to the masonic norm, it must also be acknowledged that such benevolent enterprises constitute the best of the Christian welfare ethic.

The Northern Jurisdiction was formed in 1867 and its headquarters are in Lexington, Massachusetts. It includes the 15 States east of the Mississippi River and north of the Mason–Dixon Line and the Ohio River, including Delaware. Also largely concerned with children's learning difficulties, the Northern Jurisdiction has 47 centres providing free, multi-sensory reading and written language tutorial services. The Southern Jurisdiction encompasses the 35 remaining states, the District of Columbia and the United States territories and possessions. The first *Scottish Rite* Supreme Council (Southern) was founded in Charleston, South Carolina, in 1801.

Outside the United States and its provinces, Ancient and Accepted *Scottish Rite* Freemasonry is also popular in Canada. Additionally, it is operative in Australia and New Zealand. In terms of its relationship with Craft Freemasonry, one cannot do better than to summarize in the words of the Southern Jurisdiction USA Orient (State) of California, whose informative website has many useful links:

> The *Scottish Rite* shares the belief of all masonic organizations that there is no higher degree than that of Master Mason. The degrees are in addition to, and in no way 'higher' than those of Blue Lodge or Craft Lodge Masonry. *Scottish Rite* degrees simply amplify and elaborate on the lessons of the Craft.[6]

The Franklin Foundation

The precise date and place for the formal introduction of any Rite of Freemasonry into America have long been matters of debate. Opinions are split as to whether it was Philadelphia in 1730 or Boston in 1733. Either way, the grants of purpose are each generally understood to have come from the Grand Lodge of England.

The positions seems to be that on 5 June 1730, one Daniel Coxe received a grant as Grand Master of the Provinces of New York, New Jersey and Pennsylvania. Then, on 13 April 1733, a certain Henry Price received a grant as Provincial Grand Master of New England and its territories. The accounts of what happened next in each case were debated throughout the 1923 issues of the masonic journal *The Builder*.[7]

It was initially stated that, although Coxe was the first to receive his warrant, he was not the first to exercise it because he spent the period between 1730 and 1733 in England. New Jersey Supreme Court records then revealed that he was actually back in America for some of the intervening period, but there was still no evidence that he exercised his masonic right before returning again to England. On 30 July 1733, Henry Price organized the Provincial Grand Lodge of Massachusetts, and duly constituted The First Lodge of Boston, which subsequently became St John's Lodge.

Since Daniel Coxe had apparently made no use of his warrant, the Grand Lodge of England cancelled his privilege, and extended Henry Price's authority to cover all of North America in August 1734.[8] Then, on 28 November that year, Benjamin Franklin applied to Price for recognition of the Lodge of St John in Philadelphia, which had been operating independently from 1730.[9] It would seem, therefore, that formalized American Freemasonry was commenced in Boston in June 1733, followed by Philadelphia at the end of 1734. On Friday 24 February 1735, the *Boston Gazette* reported:

> On Friday last was held a Grand Lodge of that Antient and Honorable Society of Free and Accepted Masons at the *Bunch of Grapes* tavern in King Street, where Mr Henry Price, Grand Master of His Majesty's dominions in North America, nominated and appointed his Grand Officers for the ensuing year, viz. Andrew Belcher Esq., Deputy Grand Master; Mr James Gordon and Mr Frederick Hamilton, Grand Wardens for this Province [Massachusetts]; and Mr Benjamin Franklin, Provincial Grand Master for the Province of Pennsylvania.

The most important feature of this notice lies in the description of the Antient and Honorable Society of Free and Accepted Masons – the 'Antients'. It does not in any way identify the then quite separate establishment of the Grand Lodge of England – the 'Moderns' – and

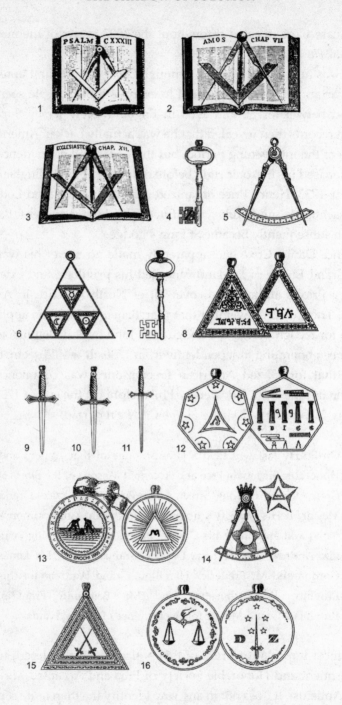

Thirty-three degrees of the Scottish Rite

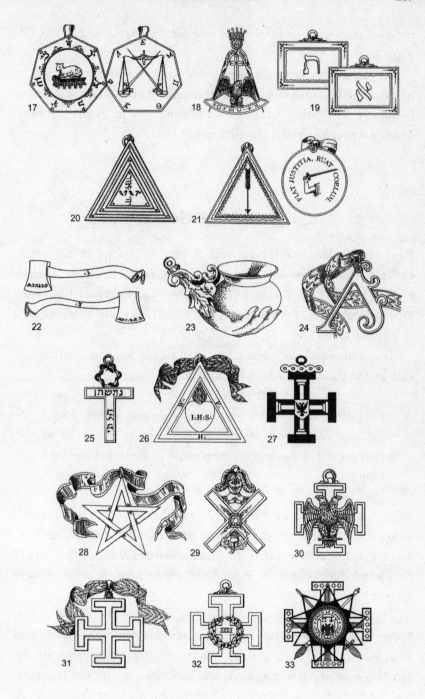

the two opposing factions were not amalgamated until 1813 (*see* page 30).

An intriguing, although most likely coincidental, masonic aspect of the name Philadelphia is that it was named after an ancient city of Lydia (*see* Revelation 1:11) in Asia Minor, now in modern Turkey, and the term *philadelphia* meant 'brother love'.[10]

Oglethorpe's Georgia

Next on the list of creations was Solomon's Lodge of Savannah, Georgia. This was established by Britain's General James Oglethorpe on 21 February 1734. It was not in the *Boston Gazette* report, but a warrant was subsequently granted by the Grand Lodge of England on 2 December 1735.[11]

The confusion over these dates led to a further round of discussion in *The Builder*, which stated in 1926:

> For many years, masonic historians have vainly tried to obtain definite information concerning the birth of the Craft in Georgia and of the date of organization of the Grand Lodge of Georgia.'[12]

What became clear in the debate was that Oglethorpe's original lodge had been formed under what were called the 'Old Customs', and this leads us to an interesting scenario that could apply to any of the early lodges of that era in America where there are apparent conflicts of dating.

Eleanor Oglethorpe (*see* chapter 5), sister of the Crown agent James Oglethorpe, who founded Georgia, built Savannah and established Solomon's Lodge, was an enthusiastic leader of the Jacobite movement in England, and described as a 'keen conspirator'.[13] Married to a French nobleman, she was the Marquise de Mézières, but spent much time in England living at General James's

Westbrook House in Godalming, Surrey. Eleanor had been raised at the Stuart court of St Germain-en-Laye,[14] and both she and James were connected with Stuart intrigue on both sides of the English Channel. Although James was a general in King George II's army, his military record was not good, and he was court-martialled after the 1745 Jacobite Rising for failing (purposely, it was suspected) to defeat a weak Scots force at Clifton on their northwards retreat from Derby.[15]

The fact is that James Oglethorpe never was a Grand Lodge of England Freemason. His family had long been associated with the exiled Stuart Court at its highest level, and with the national financial management of France. Any lodge that Oglethorpe founded in Savannah would have been based on the Rosicrucian model or, as is perhaps more likely, the masonic structure of the Antients – ie, the Old Custom, as stated in the Georgia records – hence the strategic December 1735 takeover by the London Grand Lodge. There was no reference to Henry Price in this warrant, and it occurred while James Oglethorpe was back in England temporarily before returning to Georgia with the Methodist missionary, John Wesley, in February 1736.

Washington and Revere

Further evidence concerning the initial use of the Antients' structure of Freemasonry in America, as against that of the Moderns of the Grand Lodge of England, comes from London's Quatuor Coronati Lodge of Research in 1994.[16]

Until the 1813 amalgamation of the Antients and Moderns, the Grand Lodge of England did not recognize the Royal Arch Chapter. And yet, on 22 December 1757, three brethren were raised to the degree of the Holy Royal Arch in Fredericksburg, Virginia. (This was the lodge where George Washington had been initiated on 4 November 1752, and raised to Master Mason on 4 August 1754.) Then, on 28 August 1769, the St Andrew's Royal Arch Chapter of Boston made America's first conferral of a Knight Templar degree.

Apparently, the lodge of St Andrew had obtained its Royal Arch charter from the Grand Lodge of Scotland in November 1762. (It should be emphasized here that a masonic Templar degree is quite distinct from the chivalric Order of the Knights of the Temple of Jerusalem.)

It is the Royal Arch which holds the ultimate key to Freemasonry. It is the rod that lay on the ground in the *The Mirrour of Policie* image (*see* page 249); it is the true 3rd degree, which is why it is regarded as an extension of that degree today, rather than being an extra degree in its own right. It is within the Holy Royal Arch that the bread, the gold, the point within a circle, the Philosophers' Stone and the Ark of the Covenant come together in a way that finally makes sense of the Golden Calf story and its alchemical connection with the Mosaic temple of the Great Ones in Sinai.

Records of the 1767 Templar conferral of William Davis in Boston show that the officers present included those of the British Army's *Glittering Star* lodge established by the Grand Lodge of Ireland. It has now been established by Quatuor Coronati that early American Freemasonry was not as reliant on the Grand Lodge of England as is often imagined. Its roots were more firmly planted in the Scots and Irish traditions of the Antients. There has been some speculation that maybe the British regimental members came across the Templar and Royal Arch degrees while stationed in Halifax, Nova Scotia, but this may simply be an effort to draw attention away from the fact that the Royal Arch tradition was then more prevalent across the Atlantic than the masonic establishment in England might wish to acknowledge. The fact is that, prior to being stationed in North America, the *Glittering Star* regiment was in Ireland from 1759 to 1765. The oldest minuted reference to the Royal Arch Chapter comes from Ireland in 1752,[17] and America adopted the degree long before it was recognized in England.

The second Royal Arch and masonic Templar in America was the silversmith Paul Revere, created at St Andrew's Chapter, Boston, on 11 December 1769. Eventually, along with his part in the Boston Tea Party and subsequent military duties in the War of Independence,

Revere also became Grand Master of the Grand Lodge of the Antients in Massachusetts.

The third to gain the Royal Arch and Templar ranks was Joseph Warren on 14 May 1770. He was the Presiding Grand Master of the Lodge of St Andrew, and the first hero of the Revolution, losing his life on the battlefield of Bunker Hill. It was said that fellow masons of the British Army marked with a sprig the place where he fell (representing the acacia sprig of Hiram Abiff). It is on this note – whether the legend is true or false – that we encounter one of the great anomalies of the War. In his capacity as Grand Master, Warren had on his staff and in his membership a good many soldiers of the British regiments stationed in and around Boston, and in this respect the St Andrew lodge was in no way unique. By the time of the War (1775–83) there were numerous American masonic lodges, all founded on the Antient tradition in liaison with the British troops. Quite suddenly, however, they found themselves in opposite camps, brother against brother, in a conflict that most of the stationed British regiments had not the heart to pursue.

Other notable members of the St Andrew Lodge were Samuel Adams, John Adams, William Dawes and Thomas Hutchinson. Nearly half of the 56 signers of the *Declaration of Independence* were Freemasons. Of the 55 Delegates to the Constitutional Convention, 31 were Freemasons, as were 33 of George Washington's 74 generals.

Scots and the New World

In the lead-up to the War of Independence, the Scottish influence in America had been enhanced significantly by virtue of a common enemy – the Georgian House of Hanover. The Jacobite Rising of 1745–6 had not ended with the Battle of Culloden. On 15 May 1746, it was decreed by Westminster that all prisoners should be taken to England for trial – specifically to London, York and Carlisle. In these places, away from the jurisdiction of the Scottish courts, the trials were superficial and the sentences brutal. In London, the prisoners were hanged and publicly disembowelled, after which their severed heads were placed on the railings at Temple Bar.

King George II's son William, Duke of Cumberland, had continued his hostility far beyond the battlefield of Drumossie Moor. In the first instance, a *Disarming Act* was passed, along with other statutes which banned the wearing of Highland dress, the playing of pipes and the use of the Scots Gaelic language. Even the traditional Clan System was overturned by the abolition of heritable jurisdictions. For 46 years after Culloden, anyone found breaking the *Acts of Abolition and Proscription* was liable to imprisonment or transportation to the colonies, if indeed he avoided being shot on sight. Any Scot deemed likely to attempt an evasion of the laws was hauled before the authorities and forced to take the extraordinary oath:

> If I do so, may I be accursed in my undertakings, family and property; may I never see my wife, nor children, nor father, nor mother, or relations; may I be killed as a fugitive coward, and lie without a Christian burial in a foreign land, far from the graves of my forefathers and kindred.[18]

From a base at Inverness, Cumberland organized a programme of subjugation across the land, and no one was safe from the vicious reprisals of the Highland Clearances. Men, women, children, livestock and property were all ruthlessly assaulted by the King's marauding soldiers. Close to 1,000 Scotsmen were sold into slavery abroad, and others simply disappeared without trace or record. Such was the savagery that, notwithstanding the Georgian victory at Culloden, there was no military pride in claiming the Battle Honour thereafter, and no regiment in the British Army now carries Culloden on its Battle Colours.

During the course of these reprisals, thousands of Scots families fled their homeland, and a great many found their way across the Atlantic Ocean to America. They had not managed to defeat the Hanoverians at home but, in assisting their colonial cousins from

1775, they certainly found a second chance. The difficulty for the Scots regiments of the British Army was that they found themselves set not only against friends and fellow masons, but also against their own countrymen who were taking up the American cause.

The Masonic Tea Party

Prior to the War of Independence, Britain had 13 colonies in North America. Each was a separate entity with its own local government, and many of the inhabitants were of Protestant British origin. The five principal urban centres were Boston, Philadelphia, New York, Charleston and Newport, through which places word came from abroad, and where there were newspapers and colleges. Land was cheap, wages were high, and overall it was a liberated environment in which the term 'American' was rarely used. People thought of themselves as Virginians, Pennsylvanians and such like. But, from 1773, all this came under financial threat when subsidies for the high British national debt were required by way of extra tax revenue from the colonies. It was not an unreasonable requirement, given that the safeguarding of American interests from the French had proved very costly, but the insensitive way in which it was managed was unacceptable.

What the Westminster Government failed to recognize – and the people of the individual colonies had yet to discover – was that America was now ready for statehood. Although the offspring had become an adult, it was still subject to parental control. But there was no need to pay for leadership and protection from outside when home rule and home defence were possible. All that was needed was for the colonies to become unified, but it took the cross-colonial masonic community to identify the potential of a fraternal relationship. They perceived a federation of colonies that could become a nation in its own right, and there is no doubt that this would have occurred by way of natural evolution. As it transpired, however, the inept parent lit the fuse of immediate rebellion and sparked a revolution.

From 1759, measures were introduced to increase the powers of British Customs officials, and to limit the use of provincial paper currency as legal tender. In 1764, a revision of the *Molasses Act* led to the *Sugar Act*, which halved the duty on imported molasses. In 1765 came the *Stamp Act*, the first directly imposed taxation, requiring a stamp on all legal documents, newspapers and periodicals. This was political dynamite because Americans did not take part in electing the Government which imposed the tax, and the mantra became, 'No taxation without representation'. Many lawyers and printers refused to comply, and the Sons of Liberty movement emerged in New York and Boston, followed by similar groups in New England, and others in the Carolinas, Virginia and Georgia. The *Stamp Act* was repealed in 1766, but then followed the *Townshend Acts* – a series of duties on glass, lead, paints, paper and tea exported to the colonies. Britain was insistent that, one way or another, the British troops in America would be paid for in America, as would the salaries of colonial officials.

The Sons of Liberty made life impossible for Customs officers, and on 30 September 1768, ships of the British Fleet, carrying around 700 troops, landed at Boston, followed shortly after by another 500 from Ireland. The Bostonians refused to house them, even though many, being sympathetic to the colonial cause, were glad to work for the privilege. In the rioting and baiting that followed, five men were killed by soldiers on 5 March 1770. John Adams spoke in the soldiers' defence at the trials, but all troops were immediately withdrawn from Boston. The *Townshend Acts* were subsequently repealed, with the exception of the tax on tea which, consequently, became the focus of a large-scale smuggling enterprise centred on Rhode Island, where tea was brought in from Holland. In the course of this, the Royal Navy patrol ship *HMS Gaspee* was lured aground and burned.

By then the East India Company had a surplus of tea and was faltering financially, so Westminster restructured affairs in order that the Company could undersell the smugglers. In September 1773, some 500,000 lbs of tea (227,000 kg) was shipped to Boston harbour, where it was felt that the residents would prefer cheaper tea to smuggled tea.

But the monopoly afforded by Britain to the East India Company for distribution throughout the colonies caused great alarm, and the merchants in New York, Philadelphia and Charlston cancelled their orders, although the Boston merchants did not. Their stance was, nevertheless, opposed by Samuel and John Adams, Josiah Quincy and John Hancock, who were determined to resist parliamentary supremacy over colonial legislatures when the three ships arrived at the end of November. The Sons of Liberty prevented any unloading, which had to be done within 20 days or the tea would be forfeit to pay Customs duties. The ships' captains sought permission to sail out of Boston with their cargo still aboard, but the officials would not allow it.

Meanwhile, a plot was being hatched at Freemason's Hall (the former *Green Dragon* tavern) where the Boston Lodge of St Andrew had its meetings. It was also the meeting place of the associated Committee of Secret Correspondence, which included the St Andrew's masons Joseph Warren and Paul Revere, and whose membership overlapped with the Sons of Liberty. It was a busy venue, with Minute books that record high numbers of regular attendees, but on the night of 16 December 1773, the St Andrew Lodge Minutes state 'Lodge closed until tomorrow evening'.[19]

On that night, Freemasons of the Lodge of St Andrew, along with those of the other groups – about 60 men in all – perpetrated a most unusual and significant historical action. Prominent in their number were John Hancock, Joseph Warren and Paul Revere. Aided by Captain Edward Proctor of the militia detachment guarding the cargo of the *Dartmouth* (who was also a St Andrew lodge member, as were a number of his men), they dressed as Mohawk Indians and boarded the ships at Griffin's Wharf, tossing 342 chests of tea into the Boston Bay (*see* plate 40). Subsequently, 12 of the party who were not St Andrew's masons joined the lodge immediately afterwards. The British Government retaliated in 1774 with a series of new measures, styled by the colonists as the *Intolerable Acts*, and the port of Boston was closed. But it was too late; the Masonic Revolution, with a view to transforming the colonies into United States, and gaining Independence from the Hanoverian Crown, had begun.

The Crown of America

In the first instance, it was not the intention of those involved to create a new-style Republic, and since Scottish traditions were very much to the fore of the masonic structure, it was planned to put in place what had been lost in Britain at the 1688 Whig Revolution a century before. Historians such as Sir Charles Petrie, Sir Compton Mackenzie, Sir Walter Scott and Alice Shield all wrote accounts of how letters and emissaries, sent from Boston, requested that Charles Edward Stuart might consider becoming King of the Americans.[20] Letters about this still exist today in the Stuart Papers at Windsor and in the *Dartmouth Papers*. (Lord Dartmouth was Britain's Secretary of State to the Colonies in the 1770s.)

These records and correspondences span a time frame from 1774 to 1780, during which period Bonnie Prince Charlie paid close attention to events in America, ordering books and buying colonial maps to follow the progress.[21] The Abbé Fabroni, Rector of Pisa University, reported that he saw letters from the men of Boston in 1775, assuring the Prince of their allegiance and requesting that he place himself at their head.[22] The problem was that Charles did not then have a legitimate heir, and he feared that if he accepted the offer on the basis of his *de jure* British royal status, the monarchy might revert to the British Crown on his death. Since this would defeat the whole object of the colonial enterprise, the Stuart commissioners advised Charles Edward against any involvement.

One of the most strikingly odd things about the War of Independence, from its outset to its conclusion, is the manner in which it was fought and finally won. It was not actually a war as such – more a series of disconnected battles and skirmishes. The colonies were not yet United States and their military forces were not a cohesively trained national unit, even though brought under General George Washington's supreme command by the Continental Congress led by John Hancock. Britain, on the other hand, had one of the world's most effective armies and centuries of military tradition. In theory it should have been a straightforward matter to put down the rebellion long before the Marquis de Lafayette and the French became involved in 1777–8. So, how and why did the British troops fare so badly in the campaign?

In the first place, it is clear that the British high command underestimated the determination and skills of the Americans, whether on the battlefield or within their intelligence network. However, such things should have been overcome once their measure was taken. The British suffered a major defeat at Saratoga in upstate New York in 1777 and Major General John Burgoyne duly surrendered the battle. But there were victories after that in places such as Savannah, Charleston and Guildford Courthouse, until finally Charles, Lord Cornwallis, suffered another massive defeat and surrendered at Yorktown on 18 October 1781. Even then, it was just another in a series of battles, and need not have decided the final outcome – but it did. Sir Henry Clinton's army was still in good shape, and the French Fleet was subsequently decimated by the British in April 1782 but, whether at high command level or on the colonial battlegrounds, the British heart was never in the campaign and, on 4 February 1783, the new regime at Westminster called a halt to the whole debacle.

The Boston Tea Party had been masterminded by Freemasons. The Continental Congress was headed by Freemasons. The Congressional Committee of Secret Correspondence was operated by Freemasons. The commander-in-chief was a Freemason, as were many of his generals and a large number of troops in the field. Independent America was founded on a masonic ideal of federation – but who had first brought them all together with such fraternal common interest? It was the officers and soldiers of the British regiments, who belonged to the very same lodges throughout the colonial states. While it was always possible for the Americans to defend their positions, it was never easy for so many of the British troops to be overtly hostile; it was the very last thing they wanted. They played out their designated roles because they had no option, but in real terms the War was lost by Britain before it was begun.

16

Debates and Monuments

Conspiracies

At this stage of the masonic story, it is a good time to consider an aspect which has been fuelled by so-called 'conspiracy theorists'. Conspiracy theorists are, in the main, sceptics. They have learned, as most people learn, that press and media reports are often slanted, that political statements are strategically contrived, and that vested interests are prevalent in all walks of life.

While most people generally accept things for what they appear – until something different is proven – conspiracy theorists consider this a complacent attitude; outside their own circles of elected acquaintance and trusted sources of information, they are naturally incredulous. Being suspicious and imaginative, they often perceive conspiracies where there are none but, on other occasions, their intuitions are may be well founded. Conspiracy theorizing is a philosophical and investigative mind-set that searches for truths and delights in uncovering veiled motives, but its mission is not meant to be destructive. In fact, the honest conspiracy theorist would always feel constructively employed.

However, there are those who move so far beyond scepticism that they even become sceptical of the sceptics! In their hunt for conspiracies, they contrive and invent conspiracies, thereby emerging as conspirators themselves. And to this end they become the perpetrators of destruction and the modern equivalents of the Inquisitional witch-finders. This is achieved by instilling fear and mistrust of everything which supports the social need. It is especially aimed against any individual or organization which might be popular, successful or in some way responsible for fulfilling public requirements. The malevolent message is that, at all levels, governments are corrupt, academia is corrupt, religion is corrupt, industry is corrupt – and the general purpose of this is to create an unstable environment wherein a power-base of sorts can be created.

Freemasonry has long been a primary target in this conspiratorial field of operation, but not in the manner that might be independently classified as anti-masonry (*see* chapter 14). On a global scale, masonic lodge membership is represented in all walks of everyday life. Companies, corporations, schools, hospitals, banks, churches, hotels, factories, shops, police forces, councils, parliaments and just about any other body, group or association that one can imagine, could well have Freemasons within its structure. Consequently, they provide a common denominator that falls easy prey to those who wish to destabilize the overall conglomerate foundation.

Although Freemasonry is not a religion, it has a similarly widespread membership, and can be subjected to the same style of attacks that are levelled against Catholics, Muslims, Jews or any other community that underpins society and its institutions. But to some people it does not matter how many children's lives have been saved or improved by the dedication of North America's 500,000 masonic Shriners, it is always possible to claim, without any proof or provocation, that such things are merely a cover for secret plots and conspiratorial activities. And there will always be a gullible audience that desires to blame everyone else for their own failings and inadequacies.

In order to create an environment of trepidation, there has to be a common enemy. The Church has Satan or the strangely defined Antichrist but, to be effective in their mission, scaremongers must ignore the Church because it promises salvation and this would defeat their objective. There has to be an adversary that is beyond clerical confrontation – someone or something that is so powerful at a secular level as to be insurmountable. In this regard, the name of a long defunct 18th-century organization from Bavaria called the Illuminists has been resurrected. Since their history has disappeared

into the mists of time, it is easy enough to claim that they now exist
as an elite group of Freemasons who prevail above all the degrees,
and are conspiring to take over the world – if they have not done so
already. With a slight shift of emphasis in the old nominal style to
create a truly Gothic image, it is claimed that these emissaries of
global damnation are called the *Illuminati*.

The Great Seal

In real terms, there is nothing sinister about the term Illuminist; it
simply means 'enlightener', and could just as easily be a fairy lamp-
lighter in a children's nursery tale. But, as we have seen, the Latin
for 'light-bringer' (*lux-fer*) was the linguistic root of 'lucifer' (*see*
page 225), and therein lies the satanic connotation which is now
applied to the term *Illuminati*. The difference between the *Illuminati*
and the Church's satanic enemy, however, is that the *Illuminati* are
said to have the Church already within their power.

The term *Illuminati* became associated with Freemasonry because a
philosophical order of Illuminists was founded in Bavaria by the ex-
Freemason Adam Weishaupt, professor of natural and canon law, and
dean of the faculty at the University of Ingolstadt, on 1 May 1776.[1]
This is the same year that is printed at the base of the pyramid on the
Great Seal of the United States: *MDCCLXXVI*, and which is accompanied by the words, *Novus Ordo Seclorum* (New Order of Ages).

So, this gives us the root source for the mysterious 'New World
Order' that many are terrified will bring about the rise of the
Antichrist. But a little investigation reveals that, by virtue of *seclorum*
(of the ages) being misidentified with 'secular' (of the world), a strategically wrong translation has been promoted in order to set the stage
for the *Illuminati* myth. When correctly translated, it turns out that
Novus Ordo Seclorum is not some catastrophic future Armageddon,
but relates to the egalitarian ideal of America's Founding Fathers
when the *Declaration of Independence* was issued on 4 July '1776' – the

The Great Seal of the United States of America – obverse and reverse

year as given on the Great Seal. *Novus Ordo Seclorum* was not used to define 'order' in terms of control. It actually relates to an order in terms of a 'series' (as in a numerical order or progression) – a New Series of Ages. It derives from Virgil's *Eclogue* 4, verse 5, which discusses a longing for an era of peace and harmony.[2]

At the end of prayers in Latin, and dating from the 2nd-century *Gloria* (a hymn of praise to the Trinity), is generally found the phrase *secula seculorum* – literally 'for ever and ever' (ages of ages), followed by 'Amen'. In classical Latin, 'world' (depending on its particular usage) would be a variant or derivative of *mundus*, but *seclorum* relates specifically to ages, centuries and generations.

Unfortunately, one figure who uses the incorrect translation and has managed to promote the 'New World Order' myth to a wide audience is the fictional symbologist Robert Langdon in the Dan Brown novel *Angels and Demons*. When discussing the dollar bill with Vittoria (the adopted daughter of a priest), Langdon explains that *Novus Ordo Seclorum* relates to a 'New Secular Order'. Since Robert Langdon is portrayed as a knowledgeable Harvard professor, many readers have forgotten that he is a fictional character in a fictional story, and have taken him at his word![3]

Apart from the coincidence of the 1776 date, there is nothing whatever to connect the *Declaration of Independence* with the Bavarian

Illuminists. It could just as easily be linked that year with the foundation of Freemasons' Hall in London, the eruption of Mount Vesuvius in Italy or the introduction of Royal Mail coaches in Scotland – they are all equally unrelated. But are there, in fact, masonic allusions in the Great Seal, as depicted on any dollar bill?

On the same day that the *Declaration* was issued, the Continental Congress formed a committee with Benjamin Franklin, John Adams and Thomas Jefferson (*see* plate 37), who were asked to prepare a device for the Great Seal. On 10 August, they reported back with a draft design that included just about everything they could think of – symbols from England, Scotland, Ireland, France, Holland, Germany and Belgium, surrounded by 13 escutcheons denoting the individual colonies which had been settled from these countries. In the form of a combined shield, the whole was supported by representations of *Liberty* and *Justice*, and surmounted by the Eye of Providence in a radiant triangular glory.

Thomas Jefferson's original drawing for the Great Seal obverse

Not surprisingly, this uninspired concept was unenthusiastically received, and the matter was referred to the Congress secretary Charles Thompson. With the aid of a heraldist, William Barton, his newly drafted design was submitted and approved in 1782.[4]

The American bald eagle on the obverse was taken from the original escutcheon as a unique representation of America (others included a rose for England, a thistle for Scotland and a *fleur de lys* for France). The eagle's shield carries 13 red and white stripes (valour and innocence), representing the 13 new states, beneath a chief of blue. In the eagle's beak is a scroll with the motto *E Pluribus Unum* ('Out of Many, One'), denoting the unification of the colonies. In the eagle's right (dexter) talon is an olive branch – a time-honoured symbol of peace – while in its left (sinister) talon are 13 arrows. In Rosicrucian terms, these could be likened to the hermetic shafts of enlightenment as clutched by the baby Jesus in Sandro Botticelli's painting *Madonna of the Book* (1483). The idea of their use in the United States design came from the arms of the united Netherlands, wherein a bunch of arrows, clutched by a lion, signified the individual provinces that broke free from Spanish dominion in the 16th century. To emphasize the importance of peace, the eagle was set with its head facing the olive branch which (again to symbolize the new states) was given 13 leaves. At the obverse crest are 13 stars on an azure field in a radiant cloud and golden glory. Although now stylized into a 1–4–3–4–1 star formation, the original design was simply one of randomly set asterisk shapes, and there is no specific pattern for the stars in Thompson's description.

On the reverse, the triangulated All-seeing Eye of Rosicrucian philosophy was also the historical Eye of Providence which had shone so well on the American cause. The unfinished pyramid is stated in the Seal explanation to represent 'strength and durability', while showing that there will always remain work to be finished. This was taken from an earlier $50 bill design by Francis Hopkinson (designer of the American flag). Contrary to popular belief, the triangle above is simply a flat triangle; it does not constitute a three-dimensional pyramidion separated from its base. The motto at the crest is *Annuit Coeptis*.

Also from Virgil, this comes from his *Georgics* (an instructional manual for farmers) and relates to 'providence in undertakings'.

A number of things are said about the Seal by those who claim it to be a message of *Illuminati* intent promulgated in the public domain by way of the dollar bill. These include:

- The truncated pyramid with the separate portion above is indicative of the letter A, thereby signifying America's intended New World Order of the *Illuminati*.
- Since Jesus holds the arrows of enlightenment in Botticelli's painting, the fact that the American eagle is facing away from them signifies America's denial of Christ.
- The Virgil motto *Annuit Coeptis*, being from Rome in pre-Christian times, is a prayer to Jupiter, and a denial of God.
- The combined elements of the Seal's roundels are black magical symbols of phenomenal power.
- The pyramid face has 72 bricks – a sacred number in ancient Babylon. It is a portrayal of the Tower of Babel.
- The pyramid is a gateway for evil Egyptian gods.
- The Seal reverse is surmounted by the Evil Eye which, in its dollar bill guise, is distributed to bring public misfortune.
- 13 is the number of those in the highest rank of the *Illuminati*.
- *Annuit Coeptis* translates as 'announcing the birth of', and relates to the son of Satan.

It is difficult to understand quite what any of this nonsense has to do with Freemasonry, but it does show that the Great Seal is actually far less masonic than many have imagined. Freemasonry is not unique in using symbols and emblems – so does heraldry, and that is primarily what is involved here. The Seal follows all the common rules for Arms design, while at the same time being distinctly American. In fact, the only symbol that is directly masonic is the All-seeing Eye, and even this was used as a Christian emblem of the ever-watchful Eye of God long before Freemasonry evolved (*see* plate 4).

The *Illuminati*

If there was a connection between America's Founding Fathers and the Bavarian Illuminists, what would it have meant in practice? In the first place they were not actually called Illuminists – that was a tag by which they became known. They were actually styled the Order of Perfectibilists. The *Encyclopedia Britannica* explains that the term *Illuminati* is an Italian rendition of Illuminists, which derives from the German *aufklärung* (enlightenment).

Adam Weishaupt, a professor of natural and canon law, and dean of the faculty at the University of Ingolstadt, was born in 1746. His background was rather unusual, since he came from a Jewish family, but was raised as a Catholic by Jesuits. A keen student of Pythagoras, he was initiated into a lodge of Freemasonry at Munich in 1774,[5] but was disappointed by the low educational standards and lack of cosmopolitan experience of his fellow masons. Despite what was happening in France, Britain, Ireland and America, the general standard of German Freemasonry at this time was poor. There was a *Rite of Strict Observance*, founded by Baron von Hund, which attempted to place a Christian interpretation on pre-Christian mysteries, and it was to this unit that Weishaupt became attached. But he soon left, and made the decision to start a more enlightened fraternity that was better suited to those who were more academically inclined.[6]

Weishaupt's particular dislike was superstition. He had suffered the effects of this from the Jesuit priests, and said that superstition encouraged bigotry and prejudice. He had suffered from prejudice too, coming from a Jewish background. His objective for the Order of Perfectibilists was to free the minds of members from such things by way of mutual study and debate. His claim, from first-hand experience, was that the conceptual religion of Christ had degenerated into a school of fanaticism and intolerance, and that those at the forefront of religious teaching were the most irreligious of all in benevolent Christian terms.[7] He drew a distinct line between Christianity and 'churchianity', maintaining that human dignity and liberty had become forfeit when Nature was abandoned in favour of control by a dogmatic Church establishment.

The Order of Perfectibilists was not a masonic institution with secrets and mysteries, although it had grades of merit and attainment within its ranks. What it promised was rational discussion and research, and within no time Weishaupt had 2,000 registered members. They not only joined in Germany, but also from France, Belgium, Holland, Denmark, Sweden, Poland, Hungary and Italy. What he had inadvertently begun was the first fully-fledged correspondence course. This led him to consider the possibility of a social structure with no national boundaries, no feudal regime to render people in servitude, and no cultural or class regulation to forge divides between races. He preached a release of free-thinking from State oppression, and a total withdrawal of Church control over matters of science and philosophy.

All things considered, Weishaupt was a well-motivated idealist and a natural revolutionary. He was a supporter of the French Revolution, and hoped that it would have a beneficial spin-off effect in Germany. Of the French conflict, he wrote:

> Salvation does not lie where strong thrones are defended by swords, where the smoke of censers ascends to heaven, or where thousands of strong men pace the rich fields of harvest.[8]

Unsurprisingly, none of this was popular with the secular or clerical authorities, but Weishaupt's idealistic dream of equal rights was too big to be of any real concern – that is, until his group decided that they were themselves guilty of those very things they preached against. How could there be fairness and harmony in society if it did not exist within their own organization? Where were the women? The Order of Perfectibilists therefore opened its doors to female members, and the ranks swelled yet again with those who took a new message into the outside world. They called it 'feminine equality'.

This was the last straw. Such a thing had never been heard of in the 1780s, and the authorities rose up to confront Adam Weishaupt.

He was accused of breaking God's laws and plotting to overthrow the Church. Every charge in the book, from heresy to treason, was hurled at him, and, in 1784, he was banished from the country. His Illuminists (as they had become popularly known) were subsequently proscribed by Duke Karl Theodore of Bavaria, and the Order was terminated. Meanwhile, Weishaupt found asylum with Duke Ernst of neighbouring Gotha, where he lived until his death in 1811.

But were the Founding Fathers of America actually influenced in any way by the *Illuminati*? It is possible, but very unlikely. Indeed, the July 1776 *Declaration of Independence* was signed less than two months after Weishaupt's Order had been established. The link which is cited by so many who insist that the *Illuminati* now control America stems from an event in 1798. On 9 March of that year, long after the Perfectibilists had been disbanded, the Congregationalist minister Jedediah Morse made an announcement at the New North Church in Boston. In a treatise by the Jesuit Abbé Augustus Burruel, Morse stated that the European *Illuminati* were conspiring to overthrow the rights and liberties of America's newly acquired status. What the book actually stated was in reference to the French Revolution: 'Princes and nations shall disappear from the face of the Earth ... and this revolution shall be the work of secret societies.' Morse's theory was heightened, nevertheless, by another book, *Proofs of a Conspiracy Against all the Governments of Europe*, by Dr John Robison of Edinburgh.[9] Once again, this had nothing to do with America – simply that the monarchies of Europe were, at that time, under threat from a wave of anti-clerical republicanism.

Rev Morse had somehow forgotten that America was already free of British monarchical constraint, and that the United States was constituted as a federal republic over which European governments had no control. For a short time his fears were newsworthy and gained some press coverage when he accused Thomas Jefferson of being an *Illuminati* agent. In the event, the Morse absurdity was short-lived, but it reared its head again when John Kennedy,

America's first Catholic president, was assassinated in 1963. How could this possibly happen unless it was the retribution of the Bavarian *Illuminati*? From that moment, things became ever more exaggerated, and reached a point in July 1969 when a left-wing Chicago newspaper blamed the *Illuminati* for America's growing drugs problem, stating:

> The possibility that Adam Weishaupt killed George Washington and took his place, serving as our first President for two terms, has now been confirmed ... The two main colors of the American flag are red and white; these are also the official colors of the Hashishism. The flag and the *Illuminati* pyramid have thirteen divisions. Thirteen is, of course, the traditional code for marijuana![10]

Such lunacies did not stop in 1969. Even now, articles of this type are cited as if they are part of some authoritative archive. Much of what is unpopular that happens in America is blamed on the *Illluminati*, but the problem is that no one can identify where the supposed conspiratorial plots are hatched. It must all be done in secret, behind closed doors – and that, of course, resolves into just one possibility: the Freemasons. They must be the *Illuminati*!

That apart, it is perhaps relevant to ask whether there any similarity between Weishaupt's ideals and those of the Founding Fathers. His desires were for national equality, sexual equality, freedom from feudal constraints and freedom from Church controls. Certainly the two were similar, as were the mutual concepts of revolution to achieve those ends. The only difference was that the Americans *had* their revolution and won their freedoms, but neither was achieved by Weishaupt.

By 1792 a similar mood to Weishaupt's ideal was indeed emerging in Philadelphia and New England as a spin-off from the French Revolution. In that year, Samuel Jennings, a Pennsylvanian artist living in London, produced his painting *Liberty Displaying the Arts and Sciences*. Commissioned by the directors of the Library

Company of Philadelphia (where it is still displayed),[11] the work features *Liberty*, with a broken chain at her feet, in a setting of masonic iconography concerning the Liberal Arts (*see* plate 42). It was 73 years before slavery was abolished by Abraham Lincoln, but *Liberty* (in her *Marianne* guise) is seen proffering a grey book to a group of freed slaves, while others celebrate at the liberty pole outside. The book that *Liberty* presents is actually the Library Company's catalogue of the era – a potent statement of intent that the whole world of books and the knowledge contained therein would become available to all.

It is now possible to see why the designers of the United States are claimed to have been *Illuminati*, and are consequently accused of godlessness and sinister practice. These are precisely the charges that were levelled by the feudal aristocracy and fanatical priests against Weishaupt. Those who level such accusations today against the Founding Fathers of America are, of course, perfectly free to do so, but at the same time they must also be prepared to recognize that they are placing themselves in the ranks of racial exploiters, sexual discriminators and religious extremists.

The historical *Illuminati* were never in a position to wield any power over anyone. They influenced the thinking of a great many people, and possibly assisted the mind-set for the French Revolution, but they never once influenced any government except against themselves. The measure of their success can be notionally perceived in hindsight, but at the time they were a failed Order, and were totally non-existent by the late 1780s. As for their attachment to Freemasonry, it too was non-existent; Weishaupt founded the group specifically because he was unimpressed with German Freemasonry. It is impossible to presume that, in the context of all this, the *Illuminati* managed to contrive a powerful New World Order, and have since been running a conspiratorial global network for the past 200 years. The *Illuminati* simply do not exist, neither in the top echelons of Freemasonry, nor anywhere else.

Masonic Memorials

The draft *Constitution* of the United States of America was approved and signed by 39 of 42 delegates on 17 September 1787. By the following 25 June it was ratified by the individual States, and Maryland ceded 10 square miles to become the District of Columbia, which would embrace the new Federal capital.

George Washington was elected the first President on 4 February 1789, with John Adams as his vice president. Robert Livingstone, Grand Master of the New York Grand Lodge administered the oath at the inauguration on 30 April, using the Bible from St John's Lodge of New York. Other notable Freemasons in attendance were the marshal, Jacob Morton, and the presidential escort, Morgan Lewis.[12]

On 18 September 1793, the cornerstone of the Capitol was laid. The Maryland lodges were in attendance, along with Washington's own Alexandria Lodge No 22 from Virginia. The silver trowel and walnut square used by the President for the occasion are now in the Alexandria–Washington Replica Lodge Room at the George Washington Masonic National Memorial. The front lawn of this impressive museum and library centre (which we shall revisit in the next chapter) boasts a ground sculpture of the largest square and compasses in the world, and a massive bronze statue of George Washington commands the Memorial Hall.

With a completely free aspect, the Capitol and White House were set within an elaborately conceived geometrical layout that became Washington, DC. Designed in 1791 by the architect Pierre Charles L'Enfant, in collaboration with George Washington and Thomas Jefferson, the city emerged as a masterwork in masonic design. This related to the streets in their relationship with one another, and to the buildings and their individual architecture; also to their strategic positioning and, again, their locational relationships. There are no fewer than 20 complete zodiacs in the design, each one mysteriously connected to specific star patterns, as detailed in the recently published research of David Ovason.[13]

Benjamin Latrobe, a principal architect of the Washington Capitol, was a Freemason, and the building abounds in Ionic, Doric and Corinthian columns, which (as the three primary supports of lodge ritual) represent wisdom, strength and beauty. Latrobe's design for the House of Representatives includes a starry canopy, defined as the 'cover of the lodge'. The columns in the Senate vestibule have chapiters depicting corn, while the vestibule itself leads to a masonic winding staircase, and the Senate wing pediment, entitled *Progress of Civilization*, includes sheaves of wheat – the masonic symbols of plenty.

The great dome of the Capitol, surmounted by the statue of *Freedom*, is among the most famous man-made landmarks in America, and the Rotunda beneath is the Capitol's main circulation arena. With a diameter of 96 ft (*c.* 29 m) and a height of 180 ft (*c.* 55 m), it is an extraordinarily ambitious architectural work that progressed over many years. The original dome was replaced from 1856, along with other structural extensions, by the project's fourth architect Thomas Walter. The dome's interior was finished in 1866, embodying the wonderful concave ceiling fresco, *Apotheosis of Washington*, by the Italian artist Constantino Brumidi. Recently cleaned and restored in the 1980s, the work is rich in masonic and alchemical imagery, including Hermes with his caduceus and a bag of gold.

Also in the Washington city complex is the imposing *Scottish Rite* headquarters, the House of the Temple, which contains the Executive Chamber of the Supreme Council. Nearby is the Grand Lodge of the District of Columbia, with its extensive library and museum. But of all the masonic edifices, the best known and most visually striking has to be the 500-ft white marble obelisk of the Washington Monument.[14]

The enormous Symington marble cornerstone was ceremonially dragged through the streets by anyone who could attach a line to the cumbersome truck from the rail yard, and it was set in position near to the cross-axis of the Capitol and the White House on Sunday 4 July 1848.[15] The ceremony was conducted by Benjamin B French, Grand Master of the Grand Lodge of the District of Columbia, who wore an apron and sash that had belonged to President Washington,

Hermes in the *Apotheosis of Washington*

and used the same gavel that he had used for the Capitol event in 1793.

The erection of the Monument was a long and fraught process, as the large marble blocks had to be taken to ever-increasing heights. During the course of this, 190 memorial stones were donated from around America and from other countries, to be built into the interior walls. One was even sent from Rome by Pope Pius IX, but on the night of 6 March 1854 it was stolen, and has never since been found.

Seven years after commencement, the main construction was complete. The aluminium pyramidion was lowered into position on 6 December 1884, and the Monument was dedicated on 22 February 1885. It then took a further three years to build, fill and complete the terrace, and from 1889 the Washington Monument became a focus for visitors worldwide. Not strictly an obelisk in the Egyptian sense of a single hewn block of stone, the Monument is a sky-scraping building with a number of landings and an inner stairway. When first opened to the public, a steam-driven elevator was operational, but of the 122,000 visitors in 1889, some 52,000 preferred to climb the 898 steps to the top, where windows overlook the city. Then, in 1901, a new electric elevator was installed, and the edifice was permanently lit for aircraft safety from 1929.

Aerial view of the Washington Monument

For all its ground-level magnificence, the true magic of the Monument obelisk does not lie in its imposing height, its gleaming marble or in any of those aspects of the magnificent engineering. These things alone do not render it as a masonic edifice, even though the stonemasonry is impressive. The important function of the Washington Monument is that it conveys the single most important of all masonic devices – that within which the lost secret of Freemasonry has always been held. The obelisk is not a stand-alone feature; it incorporates within its whole the all-important round terrace which is so large that it took three years to build. It is from overhead that the true nature and purpose of the Monument can be seen, and from the sky directly above, day or night, it appears as no more nor less than a gigantic edifice of Light – a point within a circle ⊙.

19

The Royal Art

A Loss of Context

The biggest single hindrance to masonic study these days is caused by the variability of its texts. Rules concerning ritual have not been strict enough, and even simple adjustments have caused losses in the original emphasis and intent. Lodges have been allowed certain freedoms of interpretation, in terms of modernization, focus and vernacular revision. But, in reality, no matter how old-fashioned or outmoded any original text might appear, it was meant to be conveyed and continued as written – not adjusted to suit the requirements of a subsequent era.

It should always be assumed that individually chosen words are as important as their overall contexts, because changing a single word can so easily alter the context itself. Take, for example, the Bible's New Testament entries in Matthew 13:55 and Mark 6:3. They each describe Jesus' father, Joseph, as being an *ho tekton*. This translates directly into English as 'master of the craft' – precisely as the distinction is used in Freemasonry. But following the initial translation it was decided that, since Joseph was not a Freemason, then a different interpretation was required and the term 'carpenter' was inserted instead. By virtue of this, the prestigious royal genealogy attributed to Joseph in Matthew 1:1–16 was completely undermined, and his social standing, along with that of Jesus, has been misconstrued ever since. Even if Joseph was not a Freemason, he was indeed described as an *ho tekton* in Greek, and a *naggar* in Aramaic –

both of which identify a most scholarly and learned man. Neither description has anything whatever to do with woodwork.[1]

Even though James Anderson claimed that much had been lost prior to 1717, what did exist were those remnants of original masonic ritual that were performed at *The Apple Tree* and the *Goose and Gridiron* – along with the Antients' ceremonial from the *Black Lion* and *The Shakespeare*. The former were adapted and amended, however, by Anderson and Desaguliers, while the latter fell to equally unscrupulous interpreters in 1813. Thus, it is fair to say that just as much has been lost since 1717 as was lost before. Any attempt to unravel old truths from today's masonic ritual is as unlikely to succeed as would a quest to discover Joseph's ancestors from a base of understanding that he was a 1st-century carpenter.

A Masonic Code

Documents and books written in the English language from the time of Shakespeare and Bacon are markedly different to those written before that era. The English language not only changed considerably in structure, but also its vocabulary increased substantially during this period. From comparative studies of the King James translation of the Bible (1611) and Shakespeare's first Folio (1623), it appears that the nation's vocabulary increased by 100 per cent. That is to say, half the words that were in use afterwards were not in regular use before. New words were either invented, or obscure words were adjusted and brought into everyday use. Shakespeare is personally credited with having coined some 2,000 words, including *critical, leapfrog, majestic, dwindle* and *pedant*. He also introduced any number of clichés and catchphrases that are still in regular use, such as 'one fell swoop', 'flesh and blood' and 'vanish into thin air'.

Prior to that, the language of England was a strange and garbled mixture of Latin corruptions, Greek variants and misused French interlaced with some Norse jargon, all based on a crude Germanic dialect from Anglo-Saxon times. A quick comparison can easily be made by comparing the vocabulary of Chaucer with that of Shakespeare. A good example is provided by the familiar *Lord's Prayer* which, in John Wycliffe's 1384 Bible translation, was rendered as:

> Oure fadir þat art in heuenes halwid be þi name;
>
> þi reume or kyngdom come to be.
>
> Be þi wille don in herþe as it is dounin heuene.
>
> yeue to us today oure eche dayes bred.
>
> And foryeue to us oure dettis þat is oure synnys
>
> as we foryeuen to oure dettouris þat is to men þat han synned
>
> in us.
>
> And lede us not into temptacion but delyuere us from euyl.[2]

By virtue of the limitations of old alphabets, letters had been used in a peculiar fashion. As above, the 'v' phonetic was often written as 'u'. The reverse was the case in Latin with 'u' written as 'v'. The Old English þ, which eventually became written as 'y', was pronounced 'th', as in *ye* for *the*, whereas the reverse occurred with such words as *thou*, eventually becoming *you*. France had no 'w' in its alphabet, and so the Scots name *Stewart* was rendered as *Stuart*. It was introduced with that new spelling for the Royal House of Stewart by Mary, Queen of Scots, during her reign as Queen of France.

Then there were the much used 'I' letters because there was no 'J' in the Latin alphabet. In contrast, the Nordic language had a 'j' that was pronounced 'ea' (something close to a 'y'). Hence, the Norse *jarl* eventually became *earl* in English, whereas 'y' was commonly used in place of 'i' to denote the phonetic as in *rise*, against the short-i of *ink*. However, 'y', as in dainty, was often rendered as 'ie' to convey the right sound, and other dipthongs were similarly used.

If there is an individual work that marks the turning point, it appears to be Edmund Spenser's *The Shepheardes Calendar* in 1579, when lyrical poetry created the need for a more constant format.[3] It is in this work (a pastoral poem of the months of the year in terms of their relationship to the span of a lifetime cycle) that Spenser claimed he strove for a language more purely English than the 'gallimaufry and hodge podge of al other speeches'. From the *Aprill Laye* comes:

> Now ryse vp Elisa, decked as thou art
> in royall aray;
> And now ye daintie Damsells may depart
> eachone her way,
> I feare, I haue troubled your troupes to longe.
> Let dame Eliza thanke you for her song.

Referring to Queen Elizabeth as both Elisa and Eliza, this verse marks the formal spelling change from *Elisabeth* to *Elizabeth*, although by then the Queen had herself been using the new spelling for a while. Also, in the first line we have the word *thou*, which in the last line has become *you*.

What made all of this so important at the time was the great emphasis on verse patterns. This was not just a matter for written poetry, wherein standardizations or clever variables were necessary for metre or rhyme, but in plays such as those by William Shakespeare. These were also constructed in verse sequences – as indeed was the King James Bible.

Masonic ritual, which stemmed from this era, was similarly constructed. But, whereas Shakespearean verse does not work when amended to our currently evolved use of language, neither does the Bible retain its dimensional accuracy when 'modernized' in so-called updated editions. It was expected, nonetheless, that masonic ritual could withstand such corruption – but it cannot, and it does not. Only in its original form can the ritual maintain its intended meaning, and this extends to the great importance of line ends and beginnings, as well as to the precise original words.

Spenser and others of the Baconian group were senior members of the latter Elizabethan and early Stuart Secret Service (*see* chapter 13) and, from the time of John Dee, they were masters of codes and ciphers. These were cleverly used in Shakespeare's plays – sometimes with purpose, but often just for amusement. The strategic use of capital letters (just as Spenser wrote *Damsells* mid-line instead of *damsels*) was very much a part of this, as was the significance of where a line might begin or end. There was no better way of ensuring that line starts and ends did not get changed in future transcriptions than by constructing messages and other prose sequences in verse patterns. Then with the addition of rhyming or the use of iambic pentameter, there was little allowance for alteration, and the emphases were preserved.

Shakespeare's works are loaded with capital letter manipulations in a form that he called 'cogging'. (To *cog* dice is to make them fall in a particular way.[4]) From the time of the first folio of his work, all subsequent editions have been corrupted by editors and publishers who thought they were making improvements or corrections (much as has happened with the ritual of Freemasonry). An importance of the first folio is that, apart from Capital Letters, many others were printed as **bold** letters – or perhaps lines were broken in what others have since considered to be an incorrect manner. There are so many examples, it would take a book in itself to discuss them, but just a few will suffice here to show how it works. In *A Midsummer Night's Dream*, Titania states:

> Thou shalt remaine here, wither thou wilt or no.
> I am a spirit of no common rate:
> The summer still doth not tend upon my state,
> And I doe love thee; therefore goe with me.
> Ile give thee fairies to attend on thee;
> And they shall fetch thee jewels from the deepe ...[5]

With the inclusion of the boldly printed '**n**' in the fourth line, the capital letters of the line beginnings spell out the name Titania.

A slightly more complex form of cogging was often used, wherein the relevant letters were not necessarily in the correct order. Sometimes they were wholly anagrammatical. From the 1609 quarto of Shakespeare's *Sonnets*,[6] a verse concerning Adonis (as underlined), reads:

And you, but one, can every shadow lend.

Describe <u>Adonis</u>, and the counterfeit

Is poorly imitated after you

On Helen's cheek all art of beauty set.

A rearrangement of the first and bold letters in this case reaffirms the name Adonis. Such anagrams could become very intricate, not just set at the beginnings of lines, but with capitals or unusually printed letters within the body of lines. French and Latin words were also used to add a more obscure aspect to the coding. A good example comes again from *A Midsummer Night's Dream* in a conversation between Egeus and Theseus:

My Lord, this is my daughter heere asleepe,

And this Lysander, this Demetrius is,

This Helena, old Nedars Helena,

I wonder of this being here together.

No doubt they rose up early ...[7]

In this instance, based on the thought emphasis of the last line (the first of Theseus), the initial Capitals spell out the word *MATIN* – French for 'morning'. This would be totally lost if a modernization changed the last line to 'Doubtless they rose up early ...'

These examples are simplistic, but the cogging cipher becomes sophisticated and complex in much of Shakespeare's and Bacon's work. This serves to make the point that what the writer writes is precisely what is meant to be conveyed. Its structure and grammar can sometimes be improved, but it cannot necessarily be adjusted or interpreted without the chance of losing or distorting the original intent.

This form of cogging was known to the originators of formalized Freemasonry in the early 1700s and this is demonstrated by its use in a 1704 document known as the *Roll of the Newcastle College of Rosicrucians*. This is held within the manuscripts of James

Anderson's *Old Charges* of the Craft. More important than the Newcastle MS, the cipher is also extant from much earlier times, appearing in a document from York in 1630, and another from as far back as 1600 at the very height of the Shakespearean era.[8] A manuscript of Rosicrucian Charges was found when the old Norman castle of Pontefract in Yorkshire was demolished in 1649. Used as a Royalist fortress during the Civil War, Pontefract Castle was an archive for all manner of Stuart-related documents that were lodged there for safe-keeping. The Charge from 1600 reads:

> Much might be said of the noable Artt;
> A craft that's worth estieming in every part.
> Sundrie nations, noables, and kings also,
> O, how they sought its worth to know.
> Nimrod and Solomon, the wisest of all men,
> Reason saw to love this Science then.
> I'll say no more, lest by my shallow verses, I
> Endeavouring to praise should blemish Masonrie.[9]

In the same way as *A Midsummer Night's Dream*, *The Tempest* and *Love's Labour's Lost*, masonic rituals were constructed, and are still performed, as plays. But their scripts have been amended and modified. Thus, although the staging (whether the death of Hiram Abiff or something else) is superficially preserved, the intended deeper meanings have been ignored and forgotten, if not lost altogether. The only way to discover their ultimate truths and emphases with any precision would be to find the originals in the way that they were first written, with the intended wording and its format, aided by the correct line breaks, the strategic use of capitals, intentional variations in spelling, and suchlike. Endeavouring to work from anything later than the primary texts can only be guesswork. And like reading, say, 'Doubtless' for 'No doubt', it can mean much the same on the surface, but the express purpose of the original would not be discovered.

Notwithstanding all medieval trade guild practice, the actual masonic texts that were revived and adjusted from 1717 first emanated in the Shakespearean era, and were most likely Baconian in origin. They were based on Rosicrucian philosophies, and became a bedrock of the Stuart Royal Society of Christopher Wren and his colleagues. By the time of Isaac Newton's presidency of the Society from 1703, the key original texts had disappeared, and he spent his life searching for the hidden secret of the ancient Royal Art, remaining always in the shadow of Solomon. When the new-style Freemasonry was born from its base of the London Guilds and Livery Companies, it was already lacking in the real substance of its birthright, and those concerned knew it at the time. This takes us back to where this book began, with James Anderson's statement in 1723 that:

> ... very little has come down to us that testifies the English masonic tradition before the latter 17th century. Many of the Fraternity's records of Charles II's and former reigns were lost in the next and at the Revolution of 1688.

The greatest of all misunderstandings arose in the way that modern Freemasonry became described as 'speculative', as opposed (or so it was perceived) to 'operative' stonemasonry. But a Freemason (*frère maçon*) was never an 'operative stonemason'; he was once an 'operative Freemason', and it was in relation to this legacy that the emergent dining-club fraternity was 'speculative'. Freemasonry never had anything to do with wages, conditions of labour or hacking bits of stone. It was an accomplished art with a scientific root. Citing the Shakespearean *Old Charge of Masonrie* once again:

> Nimrod and Solomon, the wisest of all men,
> Reason saw to love this Science then.

The Powder of Projection

What then was the Royal Art of King Solomon that dated back to Nimrod of Mesopotamia and was held in such high esteem? As we saw in chapter 15, it is alluded to in the Greek *Septuagint*. This is the oldest of all extant Old Testament Bible texts from the 3rd century BC, whereas the currently used Hebrew version dates only from the 10th century AD, and is actually 500 years 'newer' than the Christian New Testament.[10]

In describing the immense golden wealth of King Solomon, the *Septuagint* explains that King Huram of Tyre supplied him with alluvial gold from the mines of Ophir, near Sheba, along with many other favours.[11] Even the Queen of Sheba herself brought Solomon 120 talents of gold.[12] It is said that 'the weight of gold which came to Solomon in one year was six hundred and sixty six talents of gold'.[13] It was for this reason that when the astonishing alchemical science of King Solomon (then known as the *Mosaico-Hermetic Art*) was condemned by the 4th-century Christian bishops, the Revelation of St John was doctored so that this number became the designated mark of the beast: six hundred, threescore and six.[14] This number of golden talents (one year's supply to King Solomon) is equivalent to about 30 tons – with a value today of around $250 million.[15]

King Huram was extremely wealthy and powerful, but he needed to trade with Solomon of Judah to obtain one particular product, as did the Queen of Sheba and the Jordanian kings of Petra. To this end, Huram helped Solomon build the ships of his Red Sea fleet, based at Ezion-geber. This enabled Solomon to enter the lucrative horse trade, as a result of which he had 40,000 stalls of horses for his chariots and 12,000 horsemen.[16] Noted for his wisdom and philosophical writings, the Jerusalem Temple was the high point of Solomon's fame, which he built near King David's palace to house the Ark of the Covenant. Once again Huram of Tyre assisted with this, supplying designers, craftsmen, and materials – the director of operations being Hiram, a skilled artificer in metals known to Freemasons as Hiram Abiff.[17] In return for this, the Phoenician king did not ask for money or any other form of trade; instead he asked that Solomon should 'give bread to my household'.[18]

This takes us back to the ancient Mesopotamian *shem-an-na* (the highward fire-stone) of Nimrod, and to the Karnak temple relief of Tuthmoses III which displays the treasures of Egypt in about 1450 BC. As shown in the diagram below (*see also* chapter 11), the cone-shaped objects – strategically set alongside two obelisks – are listed as being made of gold, but are classified as 'white bread'.

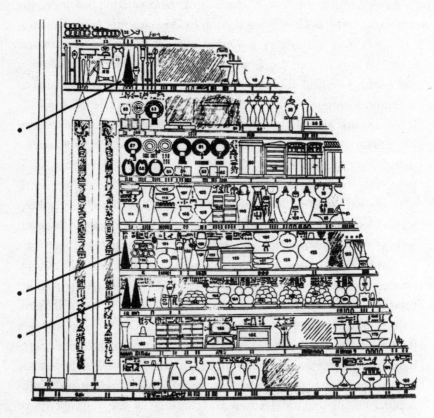

Section of the Egyptian treasure relief of Tuthmoses III at Karnak

The mysterious white powder that was discovered by Flinders Petrie at the Mount Horeb temple of Sinai in 1904 was also coupled with inscribed references to 'bread', accompanied by numerous carved reliefs of related presentations to pharaohs and gods in a sacred location termed the House of Gold. The wall inscriptions describe the substance being 'the gold of reward' and a 'giver of life', but it was also classified as a 'precious stone'.

Alexandrian hermetic documents describe the magical Paradise Stone that was heavier than the gold from which it was made, and yet could be lighter than a feather. Alchemists and chemists of the Middle Ages and Renaissance times, such as Flamel and Philalethes, wrote about the Philosophers' Stone, which they said was made from gold, but had the appearance of a very fine powder. The Elizabethan magus John Dee recorded the exotic powder of projection, and the Royal Society philosopher, Robert Boyle, commented on its strange anti-gravitational behaviour (*see* chapter 4).

Before the age of King Solomon, Moses was said to have burned the Golden Calf and transposed it into a powder which he mixed with water and fed to the Israelites. As we have seen, this Exodus story is bound up with a parallel white substance called *manna*, which Moses told the Israelites was 'bread', and yet *Manna* was the title of the alchemical treatise that Isaac Newton found so intriguing 3,000 years later (*see* page 146). Paramount in all this, the recurring graphic symbol was always the ancient glyph for Light – a point within a circle ⊙ – just as prevails in the masonic tradition. It is referred to as 'the centre' (the eye), and is said to be where the greatest of all secrets is held. This was alluded to in the *Theater of Fine Devices* emblem of the man in the centre of the Chartres labyrinth (*see* page 260). The symbol was so poignant that Robert Fludd even made his own drawing, showing the compasses (one of the Great Lights of Freemasonry) delineating the ultimate Great Light of the Lost Secret.

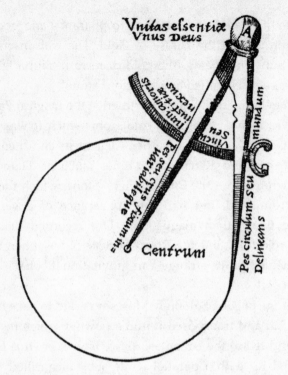

Robert Fludd's 16th-century drawing of the Great Light

The Ark of the Covenant

Of all the venerated treasures of the ancient Israelites, the most revered was the Ark of the Covenant. This 4-ft coffer was made for Moses from gold plate, with a solid gold lid and cherubs, by Bezaleel at the mountain temple in Sinai. It was transported hundreds of miles to Jerusalem, where the Temple of King Solomon was built specifically to house it in the Holy of Holies. Meanwhile, en route with Joshua and the Israelites, the Ark played a part in a number of battles, when it was said to have awesome powers of destruction, most notably when bringing down the walls of Jericho. With the Ark at the head of his army,[19] Joshua advised all but its Levite bearers to stay at least 1,000 yards distant (Joshua 3:3–4).

The Old Testament names some of those whom the Ark killed when they approached it inadvertently without wearing the appropriate clothes. These included Aaron's sons, Nadab and Abihu, who were speared by the fire which leapt from the Ark (Leviticus 10:1–2), while Uzzah the carter was struck dead the moment he touched it (1 Chronicles 13:10–11). On another occasion, an accident caused the Ark to blaze its fire in their own midst, killing some of the Israelites (Numbers 11:1). Soon afterwards, the importance of the Ark in battle becomes clear when, having left it at a base camp, a company of Israelites was routed by Amalekite warriors (Numbers 14:44–45).

The Ark's story is continued throughout the balance of the Old Testament, and its presence is related to all the succeeding Kings of Judah until 586 BC. King Hezekiah (12th lineal descendant of Solomon) was said to have prayed before the Ark (2 Kings 19:15). In the subsequent reigns of Kings Manasseh and Amon, the Ark was retained in a Levite sanctuary. Later, when recounting the reign of Hezekiah's great-grandson, King Josiah of Judah, 2 Chronicles 35:3 relates how, more than 360 years after Solomon built the temple, Josiah decided that the Ark should be returned to its proper abode. '[He] said unto the Levites that taught all Israel, which were holy unto the Lord, Put the holy ark in the house which Solomon the son of David king of Israel did build; it shall not be a burden upon your shoulders.' Subsequently, it was hidden by the high priest Hilkiah and his son Jeremiah at the time of Nebuchadnezzar's invasion and destruction of the Temple.[20]

Together with all this, it must be remembered that the Ark of the Covenant is the masonic crest emblem of the arms of the United Grand Lodge of England. It is the paramount device of the masonic secret, and is of particular relevance to Royal Arch Freemasonry – the add-on Chapter of the 3rd degree. More correctly, the Royal Arch should be a part of the 3rd degree, if not actually constituting the degree itself, instead of the death and burial of Hiram Abiff.

In chapter 11 we looked at certain aspects of the linguistic root of the Greek word ark, with its equivalent being the Latin arca (a box or chest). Returning to this etymology, it is possible to see that in

The Royal Arch – by Laurence Dermott, 1783

France *arca* became *arche*. This moved into English use in the early Middle Ages, and William Caxton's 1483 printing of *The Golden Legend* by Jacapo de Voragine refers to the Ark of the Covenant as the 'Arche of the Testaments'. Subsequently, the word *arche* became *arch*, and then *arc*, which is the proper English form of *ark* today.[21] In 1783, Laurence Dermott, Secretary of the Antient Grand Lodge of England (the Antients prior to their amalgamation with the Moderns), drew up his Royal Arch representation, in which the Ark was the central focus of the imagery.

In biblical terms, the power of the Ark was said to be the Ark-light which emanated from between the golden cherubim, and sent out spears like bolts of lightning. This was dignified as being the ultimate manifestation of God's 'presence'. In fact, the Bible states that 'God is Light'.[22] Also (*see* chapter 13), the 'bread' of the white powder gold was itself called the 'bread of the presence'.[23]

The description of 'fire', with which Moses was said to have burned the Golden Calf is seemingly ambiguous since centuries of scholars have debated how the burning of gold could possibly create a powder. We now know that 'ark' (*arca*) – a storage box – is linguistically synonymous with 'arc' (*arcus*) – a bow-shape as manifested in electronic arcing. It is from this combination of storage and energy production that arc lamps were developed from 1822 by the British chemist Sir Humphrey Davy. His use of positive and negative poles replicated the action of the biblical cherubim, with the ultimate power of the light being 'at the centre' of the arc. By 1910, it was announced that some 20,000 arcs had been installed in British cities and, some 3,500 years after the time of Moses, sparking light-giving devices were once again being called 'arcs'.

The construction of the Ark, as given in Exodus 37:1–9, is precisely that of a modern electrical capacitor, and would have been capable of drawing enough energy into storage from the atmosphere to produce many tens of thousands of volts. Exodus 37:1–2 explains: 'And Bezaleel made the ark of shittim wood ... and he overlaid it with pure gold within and without.' Here, then, are the necessary components: two plate-layers of gold (an excellent electrical conductor), sandwiching a non-conductive dielectric insulator of acacia wood. Exodus 37:7 continues: 'And he made two cherubims of gold', placing one at each end of the mercy seat (the box top). These were the uppermost outer electrodes, needing only for each pole to be connected to its respective golden plate-layer. Even at low electrical potentials, such a device would become highly charged.

The art of metals' transmutation and the defiance of gravity was the science of light manipulation – the arc which the Master Craftsmen had termed the *camu-lôt* (curved light). It was the root of all things magical and alchemical, and in Britain the courts which practised the art in places such as Colchester, Caerleon and Carlisle were known as the courts of *Camu-lôt* (Camelot).

To finally solve the mystery of the Royal Art, it is necessary to discover how the Therapeutate priests of Tuthmoses, the Great Ones of the House of Gold, Moses, King Solomon and others used high-voltage electrical fire to transform gold into an exotic white powder that became the magical 'stardust' of romantic legend. To understand the Lost Secret, we need to know how this powder was medically beneficial, and how it had the power to defy gravity with its weight-changing structure.

20

Discovering the Secret

Hell Fire!

In pride of place in the Royal Arch room at the George Washington Masonic National Memorial in Alexandria, Virginia, is an impressive reproduction of the Ark of the Covenant (*see* plate 36). Set within a limestone arch, it is not dissimilar to the Laurence Dermott portrayal (*see* page 330). This sets the scene for the link between America's Founding Fathers and what was termed their 'Old Custom' of Scots and Irish Freemasonry (as distinct from the new styles that were introduced by the United Grand Lodge of England and the *Scottish Rite* of Chevalier Ramsay). The key figure in this was Benjamin Franklin, whose St John Lodge in Philadelphia was operative from 1730, long before the Royal Arch ritual was embraced by the mainstream of English workings.

Originally a Philadelphia printer, Franklin became America's Ambassador to France in 1776, and had previously been inducted as a Fellow of London's Royal Society on 24 November 1757. This followed his extraordinary work with lightning rods and electricity.[1] Having distinguished between negative and positive currents, while determining that lightning was itself a form of electrical energy, Benjamin Franklin was in the best position to understand the nature of arkite (arcane) technology. Indeed, it was for this reason that he attracted widespread interest in France, where he was a regular attendee of the Académie Française[2] and a welcome guest of the Royal Court (*see* plate 38). In England he became involved with the Royal Society's offshoot lodge at High Wycombe, the Knights of St Francis of Medmenham Abbey, commonly known as the Hell Fire Club. Becoming a close colleague of the founder, Sir Francis Dashwood (*see* plate 27), Franklin was an active member for five years from 1757.[3]

The original Hell Fire Club had been in St James's, London, and was run by Philip, Duke of Wharton, before he became Grand Master of the Grand Lodge of England. Being an undercover Jacobite cell, the Hell Fire Club's secret Chapter House operated behind a mask of pseudo depravity, but it was from beyond this contrived veil that Dashwood and Franklin produced their revised *Book of Common Prayer* for the Anglican Church, while others of the group, like the prominent journalist John Wilkes, fought his campaign for public liberty and freedom of the press. Wilkes was applauded by Franklin because of the stand taken by his newspaper, *The North Briton*, in favour of the American cause.[4]

Despite being Britain's Chancellor of the Exchequer from 1761, Francis Dashwood, Lord Despencer, was acquainted in Europe with Prince Charles Edward,[5] who was Head of the Royal House of Stuart when Benjamin Franklin first went to France in 1776. While in the Languedoc region, Franklin became involved with the Rosicrucian fraternity of the *Bonnie Prince* and his mentor, the Count of St Germain, establishing the masonic Order which eventually became formalized as the Commandery of Carcassonne.[6] The records of the Order are now held by the Grand Orient de France.

This would doubtless have led Franklin to become aware of an ancient Rosicrucian philosophy which the Templars had called *Ormus.*[7] As a founder and first secretary of the American Philosophical Society, such matters were of great interest to the emergent scientist, especially since his fellow mason, St Germain, was at the forefront of philosophical education in Paris. As a leading Templar of the ancient and hermetic *Rite of Philalethes*, the Count was subsequently an elected delegate of the Paris Grand Convention of Masons.[8]

TABLEAU
DES OFFICIERS ÉLUS PAR LA R∴ L∴
DES COMMANDEURS DU TEMPLE,
A L'O∴ DE CARCASSONNE,

Pour diriger ſes Travaux depuis le 24ᵉ jour du 4ᵉ mois de l'an de
G∴ L∴ 5785, juſqu'à pareil jour de l'an 5786.

N∴ DE FAMILLE.	QUAL∴ CIVILES.	QUAL∴ MAÇONIQUES.
F∴ Le Docteur Franklin,	Ambaſſadeur des Etats-Unis de l'Amérique,	*Vénérable d'honneur.*
F∴ De Valette,	Conſeiller du Roi, Magiſtrat en la Sénéchauſſée & Siége Préſidial de Carcaſſonne,	*Vénérable.*
F∴ Astoin,	Avocat au Parlement,	*Premier Surveillant.*
F∴ L'Abbé Meric de Rieux,	Prieur de Notre-Dame de Roumanou, Avocat au Parlement,	*Second Surveillant.*
F∴ Nicolas-Alexis Prince de Gallitzin,	. . . .	*Ex-Vénérable d'honneur.*
F∴ Sarran,	Receveur du Canal de Languedoc, au Port de Foucaud,	*Ex-Maître.*
F∴ Cazes,	Avocat au Parlement,	*Orateur.*
F∴ Vidal de Sᵀ-Martial,	Avocat au Parlement,	*Secrétaire.*
F∴ Gourg,	Procureur au Sénéchal & Siége Préſidial de Carcaſſonne,	*Tréſorier.*
F∴ David de Lafajeole,	Conſeiller du Roi, ſon Lieutenant-Particulier au Sénéchal & Siége Préſidial de Carcaſſonne,	*Premier Expert.*
F∴ Rebouilh,	Doĉteur de la Fa	
F∴ David de Lafajeole		

Commanders of the Temple of Carcassonne, 1786,
with Benjamin Franklin's name at the top of the list

Plans were laid at this time to bring notable French Templars such as the Marquis de Lafayette into the American Revolution, and they set up conspiratorial headquarters at one of Count St Germain's workshops – the old Templar preceptory at Bézu in Languedoc. Grand Orient records detail the Count as being President of the Parliament of the Temple. The net result of the establishment was that, in conjunction with Jacobite Royal Society members in London and adherents at the Académie Française, aspects of the strategy for the War of Independence were formulated at Carcassonne, and the French joined the American campaign in 1778.

The Magic of *Ormus*

The scientific art of *Ormus* related to a quintessential form of gold, the anti-gravitational properties of which had been of significant value in the Templars' construction of the *Notre Dame* cathedrals of France. It was used in the manufacture of the brilliant Gothic stained-glass windows which retain their own luminosity. They were designed by Persian philosophers of the school of Omar Khayyãm, who explained that their method of glass production incorporated the *Spiritus Mundi* – the cosmic breath of the universe. When discussing Templar glass in the 16th century, the hermeticist Sancelrien Tourangeau confirmed that it was a product of the Philosophers' Stone, and wrote:

> Our Stone has two more very surprising qualities. The first, with
> regard to the glass, to which it imparts all sorts of interior colours,
> as in the windows of Sainte-Chapelle at Paris and those in thy
> churches of Saint-Gatien and Saint-Martin in the city of Tours.[9]

To manufacture the exotic *Ormus* material (the white 'bread' of the highward fire-stone, which had been made so long before by Moses and Solomon) the Templars required a supply of easily accessible alluvial gold. They had found this at Bézu, where the land was rich in near-surface gold from old mine workings – precisely what they needed for the transmutation process. To gain access to this, the landowner Bertrand de Blanchefort was brought into the Order soon after they returned from Jerusalem, and he was rewarded with the Grand Mastership in 1153.

Fulcanelli referred to hermetic transmutation as the wisdom content of the Golden Fleece. Just a century or so ago, he wrote that 'the fable of the *Golden Fleece* is a cryptic story of the whole hermetic work, which is to produce the Philosophers' Stone',[10] and in more recent times the Swiss analytical psychiatrist Carl Gustav Jung made a similar association in his book *Psychology and Alchemy*.[11] In 1598, a text entitled *Aureum Vellus* (Golden Fleece) was published in Germany by the philosopher Salomon Trismosian.[12] He wrote that, contrary to the romantic notion of the woolly ram's skin of perceived mythology, the historical Fleece was actually a skin in the sense of a vellum. Indeed, the etymology confirms this, with the English word 'fleece' stemming from the Middle High German *vlûs*, which related simply to a sheep's skin. The Golden Fleece, stated Trismosian, was a parchment which contained the secrets of gold and the Philosophers' Stone from 'the kings and sages of the Egyptians, Arabs, Chaldeans, and Assyrians'.

The term *Ormus* was directly related to Ormuzd (Ahura Mazda), the Persian God of Life and Light. It is significant that the rediscovery of the creative process a couple of decades ago resulted in the Philosophers' Stone being classified by modern physicists as *ORMEs* – Orbitally Rearranged Monatomic Elements. The Royal Art is the alchemical process which transposes Transition Group-1 metals into a single atomic state. Rendered as a fine white powder and classified as 'exotic matter', the substance has unique anti-gravitational and superconductive attributes, just as the bygone philosophers had claimed. It is now also known that this extraordinary substance has precisely the qualities attributed to it by the Therapeutate priests of Tuthmoses, and it will resonate with human DNA to stimulate hormonal production, synchronize the left and right hemispheric brain function, and enhance the immune system.

The complete story of this 'powder of projection' is related, from ancient to modern times, in my book *Lost Secrets of the Sacred Ark*. In essence, however, it is manufactured from such noble metals as gold, platinum, iridium, rhodium, palladium, ruthenium and osmium by means of a process which separates the individual atoms from their metallic bonds. The resultant powder is a substance not to be found anywhere on the Periodic Table of Elements, and which no longer analyzes as being a metal of any sort. It becomes a unique form of silica.

In 1989, Dr Hal Puthoff, director of the Institute for Advanced Studies in Austin, Texas, produced an article for the *Physical Review* entitled 'Gravity as a Zero-point Fluctuation Force'.[13] He explained that when physical matter begins to resonate in another dimension outside our own familiar space-time, it loses four-ninths (44 per cent) of its weight. This is precisely what was discovered in respect of *ORMEs* gold during a process of spectroscopic electrical arcing. Initially, it will always weigh just 56 per cent of the gold weight from which it is made. Further heating and cooling will, however, produce exactly the results described by the ancient Alexandrians. The more it is cooled, the heavier it becomes – to the point that it will outweigh its original gold by many hundreds of per cent. The same applies in reverse. When heated, it can reach a state where it defies gravity entirely, weighing less than nothing.[14] At this point the sample will disappear altogether from vision, having completed its extra-dimensional resonance so that it moves entirely into another realm of space-time, but can be retrieved again on cooling.

The white powder of projection is now being researched for industrial use in terms of its fuel-cell capabilities because it is superconductive and can attract, store and distribute high-volume energy. Also, the world of medicine has become fascinated by its future potential to cure immune system deficiencies and cellular breakdown as in AIDS and cancer conditions. The secret of its operation lies in a particular light-wave which exists at the nuclear centre ⊙. It is a slow wave-form light, which resonates precisely with the light frequency of human DNA and constitutes the very Light of Life itself.

In the May 1995 issue of *Scientific American*, the effect of the platinum-group metal ruthenium was discussed in this context. It was pointed out that when single ruthenium atoms are placed at each end of a short strand of DNA, the helix becomes 10,000 times more conductive. It becomes, in effect, a superconductor. For some time, chemists had suspected that the double helix might create a highly conductive path along the axis of the molecule, and here was confirmation of the fact.[15] Similarly, the *Platinum Metals Review*[16] has featured regular articles concerning the use of Transition Group-1 elements in the treatment of cancers. These are caused through the abnormal and uncontrolled division of body cells, but can be made to relax and become corrected.[17]

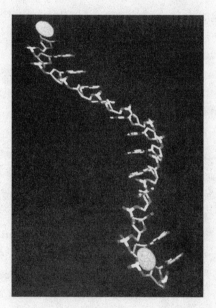

Graphic of single *Ormus* atoms attached to short-strand DNA

During recent years, heightened interest has led to numerous articles in medical and scientific journals, expounding on the puzzling attributes of monatomic (single-atom) gold nanotechnology. And, in May 2003, the Equity Gold Trust's prospectus for the Securities and Exchange Commission in Washington, DC, stated:

> Future applications for gold catalysts are in pollution control, clean energy generation and fuel cell technology. In addition, work is under way for the use of gold in cancer treatment.[18]

Elements of Construction

The *Ormus* material is not just the Philosophers' Stone, it is also the mythological Phoenix which burns to ashes, and from which is born a new enlightenment. At a temperature of 1,160°C it moves through a stage of being a brilliantly clear gold glass which is highly super-conductive – precisely as the *tchām* coverings of the obelisk pyra-midions and pyramid capstones were described.

But what has all this to do with stonemasonry and temple build-ing? Possibly a great deal – although not in straightforward terms of stone-cutting and assembly. It is more to do with the unique technol-ogy of the construction process.

Following the destruction of King Solomon's original Temple, another was built on the same site by Prince Zerubbabel after the Israelites' Babylonian captivity. This second Temple was subse-quently enlarged by the Hasmonaean rulers of Jerusalem in the 2nd century BC, and was then considerably extended a century or more later by King Herod the Great. It was, at that time, the largest man-made building complex in the classical world.[19] Herod's final construction occupied a space of some 144,000 sq m, compared with 30,000 for the Acropolis in Athens.[20] It had an outer wall that was 16 ft thick (nearly 4.9 m) and many of its stones weighed between 50 and 100 tons apiece. In his awestruck description of the edifice when writing in the 1st century AD, Flavius Josephus used such words as 'incredible', 'immense' and 'amazing'.[21] In the wall structure that remains today, there are still massive corner-stones weighing over 80 tons each and over 100 ft (30 m) above ground level.[22] The question that arises is: How did the masons lift them into position?

Similarly, the architecture of the *Notre Dame* cathedrals of France – those majestic Gothic Templar edifices built by the Children of Solomon – was considered impossible, phenomenal, and still baffles architects today. The pointed ogives reach incredible heights, span-ning logically insurmountable space, with flying buttresses and thinly ribbed vaulting. Everything pulls upwards and, despite the thousands of tons of richly decorated stone, the overall impression is one of magical weightlessness.

In addition, there are the most ancient of all massive structures: the Giza pyramids of Egypt. Were the massive stone blocks raised to great heights with such accuracy by hundreds of thousands of slaves using nothing but ropes and ramps over an undefined period of time, as is the common speculation? As unsuccessful latter-day attempts to replicate that process have proven, they clearly were not. To construct an inclined plane to the top of the Great Pyramid at a gradient of 1:10 would have required a ramp of 4,800 ft (c. 1,460 m) in length, with a volume three times greater than that of the pyramid itself.

The three pyramids of Giza are assigned as the pharaonic tombs of Khufu, Khafre, and Menkaure, yet for all the investigation of their known internal and subterranean chambers and passages, no bodily remains have been found in these monuments, nor have the bodies of these Old Kingdom pharaohs been found anywhere else. In the secret repository of the King's Chamber within the Great Pyramid, age-old tradition relates that the builders had placed 'instruments of iron, and arms which rust not, and glass which might be bended and yet not broken, and strange spells'.[23] But what did the first explorers of the 9th-century Caliph Al-Ma'mun find, having tunnelled their way into the sealed chamber? The only furniture was a lidless, hollowed granite coffer,[24] containing not a body, but a layer of a mysterious white powdery substance. This was determined to be grains of feldspar and mica,[25] which are both minerals of the aluminium silicate group. During the course of the recent white powder research, aluminium and silica were two of the constituent elements revealed by conventional analysis of a granular sample known to be a 100 per cent platinum-group compound.

In reality, the pyramid building process might have been far more straightforward than has been imagined, and a good deal now points to the possibility that such constructions were aided by the technology of the superconductive fire-stone. This would certainly account for the large volume of its manufacture at the Mount Serâbît temple of Hathor in Sinai. In fact, the very word 'pyramid' derives from the

Greek *pyr*, which means 'fire' (whence *pyre* and *pyro*), denoting that the pyramids were, in one way or another, 'fire-begotten'.[26]

Following initial experiments during the 1980s, further tests have revealed that since monatomic elements are capable, under thermo-gravimetric procedures, of falling to zero weight, they act in opposition to all the laws of gravity. The point has been made that because gravity determines space-time, then elements which can defy gravity are capable of bending space-time.[27] But there is rather more to monatomic elements than that. In addition to weighing less than nothing, the laboratory pan in which such experiments are conducted can also be caused to weigh less than nothing. Thus, the powder is capable of transposing its own weightlessness to its host, which might be a pan – or might very well be an enormous block of stone, especially since some stones contain their own monatomic elements. A fact worth considering is that, apart from being called *Ormus* and 'highward fire-stone', this magical powder of projection was also called *shem-an-na*, abbreviated in biblical lore to *manna* (*see* page 229). Isaac Newton was particularly fascinated by the alchemical treatise, *Manna*, and it was he who discovered and expounded the *Law of Gravity*.

The Lord of Light

Although attached as a Chapter to the 3rd degree of the Craft, Royal Arch Freemasonry emerged from a very different culture, which had nothing to do with Hiramic ritual.[28] Royal Arch members are styled Companions rather than Brethren,[29] and its tenets and symbols have a positive alchemical aspect which is more akin to Rosicrucian metaphysical philosophy. One of its key differences is that, instead of being concerned with lifting a dead Master from an ignominious grave, it has a distinct crypt legend as its theme. It is partially rooted in Old Testament lore, but also has a parallel origin from Templar Europe in much later times, with elements of a tradition concerning knights of the crusading era who discovered a secret vault in Jerusalem.

Documents pre-dating the 1723 English *Constitutions* specify no less than 23 times that the Royal Arch is about the cultivation of a *Royal Art* – each time written in capitals or italics.[30] Also from the early ritual comes the question: 'Whence comes the pattern of an arch?', to which the correct ceremonial answer is 'From a rainbow'.[31] This is perfectly in keeping with the 'curved light' emblem of the alchemical House of Camu-lôt (*see* page 331). It can also be seen in plate 29 as a prominent design feature of Mozart's 18th-century lodge in Vienna.

One of the symbolic words in Royal Arch ritual, said to have been discovered in a First Temple vault when the foundation was being prepared for Zerubbabel's second Temple, is *Jah-Bul-On*. Engraved on a gold plate, it is reckoned to be a combination of words, meaning 'I am the Lord, Father of All' – sometimes lengthened to 'I am and shall be; Lord in Heaven; Father of All'.[32] Whatever the case, *Jah-Bul-On* relates to the Great Architect of Freemasonry – *Jah* as in Psalm 68:4 ('I am'),[33] *Bul* (Canaanite: 'Lord'), and *On* (House of the Sun),[34] which translates to 'I am/the Lord/On'. However, the term *On* (as mentioned in Genesis 41:45 in relation to Heliopolis) was specifically related to Light. A more accurate translation of *Jah-Bul-On* would therefore be, 'I am the Lord of Light.'

With Light the predominant requirement in its greater and lesser forms throughout all masonic ritual, there are indeed some key pointers to old secrets within the Royal Arch ceremony. The ceremony arrived in 18th-century England from Ireland and Scotland as a remnant of a more philosophical branch of Freemasonry, which had otherwise been exiled. Since speculative Masonry of the original Scottish style evolved directly from a Templar legacy in the Gaelic realms, it is clearly the case that its importance was a Templar importance, and its secrets were Templar secrets. Undoubtedly, the Jerusalem Temple was of great significance to the early Knights Templars, but not because it was Solomon's project, nor because Hiram Abiff was murdered there. It was important because of what they unearthed at the Jerusalem site and brought back to the West in 1127 (*see* page 105).

Rather than referring to Hiram Abiff's lodge at Solomon's Temple (as given in the 3rd degree), the Royal Arch ritual points to an earlier event. In this instance, it is related that the First or Holy Lodge was held 'at the foot of Mount Horeb in the wilderness of Sinai', with Moses, Aholiab (son of Aaron), and Bezaleel presiding.

Also engraved on the golden plate were two integrated geometric shapes: a triangle within a circle. Graphically, these are depicted as a pair of concentric figures in the surround of a square – essentially three shapes in all: a circle, a square and a triangle. The ritual relates that the secret of this is 'more precious than rubies, and all the things thou canst desire are not to be compared with her ... She is a tree of life to them that lay hold upon her ...' (Proverbs 3:15–18.)

In chapter 5 we looked at the hermetic work known as the *Rosarium Philosophorum*, (The Rosary of the Philosophers) published in 1550 within the alchemical volume *De Alchemia opuscula complura veterum philosophorum*.[35] In respect of the Philosophers' Stone, it states that its emblem is drawn by means of a circle, a square and a triangle. The graphic symbol of the Philosophers' Stone (*see* page 69), as determined by the *Rosarium Philosophorum*, is therefore similar to the Royal Arch graphic discovered in the Jerusalem Temple vault. All things considered, it seems likely that Royal Arch ritual is a legacy from the 12th-century Templar excavations in Jerusalem, although modern ritual links the vault discovery to masons at the time of Zerubbabel's Second Temple (*c.* 536–20 BC).

While the Ark of the Covenant was itself a prerequisite for manufacturing the sacred Stone of the white powder gold in the days of Moses and Solomon, it was also a storage receptacle for the substance, and the Bible tells of 'the ark of the covenant overlaid round about with gold, wherein was the golden pot that had the manna'.[36] Given the superconductive attributes of *Ormus*, the Ark would itself have become more than a powerful capacitor; it would have been a generative superconductor. Consequently, there is no reason to doubt any of the biblical statements concerning the Ark's ability to levitate and emit violently destructive forces, whether as straightforward light beams or as harmful rays.

Ark of Gold

Once again (as with the pyramid building potential of *Ormus*) we find ourselves in the realm of phenomenal levitation. Numbers 10:33–36 states: 'As they travelled, the Ark was sent on before them.' There are many other references to the Ark levitating and moving of its own accord,[37] while the *Freemasons' Book of the Royal Arch* states that, when in the Holy of Holies of the Temple in Jerusalem, the Ark remained out of contact with the earth – hovering three-fingers' distance above the ground.[38] Strange as this might seem, basic calculations show that the common pictorial image of four Levites carrying the Ark suspended on a couple of poles is a physical impossibility (*see* plate 24).

The mercy seat (lid) of the Ark of the Covenant is given in the description of Exodus 37:1–9 as covering the whole coffer, from corner to corner within the perimeter crown. At the lowest estimate of cubit conversion it was 45 in long and 27 in wide (*c.* 113 x 68 cm).[39] To avoid sagging beneath the two golden cherubs, it would need to have been relatively thick, and it was said to have been of pure gold (24 carat).[40] Jewish tradition relates that the mercy seat was a palm-span in depth,[41] which is recorded at 3.5 in (*c.* 8.25 cm). This would seem about right to support the soft metal slab over an empty space on a rigid box-frame, but it is worth getting this volume of gold into a physical perspective.

The weight of gold is expressed in troy ounces, with a troy ounce equivalent to 1.097 *avoirdupois* ounces (*c.* 31.10 gm). A cube of gold with 11.7 mm edges weighs 1 troy ounce, and the Ark lid contained around 39,581 such cubes. Its total weight was therefore around 2,714 lb (1,231 kg). This is an astonishing amount of gold, with a current market value of about US \$10.5 million.

The World Gold Council advises that 24-carat gold has a specific density of 19.32 gm/cm^3. So, by applying this for a more precise calculation, a marginally lower weight of 2,700 lb (*c.* 1,224 kg) is ascertained.[42] Hence, the Ark lid weighed over a ton, notwithstanding the cherubim or the coffer itself, which was double-plated inside and out with gold.[43] Since the Ark was said to have been lifted by wooden shafts onto its transport by four men, it would need to have been far lighter than this unless levitational powers were employed.

The Levitical Solution

Levitation is the raising and suspension of a material substance in defiance of gravity. Feats of natural levitation are difficult to comprehend because material objects are, of course, subject to the downward thrust of gravity. Nevertheless, this thrust can be defied by an opposing force which is seemingly of no comparative consequence. All magnets, no matter how small, can lift metallic objects with a greater force than the Earth's entire gravitational thrust can muster in opposition. Notwithstanding this, the magnet would itself drop to the ground if let go. Hence it is the motive energy applied to an object, rather than the object itself, which is crucial to levitation.

The word 'levitate' stems immediately from the Latin *levis*, meaning 'light' in terms of gravitational attraction. The opposite word is *gravis*, meaning 'heavy'. Similarly related to the raising of weight is the English verb 'to lever', which also derives from the same *levis* root. A mechanical device that grips heavy stones for lifting is called a 'lewis' – once again this is rooted in the Latin *levis*.[44] The 'lewis' is a feature of some masonic workings, and the related proper name, Lewis, is given symbolically to the son of a mason (between the ages of 18 and 21) who is in waiting to become an Entered Apprentice. The movement towards Master Mason status is called 'raising', and this is symbolized by the raising of the body of Hiram Abiff. Indeed, the whole masonic process is based on an upward movement towards the Light, with Jacob's ladder and the winding staircase being the Hiramic equivalents of the 1st and 2nd degrees.

In biblical lore, an equivalent name to Lewis is Levi, which stems in Hebrew from *lewî*, which signifies 'gravitating towards'. The Latin parallel is *levitas*, for which the immediate and familiar synonym is *levite*. The Levites were said in the Old Testament to be the male descendants of Levi, who were granted holy status by Moses along with the priestly sons of Aaron – but the Levites were not necessarily priests, although they were considered priestly. On numerous occasions, Flavius Josephus refers in his *Antiquities of the Jews* to 'the priests *and* the levites'.[45] The precise status of the Levites is difficult to assess, but the book of Numbers 18:2, 4 describes how they were selected to join the priests of Aaron. Their function is precisely given, however, in that it was their duty to keep charge of the Tabernacle and its accoutrements including the Ark of the Covenant.[46] The *Lutterworth Dictionary of the Bible* explains that Levites were the equivalent of a 'trade guild', with a particular know-how and special skills.[47]

In all instances, it is the Levites who are the guardians and bearers of the Ark. Their particular qualification was in knowing how to perform these functions, and in these respects certain Levites were indeed classified as priests.[48] Deuteronomy 31:25, Joshua 3:3, 3:6 and 8:33 each relate to the Levites 'bearing' or 'taking up' the Ark. They were in charge of its *levis* (raising), and were thus its levitators. The terms *levis*, Levite and 'levitate' are synonymous, and are all rooted in the science of low gravitational weight. Since the Ark was far too heavy to be lifted and carried by ordinary means, they had (in masonic terms) to become its Lewis. For this task, special clothing was worn and the apron of Freemasonry (*see* page 122) was derived from the protective *ephod* apparel of the Levite guardians of the Ark.[49]

In plate 7 a Lewis tackle is seen on the trestle table of Grand Lodge. This has been enlarged in the figure below, and it symbolizes (in the best terms known to those at the time of Anderson's *Constitutions*) what Freemasonry is all about – the art of 'raising'. But it hardly constitutes an impressive Royal Art in the manner portrayed. The true Royal Art is depicted in the adjacent image – the art of the Levite levitators. This is a modern example of superconductive levitation, and is precisely what can be achieved with the science of *Ormus*. It does not matter whether one uses the terms 'white powder gold', *shem-an-na*, 'highward fire-stone', *manna*, 'powder of projection' or Philosophers' Stone – the resultant attribute is the same. It is a superconductor,

A masonic Lewis and tackle from Anderson's 1784 *Constitutions* (left),
and an example of modern superconductive levitation (right)

which retains no magnetic potential within itself, and which repels all
other magnetic forces. The secret of its operation is a low-frequency
wave of Light which sits at its centre ⊙.

On numerous occasions in the Old Testament, God is said to
reside between the cherubim of the Ark,[50] and was claimed to be present within its lightning. The Ark was classified as a 'dangerous
trust' for the Levites,[51] and philosophical Judaism has always centred its awe on the 'tube of fire' and the 'sparks that issued from
the cherubim', rather than on the magnificence of the box itself.[52] The
Ark of the Covenant was a powerful electronic arcing device – the
provider of the 'fire' with which Moses burned the Golden Calf. As a
storage facility for the *Ormus* powder, it also became a superconductor in its own right, with the ability to ride on its own Meissner
Field. (Excluding all external magnetic fields, this diamagnetic effect
was named after the German physicist Walter Meissner, who published the discovery in 1933.)

The original lost secret of Freemasonry – or at least one of them –
appears to be the very secret that facilitated the construction of the
Giza pyramids and the building of the Jerusalem Temple. It was a
levitical technology from the earliest of times, and one which is only
now being rediscovered by modern science. Although little to do
with medieval trade guilds outside those with immediate Templar

connections in France, it was wholly connected with the building of stone edifices that would have been impossible by any other means. The technique was one of superconductive levitation, and the route to it – as was well known to Robert Boyle, Christopher Wren, Isaac Newton and all those who strove to unravel its mystery – was the very substance that became the Holy Grail of their scientific pursuit. It was the time-honoured *Mat-benu* (the Light of the Stone) of the Mason Word, combined with the extraordinary properties of Orbitally Rearranged Monatomic Elements, once known to all as the Philosophers' Stone.

Despite all the bewildering and seemingly naive rituals of modern Freemasonry, its physical aspect has been preserved in the terminology of its definition: The Craft, described by the *Oxford English Dictionary* as 'a skill in a practical art'. The skills of the Master Craftsmen on which the philosophy was founded were switched in emphasis from the practical to the personal, and became so veiled by confusing allegory that the original purpose was lost and forgotten. This is not to say that the benevolent ideals of today's fraternity are anything less than commendable, but they are not what Freemasonry was concerned with before the 18th century.

No matter what route one takes in following masonic evolution – whether from the Rosicrucian movement, the Knights Templars, the mystery schools of Egypt, or the specialist trade guilds of Europe – skills in practical sciences and natural philosophies are constantly to the fore. If true masonic intent has been pursued in any environment down to the present day, then it has occurred, albeit perhaps unwittingly, precisely where Sir Christopher Wren left it – within the membership of the Royal Society and other such academies around the world.

Through ongoing research in many fields, modern science is now catching up with technologies that were known and practised (even if not fully understood) in the distant past. Such things as were deemed to be 'magic' were condemned by fearful religious establishments, and particularly so during the puritanical 1600s which led to the adepts of alchemy and hermetic philosophy becoming secretive, 'invisible' societies. *Nathan Bailey's Etymological Dictionary* of 1736 discusses magic, however, as follows:

> A useful science, teaching the knowledge and mutual applica-
> tion of active bodies with passive, so as to make many excellent
> discoveries, called natural philosophy.

The natural philosophical secrets of Freemasonry were lost when the magic of its enterprise was subsumed by a strategically con- trived fear of the unknown, when the quest for knowledge was forsaken by those who held the reins of control. But now the magic has returned, emerging from the shadow of Solomon, and with a scientific awareness of nuclear states, superstrings, nanotechnol- ogy and parallel dimensions, the Light is being pursued towards a proverbial vanishing point which is also its point of emanation ⊙. It is here 'at the centre' that the ultimate universal secret waits still to be found.

NOTES AND REFERENCES

Chapter 1

1 New York was previously called New Amsterdam until James Stuart wrested it from the Dutch in 1664.
2 Sir Charles Petrie, *The Stuarts*, Eyre and Spottiswoode, London, 1937, ch 8, p 336.
3 The 1647 *Declaration for Liberty of Conscience* is cited in full in HRH Prince Michael of Albany, *The Forgotten Monarchy of Scotland*, Element Books, Shaftesbury, 1988, and Chrysalis Vega, London, 2002, Appendix II, pp 348–50.
4 *Ibid*, ch 10, pp 147–48.
5 An account of this sequence of events is given in Marquis de Ruvigny et Raineval, *The Jacobite Peerage, Baronetage, Knightage and Grants Of Honour* (1921), facsimile reprint Charles Skilton, London, 1974, Appendix II.
6 Two opposing political groups (parties) were operative at Westminster, and they were each defined by a nickname foisted upon them by the other. They were the *Whigs* (rustlers) and the *Tories* (thieves). The latter were the inheritors of the Stuart Royalist position, and the Whigs were essentially those of the wealthy land-owning aristocracy.
7 *Nineteenth Century Review*, London, September 1897.
8 Details of the Vatican discovery and the papal intrigue behind the Orange invasion were revealed by the Italian historical journalists, Rita Monaldi and Francesco Sorti.
9 Genesis 28:12.
10 W Kirk MacNulty, *Freemasonry*, Thames & Hudson, London, 2003, p 23.
11 Michael White, *Isaac Newton, the Last Sorcerer*, Fourth Estate, London, 1997, ch 7, p 159.
12 The details and dimensions of Solomon's Temple are given in the Old Testament books, 1 Kings 6–7 and 2 Chronicles 3–4.
13 M White, *Isaac Newton, the Last Sorcerer*, ch 7, p 159.

Chapter 2

1 John Hamill, *The Craft*, Crucible, London, 1986, ch 2, pp 27–8.
2 *Oxford Compact English Dictionary* (Oxford Word Library: OWL Micrographic), Oxford University Press, Oxford, 1971 – Freemason.
3 David Stevenson, *The Origins of Freemasonry*, Cambridge University Press, Cambridge, 1988, Intro, p 1.
4 The *Regius* MS is No 17, A1 in the British Museum Register. It is also known as the *Halliwell Manuscript*, and is referred to in the Royal Library catalogue as *Constitutiones Artis Gemetrie Secundum Euclidem*.
5 The *Matthew Cooke* MS is listed as Additional MS 23/198.
6 Flavius Josephus, *Antiquities of the Jews* (trans, William Whiston), Milner & Sowerby, London, 1870, bk I, ch 2:3.

7   James Hastings (ed), *Dictionary of the Bible*, T & T Clark, Edinburgh, 1909 –
    Pillars.
8   Manly P Hall, *The Secret Teachings of All Ages*, Philosophical Research Society,
    Los Angeles, CA, 1989, p CLXXIII.
9   *The Catholic Encyclopedia*, Robert Appleton, New York, 1910, vol 1 – The
    Seven Liberal Arts.
10 *Ibid*, vol XII – Rabanus Maurus.
11 Laurence Gardner, *The Magdalene Legacy*, Thorsons–Element/HarperCollins,
    London, 2005, *passim*.
12 Geoffrey Keynes, 'Newton the Man' in *The Royal Society Newton Tercentennary
    Celebrations*, Cambridge University Press, Cambridge, 1947, p 27.
13 J Hamill, *The Craft*, ch 2, p 40.
14 Gordon Donaldson and RS Morpeth, *A Dictionary of Scottish History*, John
    Donald, Edinburgh, 1977 – Anne.
15 J Hamill, *The Craft*, ch 1, p 16.
16 Ezekiel 1:10.
17 A good overview of the Antients and Moderns is given in Bernard E Jones,
    Freemasons' Book of the Royal Arch, Harrap, London, 1957, chs 4 and 5, pp 52–68.
18 D Stevenson, *The Origins of Freemasonry*, ch 6, p 144.
19 Michael Howard, *The Occult Conspiracy*, Rider, London, 1989, ch 1, p 16.
20 HL Haywood, 'Freemasonry and the Comacine Masters – Part VI' in *The
    Builder*, National Masonic Research Society, October 1923, vol IX, no 10.

Chapter 3

1   Robert Lomas, *Invisible College*, Headline, London, 2002, ch 5, p 85.
2   J Hamill, *The Craft*, ch 2, pp 30–1.
3   CH Josten, *Elias Ashmole*, Ashmolean Museum and the Museum of the
    History of Science, Oxford, 1985, p 3.
4   D Stevenson, *The Origins of Freemasonry*, ch 5, pp 86–7.
5   Barbara J Shapiro, *John Wilkins 1614–1672*, University of California Press,
    Berkeley, CA, 1969, ch 4, pp 113–14.
6   Frances A Yates, *The Rosicrucian Enlightenment*, Paladin, St Albans, 1975, ch
    13, p 223.
7   D Stevenson, *The Origins of Freemasonry*, ch 5, p 102.
8   The two key works by Eirenaeus Philalethes are: *Introitus apertus ad occulusum
    regis palatium: Open entrance to the closed palace of the King – Secrets Revealed*,
    Musaeum Hermeticum, Amsterdam, 1667; and *Tres tractatus de metallorum
    transmutatione – Brief Guide to the Celestial Ruby*, Musaeum Hermeticum,
    Amsterdam, 1668.
9   Roger Sherman Loomis, *The Grail: From Celtic Myth to Christian Symbolism*,
    University of Wales Press, Cardiff, 1963, ch 13, pp 212–13.
10 Richard Chartres and David Vermont, *A Brief History of Gresham College*,
    Gresham College, 1997, p 7.
11 FA Yates, *The Rosicrucian Enlightenment*, ch 13, p 223.

12 Benjamin Woolley, *The Queen's Conjuror*, HarperCollins, London, 2001, Epilogue, p 325.

13 HRH Prince Michael of Albany, *The Forgotten Monarchy of Scotland*, ch 5, p 65. *See also* Keith B Jackson, *Beyond the Craft*, Lewis Masonic, London, 1980, p. 61.

14 A facsimile edition of Thomas Sprat, *History of the Royal Society*, was published by Routledge, London, 1959.

Chapter 4

1 'Nicholas Stone and the Mystery of the'Acception' by Matthew Scanlan, MA, former assistant curator at the library and museum, Freemasons' Hall, London, in *Freemasonry Today*, Bury St Edmunds, Issue 12, July 2001.

2 Evelyn diary published: Guy de la Bédoyère (ed), *The Diary of John Evelyn*, Boydell Press, Woodbridge, 1995.

3 Tom Griffith (ed), *The Concise Pepys*, Wordsworth, Ware, 1997.

4 Henry W Robinson (ed) *The Diary of Robert Hooke*, Taylor & Francis, London, 1935.

5 Books concerning individual members of the early Royal Society are numerous. The most comprehensive biography concerning Robert Hooke (outside his own diary) is Stephen Inwood, *The Man Who Knew Too Much*, Macmillan, London, 2002.

6 M White, *Isaac Newton, the Last Sorcerer*, ch 7, pp 138–9.

7 Michael Hunter, *Robert Boyle, Scrupulosity and Science*, Boydell Press, Woodbridge, 2000, ch 5, pp 108–9.

8 B Woolley, *The Queen's Conjuror*, ch 18, pp 190–1.

9 J Hamill, *The Craft*, ch 2, p 30.

10 D Stevenson, *The Origins of Freemasonry*, ch 6, p 137.·

11 Recommended reading concerning the work of John Harrison is Dava Sobel, *Longitude*, Fourth Estate, London, 1995.

12 Richard Nichols, *Robert Hooke and the Royal Society*, Book Guild, Lewes, 1999, ch 5, pp 31–2.

13 *The Diary of Samuel Pepys* (*see* note 3) is the best source of information concerning the plague and fire in London.

14 The London Monument is often credited to Christopher Wren, but Wren's design was for a smooth column of different diameter. *See* Margaret 'Espinasse, *Robert Hooke*, Wm Heinemann, London, 1954, ch 5, pp 96–7.

15 J Hamill, *The Craft*, ch 1, p 17.

16 M White, *Isaac Newton, the Last Sorcerer*, ch 5, p 96.

17 *Ibid*, ch 7, pp 149–50. For an overview of Newton's beliefs, *see* also Frank E Manuel, *The Religion of Isaac Newton*, Clarendon Press, Oxford, 1974; for information concerning his alchemical pursuits, *see* Betty JT Dobbs, *The Foundations of Newton's Alchemy*, Cambridge University Press, Cambridge, 1974.

18 William Stukeley, *Memoirs of Sir Isaac Newton's Life* (ed, A Hastings White), Taylor & Francis, London, 1936, pp 19–20.

19 D Stevenson, *The Origins of Freemasonry*, ch 9, p 223.

20 The rebuilding of St Paul's, and Christopher Wren's activities between 1666 and 1708 are well described in Adrian Tinniswood, *His Invention So Fertile*, Jonathan Cape, 2001, ch 9, p 164 and ch 17, p 348.

Chapter 5

1 Richard Neve, *The City and Country Purchaser and Builders' Dictionary: or the Compleat Builders' Guide*, Philomath, London, 1703, p 143.

2 Bernard E Jones, *Freemasons' Guide and Compendium*, Harrap, London, 1950, p 152 and notes, pp 147–61.

3 M White, *Isaac Newton, the Last Sorcerer*, ch 6, p 121.

4 This work was originally published as Part II of *De Alchemia Opsuscula complura veterum philosophorum*, Frankfurt, 1550.

5 In Adrian Gilbert, *The New Jerusalem*, Bantam, London, 2002, ch 12, pp 222–3, the author suggests, probably quite correctly, that this female depiction of London alludes to the biblical distress of Jerusalem: 'How does the city sit solitary, that was full of people! how is she become a widow! she that was great among the nations, and princess among the provinces, how is she become tributary!' (Lamentations 1:1).

6 *Ibid*, ch 12, pp 227–37 for good information concerning the inherent geometry of this image and its wider context.

7 Gregory of Tours, *A History of the Franks* (trans, Lewis Thorpe), Penguin, London, 1964, provides a 6th-century contemporary history of the early Merovingian dynasty. For a latter-day perspective, *see* JM Wallace-Hadrill, *The Long Haired Kings*, Methuen, London, 1962. A genealogical chart of the Merovingian Kings is given in Laurence Gardner, *Bloodline of the Holy Grail*, Thorsons–Element/HarperCollins, London, 2002, pp 335–7.

8 J Hamill, *The Craft*, ch 1, pp 20–1.

9 *Ibid*, ch 3, pp 44–5.

10 Donald Nichols, 'The Welsh Jacobites' in *Transactions of the Honourable Society of Cymmrodorion 1948*, London, 1948, p 472.

11 Sir Charles Petrie, *The Jacobite Movement – The Last Phase*, Eyre & Spottiswoode, London, 1950, ch 16, p 416.

12 Fitzroy Maclean, *Bonnie Prince Charlie*, Weidenfeld and Nicolson, London, 1988, ch 19, p 332.

13 Andrew Lang, *Prince Charles Edward Stuart*, Longmans, London, 1903, ch 5, p 336.

14 *Ibid*, ch 4, p 310.

15 G Roberts, *Aspects of Welsh History*, University of Wales Press, Cardiff, 1969, pp 63–8. *See also* F Jones, 'Taliaris' in *Archaeologica Cambrensis*, CXVII, 1968, pp 157–71.

16 JP Jenkins of Clare College, Cambridge, 'Jacobites and Freemasons in Eighteenth-century Wales' in *The Welsh History Review*, University of Wales, Aberystwyth, vol 7, no 4, Dec 1977, p 393.

17 George Rudé, *Wilkes and Liberty*, Oxford University Press, Oxford, 1972, pp 178–9.

18 AG Prys-Jones, *The Story of Carmarthenshire*, Christopher Davies, Swansea, 1959, vol II, ch 32, p 309.
19 Sir John E Lloyd, *A History of Carmarthenshire*, London Carmarthen Society, 1939, p 40.
20 J Hamill, *The Craft*, ch 3, p 46.
21 *Ibid*, ch 3, p 47.
22 Brig AFC Jackson, *Rose Croix*, Lewis Masonic, London, 1980, ch 12, p 111.
23 *Ibid*, ch 12, p 116.
24 HRH Prince Michael of Albany, *The Forgotten Monarchy of Scotland*, ch 17, p 253.
25 J Hamill, *The Craft*, ch 3, pp 49–50.
26 *Burke's Peerage, Baronetage and Knightage*, Burke's Peerage, London, 1970 –The Royal Lineage: Kings of England: George III.
27 Brig AFC Jackson, *Rose Croix*, ch 14, pp 148–9.
28 HRH Prince Michael of Albany, *The Forgotten Monarchy of Scotland*, ch 16, p 243.
29 George S Draffen, *Pour La Foy – A Short History of the Great Priory of Scotland*, 1949, fac. CD-Rom, Grand Lodge of Scotland, Edinburgh, ch 5, p 44.
30 J Hamill, *The Craft*, ch 4, p 65.

Chapter 6

1 J Heron Lepper and Philip Crossle, *History of the Grand Lodge of Free and Accepted Masons of Ireland*, Dublin 1925, p 147, note 1.
2 Burke's Peerage, 1840 edition – Doneralie.
3 The Transactions of the Quatuor Coronati Research Lodge in London, No 2076, United Grand Lodge, vol 8, 1895, pp 16–23, relate that this portrait was then in the collection of Lady Castletown. Attempts have been made to suggest that Elizabeth St Leger (later Mrs Aldworth) could not have been initiated until c. 1734, after the Grand Lodge foundation. The family records, however, show otherwise. In any event, it makes little difference; the important fact is that she was a Freemason even though tradition has it that women were not admitted.
4 D Stevenson, The Origins of Freemasonry, ch 9, p 230, note 34.
5 Michael Baigent and Richard Leigh, *The Temple and the Lodge*, Corgi, London, 1990, ch 11, pp 228–9.
6 Grand Lodge of Ancient Free and Accepted Masons of Scotland website <http://www.grandlodgeofscotland.com>
7 J Hamill, The Craft, ch 3, p 51.
8 Ibid, ch 3, p 54.
9 The Catholic Encyclopedia, vol XIII – Marquess of Ripon.
10 Clement XII, *In Eminenti*, 28 April 1738
Benedict XIV, *Providas*, 18 May 1751
Pius VII, *Ecclesiam*, 13 September 1821
Leo XII, *Quo graviora*, 13 March 1825
Pius VIII, *Traditi*, 21 May 1829

Gregory XVI, *Mirari*, 15 August 1832

Pius IX, *Qui pluribus*, 9 November 1846

Pius IX, *Quibus quantisque malis*, 20 April 1849

Pius IX, *Quanta cura*, 8 December 1864

Pius IX, *Multiplices inter*, 25 September 1865

Pius IX, *Apostolicæ Sedis*, 12 October 1869

Pius IX, *Etsi multa*, 21 November 1873

Leo XIII, *Humanum genus*, 20 April 1884

Leo XIII, *Præclara*, 20 June 1894

Leo XIII, *Etsí nos*, 15 February 1882

Leo XIII, *Ab Apostostolici*, 15 October 1890

Leo XIII, *Annum ingressi*, 18 March 1902

11 The Catholic Encyclopedia, vol IX – Masonry.

12 In American rituals, 'the greatest and best men of all ages' is substituted for 'monarchs'.

13 J Hamill, *The Craft*, ch 3, p 57.

14 Brig ACF Jackson, *Rose Croix*, ch 1, p 5.

15 Melville Henri Massue, 9th Marquis de Ruvigny et Raineval, *The Jacobite Peerage, Baronetage, Knightage and Grants of Honour*, Intro pp ix–xxi.

16 HRH Prince Michael of Albany, *The Forgotten Monarchy of Scotland*, ch 18, p 274.

17 Armoises, Madame Olivier des, *Un rapport sur la mort etrange du 4ieme Comte d'Albanie le Prince Charles Benoix Stuart a Monsieur le Ministre des Affaires Etrangere a Paris*, Paris 1898.

18 MH Massue de Ruvigny, *The Jacobite Peerage, Baronetage, Knightage and Grants of Honour*, Intro, p xxi and note.

19 John Lane, *Masonic Records 1717–1894*, United Grand Lodge of England, London, 1895; and S Pope, *The Development of Freemasonry in England and Wales*, Ars Quatuor Coronatorum, London, 1956, pp 129–31.

20 The foundation stone for the present theatre at Stratford was also laid with masonic honours in 1929 by the Provincial Grand Master, Lord Ampthill, The Freemason, 6 July 1929, pp 13, 16.

21 Ibid, 29 May 1880, pp 238–41, and 21 July 1883, pp 370–2.

22 Ibid, 22 January 1887, pp 38–9.

23 J Hamill, *The Craft*, ch 3, pp 57–8.

24 The symbolic penalties of obligation are those of 'having my throat cut across, my tongue torn out and, with my body, buried in the sands of the sea'.

25 Ibid, ch. 3, p 59.

Chapter 7

1 *The Oxford Concise English Dictionary* (ed, Della Thompson), Oxford University Press, Oxford, 1995 – Tailor.

2 Such phonetically based linguistic variations, as applied to Freemasonry, are more fully discussed in John Robinson, *Born in Blood*, Guild Publishing, London, 1989, ch 17, pp 224–34.

3 J Parnell McCarter, *Reformed Historical Studies on the Enlightenment Era and its Aftermath – a Teacher's Manual*, Historicism Research Foundation, The Puritan's Home School Curriculum, Jenison, MI, 2003, Chap Test 3, p 20 and Summary Test, p 56.

4 Jacques Henry, *Mozart Frère Maçon – la symbolique maçonniquedans l'oeuvre de Mozart*, Éditions Alinea, Aix-en-Provence, 1991.

5 Louis Charpentier, *The Mysteries of Chartres Cathedral*, Research Into Lost Knowledge Organization, and Thorsons, Wellingborough, 1992, ch 18, pp 144–51.

6 J Robinson, *Born in Blood*, ch 17, p 227.

7 King David was married to Maud de Lens, and his sister Mary was married to Eustace III, Count of Boulogne, the brother of Godefroi de Bouillon.

8 HRH Prince Michael of Albany, *The Forgotten Monarchy of Scotland*, ch 3, pp 31–2.

9 JSM Ward, *Freemasonry and the Ancient Gods*, Simpkin Marshall, London, 1926, ch 13, p 300.

10 L Charpentier, *The Mysteries of Chartres Cathedral*, ch 8, p 69.

11 Palestine Exploration Fund, 2 Hinde Mews, Marylebone Lane, London, W1U 2AA.

12 Leen and Kathleen Ritmeyer, *Secrets of Jerusalem's Temple Mount*, Biblical Archaeological Society, Washington DC, 1998, ch 5, p 83.

13 These artifacts are now held by the Scottish Templar archivist, Robert Brydon, at Roslin, near Edinburgh. *See* Christopher Knight and Robert Lomas, *The Hiram Key*, Century, London, 1996, ch 13, p 267.

14 Michael Swanton (trans), *The Anglo Saxon Chronicle*, JM Dent, London, 1997 – Peterborough MS (E) 1128, p 259.

15 The *Latin Rule* is reproduced as a translation in Malcolm Barber and Keith Bate, *The Templars*, Manchester University Press, Manchester, 2002, pp 31–54.

16 This letter is reproduced as a translation in Conrad Greenia, 'In Praise of the New Knighthood' in *Bernard de Clairvaux Treatises*, Cistercian Publications, Kalamazoo, MI, 1977, vol 3, pp 127–45.

17 M Barber and K Bate, *The Templars*, pp 67–73.

18 HRH Prince Michael of Albany, *The Forgotten Monarchy of Scotland*, ch 5, p 61.

19 Brig ACF Jackson, *Rose Croix*, App III, p 250.

20 2 Kings 22:8 and 2 Chronicles 34:15.

21 *The Catholic Encyclopedia*, vol II – Benedict XI; and vol XIV – Toulouse.

22 The word 'heresy' is defined as a belief or practice contrary to the orthodox doctrine, but it actually derives from the Greek *hairesis*, meaning 'choice'. Thus, a charge of heresy was a denial of the right of choice.

23 HRH Prince Michael of Albany, *The Forgotten Monarchy of Scotland*, ch 5, pp 61–2.

24 The excommunication of Scotland as a nation was not repealed until 1323. This followed Robert the Bruce's defeat of Edward II at Bannockburn in 1314 and the drawing up of the Scottish Constitution (the *Declaration of Arbroath*) in 1320. Subsequently, in 1328, the *Treaty of Northampton* confirmed Scotland's independence under King Robert I.

25 The Franco-Scots *Auld Alliance* was one of the longest standing arrangements in the history of Europe, whereby (until 1906) Scots entered France as
French citizens, and vice-versa.

26 JSM Ward, *Freemasonry and the Ancient Gods*, ch 13, p 303.

27 From 1314, Robert's brother, Edward Bruce, was King of Ireland until his
death in 1318.

28 JSM Ward, *Freemasonry and the Ancient Gods*, ch 13, p 300.

29 Jacques de Molay was executed on 18 March 1314.

30 Keith B Jackson, *Beyond the Craft*, p 61.

31 HRH Prince Michael of Albany, *The Forgotten Monarchy of Scotland*, ch 8, pp
125–6.

32 *The Mail on Sunday*, 20 June 1997.

33 RF Gould, *Gould's History of Freemasonry*, Caxton, London, 1933, Intro.

34 L Charpentier, *The Mysteries of Chartres Cathedral*, ch 18, p 145.

35 The *Notre Dame* ground-plan made use of ley lines and Mother Earth locations in which the terrestrial forces were heightened by deep underground
caverns or wells.

36 A dolmen usually comprises two upright stones with a horizontal capstone
across the top, as at Stonehenge. From prehistoric times, dolmens were used
as gigantic resonators (much like sound-boxes used to amplify acoustic
musical instruments) to boost the properties of the Earth's telluric current.

37 Mary Sworder (ed), *Fulcanelli: Master Alchemist: Le Mystère des Cathédrales*,
Brotherhood of Life, Albuquerque, NM, 1986, ch 3, p 42.

Chapter 8

1 *Ars Quatuor Coronatorum*, The Transactions of Quatuor Coronati Lodge No
2076, United Grand Lodge of England, vol 74, 1961, pp 133–7.

2 F Josephus *The Antiquities of the Jews*, bk III, ch VII:5. *See* also 1 Samuel 2:18.

3 J Hastings, *Dictionary of the Bible*, under Dress – item: Apron.

4 Werner Keller, *The Bible as History* (trans, William Neil), Hodder & Stoughton,
London, 1956, p 72.

5 *Ibid* – Brass.

6 F Josephus, *The Antiquities of the Jews*, bk VII, ch III:4.

7 Albert Mackey, *Encyclopedia of Freemasonry* (facsimile 1909 edn), Kessinger,
Kila, MT, 2003.

8 *Baabanim* and *vebagneisim*.

9 This document, dated 14 October 1726, was written by an otherwise
unknown author named Thomas Graham, and entitled *The Whole Institution
of Free Masonry Opened and Proved by the Best of Tradition and still some
Reference to Scripture.*

10 Alex Horne, *King Solomon's Temple in the Masonic Tradition*, Aquarian Press,
London, 1971, ch 14, p 341.

11 As well as relating to 'Marrow on the bone' or 'It stinketh', other interpretations of *Mahabyn* are 'What! the builder?' and the Irish catechism interpretation, 'Matchpin'. *See* D Stevenson, *The Origins of Freemasonry*, ch 6, p 149.

12 For details of these various interpretations, see Manly P Hall, *The Secret Teachings of All Ages*, Philosophical Research Society, Los Angeles, CA, 1989, p LXXVIII–IX, The Hiramic Legend.

13 A Horne, *King Solomon's Temple in the Masonic Tradition*, ch 14, pp 280–345.

14 The *ephod* has a number of mentions in Exodus 9.

15 The Bible gives all its related measurements in cubits – a loose standard based upon a forearm's length from elbow to fingertip. The measurement was therefore a variable, ranging from 18 inches to 22 inches. Within this range, there were differences between Egyptian, Hebrew, and Sumerian cubits. Other variables were Royal cubits, Sacred cubits, and Angelic cubits. For our purposes, the minimum 18-inch cubit has been used throughout (*c.* 46 cm).

16 It has been suggested that the said definition of 'boards' is perhaps a mistranslation for 'frames', but the old technical terms are obscure, so it is difficult to tell which is the more accurate. *See* J Hastings, *Dictionary of the Bible –* Tabernacle 5c.

17 A Horne, *King Solomon's Temple in the Masonic Tradition*, ch 14, p 340.

18 WK MacNulty, *Freemasonry*, p 16.

19 *Ibid*, pp 22–3.

20 *Ibid*, p 28.

Chapter 9

1 The Scottish Parliament consisted of Barons, Burgesses and Nobles, and was therefore called the *Three Estates*.

2 HRH Prince Michael of Albany, *The Forgotten Monarchy of Scotland*, ch 6, p 94.

3 St Anthony was the founder of Christian monasticism in Egypt, AD c. 300.

4 The General Register Office for Scotland is at the New Register House, 3 West Register Street, Edinburgh EH1 3YT.

5 The Library of the Faculty of Advocates of the Scottish Bar (est 1532) is at: Advocates Library, Parliament House, Edinburgh EH1 1RF.

6 The 17th-century seal of the Knights Templars and Canons of St Anthony can be seen at <http://www.graal.co.uk/affiliates.html>.

7 The Royal Society, 6–9 Carlton House Terrace, London SW1 5AG.

8 Thomas Sprat, *History of the Royal Society*, J Allestry and the Royal Society, London 1667.

9 M White, *Isaac Newton, The Last Sorcerer*, ch 7, pp 158–62.

10 Frank E Manuel, *The Religion of Isaac Newton – The Freemantle Lectures 1973*, Clarendon Press, Oxford, 1974, ch 4, pp 93–4.

11 Aspects of Isaac Newton's theories concerning the Temple of Solomon, especially his notion that the Temple was a microcosmic model, are discussed in Betty JT Dobbs, *The Janus Face of Genius: The Role of Alchemy in Newton's Thought*, Cambridge University Press, Cambridge, 1991.

12 MS 33 (SL44/R19) in the Keynes MSS Collection, King's College Library, Cambridge.

13 M White, *Isaac Newton, The Last Sorcerer*, ch 7, p 140.

14 FA Yates, *The Rosicrucian Enlightenment*, ch 9, pp 165–6.

15 *Ibid*, ch 15, p 250.

16 J Hamill, *The Craft*, ch 2, pp 30–1.

17 *See also* Alex Lawrie, *History of Freemasonry*, Longman & Rees, London, 1804.

18 Templars entering this Order today are dressed as pilgrims returning from Compostela, Spain, with the clamshell badges of Santiago [*Sant Iago* = St James] on their hats.

19 D Stevenson, *The Origins of Freemasonry*, Introduction, p 8.

20 *Ibid*, ch 3 p 47.

21 *Ibid*, ch 4, p 59.

22 *Ibid*, ch 5, p 86.

23 The subject of Camillo's Theatre concept is discussed in Frances A Yates, *Theatre of the World*, University of Chicago Press, Chicago, 1969.

24 Frances A Yates, *The Art of Memory*, University of Chicago Press, Chicago, 1966, pp 130–1.

25 Marcus Vitruvius Pollio.

Chapter 10

1 Recommended reading concerning medieval Flemish heraldry and Scotland is Beryl Platts, *Scottish Hazard*, Proctor Press, London, 1985 (part 1), 1990 (part 2).

2 Sir Iain Moncrieffe, *The Highland Clans*, Barrie & Jenkins, London, 1982, p 219. *See also* GWS Barrow, *The Kingdom of the Scots*, Edward Arnold, London, 1973, ch 11, p 318.

3 A genealogical chart of St Clair (Sinclair) heritage from the 7th to the 14th century is given in the 1st edition (only) of Laurence Gardner, *Bloodline of the Holy Grail*, Element Books, Shaftesbury (and Element Inc. USA), 1996, Appendix V, pp 427–31.

4 The 1916 Rhind Lectures of the Society of Antiquaries of Scotland, were published under the auspices of the Royal Celtic Society and the University of Edinburgh as William J Watson, *The History of the Celtic Place Names of Scotland*, William Blackwood, London, 1926.

5 Richard Augustine Hay, *The Genealogie of the Sainteclairs of Rosslyn* (ed, RLD Cooper; trans, J Wade), Grand Lodge of Scotland, Edinburgh, 2002.

6 *Knights Templar and Freemasonry*, Friends of Rosslyn brochure, 1993.

7 Andrew Sinclair, *The Sword and the Grail*, Crown, New York, NY, 1992, chs 9–11, pp 108–50.

8 M Baigent and R Leigh, *The Temple and the Lodge*, ch 8, p 351.

9 Robert Brydon, *Rosslyn and the Western Mystery Tradition*, Rosslyn Chapel Trust, Roslin, 2003, Intro.

10 A photograph of Michelangelo's Moses is included in the plate section of Laurence Gardner, *Genesis of the Grail Kings*, Transworld/Bantam, London, 1999.

11 The word Viking derived from *Wiking* because there was no 'w' or 'u' in the Latin alphabet, only a 'v'. The inherent *Wi* syllable meant 'contentious' or 'warlike'. Thus, the Vikings were *Wi-kings* = Warlike kings. *Oxford Compact English Dictionary* under Vikings and Wi.

12 Hargrave Jennings, *The Rosicrucians – Their Rites and Mysteries*, Routledge, London, 1887, ch 12, p 107.

13 Geza Vermes, *The Complete Dead Sea Scrolls in English*, Penguin, London, 1998, p 85.

14 A photograph of the Melchizedek statue at Chartres is included in the plate section of Laurence Gardner, *The Magdalene Legacy*.

15 R Brydon, 'The Chapel Builders' in *Rosslyn and the Western Mystery Tradition*, Rosslyn Chapel Trust, Roslin, 2003.

16 Philip Coppens, *The Stone Puzzle of Rosslyn Chapel*, Frontier, Enkuizen, NL, 2004, ch 8, p 77.

17 Christopher Knight and Robert Lomas, *The Hiram Key*, Century, London. 1996, ch 15, p 307

18 A Sinclair, *The Sword and the Grail*, ch 7, pp 86–8.

19 Tim Wallace Murphy and Marilyn Hopkins, *Rosslyn*, Element, Shaftesbury, 1999, ch 1, p 17.

20 Henri and HA Frankfort, *Before Philosophy*, Penguin, London, 1951, pp. 240–8.

21 Robert Graves, *The White Goddess*, Faber & Faber, London, 1961, ch 16, pp 286–7.

22 Henri Frankfort, *Kingship and the Gods*, University of Chicago Press, Chicago, 1948, Epilogue, p 343.

23 Sir Lancelot CL Brenton (trans), *The Septuagint*, Samuel Bagster, London, 1851.

24 *The Historic Enigma: Rosslyn Chapel* (Rosslyn Chapel visitor pamphlet), Friends of Rosslyn, Roslin (undated).

25 Sir Iain Moncrieffe, *The Highland Clans*, p.220.

26 A Sinclair, *The Sword and the Grail*, ch 7, pp 77–8.

27 The full sequence of events concerning Columbus, the Drummonds and Sinclairs is given by Ian F Brown in 'The Sinclair/Columbus Connection – The Drummonds of Madeira and Christopher Columbus' in a special issue of *The Sinclair Genealogist*, extracted from the *Glasgow and West of Scotland Family History* spring newsletter, Glasgow, 1993 pp 4–9.

Chapter 11

1 Good images of Emulation boards can presently be seen in the Tracing Boards section of the Grand Lodge of British Columbia web site: http://freemasonry.bcy.ca

2 Andrew Sinclair, *The Secret Scroll*, Birlinn, London, 2002, ch 15, pp 203–5.

3 George William Speth, 'The Kirkwall Scroll' in *Ars Quatuor Coronatorum*, vol 10, Quator Coronati Lodge, London, 1897.

4 Exodus 37:2–15.

5 Exodus 32:2–4.

6 1 Kings 10:10–11.

7 1 Kings 10:14–21.

8 Genesis 14:18. In line with the Last Supper communion of Jesus, Melchizedek presented Abraham with the bread and wine of the covenant.

9 Exodus 16:15.

10 Solomon was the son of King David of Bethlehem. Hebrew: *Beth-le-hem* = House of bread – ie, David of the House of Bread. See J Hastings, *Dictionary of the Bible* – Bethlehem.

11 1 Kings 7:48.

12 *Septuagint* 3 Kings 5:7 and 10:11 confirm that King Huram of Tyre supplied the raw gold from the mines of Ophir, near Sheba, while his requirement in return for this and all his favours was that Solomon should 'give bread to my household'.

13 Matthew 26:26.

14 Hebrews 9:4.

15 Exodus 31:3–4, and 1 Kings 7:14.

16 In discussing Bezaleel and the Ark, particular reference is made to this Egyptian bas-relief in Immanuel Velikovsky, *Ages in Chaos*, Sidgwick & Jackson, London, 1952, ch 4, p 160.

17 KB Jackson, *Beyond the Craft*, pp 13–16.

18 *Ibid*, p 18.

19 In its original form, the Old Testament was written in a Hebrew style consisting only of consonants. In parallel with this, a Greek translation emerged in about 270 BC for the benefit of the growing number of Greek-speaking Hellenist Jews. This became known as the *Septuagint* (from the Latin *septuaginta*: seventy) because 72 scholars were employed in the translation. Some centuries later, a Latin version of the Bible, known as the *Vulgate* (because of its vulgar or common use) was produced around AD 385 by St Jerome for use in the Christian Church (including the New Testament). Then a revised Hebrew Old Testament (on which today's Jewish Bible is based) was introduced by Masoretic scholars in around AD 900. It was, however, the older and more reliable *Septuagint* that was used for translating the King James Authorized English-language edition, issued in 1611.

20 J Hastings, *Dictionary of the Bible* – Ark.

21 This work is correctly entitled *Sa nagba imurur* (He who saw Everything). *See also* Leonard Cottrell, *The Land of Shinar*, Souvenir Press, London, 1965, p 42.

22 Uta-napishtim of Shuruppak reigned about 4000 BC.

23 Alexander Heidel, *The Gilgamesh Epic and Old Testament Parallels*, University of Chicago Press, Chicago, IL, 1949, ch 1, p 15.

24 Peter Lemesurier, *The Great Pyramid Decoded*, Element Books, Shaftesbury, 1977, ch 9, p 261.

25 Rev George H Schodde (trans), *The Book of Jubilees*, EJ Goodrich, Oberlin, OH, 1888.

26 Samuel Noah Kramer, *History Begins at Sumer*, Thames & Hudson, London, 1958, pp 214, 260.

27 A Heidel, *The Gilgamesh Epic and Old Testament Parallels*, ch 2, p 105.

28 *Epic of Gilgamesh*, Tablet XI:19–31.

29 *Atra-hasis Epic*, Tablet fragment IV, column 4.

30 *Ibid*, p 107.

31 Thorkild Jacobsen, *The Treasures of Darkness – A History of Mesopotamian Religion*, Yale University Press, New Haven, CT, 1976, ch 4, p 108.

32 Samuel Noah Kramer, *Sumerian Mythology*, Harper Bros., New York, 1961, ch 2, p 53, and ch 5, p 115, note 53.

33 SN Kramer, *History Begins at Sumer*, pp 164–5.

34 The subjects of Nîn-kharsag, the Flood, and various other aspects of Old Testament History as originally written, are dealt with fully in Laurence Gardner, *Genesis of the Grail Kings*, Transworld/Bantam, London, 1999.

35 'Tapping Crops' Genetic Wealth' in *Scientific American*, August 2004, pp 28–33.

36 The Patrick Foundation, PO Box 72, Cirencester, Gloucestershire, GL7 6YG.

37 The story of Woolley's Iraq expedition for the British Museum and the University of Pennsylvania is told in Sir C Leonard Woolley, *Ur of the Chaldees*, Ernest Benn, London, 1929.

38 EA Speiser (ed), *The Anchor Bible – Genesis*, (translation from Hebrew text), Doubleday, Garden City, NY, 1964, ch 2, p 16.

39 Georges Roux, *Ancient Iraq*, George Allen & Unwin, London, 1964, ch 7, p 95.

40 The *Enûma elish* is named in accordance with its opening words 'When on high'. It was first composed around 3,500 years ago. *See* Alexander Heidel, *The Babylonian Genesis*, University of Chicago Press, Chicago, IL, 1942, ch 1, p 14.

41 *Adâpa Tablet*, Fragment IV.

42 A Heidel, *The Babylonian Genesis*, Appendix, p 152, and p 153 note 23.

43 F Josephus, *Antiquities of the Jews*, bk I, 1:2.

44 Robert Alter (trans), *Genesis*, WW Norton, New York, NY, 1996, ch 3, p 15.

45 SN Kramer, *History Begins at Sumer*, p 210.

Chapter 12

1 J Hastings, *Dictionary of the Bible* – Jachin and Boaz.

2 Peter A Clayton, *Chronicles of the Pharaohs*, Thames and Hudson, London, 1994, p 217.

3 Obelisk stems from the Greek *obeliskos*, meaning a 'spit' – *The Oxford Compact English Dictionary*. They are four-sided, tall thin, tapering monuments with apex pyramidions – ie, shaped like a spit.

4 The Lateran obelisk is 32.18 m (37 m with its base), and was originally 36 m (118 ft). Its weight is 455 tons.

5 The obelisk that would have been the tallest still lies in a trench at Aswan, having been abandoned when fissures became apparent in the stone.

6 The Wimborne monument is just 22 ft (*c.* 6.7 m) and 6 tons. There is also a 6-ft altar obelisk of Amenhotep II in the Oriental Museum at the University of Durham.

7 D Stevenson, *The Origins of Freemasonry*, ch 5, p 79.

8 A good account of Kircher's life and times is given in Paula Finden, *Athanasius Kircher: The Man Who Knew Everything*, Routledge, London, 2003.

9 *The Catholic Encyclopedia*, vol VIII – Athanasius Kircher.

10 This work is available in translation as George Boas (ed) *The Hieroglyphics of Horapollo*, Princeton University Press, Princeton, NJ, 1993.

11 The Rosetta Stone is in the British Museum, London.

12 An ornamental, oval-shaped hieroglyphic inscription denoting a royal name.

13 For details of this event, along with those of other obelisk removals and erections, *see* Burn Dibner, *Moving the Obelisks*, Burndy Library, New York, NY, 1950.

14 M Howard, *The Occult Conspiracy*, ch 1, p 10.

15 Flavius Josephus, *Against Apion*, Milner & Sowerby, London, 1870, I:26–7.

16 F Josephus, *Antiquities of the Jews*, bk II, 10:2.

17 James Henry Breasted, *The Dawn of Consciousness*, Charles Scribner's Sons, New York, NY, 1934, p 350. *See also* Ahmed Osman, *Moses, Pharaoh of Egypt*, Grafton/Collins, London, 1990, ch 6, p 66.

18 Sigmund Freud, *Moses and Monotheism*, Hogarth Press, London, 1939, pp 12–13.

19 Sir WM Flinders Petrie, *Researches in Sinai*, John Murray, London, 1906, ch 14, p 200.

20 The Authorized *Oxford Concordance Bible*, Oxford University Press, Oxford – On.

21 Spencer H Lewis, *The Mystical Life of Jesus*, Ancient and Mystical Order Rosae Crucis, San Jose, CA, 1982, ch 11, pp 191–2.

22 Barbara Thiering, *Jesus the Man*, Transworld/Doubleday, London, 1992, ch 9, pp 51, 55.

23 Flavius Josephus, *Wars of the Jews*, Milner & Sowerby, London, 1870, bk II, VIII:6.

24 Labib Habachi, *The Obelisks of Egypt*, J M Dent, London, 1978. ch 3, p 49.

25 Philip S Callahan, *Paramagnetism*, Acres, Metairie, LA, 1995, ch 7, pp 61–72.

26 Philip S Callahan, *Ancient Mysteries, Modern Visions*, Acres, Austin, TX, 2001, chs 3–4, pp 26–52.

27 An extensive region bordering the Black Sea.

28 Geoffrey Keating, *The History of Ireland*, 1640 – reprinted by Irish Texts Society (trans, David Comyn and Rev PS Dinneen), London 1902–14, vol II, pp 20–1.

29 The name was later corrupted by the 4th-century Eusebius of Caesarea, to Cencheres, and given in the Irish register as Cincris. *See* Clive Carpenter, *The Guinness Book of Kings, Rulers and Statesmen*, Guinness Superlatives, Enfield, 1978, p 68.

30 PA Clayton, *Chronicle of the Pharaohs*, p 120.

31 Sir Ernest A Wallis Budge (trans), *The Book of the Dead*, University Books, New York, NY, 1960, p 201.

32 Geoffrey Keating, *The History of Ireland*, vol II, p 17.

33 *Ibid*, vol I, p 233.

34 In particular, *see* Ahmed Osman, *Stranger in the Valley of Kings*, Souvenir Press, London, 1987. Also his *Moses, Pharaoh of Egypt*.

35 L Habachi, *The Obelisks of Egypt*, ch 3, p 48.

36 Sir Ernest A Wallis Budge, *Cleopatra's Needle and Other Egyptian Obelisks* (1926), rep. Dover Publications, New York, NY, 1990, pp 26–38.

37 Pierre Lacau, 'L'Or dans l'architecture égyptienne' in *Annales du Service des Antiquités de l' Égypte*, Cairo, No 53, 1956, pp 241–7.

38 Raphael Patai, *The Jewish Alchemists*, Princeton University Press, Princeton, NJ, 1994, ch 2, pp 30–40.
39 *Ibid*, ch 11, p 150.
40 Laurence Gardner, *Lost Secrets of the Sacred Ark*, HarperThorsonsElement, London 2003.
41 Alan Gardiner, *Egyptian Grammar*, Griffith Institute, Ashmolean Museum, Oxford, 1957, 24:32.
42 Sir WMF Petrie, *Researches in Sinai*, ch 6, p 72.
43 *Ibid*, ch 6, p 85.
44 Kenneth Anderson Kitchen, *Ramesside Inscriptions*, Basil H Blackwell, Oxford, 1975, p 1.
45 Sir WMF Petrie, *Researches in Sinai*, ch 7, p 101.
46 Jaroslav Cerny (ed), *The Inscriptions of Sinai*, Egypt Exploration Society, London, 1955, vol 2, ch 1, p 9.
47 *Ibid*, vol 2, ch 5, p 119.
48 *Ibid*, vol 2, ch 5, p 205.
49 Ernest A Wallis Budge, *Hieroglyphic Texts from Egyptian Stelae*, British Museum, London, Part 1, 1911, Stela 569. (This series has been continually produced, with Part 12, edited by M L Bierbrier, issued in 1993).
50 Eirenaeus Philalethes, *Introitus apertus ad occulusum regis palatium: Open entrance to the closed palace of the King – Secrets Revealed*, Musaeum Hermeticum, Amsterdam, 1667.
51 Eirenaeus Philalethes, *Tres tractatus de metallorum transmutatione – Brief Guide to the Celestial Ruby*, Musaeum Hermeticum, Amsterdam, 1668.

Chapter 13

1 D Stevenson, *The Origins of Freemasonry*, ch 6, p 127.
2 J Hamill, *The Craft*, ch 2, p 33.
3 *Ibid*, ch 6, p 133.
4 Sir Thomas Browne, *Religio Medici and Other Works* (ed, LC Martin), Clarendon Press, Oxford. 1964, pp 16, 294.
5 Whereas the Egyptians referred to their monarchs as kings, the Greeks introduced the term *pharo* (pharaoh). Its root was in the word *phare*, meaning 'great house'. It is the same word from which the English word fairy derives.
6 Francis Bacon, *The Proficience and Advancement of Learning, Divine and Human*, Printed for Henri Tomes; To the King in London, 1605, bk II, V:1.
7 *Ibid*, bk II, VI:5.
8 'The Mason's Confession' or Dundee Manuscript 1727, in the *Scots Magazine*, vol xvii, Sands, Donaldson, Murray and Cochran, Edinburgh, March 1755, pp 132–7.
9 George V Tudhope, *Bacon Masonry*, University of California Press, Berkeley, 1954, ch 2, p 8.
10 L Habachi, *The Obelisks of Egypt*, ch 1, p 3.
11 *Ibid*, ch 1, p 5.

12 C Knight and R Lomas, *The Hiram Key*, pp 103–6.
13 Richard Carlyon, *A Guide to the Gods*, Heinemann/Quixote, London, 1981, pp 278–9, item: Hu.
14 L Habachi, *The Obelisks of Egypt*, ch 2, p 13.
15 *Ibid*, ch 1, p 5.
16 *Oxford Concise English Dictionary* – Techno and Technology.
17 Kenneth Grant, *The Magical Revival*, Skoob Books, London, 1991, ch 7, p 123.
18 *Complete Oxford English Dictionary* (etymology), items: (a) phoenician, (b) phoenix 1, and (c) phoenix 2.
19 As Annu it was also known as Innu, or Innu Mehret. *See* Sir EAW Budge, *The Book of the Dead*, pp 1, 201. *See also* Graham Hancock, *Fingerprints of the Gods*, William Heinemann, London, 1995, ch 41, p 360.
20 T Jacobsen, *The Treasures of Darkness*, ch 4, p 95.
21 Sir Charles Leonard Woolley, *The Sumerians*, WW Norton, London, 1965, p 29.
22 There are numerous references to this effect in Shimon bar Yochai, *The Zohar* (ed, Rabbi Michael Berg), The Kabbalah Centre, New York, NY, 2003, Intro. pp xxii–lxxvii.
23 *Oxford Concise English Dictionary* – Lucifer.
24 Elaine Pagels, *The Origin of Satan*, Random House, New York, 1995, ch 2, p 48.
25 John Milton, *Paradise Lost*, Jacob Tonson, London, 1730, Book 10, lines 425–6.
26 The invention of the satanic myth is discussed in Laurence Gardner, *Realm of the Ring Lords*, HarperThorsonsElement, London, 2003, ch 13, pp 162–6.
27 MP Hall, *The Secret Teachings of All Ages*, p LXXIX.
28 For example, the confession 'I have not killed' was transcribed to the decree 'Thou shalt not kill'; 'I have not stolen' became 'Thou shalt not steal'; 'I have not told lies' became 'Thou shalt not bear false witness', and so on.
29 JH Breasted, *The Dawn of Consciousness*, p 371.
30 *Ibid*, pp 377–8.
31 Examples of Proverb comparisons with the wisdom writings of Amenemope are given in Laurence Gardner, *Genesis of the Grail Kings*, Transworld/Bantam, 1999, Chart Appendix, p 261.
32 RS Loomis, *The Grail: From Celtic Myth to Christian Symbolism*, ch 13, p 210.
33 A good text in this regard is Wolfram Von Eschenbach, *Parzival* (ed, Hugh D Sacker), Cambridge University Press, Cambridge, 1963.
34 A sister language to the Vedic Sanskrit of India.
35 RS Loomis, *The Grail: From Celtic Myth to Christian Symbolism*, ch 13, pp 212–13.
36 *Septuagint* 1 Kings (1 Samuel) 21:6. The books of 1 Samuel and 1 Kings are the same book in the *Septuagint*, as are 2 Samuel and 2 Kings. Whereas the King James Bible has only two books of Kings, the *Septuagint* has four.
37 F Josephus, *The Antiquities of the Jews*, bk III, 1:6.
38 Before modern science discovered the phenomenon of white-powder gold in the 1980s, the manna which fell to the ground like snow, and which was eaten by the Israelites in Sinai was suggested to be a resinous secretion from the tamarisk tree. Crystalline grains of tamarisk resin were recorded in 1483 by Breitenbach, Dean of Mainz, who confirmed that they blew around like

small beads at daybreak. The German botanist G Ehrenburg explained in 1823 that tamarisk trees exuded the white crystals when attacked by a particular type of plant louse native to Sinai. *See* W Keller, *The Bible as History*, pp 129–31. Had this actually been the case, however, the Israelites would have known precisely what it was, and would not have asked the question, 'What is this?' – '*Manna?*'

39 Complete texts from about 1425 BC based on earlier texts from the 3rd millennium BC. *See* Sir EAW Budge (trans), *The Book of the Dead*, pp ix, 3.

Chapter 14

1 E Pagels, *The Origin of Satan*, ch 2, p 39.
2 *See* 'Israel' item in Paul Carus, *The History of the Devil*, Gramercy Books, New York, NY, 1996, pp 70–1.
3 Luke 22:3 and John 13:27.
4 Mark 3:23 and Luke 11:18.
5 For instance, Acts 5:3, 26:18, Romans 16:20 and 1 Corinthians 5:5.
6 Revelation 2:9.
7 Revelation 12:9, 20:2, 20:7.
8 *See also* Mark 8:33.
9 *See also* Luke 4:5–13.
10 Yuri Stoyanov, *The Hidden Tradition in Europe*, Arkana/Penguin, London, 1994, *passim* on Dualism.
11 Rev SC Malan (trans), *The Book of Adam and Eve* (from the Ethiopic text), Williams & Norgate, London, 1882.
12 Sir Ernest A Wallis Budge (trans), *The Book of the Cave of Treasures*, The Religious Tract Society, London, 1927.
13 Sir Ernest A Wallis Budge (trans), *The Book of the Bee* (from the Syriac text), Clarendon Press, Oxford, 1886.
14 Phyllis Siefker, *Santa Claus, Last of the Wild Men*, MacFarland, Jefferson, NC, 1997, ch 4, pp 65–6.
15 A further entry from 2 John 1:7 states: 'For many deceivers are entered into the world, who confess not that Jesus Christ is come in the flesh. This is a deceiver and an antichrist.'
16 Leonard RN Ashley, *The Complete Book of Devils and Demons*, Robson Books, London, 1997, ch 1, p 15.
17 Richard Sandbach, *Understanding the Royal Arch*, Lewis Masonic, Hersham, 1992, ch 1, p 1.
18 A complete edition of the work exists as Diana Vaughan, *Mémoires d'une Ex-Palladiste Parfait Initiée, Indépendant Publication mensuelle Cesi este un æuvre de bonne foi* (ed, A Pierret), Paris (undated).
19 A version of this work is now available as Arthur Edward Waite, *Devil Worship in France with Diana Vaughan and the Question of Modern Palladism*. Red Wheel/Weiser, York Beach, ME, 2003.
20 The meeting was reported by Edmond Frank in *l'Illustration*, Paris, No 2827, 1 May 1897.

21 Stephen Knight, *Jack the Ripper, The Final Solution*, reprinted in paperback: HarperCollins, London, 1979.
22 Stephen Knight, *The Brotherhood – The Secret World of the Freemasons*, reprinted in paperback: HarperCollins, 1994.

Chapter 15

1 The new theatre opened in 1932, and in 1961 was renamed the Royal Shakespeare Theatre after the Royal Shakespeare Company was formed by Peter Hall in 1960.
2 When the UGLE Grand Master is a member of the Royal Family, a Pro Grand Master is appointed to act in his stead. Rather more than a deputy, he becomes the acting or executive Grand Master.
3 *Nathan Bailey's Etymological English Dictionary*, 1721 – *commonweal* relates to common land or land for 'public benefit or advantage'.
4 The Pythagoras Theorem.
5 'Unto you it is given to know the mystery of the kingdom of God; but unto them that are without, all these things are done in parables' (Mark 4:11).
6 Richard Deacon, *A History of the British Secret Service*, Grafton Books, London, 1982, ch 1, pp 23–4.
7 *Ibid*, ch 2, p 34.
8 *Ibid*, ch 2, p 40.
9 Robin Brumby, *Doctor John Dee: The Original 007*, Academic Board of Dacorum College, Hemel Hempstead, 1977, ch 1, p 1.
10 R Deacon, *A History of the British Secret Service*, ch 2, p 43.
11 *Ibid*, ch 2 pp 51–2.
12 The Marlowe Society <http://www.marlowe-society.org/>. In practice, the Elizabethan Star Chamber was virtually an executionary court in which trials were for show since the outcomes had already been decided.
13 Peter Dawkins, *Dedication to the Light*, Francis Bacon Research Trust, Coventry, 1984, pp 141–2.
14 For further information in this regard, *see* Alfred Dodd, *Shakespeare, Creator of Freemasonry*, Rider, London, 1937.
15 Francis Bacon, *The Philosophical Works of Francis Bacon* (ed, Peter Shaw), JJ & P Knapton, London, 1733.
16 EK Chambers, *William Shakespeare*, Clarendon Press, Oxford, 1930, vol 2, p 343.
17 FA Yates, *The Rosicrucian Enlightenment*, ch 2, pp 51–2.
18 Frances A Yates, *Giordano Bruno and the Hermetic Tradition*, University of Chicago Press, Chicago, IL, 1964, ch 14, p 274; ch 21, pp 422–3.
19 *Ibid*, ch 21, pp 414–16.
20 M White, *Isaac Newton – The Last Sorcerer*, ch 4, pp 75–6.
21 FA Yates, *The Rosicrucian Enlightenment*, ch 13, pp 212–13.
22 Samuel Pepys, *The Illustrated Pepys* (ed, Robert Latham), Penguin, London, 2000, entries 14–25 May 1660, pp 25–7.
23 P Coppens, *The Stone Puzzle of Rosslyn Chapel*, ch 8, p 71.
24 Yatri, *Unknown Man*, Sidgwick & Jackson, London, 1988, p 86.

25 The human spine contains 24 individual vertebrae (7 cervical, 12 thoracic, and 5 lumbar), plus the separately fused sections of the sacrum and the coccyx, which contain 5 and 4 vertebrae, respectively. These total 33 in all.
26 MP Hall, *The Secret Teachings of all Ages*, p LXXIX.
27 *Ibid*, p XIX. Descartes shares with Francis Bacon the honour of founding the systems of modern science and philosophy. He was the discoverer of analytical geometry and the founder of the science of optics.
28 Serena Roney-Dougal, *Where Science and Magic Meet*, Element Books, Shaftesbury, 1993, ch 4, p 91.
29 Colin Wilson and John Grant, *The Directory of Possibilities*, Webb & Bower, Exeter, 1981, p 144 – Pineal Eye.
30 Debbie Shapiro, *The Body Mind Workbook*, Element Books, Shaftesbury, 1990, ch 3, p 49.
31 Copy at the British Library – Record Number 19237. Shelfmark 521.g.i.
32 The poem was published in 1573. *See* J Thomas Looney (ed), *Shakespeare Identified*, Cecil Palmer, London, 1920, vol 1, p 572.
33 Queen Marguerite (1492–1549) was also a poet and the renowned author of the *Heptameron* – 72 stories of cheating and revenge, patterned after Giovanni Boccaccio's *Decameron*.
34 Thomas Sprat, *History of the Royal Society of London for the Improving of Natural Knowledge* (reprint of 1667 edition), Routledge & Kegan Paul, London, 1959.
35 Lord Macaulay, *Critical and Historical Essays*, London, 1862, vol 1 – reprinted from *The Edinburgh Review* of July 1837.
36 Margery Purver, *The Royal Society, Concept and Creation*, Routledge & Keegan Paul, London, 1967, ch 2, pp 22–3.
37 A Mackey, *Encyclopedia of Freemasonry* – Shakespeare.

Chapter 16

1 The Drapers' Company website is at <http://www.thedrapers.co.uk>.
2 Details of Templar acquisition in London are given in chapter 7 – A Sovereign Order.
3 *Concise Oxford English Dictionary* – Mystery.
4 The same word in today's French is *métier* – *Larouse Pocket French Dictionary*, Larousse, London, 1994.
5 The City & Guilds website is at <http://www.city-and-guilds.co.uk>.
6 E Thornton Cook, *Their Majesties of Scotland*, John Murray, London, 1928, ch 22, p 397.
7 A comprehensive schedule of individually named votes for and against the 1707 Act of Union is given in HRH Prince Michael of Albany, *The Forgotten Monarchy of Scotland*, Appendix III, pp 351–4. (*See* under 'Forgotten Monarchy' <http://www.Graal.co.uk>.)
8 A full and concise overview of events surrounding the Act of Union is given in GS Pryde, *The Treaty of Union Between Scotland and England 1707*, Thomas Nelson, London, 1950.

9   Details of other famous Scottish Freemasons, and of Scottish Freemasonry in general, can be found on the Grand Lodge of Ancient Free and Accepted Masons of Scotland website <http://www.grandlodgeofscotland.com>.

10 *Burke's Peerage, Baronetage and Knightage*, Burke's Peerage, London, 105th edition, 1970 – Wharton.

11 Frank McLynn, *The Jacobites*, Routledge & Kegan Paul, London, 1985, ch 8, p 140.

12 J Hamill, *The Craft*, ch 3, p 47.

13 For example: *Ibid*, ch 3, p 45.

14 Sir Compton Mackenzie, *Prince Charlie and his Ladies*, Cassell, London, 1934, pp 199–200.

15 Frank McLynn, *Charles Edward Stuart*, Routledge, London, ch 37, p 532.

16 F McLynn, *The Jacobites*, ch 8, p 140.

17 Alec Mellor, *La chartinconnue de la franc-maçonnerie chretienne*, Tours, 1965, pp 119–20.

18 F McLynn, *Charles Edward Stuart*, ch 37, p 533.

19 Carlo Francovich, *Storia massoneria in Italia*, Florence, 1974, p 220.

20 *Ibid*, ch 37, pp 534–5.

21 HRH Prince Michael of Albany, *The Forgotten Monarchy of Scotland*, ch 13, p 184.

22 *See* Andrew Lang, *Historical Mysteries*, Thomas Nelson, London, 1904, The Count of St Germain (Rosicrucian Chancellor of Charles Edward Stuart) was the son of Juan Tomazo Enriquez de Cabrera, Conte de Melgar of Castille, and Maria Anna, dowager Queen of Spain and widow of King Carlos II. The Prussian Church Register of Eckernforde records his death on 27 February 1784, and burial on 2 March.

23 David Loth, *Lafayette*, Cassell, London, 1952, ch 4, p 36.

24 The *Quatuar Coronati* were Four Crowned martyrs – Christian stonemasons named Claudius, Castorius, Symphorianus and Nichostratus, who were persecuted by Emperor Diocletian in the 3rd century.

25 He was described in a Commissioners of Excise report dated 7 May 1745 as 'William Harper, Episcopal Minister at Bothkiner ... very active in aiding and assisting the rebels, and waited for the Pretender's son at Falkirk'.

26 HRH Prince Michael of Albany, *The Forgotten Monarchy of Scotland*, ch 13, pp 183–4.

27 D Loth, *Lafayette*, ch 13, p 206.

28 *Ibid*, ch 16, p 244.

29 *Beaux Arts Magazine*, Freemasonry Museum edition, in association with the Grand Orient de France, Paris, 2000, p 15.

30 *Ibid*, p 27.

31 A full account of the Marian history of La Sainte-Baume and the Languedoc Abbey of St Maximus is given in Laurence Gardner, *The Magdalene Legacy*, HarperCollins/Thorsons–Element, London, 2005.

32 ECM. Begg, *The Cult of the Black Virgin*, Arkana, London, 1985, ch 4, p 103.

Chapter 17

1 For Jacobite Freemasonry in 18th-century France, *see* P Chevalier, *Les·ducs sous l'Acacia*, Paris, 1964, and *La première profanation du temple maçonnique*, Paris, 1968. For the Jacobite role in Spain, *see* JAF Benimeli, *La masonería española en al siglo 18*, Madrid, 1974, esp. pp 48–65. For Italy, *see* C Francovich, *Storia massoneria in Italia*.

2 Brig. ACF Jackson, *Rose Croix*, ch 2, p 17.

3 *Ibid*, ch 1, p 1.

4 Ramsay had delivered an earlier version of the oration, called the Epernay version because its details were found in the Epernay archives. It was entitled 'Discourse given at the St John's Lodge on 26 December 1736', and had a more Jewish flavour than the subsequent Grand lodge oration.

5 J Cuthbert Hadden, *Prince Charles Edward*, Sir Isaac Pitman & Sons, London, 1913, ch 18, p 285.

6 Orient of California website <http://www.scottishritecalifornia.org>.

7 Various correspondents in *The Builder*, 1923 – especially April, November and December.

8 It was claimed in November 1923 that a letter had been written by a Henry Bell of Lancaster, PA, to a Dr Thomas Cadwallader on 17 November 1754. It indicated that, on behalf of the unofficial *Tun Tavern* lodge in Philadelphia, he had applied to the Grand Lodge of England for a charter in the fall of 1730, but was advised to contact Daniel Coxe, as a result of which the request was granted. The problem was that the said letter and the response to it were matters of hearsay because they could neither be produced nor confirmed. They were reckoned to have been lost in 1873.

9 In 1730, Benjamin Franklin reported in his *Pennsylvania Gazette* that there had been masonic meetings in Philadelphia.

10 Philadelphia, about 28 miles from Sardis, was named by Attalus Philadelphius of Pergamus before 138 BC. *See* J Hastings, *Dictionary of the Bible* – Brother Love, and Philadelphia.

11 On 13 December 1733 the Grand Lodge of England had announced its intention to send distressed masons out to the new colony.

12 *The Builder*, July 1926 – Volume XII, Number 7.

13 F Maclean, *Bonnie Prince Charlie*, ch 20, pp 332–3.

14 F McLynn, *The Jacobites*, ch 7, p 115.

15 Sir C Petrie, *The Jacobite Movement – Last Phase*, ch 5, p 102.

16 Quatuor Coronati Lodge 2076, *Ars Quaturo Coronatorum* Transactions, London, vol 107, 1994.

17 KB Jackson, *Beyond the Craft*, pp 9–10.

18 HV Morton, *In Search of Scotland*, Methuen, London 1929, ch 5, p 133.

19 M Baigent and R Leigh, *The Temple and the Lodge*, ch 16, pp 302–3.

20 Sir C Petrie, *The Jacobite Movement – The Last Phase*, ch 8, p 174.

21 *Ibid*, ch 8, p 175. *See also* Sir Compton Mackenzie, *Prince Charlie*, Daily Express Publications, 1932, ch 12, p 133.

22 Alice Shields, *Henry Stuart, Cardinal of York*, Longmans, London, 1908, ch 16, pp 213–14. *See also* Rev L Dutens, *Mémoires d'un voyageur qui se repose*, Cox Sons & Baylis, London, 1807, vol III, p 30.

Chapter 18

1 M Howard, *The Occult Conspiracy*, ch 3, p 61.
2 For the complete story of the Great Seal of the United States, *see* Eugene Zieber, *Heraldry in America*, Greenwich House, New York, NY, 1895.
3 Dan Brown, *Angels and Demons*, Corgi, London, 2001, ch 31, p 135.
4 The United States Institute of Heraldry is at 9325 Gunston Road, Fort Belvoir, VA 22050–5579.
5 The Strict Observance Lodge of Theodore of Good Council.
6 An account of the Order of Perfectibilists is given in *Einige Originalschriften des Illuminaten Ordens*, Government of Bavaria, Munich, 1787.
7 Vernon Stauffer, *New England and the Bavarian Illuminati* (New York, 1919) – reprinted by Invisible College Press, Woodbridge, VA, 2005, ch 3, pp 140–1.
8 M Howard, *The Occult Conspiracy*, ch 3. pp 62–3.
9 John Robison, *Proofs of a Conspiracy Against all the Governments of Europe* –1801 edition reprinted by the Christian Book Club of America, Hawthorn, CA, 1961.
10 'Mayor Daley Linked with Illuminati' in *Spark*, Chicago, vol 2, no 9, July 1969.
11 The Library Company of Philadelphia was founded in 1731 at the instigation of Benjamin Franklin. It was the largest public library in America until the 1850s, and is now an independent research library with one of the nation's premier collections of early American documents.
12 M Baigent and R Leigh, *The Temple and the Lodge*, ch 19, p 349.
13 David Ovason, *The Secret Architecture of Our Nation's Capital*, HarperCollins/Perennial, New York, NY, 2002.
14 For recommended reading, *see* George J Olszewski, *A History of the Washington Monument 1844–1968*, Office of History and Historic Architecture, Washington, DC, 1971.
15 It could not be placed precisely at the cross-axis as hoped, because the ground was not firm enough at that point.

Chapter 19

1 Wilson, AN, *Jesus*, Sinclair Stevenson, London, 1992, ch 4, p 83.
2 Word Origins <http://www.wordorigins.org/histeng.htm>
3 Alfred Dodd, *Secret Shakespeare*, Rider, London, 1951, p 19.
4 *Ibid*, p 22.
5 Titania in Act III, Scene I.
6 Sonnet 78 in the MS order; LIII in the 1609 Quarto, line 4.
7 Act IV, Scene I.
8 Details of these Charges are given as they appear chronologically in John Yarker, *The Arcane Schools – A Review of their Origin and Antiquity, with a*

General History of Freemasonry, and its Relation to the Theosophic, Scientific and Philosophic Mysteries, William Tait, Belfast, 1909.

9 In the 1600 Pontefract version, this anagrammatical verse is written by one William Kay to a Robert Preston. The 1630 York example was accompanied by a mahogany rule bearing the name of John Drake. The 1704 Newcastle MS is addressed by Richard Steed to Joseph Claughton.

10 In about the year 900, the old Hebrew text (which does not now exist) emerged in a new form, produced by Jewish scholars known as the Massoretes because they appended the *Massorah* (a body of traditional notes) to the text. The oldest existing copy of this comes from little more than 1,000 years ago, in 916. It is Known as the *Codex Petropolitanus*.

11 *Septuagint* 3 Kings 10:11.

12 *Ibid*, 3 Kings 10:10.

13 *Ibid*, 3 Kings 10:14.

14 New Testament Revelation 13:8.

15 One talent of gold = 108 lbs *avoirdupois*: J Hastings, *Dictionary of the Bible* – Money. One ton = 2,240 lbs.

16 King James Authorized Old Testament, 1 Kings 4:26.

17 *Ibid*, 1 Kings 7:13–14.

18 *Septuagint* 3 Kings 5:7.

19 Werner Keller, *The Bible as History* (trans, William Neil), Hodder & Stoughton, London, 1956, ch 15, pp 157–8.

20 In the 1300s, an anonymous Ethiopic book was published, entitled *Kebra Nagast* (Glory of the Kings). During this era of European infiltration into African countries, the object of the work was to establish the pretence of an ancient Judaeo-Christian culture in old Abyssinia. It claimed that the kings of that country had descended from a certain Menyelek, who was the hitherto secret son of King Solomon and the Queen of Sheba. Not only that, but Menyelek had apparently stolen the Ark and carried it to Ethiopia. Amazingly, the legend lives on to this day, encouraged by the Ethiopian Orthodox Church and the Axum tourist industry. The relic is said to be kept in a crudely erected 1960s chapel to which entry is, not surprisingly, prohibited, and no one (not even the Patriarch) has ever seen it. The book is available in translation as Sir EA Wallis Budge, *Kebra Nagast* (*The Queen of Sheba and her only son Menyelek*), Oxford University Press, Oxford, 1932. A full account of the Ethiopian tradition is given in Graham Hancock, *The Sign and the Seal*, Heinemann, London, 1992.

21 All etymological and linguistic references are as per the *Oxford Concise English Dictionary*.

22 From the First Epistle of John – 1 John 1:5.

23 *Septuagint* 1 Kings (1 Samuel) 21:6.

Chapter 20

1 David T Morgan, *The Devious Doctor Franklin, Colonial Agent*, Mercer University Press, Macon, GA, 1999, ch 1, p 15.

2 James Breck Perkins, *France in the American Revolution*, Cornerhouse, Williamstown, MA, 1970, ch 7, p 140.

3 Geoffrey Ashe, *The Hell-Fire Clubs*, Sutton, Stroud, 2000, ch 9, pp 140–1.

4 Phillips Russell, *Benjamin Franklin: The First Civilized American*, Brentano's, New York, NY, 1926, ch 24, p 218.

5 G Ashe, *The Hell-Fire Clubs*, ch 6, p 103.

6 Records of the Commandery of the Temple of Carcassonne are held in the bibliothèque collection of the Grand Orient de France, and Les archives secrètes des francs-maçons, in Paris.

7 Michael Baigent, Richard Leigh and Henry Lincoln, *The Holy Blood and the Holy Grail*, Jonathan Cape, London, 1982, ch 5, p 92.

8 N Deschamps, *Les Sociétés Secrètes et la Société ou Philosophie de l'Histoire Contemporaine*, vol II, Paris, 1881, p 121.

9 L Charpentier, *The Mysteries of Chartres Cathedral*, ch 17, pp 137–43 gives a good overview of the properties of Gothic stained glass.

10 Antoine Faivre, *The Golden Fleece and Alchemy*, State University of New York Press, New York, NY, 1993, ch 2, p 53.

11 Carl Gustav Jung, *Psychology and Alchemy*, Routledge, London, 1980, part 2, ch 3, pp 158–9, and part 3, ch 5, p 370. A commentary concerning Jung and Jason is given in Joscelyn Godwin's Foreword to Faivre, Antoine, *The Golden Fleece and Alchemy*, pp 1–6.

12 Raphael Patai, *The Jewish Alchemists*, Princeton University Press, Princeton, NJ, 1994, ch 20, p 268.

13 HE Puthoff, 'Gravity as a Zero-point Fluctuation Force' in *Physical Review A*, 1 March 1989, vol 39, no 5.

14 Scientific reports, testing procedures, and full analytical details of all experiments and their results over a 20-year period are given in L Gardner, *Lost Secrets of the Sacred Ark*.

15 David Patterson, 'Electric Genes' in *Scientific American*, May 1995, pp 33–4. Superconductors are used for brain scanning and can even measure thoughts. A superconductor is sensitive to magnetic fields of minute proportion. Unlike electric conductivity, superconductivity does not require physical contacts.

16 A quarterly publication of Johnson Matthey plc, 40–42 Hatton Garden, London EC1N 8EE.

17 For example: 'Anti-tumour Platinum Coordination Complexes' in *Platinum Metals Review*, vol 34, no 4, 1990, p 235.

18 As filed by the Equity Gold Trust (World Gold Trust Services LLC) on 13 May 2003 with the Securities and Exchange Commission, Washington, DC, Registration No.333–.

19 L and K Ritmeyer, *Secrets of Jerusalem's Temple Mount*, ch 5, p 57.

20 Shimon Gibson and David M Jacobsen, *Below the Temple Mount in Jerusalem*, Tempus Reparatum, Oxford, 1996, Preface p vii.

21 F Josephus, *The Antiquities of the Jews*, bk XV, 11:5.

22 L and K Ritmeyer, *Secrets of Jerusalem's Temple Mount*, ch 3, pp 47, 49.

23 G Hancock, *Fingerprints of the Gods*, ch 35, p 298.

24 IES Edwards, *The Pyramids of Egypt*, Viking, New York, NY, 1986, p 115.

25 G Hancock, *Fingerprints of the Gods*, ch 38, p 330.

26 Hargrave Jennings, *The Rosicrucians: Their Rites and Mysteries*, Routledge, London, 1887, pp 4, 108, 225.

27 *Nexus* magazine, David Hudson lecture transcript: part 2, November 1996, p 38.

28 For further reading in this regard, *see* BE Jones, *Freemasons' Book of the Royal Arch*, ch 3, p 20 ff.

29 Richard Sandbach, *Understanding the Royal Arch*, Lewis Masonic, Hersham, 1992, ch 8, p 36.

30 BE Jones, *Freemasons' Book of the Royal Arch*, ch 3, p 36.

31 *Ibid*, ch 11, p 132.

32 C Knight and R Lomas, *The Hiram Key*, ch 13, pp 264–5.

33 *Jah* is inherent in *Hallelujah*: Praise the Lord.

34 HS Lewis, *The Mystical Life of Jesus*, pp 191–2.

35 Fergusson MS 210: *De Alchemia Opuscula complura veterum philosophorum*, Frankfurt, 1550.

36 Hebrews 9:4.

37 Louis Ginsberg, *Legends of the Jews*, Johns Hopkins University Press, Baltimore, MD, 1998, vol 3, p 243.

38 BE Jones, *Freemasons' Book of the Royal Arch*, George G Harrap, London, 1957, ch 11, p 137.

39 1 cubit = 18 inches. The Ark lid was 2.5 cubits x 1.5 cubits.

40 There are seven nouns in the Bible which have the meaning 'gold'. They are: *zahav, paz, ketem, harus, s'gor, ophir, baser*. Among the adjectival references, *zahav tahor* referred to 'pure gold' (ie, 100 per cent) as applicable to the lid of the Ark. The *Midrash* defines 'pure gold' as gold which does not diminish on melting. *See* Raphael Patai, *The Jewish Alchemists*, ch 3, pp 41–6.

41 Moshe Levine, *The Tabernacle: Its Structure and Utensils*, Soncino Press, Tel Aviv, 1969, p 88.

42 The World Gold Council is a non-profit association of gold producers world-wide, headquartered in London, with offices in all major markets. All information in this chapter section is obtained from the World Gold Council, 45 Pall Mall, London SW1Y 5JG.

43 1 ton = 2,240 lb/1,016.05 kg.

44 All etymological information in this section is from the *Oxford Concise English Dictionary* and the *Oxford Compact English Dictionary*.

45 For example, F Josephus, *Antiquities of the Jews*, bk IV, 4:3, 8:8, 8:44.

46 J Hastings, *Dictionary of the Bible* – Levite.

47 Watson E Mills (ed), *Lutterworth Dictionary of the Bible*, Lutterworth Press, Cambridge, 1994.

48 Joshua 3:6.

49 J Hastings, *Dictionary of the Bible*, under Dress – item: Apron. *See also* chapter 8 – The Masonic Apron.

50 1 Samuel 4:4, 2 Samuel 6:2, 1 Chronicles 13:6, Psalm 80:1, Psalm 99:1, Isaiah 37:16.

51 L Ginsberg, *Legends of the Jews*, vol 3, p 228.

52 *Ibid*, pp 157, 210.

MASONIC AND MONARCHICAL TIMELINE

ENGLAND	SCOTLAND
Norman	*Celtic*
William I 1066–87	Malcolm III Canmore 1058–1093
William II 1087–1100	Donald Ban 1093
	Duncan II 1094
	Donald Ban (restored) 1094–7
	Edgar 1097–1107

1095–9 First Crusade led by Godefroi de Boullion into the Holy Land

Henry I 1100–35	Alexander I 1107–24

1114 Monastic military unit under Hugues de Payens become the Poor Knights of Christ and the Temple of Solomon (Knights Templars)

1118 Templar Grand Knights of St Andrew instituted by King Baldwin II of Jerusalem – styled Guardian Princes of the Royal Secret

1127 Knights Templars return to France from Jerusalem

1128 Council of Troyes. Bernard de Clairvaux, Patron of the Templars.

Hugues de Payens, Grand Master of Templars, meets with King David I of Scots and establishes Templar preceptory on South Esk in Scotland

Stephen de Blois 1135–54	David I 1124–53

1139 Pope Innocent II grants the Knights Templars international sovereignty

1144–5 Templars granted rights to consecrate land and collect taxes

1147 Templars of the Royal Ark establish the Paris Chapter House

Plantagenet

Henry II 1154–89	Malcolm IV 1153–65

1161 Templar headquarters established in Fleet Street, London

Gothic cathedrals built in France by masonic guilds, including the Children of Solomon, through the 12th and 13th centuries

Richard I 1189–99	William I (the Lion) 1165–1214
John 1199–1216	Alexander II 1214–49
Henry III 1216–72	Alexander III 1249–86

1245 *Bible Moralisée* published in France

Edward I 1272–1307   **Margaret (of Norway) 1286–90**

1291 End of the eight Crusades

                                     John Baliol 1292–6
Edward II 1307–27   **Robert I (Bruce) 1306–29**

1307 Templars persecuted by Pope Clement V and King Philip IV of France

1312 Templars outlawed in Europe and England (not effective in Scotland)

1314 Execution in Paris of Jacques de Molay, Grand Master of Knights Templars.

Battle of Bannockburn – Templar troops under command of Chevalier Hugues de Crecy

1317 Robert I (Bruce) constitutes Templars as Elder Brethren of the Rosy Cross

Templars in Portugal reincorporated as the Knights of Christ by King Dinis (ratified by John XXII in the following year)

1320 Scotland's written Constitution, the *Declaration of Arbroath*

Edward III 1327–77   **David II 1329–71**

1348 Order of the Garter constituted by Edward III of England

Stewart

Richard II 1377–99   **Robert II 1371–90**

1384 John Wycliffe's English Bible translation

*c.*1390 The masonic *Regius Manuscript* (England)

1394 Prince Henry the Navigator installed as Grand Master of the Knights of Christ in Portugal

1398 Sinclair Fleet sails from Scotland to North America

Henry IV (Lancaster) 1399–1413   **Robert III 1390–1406**
Henry V (Lancaster) 1413–22   **James I 1406–37**

1416 French chemist Nicolas Flamel described the Philosophers' Stone as a 'fine powder of gold'

Henry VI (Lancaster) 1422–61   **James II 1437–60**

1429 Order of the Golden Fleece constituted by Philip of Burgundy

1435 Early use of the term 'free mason' in England

1441 William Sinclair of Rosslyn appointed Patron and Protector of Scottish Masons

1446 Rosslyn Chapel founded by William Sinclair (built 1450–86)

*c.*1450 The masonic *Matthew Cooke Manuscript* (England)

Edward IV (York) 1461–83   **James III 1460–88**

1472 Grant of Arms to the London Company of Freemasons

1474 onwards: Kings of Scots charter various Trade Guilds

1475 Rosslyn Charter for the Incorporation of St Mary's Chapel ratified – and St Mary's becomes Lodge No 1 in Edinburgh

Edward V (York) 1483

1488 Templars and Hospitallers jointly administered in Scotland

Richard III (York) 1483–5

Tudor

Henry VII 1485–1509   **James IV 1488–1513**

1500–20 Period of the High Renaissance in Europe

Henry VIII 1509–47   **James V 1513–42**

1517 Protest of Martin Luther in Wittenberg, Germany

1541 Reference to 'speculative' Freemasonry in Aberdeen, Scotland

Edward VI 1547–53   **Mary (Stuart) 1542–87**
Jane 1553 (9 days)   *Queen of France 1559–60*
Mary I 1553–8
Elizabeth I 1558–1603

1560 Protestant Kirk established in Scotland by John Knox

1562–8 Wars of Religion in France

1570 Elizabeth I of England excommunicated by the Pope

English Secret Service founded by Sir Francis Walsingham (formalized 1587)

1572 Altars of Rosslyn Chapel destroyed by the Kirk

1579 *The Shepheardes Calendar* published by Edmund Spenser

1582 John Dee begins his *Liber Mysteriorum* manuscripts

1583 William Schaw appointed King's Master of Works in Scotland

<u>1587 Mary, Queen of Scots, executed by command of Elizabeth I</u>

Egyptian obelisk erected at St Peter's in Rome

1590 Royal Arch working recorded in Stirling, Scotland

1590–3 Scottish *Privy Seal* records of the Knights Templars of St Anthony

1593 *The Theater of Fine Devices*, by Guillaume de la Perrière, registered at Stationer's Hall, London

1596 *Cosmographic Mystery* published by Johannes Kepler

1597 Gresham College established in London

1598 First illustration of a Freemason in *The Mirrour of Policie* by Guillaume de la Perrière

First play published by William Shakespeare, *Love's Labour's Lost*.

Globe Theatre built in London

1598–9 *Masonic Statutes* of William Schaw in Scotland.

Lodges identified at Kilwinning, Edinburgh, Stirling and St Andrews

1598 Minutes of Scottish lodge at Aitchinson's Haven, Midlothian

1599 Minutes of Scottish lodge of St Mary's Chapel, Edinburgh

1603 Union of English and Scottish Crowns

Stuart (Stewart)

James I 1603–25   **(James VI 1567–1603)**

1611 Publication of the King James Authorized Bible

1613 Elizabeth Stuart marries Frederick V, Elector Palatine of the Rhine

1614–15 Appearance of the *Rosicrucian Manifestos*

1618–48 Thirty Years War in Europe

1619 *Utriusque Geomi Historia* published by Robert Fludd

1620 Speculative masons admitted to the Worshipful Company of Masons in London

1620 Pilgrim Fathers sail from Plymouth, England, to America

1623 Sir Francis Bacon begins his *New Atlantis* (published 1627)

Publication of Shakespeare's first folio of *Comedies, Histories and Tragedies*

Charles I 1625–49   **(Charles I 1625–49)**

1628 *Sinclair Charter* references masons and trade guilds in Scotland

1632 Copernican heliocentric principle supported by Gallileo

1638 Rosy Cross linked with the Mason Word in Scotland

1641 Sir Robert Moray entered into Freemasonry at Newcastle, England

<u>1642 Outbreak of Civil War in Britain</u>

1643 *Lingua Ægyptiaca Restituta* published by Athanasius Kircher

1646 *Sloane Manuscript 3848* (British Library) relates to Freemasonry

Elias Ashmole entered into Freemasonry at Warrington, England

Ars Magna Lucis et Umbrae (The Great Art of Light and Darkness) published by Athanasius Kircher

1648 *Mathematicall Magick* published by Rev John Wilkins

1648–1742 A century of philosophical debate concerning the Golden Calf mystery

1649–63 Scottish Kirk Sessions and General Synod declare the 'unknown' Mason Word blasphemous

<u>1649 Charles I executed by command of Oliver Cromwell</u>

Charles II 1651 *(exiled)*

<u>Commonwealth declared (19 May 1649) in Britain</u>

Oliver Cromwell (Lord Protector) 1653–8
Richard Cromwell (Lord Protector) 1658–9

1650s The Invisible College active at Oxford University

1652 *Theatrum chemichum Britannicum* published by Elias Ashmole

1657 Christopher Wren appointed Professor of Astronomy at Gresham College

1660 College for the Promoting of Physico-Mathematical Experimental Learning founded at Gresham College by Christopher Wren

Stuart Restoration

Charles II 1660–85   **(Charles II 1651–85)***

1662 Wren's College granted charter by King Charles II to become the Royal Society of London for Improving Natural Knowledge

1665 War declared between England and Holland

Micrographia published by Dr Robert Hooke

Plague of the Black Death in London

1666 Great Fire of London

1667 *History of the Royal Society* published by Thomas Sprat

Philosophers' Stone again detailed as 'a fine powder of gold' in *Secrets Revealed* by Royal Society mentor Eirenaeus Philalethes

Paradise Lost issued by John Milton as a direct assault against Christopher Wren and the Royal Society

1672 Isaac Newton joins the Royal Society

1673 Sir Christopher Wren knighted by Charles II

1673–81 *Tests Acts* in England and Scotland

James II 1685–8   **(James VII 1685–8)**

1687 King James issues *Declaration for Liberty of Conscience*

Principia Mathematica published by Isaac Newton

December 1688: Invasion of England by William of Orange

King James I (VII) deposed and exiled by the Whig Revolution

Interregnum 11 December 1688 – 13 February 1689

William III (Orange) 1689–1702
and Mary II (Stuart) d. 1694

1689 Westminster *Bill of Rights* and *Declaration of Rights*

Order of the Sangréal constituted by the Royal House of Stuart

1690 Battle of the Boyne in Ireland

1692 The Glencoe Massacre by Orange troops in Scotland

1701 British *Act of Settlement* preserves the British Crown for Protestants alone

Anne (Stuart) 1702–14

1703 Isaac Newton president of the Royal Society

1705 Sir Isaac Newton knighted by Queen Anne

1707 The *Act of Union* – Scotland's Parliament is terminated and Great Britain is governed from London

1708 Rebuilding of London (fronted by Wren and Hooke) completed

GREAT BRITAIN

Hanover

George I 1714–27

1715 Jacobite Rising of James Francis Edward Stuart

(son of James II/VII) in Scotland

1717 Premier Grand Lodge of England instituted in London – the founding of modern Freemasonry from four tavern club lodges

1718 Grand Master George Payne announces that pre-1688 masonic records had been lost

1719–22 Rev Jean Theophilus Desaguliers, Grand Master of the Grand Lodge of England

1720 Old Charges from the 15th-century *Matthew Cooke Manuscript* embodied in the masonic *General Regulations*

1721 John, 2nd Duke of Montagu, installed as Grand Master of England

Robert Walpole appointed Prime Minister of King George I

1723 Philip, Duke of Wharton, succeeds as Grand Master of England

Rev James Anderson issues the *Constitutions of the Free-Masons* and confirms that the records of the Craft have been lost

1725 Grand Lodge of Ireland founded – Richard, Earl of Rosse, Grand Master

AMERICA

George II 1727–60

1727 Central Charity Fund established by Grand Lodge of England

1730 First appearance in print of the 3rd (Master Masons) degree of Craft Freemasonry and introduction of the Hiram Abiff legend

Royal Order of Scotland founded in London (formalized 1750)

> 1730 Daniel Coxe receives a grant from London as Grand Master of the American provinces of New York, New Jersey and Pennsylvania

> Lodge of St John in Philadelphia begins an independent operation

> 1733 Henry Price receives a grant from London as Provincial Grand Master of New England and its territories in America. Establishes the Provincial Grand Lodge of Massachusetts and The First Lodge of Boston – subsequently renamed St John's Lodge.

1730s Brothers of King George III, Princes Edward, William and Henry (respectively the Dukes of Gloucester, York and Cumberland) entered as Freemasons in London

1733 Grand Orient de France (French Grand Lodge) provisionally established

> 1734 Authority of Henry Price is extended throughout North America, superseding the earlier grant of office to Daniel Coxe

Benjamin Franklin obtains recognition from Price for the Lodge of St John in Philadelphia. American fraternity recorded as The Antient and Honorable Society of Free and Accepted Masons

Solomon's Lodge of Savannah established in Georgia by Britain's General James Oglethorpe, who settled the colony (Grand Lodge of England recognition obtained in 1735)

1736 Grand Lodge of Antient, Free and Accepted Masons of Scotland founded under Grand Master, William Sinclair

1737 Chev. Andrew Michael Ramsay, Orator of Grand Lodge of France, announces new-style *Scottish Rite* of Freemasonry (later exported to America)

1738 James Anderson issues revised masonic *Constitutions*

In Eminenti issued – an anti-masonic Bull of Pope Clement XII

1740–48 War of the Austrian Succession

1744 Royal Arch Chapter ritual cites biblical Moses as the first Grand Master

1745 Jacobite Rising in Britain of Charles Edward Stuart (grandson of James II/VII)

Charles Edward installed at Holyrood Abbey, Scotland, as Grand Master of Knights Templars

1746 Charles Edward Stuart defeated by troops of George II at the Battle of Culloden

1747 Chapitre Primordian de Rose Croix constituted by Charter at Arras, France, by Charles Edward Stuart and Comte de St Germain

William, 5th Lord Byron, Grand Master of Grand Lodge of England

1751 Alternative Grand Lodge foundation: The Most Antient and Honourable Fraternity of Free and Accepted Masons – the Antients. (Premier Grand Lodge becomes known as the Moderns)

1752 George Washington initiated into Freemasonry in Fredericksburg, Virginia

1752 Oldest minuted reference to the Royal Arch Chapter comes from Ireland

1756 *Constitutions* of The Most Antient and Honourable Fraternity of Free and Accepted Masons compiled by Grand Secretary, Laurence Dermott

1757 Facsimile of 15th-century *Regius Manuscript* produced for King George II

1757 Three Royal Arch raisings at Washington's lodge in Fredericksburg

Benjamin Franklin elected Fellow of Royal Society in London

George III 1760–1820

1760 Robert Jones of Glamorgan, Grand Master of the Welsh Freemasons

1761 Competitor Grand Lodge of All England established at York

 1761 Steven Morin of Bordeaux granted a patent in France to carry *Scottish Rite (Ecossais)* Freemasonry to the New World

1762 First mention in masonic texts of *Jachin* and *Boaz*, the Jerusalem Temple Pillars of King Solomon

 1762 St Andrew's Lodge, Boston, chartered for Royal Arch working by the Grand Lodge of Scotland

 1767 Henry Francken (deputized by Morin) establishes a Lodge of Perfection in Albany, New York

 St Andrew's Royal Arch Chapter of Boston makes America's first conferral of a Knight Templar degree – William Davis

1768 *Bill of Incorporation* submitted to Westminster Parliament by Premier Grand Lodge

 1769 St Andrew's Lodge, Boston, makes America's second conferral of a Knight Templar degree – Paul Revere

 1770 St Andrew's Lodge, Boston, makes America's third conferral of a Knight Templar degree – Joseph Warren

1773 Grand Orient de France (French Grand Lodge) formally constituted in Paris

 1773 Boston Tea Party arranged by Sons of Liberty and St Andrew's Lodge

 1775 American War of Independence begins

 1776 American *Declaration of Independence*, 4 July

1776 Foundation laid for Grand Lodge headquarters (*Freemasons' Tavern*) in Great Queen Street, London

Royal Order of Scotland new headquarters in Edinburgh, Scotland

 1776 Benjamin Franklin appointed American Ambassador to France

1777 Prince Charles Edward Stuart questioned about his position as Head of Jacobite Freemasons in Europe

 1778 French troops and Marquis de Lafayette, join American Revolution

1782 Prince Henry, Duke of Cumberland, installed as Premier Grand Master in London

 1783 American War of Independence ends

1784 James Anderson issues further revised masonic *Constitutions*

 1786 Benjamin Franklin a founding officer of the Templar Commandery of Cacarssonne in Languedoc, Southern France

 Grand Constitutions provided for two Supreme Councils in the USA

1787 Signing of draft *Constitution* of the United States of America – ratified 1788

1788 Masonic school for girls established by Premier Grand Lodge of England

1789 George Washington elected first President of the United States

1789–99 The French Revolution

1790 Prince of Wales (later George IV) succeeds as Premier Grand Master

1791 Thomas Dunkerley (illegitimate son of George II) forms the short-lived Supreme Grand and Royal Conclave for higher degrees in England.

1792 York Grand Lodge disbanded

1797 Prime Minister William Pitt's *Unlawful Oaths Act* (Freemasonry exempt)

1798 Charity fund for boys established in England by Grand Lodge of the Antients

1799 Prime Minister William Pitt's *Unlawful Societies Act* (Freemasonry exempt)

1801 Supreme Council of *Scottish Rite* established in Charleston, South Carolina (during presidential term of John Adams)

1804 The name 'Ancient and Accepted Scottish Rite' first appears in an agreement between the Supreme Council of France and the Grand Orient of France

1811 Scottish Grand Conclave established by Alexander Deuchar. Declared pseudo by Templar Encampment Master, Robert Martin

1813 Competitor Grand Lodges of the Antients and Moderns amalgamated at Kensington Palace, to form the new United Grand Lodge of England (UGLE)

Prince Augustus, Duke of Sussex, installed as Grand Master of United Grand Lodge. (He was previously Grand Master of the Moderns, with his brother Edward, Duke of Kent, Grand Master of the Ancients)

1813 Supreme Council Southern Jurisdiction, Charleston, ceded 15 States to a separate Northern Jurisdiction based in New York

Daniel D Tomkins (Vice President of USA under President James Monroe) elected first Northern Grand Master

1816 *Provisions* of United Grand Lodge of England and new ritual established

Ark Mariners affiliated with the Mark Masons

1819 Restructuring of *Provisions* in respect of Provincial Grand Lodges

George IV 1820–30

1822 Jean François Champollion breaks the Egyptian hieroglyphic code

1823 Emulation Lodge of Improvement founded in London

1827 Scottish Grand Conclave denounced by Grand Encampment Templars of Ireland

1828–58 Restrictive *Test Acts* repealed in England and Scotland

William IV 1830–7

1835 *Genealogie of the Sainteclairs of Rosslyn* (written in 1690 by Father Richard Augustine Hay) published in London

1836 Luxor obelisk raised in la Place de la Concorde, Paris

Victoria 1837–1901

1843 Thomas Dundas, Earl of Zetland (Shetland), succeeds as Grand Master of UGLE. Freemasons' Hall substantially rebuilt in London

>1859 Albert Pike, Grand Commander of *Scottish Rite*, Southern Jurisdiction (during presidential term of James Buchanan)

>1861–5 American Civil War between Union and Confederate States

>1864 Albert Pike, Grand Master of the Southern Jurisdiction *Scottish Rite* in Arkansas (during presidential term of Abraham Lincoln)

>1867 Northern Jurisdiction *Scottish Rite* formally established (during presidential term of Andrew Johnson)

1870 George Robinson, Lord Ripon, succeeds as Grand Master of UGLE

1874 Albert Edward, Prince of Wales (son of Queen Victoria and later King Edward VII), succeeds as Grand Master of UGLE

1877 Foundation stone for the Shakespeare Memorial Theatre at Stratford-on-Avon laid with full masonic honours

1878 *Cleopatra's Needle* (obelisk from Heliopolis) erected on Thames Embankment, London

>1881 Second *Cleopatra's Needle* (obelisk from Heliopolis) erected in Central Park, New York

1886 Quatuor Coronati Lodge of Research constituted in London

1891 15th-century *Matthew Cooke Manuscript* published in London

1897 Special United Grand Lodge of England event at Freemason's Hall, London, to celebrate the Golden Jubilee of Queen Victoria

Saxe-Coburg Gotha

Edward VII 1901–10

1901 On Edward's accession to the throne, his brother Arthur, Duke of Connaught, succeeds as Grand Master of UGLE

George V 1910–36
(Name change to Windsor 1917)

<u>1914–18 First World War</u>

1927 New Freemason's Hall built in Great Queen Street, London

Windsor

Edward VIII 1936
George VI 1936–52

<u>1939–45 Second World War</u>

1939–67 Successive UGLE Grand Masters: George, Duke of Kent; Henry, Earl of Harewood; Edward, Duke of Devonshire and, from 1952, Lawrence, Earl of Scarborough

Elizabeth II 1952–

1967 Edward, Duke of Kent (grandson of King George V and cousin to Queen Elizabeth II), succeeded as Grand Master of UGLE – current

BIBLIOGRAPHY

Adams, Duncan, *A Guide to the Tyler's Work*, Lewis Masonic, London, 1990.

Addison, Charles G, *The History of The Knights Templars*, Adventures Unlimited Press, Kempton, IL, 1997.

Albany, HRH Prince Michael of, *The Forgotten Monarchy of Scotland*, Element Books, Shaftesbury, 1988 – and Chrysalis/Vega, London, 2002.

Allen, Ian (ed), *Aldersgate Royal Art Ritual*, Lewis Masonic, Hersham, 1999.

Allyn, Avery, *A Ritual of Freemasonry*, John Marsh, Boston, MA, 1831.

Alter, Robert (trans), *Genesis*, WW Norton, New York, NY, 1996.

Anderson, James, *Constitutions of the Free-Masons (Anderson's Constitutions I), 1723*, Kessinger, Kila, MT, 1997.

— *Constitutions of the Free-Masons (Anderson's Constitutions II), 1738*, Kessinger, Kila, MT, 2004.

Anstey, Peter R, *The Philosophy of Robert Boyle*, Routledge, London, 2000.

Armoises, Madame Olivier des, *Un rapport sur la mort etrange du 4ieme Comte d'Albanie le Prince Charles Benoix Stuart a Monsieur le Ministre des Affaires Etrangere a Paris*, Paris, 1898.

Arnold, Ralph, *Northern Lights*, Catholic Book Club, London, 1959.

Ashe, Geoffrey, *The Hell-Fire Clubs*, Sutton, Stroud, 2000.

Ashley, Leonard RN, *The Complete Book of Devils and Demons*, Robson Books, London, 1997.

Bacon, Francis, *The Philosophical Works of Francis Bacon* (ed, Peter Shaw), JJ&P Knapton, London, 1733.

— *The Proficience and Advancement of Learning, Divine and Human*, Printed for Henri Tomes; To the King in London, 1605.

Baigent, Michael, Richard Leigh and Henry Lincoln, *The Holy Blood and the Holy Grail*, Jonathan Cape, London, 1982.

— *The Temple and the Lodge*, Corgi, London, 1990.

Barber, Malcolm and Keith Bate, *The Templars*, Manchester University Press, Manchester, 2002.

Barker-Cryer, Neville, *Masonic Halls of England*, Lewis Masonic, London, 1998.

— *What Do You Know About the Royal Arch?* Lewis Masonic, London, 2002.

Barrow, GWS, *The Kingdom of the Scots*, Edward Arnold, London, 1973.

Bédoyère, Guy de la (ed), *The Diary of John Evelyn*, Boydell Press, Woodbridge, 1995.

Begg, ECM, *The Cult of the Black Virgin*, Arkana, London, 1985.

Benimeli, JAF, *La masonerià española en al siglo 18*, Madrid, 1974.

Beresniak, Daniel, *Symbols of Freemasonry*, Editions Assouline, Paris, 2000.

Best, Michael R & Frank H Brightman, *The Book of Secrets of Albertus Magus*, Samuel Weiser, York Beach, MN, 1999.

Boas, George (ed), *The Hieroglyphics of Horapollo*, Princeton University Press, Princeton, NJ, 1993.

Bragg, WH (ed), *The Record of The Royal Society of London* – 4th edition, Royal Society, London, 1940.

Breasted, James Henry, *The Dawn of Consciousness*, Charles Scribner's Sons, New York, NY, 1934.

Brenton, Sir Lancelot CL (trans), *The Septuagint*, Samuel Bagster, London, 1851.

Brown, Dan, *Angels and Demons*, Corgi, London, 2001.

Browne, Sir Thomas, *Religio Medici and Other Works* (ed, LC Martin), Clarendon Press, Oxford, 1964.

Browne, William, *Highlights of Templar History*, William Mitchell, Greenfield, IN, 1944.

Brumby, Robin, *Doctor John Dee: The Original 007*, Academic Board of Dacorum College, Hemel Hempstead, 1977.

Brydon, Robert, *Rosslyn and the Western Mystery Tradition*, Rosslyn Chapel Trust, Roslin, 2003.

Budge, Sir Ernest A. Wallis (trans), *The Book of the Bee* (from the Syriac text), Clarendon Press, Oxford, 1886.

— (trans), *The Book of the Cave of Treasures*, The Religious Tract Society, London, 1927.

— (trans.) *Kebra Nagast* (*The Queen of Sheba and her only son Menyelek*), Oxford University Press, Oxford, 1932.

— (trans), *The Book of the Dead*, University Books, New York, NY, 1960.

— *Cleopatra's Needle and Other Egyptian Obelisks* (1926), rep. Dover Publications, New York, NY, 1990.

— *Hieroglyphic Texts from Egyptian Stelae*, British Museum, London, Part 1, 1911.

Bunson, Matthew E, *Encylopedia of the Middle Ages*, Facts On File, New York, NY, 1995.

Burke's Peerage, Baronetage and Knightage, Burke's Peerage, London, 105th edition, 1970.

Callahan, Philip S, *Paramagnetism*, Acres, Metairie, LA, 1995.

— *Ancient Mysteries, Modern Visions*, Acres, Austin, TX, 2001.

Callow, John, *The Making of King James II*, Sutton, Stroud, 2000.

Campbell-Everden, William P, *Freemasonry and its Etiquette*, Gramercy, New York, NY, 2001.

Carlyon, Richard, *A Guide to the Gods*, Heinemann/Quixote, London, 1981.

Carpenter, Clive, *The Guinness Book of Kings, Rulers and Statesmen*, Guinness Superlatives, Enfield, 1978.

Carr, Harry, *The Freemason at Work*, Lewis Masonic, London, 1992.

Carter, Charles, *The Preceptor's Handbook*, Lewis Masonic, London, 1994.

Cartwright, EH, *Masonic Ritual*, Lewis Masonic, Shepperton, 1985.

Carus, Paul, *The History of the Devil*, Gramercy, New York, NY, 1996.

Catholic Encyclopedia, The, Robert Appleton, New York, NY, 1910.

Cerny, Jaroslav (ed), *The Inscriptions of Sinai*, Egypt Exploration Society, London, 1955.

Chambers, EK, *William Shakespeare*, Clarendon Press, Oxford, 1930.

Charpentier, Louis, *The Mysteries of Chartres Cathedral*, Research Into Lost Knowledge Organization and Thorsons, Wellingborough, 1992.

Chartres, Richard and David Vermont, *A Brief History of Gresham College*, Gresham College, 1997.

Chevalier, P, *Les ducs sous l'Acacia*, Paris, 1964.

— *La première profanation du temple maçonnique*, Paris, 1968.

Clare, John D (ed), *Fourteenth Century Towns*, Random House, London, 1993.

Clayton, Peter A, *Chronicles of the Pharaohs*, Thames and Hudson, London, 1994.

Coil, Henry W, *Coil's Masonic Encyclopedia*, Macoy Publishing, New York, NY, 1961.

Cook, Alan, *Edmund Halley Charting the Heavens & the Seas*, Clarendon Press, Oxford, 1998.

Cook, E Thornton, *Their Majesties of Scotland*, John Murray, London, 1928.

Cooper-Oakley, Isabel, *Count of Saint-Germain*, Samuel Weiser, NY, 1970 (fac. Kessinger, Kila, MT, 1997).

Coote, Stephen, *Royal Survivor – A Life of Charles II*, Spectre, London, 1999.

Coppens, Philip, *The Stone Puzzle of Rosslyn Chapel*, Frontier, Enkuizen, NL, 2004.

Cottrell, Leonard, *The Land of Shinar*, Souvenir Press, London, 1965.

Covey-Crump, WW, *The Hiramic Tradition*, Kessinger, Kila, MT, 1998.

Curl, James Stevens, *The Art & Architecture of Freemasonry*, Overlook Press, New York, NY, 2002.

Darrah, Delmar, *The Evolution of Freemasonry*, Masonic Publishing, Bloomington, IL, 1920.

Dawkins, Peter, *Dedication to the Light*, Francis Bacon Research Trust, Coventry, 1984.

Deacon, Richard, *A History of the British Secret Service*, Grafton Books, London, 1982.

Demos, John Putnam, *Entertaining Satan, Witchcraft & the Culture of Early New England*, Oxford University Press, Oxford, 1982.

Deschamps, N, *Les Sociétés Secrètes et la Société ou Philosophie de l'Histoire Contemporaine*, Paris, 1881.

Dibner, Burn, *Moving the Obelisks*, Burndy Library, New York, NY, 1950.

Dobbs, Betty JT, *The Foundations of Newton's Alchemy*, Cambridge University Press, Cambridge, 1974.

— *The Janus Face of Genius: The Role of Alchemy in Newton's Thought*, Cambridge University Press, Cambridge, 1991.

Dodd, Alfred, *Shakespeare, Creator of Freemasonry*, Rider, London, 1937.

— *Secret Shakespeare*, Rider, London, 1951.

Donaldson, Gordon and RS Morpeth, *A Dictionary of Scottish History*, John Donald, Edinburgh, 1977.

Douglas, Hugh, *Jacobite Spy Wars*, Sutton, Stroud, 2000.

Draffen, George S, *Pour La Foy – A Short History of the Great Priory of Scotland*, 1949, fac. CD-Rom, Grand Lodge of Scotland, Edinburgh, 2002.

Duncan, Malcolm C, *Duncan's Masonic Ritual and Monitor*, Kessinger, Kila, MT, 2004.

Dutens, Rev L, *Mémoires d'un voyageur qui se repose*, Cox Sons & Baylis, London, 1807.

Dyer, Colin, *Symbolism in Craft Freemasonry*, Gale & Polden, London, 1951.

Edwards, IES, *The Pyramids of Egypt*, Viking, New York, NY, 1986.

Ellis, Aytoun, *The Penny Universities*, Secker & Warburg, London, 1956.

Eschenbach, Wolfram Von, *Parzival* (ed, Hugh D Sacker), Cambridge University Press, Cambridge, 1963.

'Espinasse, Margaret, *Robert Hooke*, Heinemann, London, 1954.

Faivre, Antoine, *The Golden Fleece and Alchemy*, State University of New York Press, New York, NY, 1993.

Fideler, David (ed), *Alexandria 2*, Phanes Press, Grand Rapids, MI, 1993.

Finden, Paula, *Athanasius Kircher: The Man Who Knew Everything*, Routledge, London, 2003.

Fox, William L, *Valley of the Craftsmen: Scottish Freemasonry in America's Southern Jurisdiction*, University of South Carolina Press, Columbia, SC, 2002.

Francovich, Carlo, *Storia massoneria in Italia*, Florence, 1974.

Frankfort, Henri, *Kingship and the Gods*, University of Chicago Press, Chicago, 1948.

Frankfort, Henri and HA, *Before Philosophy*, Penguin, London, 1951.

Franklin, Benjamin, *Autobiography of Benjamin Franklin*, Oxford University Press, Oxford, 1998.

Freud, Sigmund, *Moses and Monotheism*, Hogarth Press, London, 1939.

Fuller, Jean Overton, *The Comte de Saint-Germain*, East-West, London, 1988.

Gardiner, Alan, *Egyptian Grammar*, Griffith Institute and Ashmolean Museum, Oxford, 1957.

Gardner, Laurence, *Bloodline of the Holy Grail*, Element Books, Shaftesbury, 1996 and HarperCollins/Thorsons–Element, London, 2002.

— *Genesis of the Grail Kings*, Transworld/Bantam, London, 1999.

— *Lost Secrets of the Sacred Ark*, HarperCollins/Thorsons–Element, London, 2003.

— *Realm of the Ring Lords*, HarperCollins/Thorsons–Element, London, 2003.

— *The Magdalene Legacy*, HarperCollins/ Thorsons–Element, London, 2005.

Gattey, Charles Neilson, *Farmer George's Black Sheep*, Kensal Press, Bucks, 1985.

Gibson, Shimon and David M Jacobsen, *Below the Temple Mount in Jerusalem*, Tempus Reparatum, Oxford, 1996.

Gilbert, Adrian *The New Jerusalem*, Bantam, London, 2002.

Ginsberg, Louis, *Legends of the Jews*, Johns Hopkins University Press, Baltimore, MD, 1998.

Gould, RF, *Gould's History of Freemasonry*, Caxton, London, 1933.

— *The Concise History of Freemasonry*, Gale & Polden, London, 1951.

Grant, Kenneth, *The Magical Revival*, Skoob Books, London, 1991.

Graves, Robert, *The White Goddess*, Faber & Faber, London, 1961.

Greenia, Conrad, *Bernard de Clairvaux Treatises*, Cistercian Publications, Kalamazoo, MI, 1977.

Gregory of Tours, *A History of the Franks* (trans, Lewis Thorpe), Penguin, London, 1964.

Griffith, Tom (ed), *The Concise Pepys*, Wordsworth, Ware, 1997.

Gunther, RT, *Early Science in Oxford*, Dawsons, London, 1930.

Habachi, Labib, *The Obelisks of Egypt*, JM Dent, London, 1978.

Hadden, J Cuthbert, *Prince Charles Edward*, Sir Isaac Pitman & Sons, London, 1913.

Hale, John, *Renaissance*, Time Incorporated, New York, NY, 1965.

— *The Civilization of Europe in the Renaissance*, Atheneum, New York, NY, 1994.

Hall, Marie Boas, *The Scientific Renaissance 1450–1630*, Dover Publications, New York, NY, 1994.

Hall, Manly P, *The Lost Keys of Freemasonry*, Macoy Publishing and Masonic Supply, Richmond, VA, 1976.

— *The Secret Teachings of All Ages*, Philosophical Research Society, Los Angeles, CA, 1989.

Hamill, John, *The Craft*, Crucible, London, 1986.

Hamilton, John D, *Material Culture of the American Freemasons*, Museum of Our National Heritage, Lexington, MA, 1994.

Hancock, Graham, *The Sign and the Seal*, Heinemann, London, 1992.

— *Fingerprints of the Gods*, Heinemann, London, 1995.

Hastings, James (ed), *Dictionary of the Bible*, T & T Clark, Edinburgh, 1909.

Hauer, Christian E, Jr, *Christopher Wren & the Many Sides of Genius*, The Edwin Mellen Press, New York, NY, 1997.

Hay, Fr Richard Augustine, *The Genealogie of the Sainteclairs of Rosslyn* (ed, RLD Cooper; trans, J Wade), Grand Lodge of Scotland, Edinburgh, 2002.

Haynes, Alan, *The Elizabethan Secret Service*, Sutton, Stroud, 2000.

Heidel, Alexander, *The Babylonian Genesis*, University of Chicago Press, Chicago, IL, 1942.

— *The Gilgamesh Epic and Old Testament Parallels*, University of Chicago Press, Chicago, IL, 1949.

Henry, Jacques, *Mozart Frère Maçon – la symbolique maçonniquedans l'oeuvre de Mozart*, Éditions Alinea, Aix-en-Provence, 1991.

Horne, Alex, *King Solomon's Temple in the Masonic Tradition*, Aquarian Press, London, 1971.

Howard, Michael, *The Occult Conspiracy*, Rider, London, 1989.

Hunter, Michael, *Science & Society in Restoration England*, Cambridge University Press, Cambridge, 1981.

— *Robert Boyle, Scrupulosity and Science*, Boydell Press, Woodbridge, 2000.

— *Robert Boyle 1627–1691*, The Boydell Press, Woodbridge, 2000.

Huss, Wayne, *The Master Builders II*, Grand Lodge of Free and Accepted Masons of Pennsylvania, Pennsylvania, PA, 1988.

Inwood, Stephen, *The Man Who Knew Too Much*, Macmillan, London, 2002.

Jacobsen, Thorkild, *The Treasures of Darkness – A History of Mesopotamian Religion*, Yale University Press, New Haven, CT, 1976.

Jackson, Brig AFC, *Rose Croix*, Lewis Masonic, London, 1980.

Jackson, Keith B, *Beyond the Craft*, Lewis Masonic, London, 1980.

Jennings, Hargrave, *The Rosicrucians – Their Rites and Mysteries*, Routledge, London, 1887.

Jones, Bernard E, *Freemasons' Book of the Royal Arch*, Harrap, London, 1957.

— *Freemasons' Guide and Compendium*, Harrap, London, 1988.

Jordan, William Chester (ed), *The Middle Ages: An Encyclopedia for Students*, Charles Scribner's Sons, New York, NY, 1985.

Josephus, Flavius, *Against Apion* (trans, William Whiston), Milner & Sowerby, London, 1870.

— *Antiquities of the Jews* (trans, William Whiston), Milner & Sowerby, London, 1870.

— *Wars of the Jews* (trans, William Whiston), Milner & Sowerby, London, 1870.

Josten, CH, *Elias Ashmole*, Ashmolean Museum and the Museum of the History of Science, Oxford, 1985.

Jung, Carl Gustav, *Psychology and Alchemy*, Routledge, London, 1980.

Keating, Geoffrey, *The History of Ireland*, 1640 – reprinted by Irish Texts Society (trans, David Comyn and Rev PS Dinneen), London 1902.

Keller, Werner, *The Bible as History*, (trans, William Neil), Hodder & Stoughton, London, 1956.

Kemp, Betty, *Sir Francis Dashwood*, Macmillan, London, 1967.

Keynes, Geoffrey, *The Royal Society Newton Tercentennary Celebrations*, Cambridge University Press, Cambridge, 1947.

Kitchen, Kenneth Anderson, *Ramesside Inscriptions*, Basil H Blackwell, Oxford, 1975.

Knight, Christopher and Lomas, Robert, *The Hiram Key*, Century, London, 1996.

— *The Second Messiah*, Century, London, 1997.

Knight, Stephen, *Jack the Ripper: The Final Solution*, HarperCollins, London, 1979.

— *The Brotherhood: The Secret World of the Freemasons*, HarperCollins, 1994.

Kramer, Samuel Noah, *History Begins at Sumer*, Thames & Hudson, London, 1958.

— *Sumerian Mythology*, Harper Bros., New York, NY, 1961.

Kronenberger, Louis, *The Extraordinary Mr Wilkes*, New English Library, London, 1974.

Lane, John, *Masonic Records 1717–1894*, United Grand Lodge of England, London, 1895.

Lang, Andrew, *The Companions of Pickle*, Longmans, London, 1898.

— *Prince Charles Edward Stuart*, Longmans, London, 1903.

— *Historical Mysteries*, Thomas Nelson, London, 1904.

Laurie, William, *History of Freemasonry*, Grand Lodge of Scotland, Edinburgh, 1859.

Lawrie, Alex, *History of Freemasonry*, Longman & Rees, London, 1804.

Lemesurier, Peter, *The Great Pyramid Decoded*, Element Books, Shaftesbury, 1977.

Lepper, J Heron and Philip Crossle, *History of the Grand Lodge of Free and Accepted Masons of Ireland*, Lodge of Research, Dublin, 1925.

Levine, Moshe, *The Tabernacle: Its Structure and Utensils*, Soncino Press, Tel Aviv, 1969.

Lewis, Lesley, *Connoisseurs & Secret Agents*, Chatto & Windus, London, 1961.

Lewis, Spencer H, *The Mystical Life of Jesus*, Ancient and Mystical Order Rosae Crucis, San Jose, CA, 1982.

Lloyd, Sir John E, *A History of Carmarthenshire*, London Carmarthen Society, London, 1939.

Lomas, Robert, *Invisible College*, Headline, London, 2002.

Loomis, Roger Sherman, *The Grail: From Celtic Myth to Christian Symbolism*, University of Wales Press, Cardiff, 1963.

Looney, J Thomas (ed), *Shakespeare Identified*, Cecil Palmer, London, 1920.

Loth, David, *Lafayette*, Cassell, London, 1952.

Lyons, Sir Henry, *The Royal Society 1660–1940*, Cambridge University Press, Cambridge, 1944.

Macaulay, Lord Thomas, *The History of England*, Penguin, London, 1968.

Mackenzie, Sir Compton, *Prince Charlie and his Ladies*, Cassell, London, 1934.

Mackey, Albert, *Encyclopedia of Freemasonry* (facsimile 1909 edn), Kessinger, Kila, MT, 2003.

Maclean, Fitzroy, *Bonnie Prince Charlie*, Weidenfeld and Nicolson, London, 1988.

MacNulty, W Kirk, *Freemasonry*, Thames & Hudson, London, 2003.

Macoy, Robert, *Dictionary of Freemasonry*, Gramercy, New York, NY, 1990.

Malan, Rev SC (trans), *The Book of Adam and Eve* (from the Ethiopic text), Williams & Norgate, London, 1882.

Mannix, Daniel, *The Hell-Fire Club*, New English Library, London, 1978.

Manuel, Frank E, *The Religion of Isaac Newton – The Freemantle Lectures 1973*, Clarendon Press, Oxford, 1974.

Marrs, Jim, *Rule by Secrecy*, HarperCollins/Perennial, NY, 2001.

Marshall, Alan, *Intelligence & Espionage in the Reign of Charles II 1660–85*, Cambridge University Prerss, Cambridge, 1994.

Mathers, S Liddell MacGregor, *The Key of Solomon the King*, Routledge & Kegan Paul, London, 1972.

McCarter, J Parnell, *Reformed Historical Studies on the Enlightenment Era and its Aftermath – a Teacher's Manual*, Historicism Research Foundation, The Puritan's Home School Curriculum, Jenison, MI, 2003.

McLynn, Frank, *The Jacobites*, Routledge & Kegan Paul, London, 1985.

— *Charles Edward Stuart*, Routledge, London, 1988.

Mellor, Alec, *La chartinconnue de la franc-maçonnerie chretienne*, Tours, 1965.

Mills, Watson E (ed), *Lutterworth Dictionary of the Bible*, Lutterworth Press, Cambridge, 1994.

Milton, John, *Paradise Lost*, Jacob Tonson, London, 1730.

Moncrieffe, Sir Iain, *The Highland Clans*, Barrie & Jenkins, London, 1982.

Morgan, David T, *The Devious Doctor Franklin, Colonial Agent*, Mercer University Press, Macon, GA, 1999.

Morton, HV, *In Search of Scotland*, Methuen, London 1929.

Murphy, Tim Wallace and Marilyn Hopkins, *Rosslyn*, Element, Shaftesbury, 1999.

Neve, Richard, *The City and Country Purchaser and Builders' Dictionary: or the Compleat Builders' Guide*, Philomath, London, 1703.

Nichols, Richard, *Robert Hooke and the Royal Society*, Book Guild, Lewes, 1999.

Nicolson, Adam, *Power and Glory*, HarperCollins, London, 2003.

Olszewski, George J, *A History of the Washington Monument 1844–1968*, Office of History and Historic Architecture, Washington, DC, 1971.

Ornstein, Martha, *The Role of Scientific Societies in the 17th Century*, University of Chicago Press, Chicago, IL, 1938.

Osman, Ahmed, *Stranger in the Valley of Kings*, Souvenir Press, London, 1987

— *Moses, Pharaoh of Egypt*, Grafton/Collins, London, 1990.

Ovason, David, *The Secret Architecture of Our Nation's Capital*, HarperCollins/Perennial, New York, NY, 2002.

— *The Secret Symbols of The Dollar Bill*, HarperCollins, New York, NY, 2004.

Oxford Compact English Dictionary (Oxford Word Library: OWL Micrographic), Oxford University Press, Oxford, 1971.

Oxford Concise English Dictionary (ed, Della Thompson), Oxford University Press, Oxford, 1995.

Pagels, Elaine, *The Origin of Satan*, Random House, New York, NY, 1995.

Paine, Lauran, *Britain's Intelligence Service*, Robert Hale, London, 1979.

Painter, Sidney, *Mediaeval Society*, Cornell University Press, Ithaca, NY, 1951.

Patai, Raphael, *The Jewish Alchemists*, Princeton University Press, Princeton, NJ, 1994.

Pepys, Samuel, *The Illustrated Pepys* (ed, Robert Latham), Penguin, London, 2000.

Perkins, James Breck, *France in the American Revolution*, Cornerhouse, Williamstown, MA, 1970.

Petrie, Sir Charles, *The Stuarts*, Eyre & Spottiswoode, London, 1937.

— *The Jacobite Movement: The Last Phase*, Eyre & Spottiswoode, London, 1950.

Petrie, Sir WM Flinders, *Researches in Sinai*, John Murray, London, 1906.

Philalethes, Eirenaeus, *Introitus apertus ad occulusum regis palatium: Open entrance to the closed palace of the King – Secrets Revealed*, Musaeum Hermeticum, Amsterdam, 1667.

— *Tres tractatus de metallorum transmutatione – Brief Guide to the Celestial Ruby*, Musaeum Hermeticum, Amsterdam, 1668.

Piatigorsky, Alexander, *Freemasonry – The Study of a Phenomenon*, Harvill Press, London, 1997.

Picard, Liza, *Restoration London*, Phoenix, London, 1997.

Pike, Albert, *Morals and Dogma of the Ancient and Accepted Scottish Rite Freemasonry*, Kessinger, Kila, MT, 2004.

Platts, Beryl, *Scottish Hazard*, Proctor Press, London, 1985 & 1990.

Pope, S, *The Development of Freemasonry in England and Wales*, Ars Quatuor Coronatorum, London, 1956.

Pryde, GS, *The Treaty of Union Between Scotland and England 1707*, Thomas Nelson, London, 1950.

Prys-Jones, AG, *The Story of Carmarthenshire*, Christopher Davies, Swansea, 1959.

Purver, Margery, *The Royal Society, Concept and Creation*, Routledge & Keegan Paul, London, 1967.

Raw, Charles, *The Moneychangers*, Harvill Press, London, 1992.

Ridley, Jasper, *The Freemasons*, Constable & Robinson, London, 1999.

Ritmeyer, Leen and Kathleen, *Secrets of Jerusalem's Temple Mount*, Biblical Archaeological Society, Washington, DC, 1998.

Robbins, Alexandra, *Secrets of the Tomb*, Little Brown/Back Bay, Boston, MA, 2002.

Roberts, G, *Aspects of Welsh History*, University of Wales Press, Cardiff, 1969.

Robinson, Henry W (ed), *The Diary of Robert Hooke*, Taylor & Francis, London, 1935.

Robinson, John, *Born in Blood*, Guild Publishing, London, 1989.

— *A Pilgrim's Path: Freemasonry and the Religious Rite*, M Evans, New York, NY, 1993.

Robinson, Robert (ed), *Newton Tercentennary Celebrations*, The Royal Society, London and Cambridge University Press, Cambridge, 1947.

Robison, John, *Proofs of a Conspiracy Against all the Governments of Europe*, 1801 edition reprinted by the Christian Book Club of America, Hawthorn, CA, 1961.

Roney-Dougal, Serena, *Where Science and Magic Meet*, Element Books, Shaftesbury, 1993.

Roux, Georges, *Ancient Iraq*, George Allen & Unwin, London, 1964.

Rudé, George, *Wilkes and Liberty*, Oxford University Press, Oxford, 1972.

Russell, Phillips, *Benjamin Franklin: The First Civilized American*, Brentano's, New York, NY, 1926.

Ruvigny et Raineval, Melville Henri Massue, Marquis de, *The Jacobite Peerage, Baronetage, Knightage and Grants Of Honour* (1921), facsimile reprint Charles Skilton, London, 1974.

Sandbach, Richard, *Understanding the Royal Arch*, Lewis Masonic, Hersham, 1992.

Schodde, Rev George H (trans), *The Book of Jubilees*, EJ Goodrich, Oberlin, OH, 1888.

Schoenbrun, David, *Triumph in Paris*, Harper & Row, New York, NY, 1976.

Schrodter, Willy, *A Rosicrucian Notebook*, Samuel Weiser, York Beach, ME, 1992.

Shapiro, Barbara J, *John Wilkins 1614–1672*, University of California Press, Berkeley, CA, 1969.

Shapiro, Debbie, *The Body Mind Workbook*, Element Books, Shaftesbury, 1990.

Shields, Alice, *Henry Stuart, Cardinal of York*, Longmans, London, 1908.

— (with Andrew Lang), *The King Over the Water*, Longmans, London, 1897.

Siefker, Phyllis, *Santa Claus, Last of the Wild Men*, MacFarland, Jefferson, NC, 1997.

Sinclair, Andrew, *The Secret Scroll*, Birlinn, London, 2002.

Sinclair, Andrew, *The Sword and the Grail*, Crown, New York, NY, 1992.

Smith, Charlotte Fell, *John Dee*, Constable, London, 1909.

Sobel, Dava, *Longitude*, Fourth Estate, London, 1995.

Sora, Steven, *Secret Societies of America's Elite*, Destiny Books, Rochester, VT, 2003.

Speiser, EA (ed), *The Anchor Bible – Genesis* (translation from Hebrew text), Doubleday, Garden City, NY, 1964.

Sprat, Thomas, *History of the Royal Society of London for the Improving of Natural Knowledge* (reprint of 1667 edition), Routledge & Kegan Paul, London, 1959.

Stauffer, Vernon, *New England and the Bavarian Illuminati* (New York 1919), reprinted by Invisible College Press, Woodbridge, VA, 2005.

Stevenson, David, *The Origins of Freemasonry*, Cambridge University Press, Cambridge, 1988.

Stoyanov, Yuri, *The Hidden Tradition in Europe*, Arkana/Penguin, London, 1994.

Strayer, Joseph R (ed), *Dictionary of the Middle Ages*, Charles Scribner's Sons, New York, NY, 1985.

Stukeley, William, *Memoirs of Sir Isaac Newton's Life* (ed, A Hastings White), Taylor & Francis, London, 1936.

Swanton, Michael (trans), *The Anglo Saxon Chronicle*, J M Dent, London, 1997.

Sworder, Mary (ed), *Fulcanelli: Master Alchemist: Le Mystère des Cathédrales*, Brotherhood of Life, Albuquerque, NM, 1986.

Thiering, Barbara, *Jesus the Man*, Transworld/Doubleday, London, 1992.

Thomson, Katharine, *The Masonic Thread in Mozart*, Lawrence & Wishart, London, 1977.

Tinniswood, Adrian, *His Invention So Fertile*, Jonathan Cape, 2001.

Trow, MJ and T, *Who Killed Kit Marlow?* Sutton, Stroud, 2001.

Tudhope, George V, *Bacon Masonry*, University of California Press, Berkeley, 1954.

Velikovsky, Immanuel, *Ages in Chaos*, Sidgwick & Jackson, London, 1952.

Vermes, Geza, *The Complete Dead Sea Scrolls in English*, Penguin, London, 1998.

Waite, Arthur Edward, *Alchemists through the Ages*, Steinerbooks, New York, NY, 1988.

— *Devil Worship in France with Diana Vaughan and the Question of Modern Palladism*, Red Wheel/Weiser, York Beach, ME, 2003.

Walker, Paul Robert, *The Italian Renaissance*, Facts on File, New York, NY, 1995.

Wallace-Hadrill, JM, *The Long Haired Kings*, Methuen, London, 1962.

Ward, JSM, *Freemasonry and the Ancient Gods*, Simpkin Marshall, London, 1926.

Watson, William J, *The History of the Celtic Place Names of Scotland*, William Blackwood, London, 1926.

White, Michael, *Isaac Newton, the Last Sorcerer*, Fourth Estate, London, 1997.

Wilmshurst, CW, *The Meaning of Masonry*, Gramercy, New York, NY, 1995.

Wilson, AN, *Jesus*, Sinclair Stevenson, London, 1992.

Wilson, Colin and Grant, John, *The Directory of Possibilities*, Webb & Bower, Exeter, 1981.

Woolley, Benjamin, *The Queen's Conjuror*, HarperCollins, London, 2001.

Woolley, Sir Charles Leonard, *Ur of the Chaldees*, Ernest Benn, London, 1929.

— *The Sumerians*, WW Norton, London, 1965.

Yarker, John, *The Arcane Schools – A Review of their Origin and Antiquity, with a General History of Freemasonry, and its Relation to the Theosophic, Scientific and Philosophic Mysteries*, William Tait, Belfast, 1909.

Yates, Frances A, *Giordano Bruno and the Hermetic Tradition*, University of Chicago Press, Chicago, IL, 1964.
— *The Art of Memory*, University of Chicago Press, Chicago, IL, 1966.
— *Theatre of the World*, University of Chicago Press, Chicago, IL, 1969.
— *The Rosicrucian Enlightenment*, Paladin, St Albans, 1975.
— *The Occult Philosophy in the Elizabethan Age*, Routledge & Kegan Paul, London, 1983.
Yatri, *Unknown Man*, Sidgwick & Jackson, London, 1988.
Yochai, Shimon bar, *The Zohar* (ed, Rabbi Michael Berg), The Kabbalah Centre, New York, NY, 2003.
Zieber, Eugene, *Heraldry in America*, Greenwich House, New York, NY, 1895.

PICTURE CREDITS

Thanks must go to those below for courtesies and reproduction permissions in respect of the following photographic illustrations and copyright images:

1, 2, 3, 5, 13, 14, 21, 24, 27, 29, 31, 33, 34, 35, 37, 39, 40, 41, The Bridgeman Art Library, London. 7, 8, 10, 25, 26, 32, Collage, The Guildhall Library, Corporation of London. 9, 11, Copyright 2002 Adam McLean. 4, 6, 12, 15, 16, 17, 18, 19, 20, 22, 23, 28, 30, 38, Private Collection. 42, The Library Company of Philadelphia, PA. 36, The George Washington Masonic National Memorial, Alexandria, VA.

INDEX

Abraham 32, 164, 183, 200
Act for Rebuilding (1667) 62
Act of Abjuration 14–15
Act of Settlement (1701) 14–15
Act of Union (1707) 27, 271–2, 273
Acts of Abolition and Proscription 294
Adam 186, 193, 239, 240
Adam, Robert 88
Adâma 191–2
Adams, John 293, 297, 304, 312
Adams, Samuel 293, 297
Adamson, Henry 213–14
Adâpa Tablet 193
Adoptive Masonry 280
Aegyptica, The (Manetho) 199
Ahiman Rezon (Antient's Book of Constitutions) 29
Ainslie, James 214
Alban, St 26, 32
Albert, Prince 53
alchemy 4, 24, 35–6, 40, 43, 44, 49, 54–5, 56, 61, 146, 155, 182, 211, 220, 257, 326–7, 344, 349–50
Alchymica (Kunckel) 205
Alexander, Anthony 152
Alexander III 150, 162
Alexander the Great 218, 228–9
Alfonso of Aragon 110
Alien Act (1705) 27
All-seeing Eye 155, 257, 258, 259, 305, 306
Allegory of the Liberal

Arts (d'Antonio) 24
Alsop, Robert 274
Amen 227
Amenenope 227–8
Amenhotep III 192, 209, 210–11, 212
America 77, 233, 235, 236, 272, 281, 282–99
Cleopatra's Needle 201
Constitution 312
Freemasonry 301, 333
Great Seal 302–6
Masonic memorials 312–16
Northern Jurisdiction 285–6
Sinclair voyage (1398) 161, 172–5
Southern Jurisdiction 285, 286
American War of Independence (Revolution) 77, 233, 279–80, 292, 293, 298–9, 335
ammud 22
Ancient of Days (Blake) 16, 68
Anderson, James 5–6, 7, 18, 20, 28, 30, 32, 33–4, 36, 37, 46, 51, 57, 62–3, 87–8, 122, 134, 140, 158, 274, 318, 322–3, 324
André de Montbard 108
Angels and Demons (Brown) 303
Anglican Church *see* Church of England
Anglo-Saxon Chronicle 110
Ankhib 210
Anne, Queen 27, 65, 270–1, 272
Antediluvian Pillars 21–2
Anthony, St 143

anti-gravity 43, 332, 336, 337, 341–2 *see also* levitation
anti-masonry 233, 236–47, 301
Antichrist 241, 301, 302
Antients *see* Most Antient and Honourable Fraternity of Free and Accepted Masons
Antiquities of the Jews (Josephus) 22, 125, 193, 199, 229, 347
Anu 223, 230
Apollonius of Tyana 24
Apotheosis of Washington (Brumidi) 313
Apple Tree, The 27, 266, 318
Apprentice Pillar 167, 257
apron, masonic 122–4, 133, 347 *see also* ephod
Ararat 187
arc lamps 331
Argo 253
Ark Mariner Freemasonry 184, 187–8
Ark of the Covenant 3, 18, 113, 114, 124, 132, 133, 146, 164–5, 166, 181, 182, 183, 185, 211, 230, 325, 328–32, 333, 344, 345–6, 347–8
'ark' 185–6, 329–30
Armellini, Torquato 94
Art of Memory 156–8, 252, 255–6, 263
Ashburnham, Bertram, Lord 92, 95
Ashmole, Elias 35–6,

38, 46, 48, 140, 149
Ashnan 190
Ashur-banipal 192
Athelstan of Mercia 21, 26, 32, 33, 55–6
Atlanta Fugiens (Fludd) 68
Atra-hasis Epic 189
Aubrey, John 56
Augustine, St 233
Augustus Caesar 46, 194, 197
Auld Alliance 115
Aylmer, John 241
Aztecs 173

Bacon, Francis 44, 46, 48, 49, 144, 146, 147, 198, 219, 220, 250, 252, 257, 261, 268, 269, 322
Balcarres, Lord 40
Bannockburn, Battle of 117, 160
Barton, William 305
Baudoin I 106
Baudoin II 106, 112–13
beehive emblem 70–1
Behaim, Martin 175
benben stone 221
Benedict XI 113
Benedictine Order 142
Benn, William 274–5
Benn's Club 274–5
Bernard of Clairvaux 105, 108, 109, 110, 280–1
Bernini, Gian Lorenza 196
Bertrand de Blanchefort 336
Bezaleel 132–4, 146, 149, 182, 188, 200, 328, 331, 344
Bézu 335, 336
Bible Moralisée 216
Bill of Incorporation (1768) 76
Bill of Rights (1689) 13, 14

Bill of Security 273
Blachford, John 274
Black Death 60
Blake, William 16, 68
Board of General
   Purposes 98
Boaz and *Jachin* 83,
   125, 134, 138, 194,
   215, 223, 252, 257
'bohemians' 255–6,
   267–8
Boniface VIII 113
Bonnie Dundee
   (Viscount Graham
   of Claverhouse) 86
*Book of Adam and
   Eve, The* 240
Book of the Bee, The
   240
*Book of the Cave of
   Treasures, The* 240
Boston Lodge of St
   Andrew 297
Boston Lodge of St
   John 287
Boston Tea Party
   292, 296–7, 299
Boswell, James 150
Boulogne, House of
   108
Box Club 52, 97
Boyle, Robert 17, 40,
   41, 42, 48, 53–4, 55,
   56, 66, 145, 153,
   182, 183, 215, 218,
   327, 349
Boyle's Law 48, 56
Brahe, Tycho 256
bread of gold ('white
   bread' or 'powder
   of gold') 183, 198,
   206, 210–12, 230,
   261, 325–7, 331
Breasted, James
   Henry 199–200
*Brief Guide to the
   Celestial Ruby, A*
   (Philalethes) 211
British Army 29, 292,
   294, 295, 298–9
Brotherhood, The
   (Knight) 247
Brouncker, William,
   Viscount 48–9
Browne, Thomas 216
Bruno, Giordano
   156, 255, 268
Brydon, Robert 163

Budge, Ernest A
   Wallis 204
Builder, The 31, 287,
   290
Burgoyne, John 299
Burke's Peerage 274
Burns, Robert 88,
   272
Burruel, Augustus
   309
Byron, William, 5th
   Lord 76

Cabinet 273–4
caduceus 258
Caligula 194
Callahan, Philip 202
Calmet, Augustin 86
Camillo, Giulio 156
camu-lôt 331, 343
*Cathedral Builders,
   The* (Leader Scott)
   31–2
Catholic Church 142,
   239, 243, 245
   condemnation of
   Freemasonry 89–91
Catholic Inquisition
   30, 39, 114, 119,
   160, 161, 234, 240,
   255, 269
Catholic League
   254–5, 256
Catholicism 108,
   233–4
Catholics 8, 9, 10,
   13–14, 15, 236, 239,
   251, 268, 270, 273,
   283–4
Caxton, William 330
Celestine II 111
Celtic Church 108,
   233, 234
Cesare Minvielle 115
*Chaldean Account of
   Genesis, The* 192
Champagne, Count
   of 108
Champillon, Jean
   Francois 197, 210
*Chapitre Primordain
   de Rose Croix* 277–8
Charges, masonic
   20–6, 28, 32, 46, 53,
   57, 59, 92, 188, 222,
   323 *see also Old
   Charge of Masonrie*
Charlemagne 115

Charles I 7, 9, 20, 35,
   40, 95, 141, 152,
   255, 269, 273
Charles II of
   England 6, 7, 8, 28,
   33, 35, 38, 48, 49,
   50, 56, 60, 61, 64,
   65, 69, 71, 144, 153,
   256–7, 268, 276
Charles II of France
   25–6, 32
Charles Louis,
   Prince Palatine of
   the Rhine 45, 255,
   273
Chartres Cathedral
   105, 119, 120, 164,
   261, 327
Chaucer 319
Chemical Wedding
   (Andreae) 146
Childeric I 71
Children of Father
   Soubise 105
Children of Master
   Jacques 105
Children of Solomon
   105, 119, 140, 164,
   267, 340
Christian Church 40,
   55, 64, 170, 215,
   283–4, 301, 302, 309
   evolution of 233–6
Christian Dualism
   238–9
Christianity 4, 63–4,
   108, 217, 239–40,
   307–8
Church of England
   (Anglican Church)
   8–9, 11, 12–13, 40,
   90, 218–19, 235,
   273, 334
Church (Kirk) of
   Scotland 214, 219,
   235
Cibber, Caius 69
Cistercian Order
   108–9, 110, 142
City & Guilds
   Institute 267
Civil War, English 7,
   41, 152, 161
Clarence, Albert,
   Duke of 92
Clement V 112,
   113–14, 115, 116,
   141

Clement XII 89–90,
   276
Cleopatra (barge) 198
Cleopatra VII 194,
   197
Cleopatra's Needle 197
Clinton, Henry 299
Clovis 164
codes and ciphers
   320–4
cogging 321–3
Columbus,
   Christopher 161,
   172, 174–5
Comacine Masters
   31–2
Combe, Thomas 259
Commandery of
   Carcassonne 334
Comte de St
   Germain 117,
   277–8, 334, 335
Connaught, Arthur,
   Duke of 92, 98
conspiracy theories
   300–2
Constantius 195
*Constitutions of the
   Freemasons* (1723)
   (Anderson) 5, 7,
   17, 18, 19, 20, 21,
   28, 33–4, 57, 62–3
   70, 89, 91, 122, 127,
   257, 274, 343
   1738 revision 28, 51,
   127
   1784 revision 28–9,
   178, 257, 342
   1819 revision 89
Conway, Anne,
   Viscountess 56
Copernican
   principle 39, 44,
   250, 251–2
Copernicus 44, 45
Coriolanus 254
Cornwallis, Charles
   299
Corpus Hermeticum
   (att. Trismegistus)
   25
Cortéz, Hernán
   173
Council of Troyes
   110
'cowan' 104
Cowley, Abraham 56
Coxe, Daniel 286–7

Craft Freemasonry 10, 39, 88, 105, 124, 135–9, 140, 182, 263, 285, 286

1st degree 103, 122, 135–6, 207, 220, 221, 346

2nd degree 24, 39, 137–9, 346

3rd degree 21, 30, 105, 127, 135–6, 148, 178, 207, 249–50, 283

first documentation 26

Creede, Thomas 255

Cromwell, Oliver 7–8, 40–1, 218, 255, 269

Crown, The 26

Crusades 4, 106, 116, 142, 283

Culloden, Battle of 73, 82, 275, 277, 293, 294

Cumberland, Henry, Duke of 77, 78, 275

Cumberland, William, Duke of 294

Cycle of the White Rose 75, 92, 93

da Costa, Joseph Hippolyte 30–1, 81

Dalrymple, John 86–7

Damian, John 156

Darius, King 171

Darkness Visible (Hannah) 99

Dartmouth (ship) 297

Dartmouth Papers 298

Dashwood, Francis 334

David, King 124, 194

David I of Scots 109, 115, 118

Davis, William 292

Davy, Humphrey 331

Dawes, William 293

Dawkins, Peter 252

de Vere, Edward 259

Dead Sea Scrolls 112, 164, 200, 220

Declaration for Liberty of Conscience 9, 269

Declaration of Arbroath 271

Declaration of Independence 293, 302–3, 303–4, 309

Dee, John 45, 46, 55, 56, 156, 250–1, 255, 320, 327

Deluge, The 187

Dermott, Laurence 29, 88, 148, 330, 333

Desaguliers, Jean 127, 128, 134, 148, 158, 318

Descartes, René 258

Description of the Temple of Solomon (Newton) 18

Deuchar, Alexander 81, 82, 83

Deuchar, David 81–2

Devonshire, Edward, Duke of 99

Dionysian Artificers (Sons of Solomon) 31, 32, 81

Dionysus 31

Disarming Act 294

Discourse on Colour (Newton) 63

DNA 191, 337, 338–9

Draper's Company 265, 274

Drelincourt, Mary 75

Drummond, Elizabeth 173

Drummond, John (alias John Affonso Escorcio) 173, 174–5

Dryden, John 56

'due guard' 104

Dundas, Thomas 89

Dundee Manuscript 220

Dunkerley, Thomas 77–8

Dunstan, St 56

Dupuy, Raimond 142

East India Company 296–7

Eclogue (Virgil) 303

Edward II 86, 112, 115, 116

Edward III 123, 265

Edward VII 91–2, 93, 94, 98

Edward VIII 98

Edward the Confessor 108

Edwards, Amelia 201

Edwin of York 32

Egypt 4, 18, 25, 32, 154–5, 184, 188, 194, 197–204, 217, 221, 223, 268, 326, 341

Egypt Exploration Fund 207

Egyptian Book of the Dead 227, 229

Egyptian King List 202

Egyptian mystery schools 17, 226–7, 255, 258

Elder Brethren of the Rosy Cross 49, 117, 141, 277–8 see also Knights of the Rosy Cross

Elizabeth I 7, 45, 235, 251, 320

Elizabeth II 13

Emerald Text (Tablet) 25, 63

Encyclopedia of Freemasonry (Mackey) 126, 278

English Freemasonry see Craft Freemasonry; Grand Lodge of England; Most Antient and Honourable Fraternity of Free and Accepted Masons; United Grand Lodge of England

English language 318–20

Enki 191

Enki and the World Order 190

Enoch 21

Enochian Alphabet 182

Enochian magic 251

Enûma elish 192

Eochaid IV 115

ephod 124, 133, 347

Ephraim, St 204

Epic of Gilgamesh 186–7

Ericsson, Leif 172

Erskine, John 277

Erskine, Stuart 92, 93, 95

Esdras, Book of 170

Essenes 200

Euclid 21, 25, 32, 46 47th Proposition 46, 249

Eugenius II 111

Eve 181, 186, 188, 191, 193, 239

Evelyn, John 48, 49, 53, 60, 66

Exodus 133, 182, 183, 188, 205–6, 208, 211, 227, 229, 331, 345

Eye of God 155

Eye of Horus 155

Fabroni, Abbé 298

Fama Fraternitatis 49, 146

Fasciculus chemicus (Ashmole) 36

Fava, Bishop 243

Ferdinand, King 175

Field, Richard 259, 260

First World War 98

Fitzgerald, Edward 79

Five Points of Fellowship 128, 129–30

Flamel, Nicholas 43, 183, 227

Flavius Josephus 22, 193, 199, 200, 229, 340, 347

Flood, the 187, 188, 189

Flood myths 186–7

Floor Cloths (masonic) 177, 178 see also Kirkwall Scroll

Fludd, Robert 45, 46, 68, 255, 327

Founding Fathers of America 77, 302–3, 309, 310, 311, 333

Foxcroft, Ezekiel 146
France 17, 25, 37, 66, 79, 109, 111–12, 115–16, 233, 282, 333 see also French Freemasony
Frankfort, Henri 169
Franklin, Benjamin 77, 287, 304, 333–4
Frederick, Prince of Wales 72, 74, 77, 275
Frederick V 27, 33, 49, 144, 254, 255, 256, 273
freemason, origin of term 19–20, 103–4
Freemason, The 96, 97
Freemason's Chronicle, The 96
Freemasonry Today 51
Freemasons' Hall, London 28–9, 89, 98, 100
French, Benjamin B 313–14
French Freemasonry 6, 10, 96–7, 104–5, 112–13, 140, 279–81
Ecossais tradition 92, 113
French Rite 280
French Protestants (Huguenots) 235
French Revolution 78, 96, 279–80, 308, 309, 310, 311
French Supreme Templar Council 80, 81
frères maçons 119–21
Freud, Sigmund 199–200
Fritzer, Ingram 251–2
Fulcanelli 121, 122, 337
Fulk d'Anjou 108
Fulk de Chartres 106

Galamh of Scythia 207
Galileo 39, 45, 250, 256
Gama, Vasco da 161, 174
Gaston de la Pièrre Phoebus 114

Genealogie of the Sainteclairs of Rosslyn, A (Hay) 161
Genesis 16, 21, 22, 26, 184, 186, 193, 239, 240
genetic engineering 188, 189–93
Gentilis de Foligno 115
George I 26, 27, 33, 37, 72, 273
George II 21, 72, 77, 188, 277, 291
George III 33, 77, 80, 275
George IV 78
George V 53
George VI 98
George of Denmark 272
George Washington Masonic National Memorial 333
Georgia 290–1
Georgics (Virgil) 306
German Freemasonry 307, 311
Glencoe Massacre 86–7
Glittering Star 292
Globe, The 156, 252, 254
Gloucester, William, Duke of 77, 275
God and Nature 168–9
Godefroi de Bouillon 106, 160
Godefroi Saint Omer 108
gold 4, 43, 182–3, 188, 223, 325, 326, 345–6
Golden Calf 183, 205–7, 227, 228, 230, 327, 331, 348
Golden Fleece 122, 253, 337
Golden Legend, The (de Voragine) 330
Goose and Gridiron, The 26, 27, 65, 180, 266, 318

Gordon, Patrick 275
Graeme, William 180
Graham Manuscript 127, 134
Grand Conclave, Scotland 81
Grand Female Lodge of France 280
Grand Lodge of England (Moderns) 28, 29–30, 33, 51–2, 67, 72, 76, 77, 80, 100, 127, 134, 145, 148, 286, 287–90, 291, 334
amalgamation with Antients (1813) 30, 81, 89
conflict with Antients 29–30, 75–6, 77, 134
foundation (1717) 26, 27, 269, 274
Grand Lodge of All England (York Grand Lodge) 30, 88–9
Grand Lodge of Antient, Free and Accepted Masons of Scotland 84
Grand Lodge of Ireland 84, 292
Grand Lodge of Scotland 87, 150–1, 153, 292
Grand Lodge South of the River Trent 30
Grand Orient de France (Grand Lodge of France) 96, 280, 278, 334
gravity 55, 59, 62 see also anti-gravity
Great Architect of the Universe 15, 16, 68, 99, 216
Great Fire of London 60–1, 268
Great Sword of Deuchar 82
Greece 156, 258–9, 266
Green Man 163, 168

Gregory I 240–1
Gresham College 44–5, 47, 49, 52–3, 57, 56, 61, 62, 66, 144
Guidon de Montanor 114
Guillaume de Tyre 106
Gustav III of Sweden 276–7
Gwynne, David 75

Habachi, Labib 201
Habeus Corpus Act 79
Hacks, Charles 245
Halley, Edmond 58, 64, 256
Hamill, John 19
Hamilton, Ezekiel 276
Hamilton, George 275
Hamlet 254
Hancock, John 77, 297, 298
Hanover, House of 26, 33, 34, 51, 77, 82, 98, 180, 273, 274, 275, 293
Harewood, Henry, Earl of 99
Harper, William 279
Harrison, John 58
Hartlib Circle 56
Hathor 208, 210
Hebrew book of Jubilees 187
Heliopolis (Annu, On) 194, 196, 197–8, 199, 200, 201, 203, 212, 221, 222, 223, 230, 343
Hell Fire Club 275, 334
Helveticus, Johannes 205
Henri de Montfort 115
Henry I 110
Henry VIII 142, 234
Henry fitz Alwyn 265
Henry the Navigator 161
Herbert, Bishop 99
Heredom (Holy Mount) of

Kilwinning 118
Hermes
  Trismegistus 24,
  25, 32
Hermes-Thoth 217
Herod the Great 340
Herodotus 223
Herophilus of
  Alexandria 259
hieroglyphics,
  Egyptian 154–5,
  196–7, 210
Highland
  Clearances 294
Hilkiah 113
Hiram of Tyre
  (Hiram Abiff) 25,
  31, 32, 68, 105,
  124–7, 128–9,
  130–1, 132–4, 139,
  146, 148, 167, 188,
  194, 262, 325, 329,
  346
Histoire Ancienne
  (Rollin) 190
History of the Royal
  Society (Sprat) 49,
  262
HMS Gaspee 296
Hollar, Wenceslas 49
Holy Grail 166, 224,
  228
Holy of Holies 3, 18,
  146, 169, 182, 328,
  345
Hooke, Robert 42,
  44, 45, 47, 48, 49,
  53, 56, 57–8, 59,
  61–2, 63, 64–5, 66,
  153, 251, 256
Hooke's Law 48
Hopkinson, Francis
  305–6
House of Bread
  (Beth-le-hem) 230
House of David 194
House of Gold 211,
  212, 230, 327, 332
House of Shimtî 189,
  190
Hugues de Payens
  106, 109, 110, 115,
  160
Huram, King of Tyre
  3, 25, 125, 261,
  325–6
Hutchinson, Thomas
  293

Huygens, Christiaan
  258
Hyde, Anne 10, 270

Ibn al-Nadîm 201
Icelandic Saga, The
  172
Illuminati
  (Illuminists) 301–2,
  304, 306, 307–11
Innocent II 111
Innocent XI 14
Inquisition see
  Catholic
  Inquisition
Intolerable Acts
  (1774) 297
Invisible College 42,
  153, 250, 255
Iona 109
Ionians 31
Ireland 79, 116, 234
  Egyptian
  connection 202–4
  Protestants 15, 85,
  236, 270
  Round Towers
  201–2
  Test Act 270–1
Irish Freemasonry
  81, 84–5, 123, 228,
  333, 343
Irish Grand
  Encampment 82
Ironside, Edward
  274
Isabella, Queen 175
Israelites 25, 133,
  170–1, 181, 183,
  188, 203, 206,
  207–8, 223, 237,
  327, 328, 340
Iter Alexandri ad
  Paradisium 43,
  228–9

Jābir ibn Hayyān 25,
  205
Jachin and Boaz see
  Boaz and Jachin
Jack the Ripper
  (Knight) 247
Jacobite Peerage 92, 94
Jacobite Risings
  (1689) 86
  (1715) 37, 274
  (1745) 72, 74, 277,
  291, 293–4

Jacobites 37, 65,
  73–4, 78, 84, 87,
  272–5, 275–9, 290
Jacob's Ladder 16,
  137, 139, 221, 346
Jacques de Molay
  115, 116, 117, 131
Jah-Bul-On 343
James II of Scots 150
James III of Scots 141
James IV of Scots 40,
  118, 141, 150
James V of Scots 118,
  141
James VI of Scots (I
  of England) 7, 9,
  27, 33, 35, 49, 52,
  143, 144, 156, 235,
  248, 250, 273
James VII of Scots (II
  of England) 8–9,
  10, 11, 12–13, 36,
  60, 61, 66, 73, 84,
  86, 90, 92, 118, 162,
  273
Jefferson, Thomas
  304, 309, 312
Jenner, Henry 92, 93,
  95
Jeremiah 113
Jerome, St 240
Jesuits 307
Jesus 131, 164, 166,
  183, 220
Jewish Revolt 111
Jews 8, 10
John XXII 117
John de Soleure 117
Johnson, Samuel 74
Jones, Inigo 19
Jones, John Paul 88
Jones, Robert 75
Jonson, Ben 250
Joseph 317–18
Joshua 181, 208, 328
Jubela 128
Jubelo 128
Jubelum 128
Jubilee Grand Lodge
  92, 96
Judaeo-Christianity
  168–9, 205–6
Judaism 3, 4, 64, 217,
  239, 348
Jung, Carl Gustav
  337

Kabbalah 17

Karl Ferdinand of
  Brunswick 276
Karl Theodore of
  Bavaria 309
Karnak Brotherhood
  see Therapeutate
Karnak temple 198,
  206, 326
Keith, James 275
Kelly, Edward 251,
  255
Kennedy, John F
  309–10
Kent, Edward, Duke
  of 27, 33, 78, 81, 82,
  83, 89, 100
Kent, George, Duke
  of 98
Kepler, Johannes 256
Kepler's Laws 256
Keynes, Lord 25
Kilpatrick, Cecil 14
Kilwinning Lodge
  150–1, 152
King, William 74
King James Bible
  235, 318, 320
Kingston, James,
  Lord 84
Kingston Lacy
  monument 196,
  197
Kircher, Athanasius
  196–7, 257–8
Kirk, Robert 215
Kirkwall Scroll
  179–82, 188, 191
Knight, Stephen
  247
Knight Templar
  degree of
  Freemasonry 78,
  89, 291–2
Knights Hospitallers
  of St John 108, 115,
  140–1, 143
Knights of Christ
  161, 174
Knights of Malta 142
Knights of St
  Andrew 112–13
Knights of the Rosy
  Cross 66, 118, 121,
  144, 147, 217 see
  also Elder Brethren
  of the Rosy Cross
Knights Protectorate
  of the Sacred

Sepulchre 106
Knights Templars of Jesusalem 3–4, 49, 86, 105, 106–8, 109–11, 111–13, 141–4, 160, 161, 166, 184, 188, 220, 228, 234, 266, 273, 280–1, 336, 342, 343
Constitution (*French Rule*) 111
Constitution (*Latin Rule*) 110, 111
Constitution (1307 revision) 116
persecution 113–16, 119
in Scotland 6, 108–9, 115–18, 141, 143, 267
Knights Templars of St Anthony 143–4
Knollis, William 140–1
Knox, John 235
Knox, William 170
Kunckel, Johann 205

Lady of Life (*Nîn-tî*) 191, 193
Lafayette, Marquis de 279–80, 299, 335
Lahar 190
Lamberton, William 116
Lamech 21, 22, 32
Lapis Exillis 228
Latini, Brunetto 68
latres 21–2, 24
Latrobe, Benjamin 313
Law of Gravity 64, 342
Layard, Austen Henry 192
legal exemption 80
Legitimist Jacobite League of Great Britain and Ireland 95
Leigh, William, Lord 96, 248
L'Enfant, Pierre Charles 312
Lenglet de Fresnoy, Abbé 205
Leo XIII 90–1, 245

Leonardo da Vinci 157
Lepsius, Karl Richard 210
levitation 345–50
Levites 346–7
'lewis' 346
Lewis, Morgan 312
Liber Mystorium (Dee) 251
Liberty Displaying the Arts and Sciences (Jennings) 310–11
Library of Alexandria 112, 218
Light 207, 212, 220–2, 311, 343
Light glyph (point within a circle) 18, 112, 136, 207, 212, 220, 221, 222, 224, 316, 327, 348, 350
Lincoln, Abraham 311
Lingua Aegyptica Restituta (Kircher) 196
Livingstone, Robert 312
Lodge of Edinburgh 35
Lodge of Emulation 179
Lodge of Melrose 151
Lodge of Scone 35
Lodge of St Mary's, Edinburgh 151, 152
London City Corporations 263, 265, 274
London Company of Freemasons 36
London City Guilds 265–6, 268, 269, 274, 324
London Livery Companies 263, 265, 266–7, 274, 284, 324
Lord's Prayer 227, 319
Lost Secrets of the Sacred Ark 337
Louis de Grimoard 115
Louis XIV of France 11, 13, 276

Louis XVI 279
Louis Philippe 279
Love's Labours Lost 253, 254
low-frequency radio navigation systems 200
lucifer (lux-fer) 225–6, 242, 302
Lucifer 225
Luther, Martin 234
Lyon of East Ogil 82

Ma'at 221–2, 223
Macaulay, Thomas 262, 269
Macdonald, Flora 73, 74
Madeleine de France 118
Madonna of the Book (Botticelli) 305
Magdalene Legacy, The 280
Magic Flute, The 104
Mahabyn (*Machbenah*, *Mahabone*) 128, 129, 131, 213, 220–1, 222
Maier, Michael 255
Mainwaring, Col 149
Mair, Michael 68
Malcolm III Canmore 108, 150, 161
Manetho 199, 200, 202
Manna – a disquisition on the nature of alchemy 146, 149, 182, 327, 342
manna 164, 183, 188, 226–30, 327, 342, 347–8
Mansell, Edward 75
marbyll 21–2, 24
Margaret Atheling 108
Marianne 280
Marie, Countess of Caithness 93
Marie de Guise 166
Mark Masonry 184
Marlowe, Christopher 250, 251–2
Marshal, Henry 274

Martin, Robert 82
Marvell, Andrew 214–15
Mary, Queen of Scots 11, 72, 116, 142, 143, 251, 279, 319
Mary II 10, 13, 14, 65, 66, 85, 270
Mary de Modena 10, 11, 270
Mary Magdelene 280
Mary Rose 142
Mason Word 129, 131, 213–15, 219, 220–1, 224–5, 257, 349
masonic texts 317, 327–4
Masonry Dissected (Pritchard) 30, 127
Massachusetts, Westford grave 174
Mathmaticall Magick (Wilkins) 42, 45, 46
Matthew Cooke Manuscript 21, 22, 24, 25–6, 188
mazzebah 22
Meissner Field 348
Melchizedek (Archangel Michael) 164, 182, 183
Melville de Ruvigny, Henri 92, 93, 95, 95
Memory Theatre (Camillo) 156
Merovingian Kings 71, 164
Mesopotamia 4, 26, 164, 186, 189, 191–2, 223, 325
Meurin, Leon 243
Michelangelo 164, 196
Micmac Indians 173
Micrographia (Hooke) 58, 59, 63, 65
Middleton, William de 117
Midsummer Night's Dream, A 321, 327

Milton, John 224–5, 226

Mirrour of Policie, The 248–9, 253, 259, 292

Molasses Act (1764) 296

Monde Maçonnique, Le 96

Monmouth, Duke of 8

Montagu, John, Lord 27–8, 72, 274

Montgomery, Philip, Earl of 253

Moon pillar 253

Moray, Robert 35, 38, 39, 40, 48, 149, 153, 248, 260

Moray, William 153

More, Henry 56

Morse, Jedediah 309

Morton, Jacob 312

Moses 25, 32, 164–5, 181, 182, 185, 187–8, 200, 203, 208, 328, 332, 344, 347
and the Golden Calf 183, 204–7, 203, 227, 327, 331, 348
Egyptian identity 199–200, 203

Most Antient and Honourable Fraternity of Free and Accepted Masons (Antients) 33, 88–9, 148, 180, 283, 287–90, 291, 318, 330
amalgamation with Moderns (1813) 30, 81, 89
conflict with Moderns 29–30, 75–6, 77, 134
foundation (1751) 29

Mount Horeb *see* Serâbît temple

Mountbatten, Louis 53

Mozart 104, 343

Müller, Major 81

Murder by Decree (film) 247

Murray, Augusta 80

Murray, James 152, 277

Muses' Threnody, The (Adamson) 213–14

Music of the Spheres 64

'mysteries' 264–7

Napoleon I Bonaparte 71, 197, 280

Nathan Bailey's Etymological Dictionary 19, 225, 350

Nebuchadnezzar 113, 171, 194, 329

Neoplatonism 153–4, 157

New Atlantis, The (Bacon) 146, 261–2

New Testament 4, 64, 111, 220, 226, 227, 237–8, 239, 241, 250, 317–18, 325

New World Order 302, 311

Newton, Isaac 17–18, 25, 32, 33, 59, 63–5, 68, 139, 145–6, 149, 168, 182, 183, 218, 223, 256, 258, 268, 324, 327, 342, 349

Newton's Rings 59

Nilacus, Horapollo 197

Nimrod, King 26, 32, 188, 325, 326

Nîn-kharsag 189–93

Niul, Prince of Scythia 202, 203

Noah 24, 127–8, 129, 132, 134, 187–8, 200, 221

Noah's Ark 184–5, 186, 187

Noble Order of the Guard of St Germain 118

Nogaret, William de 113

Northern Ireland 14, 15, 236

Notre Dame cathedrals 119–21, 336, 340–1

Nova Scotia (Estotilands) 173–4

obelisks *see* pillars and obelisks

Oglethorpe, Eleanor 74, 290–1

Oglethorpe, James 74, 290–1

O'Heguerty, Pierre André 276

Old Charge of Masonrie 324

Old Testament 3, 4, 22, 29, 124, 126, 132, 139, 164, 170, 183, 184, 185, 186, 189, 193, 199, 200, 203, 208, 225, 226, 236, 237, 239–40, 325, 329, 342, 346–7, 348

Oldenburg, Henry 63

Oliphant, Laurence 279

Omar Khayyām 336

operative masonry 99
relationship with speculative 19, 36, 87, 324
transition to speculative 150, 152, 157–8, 217

Orange Order 14, 15

Orbitally Rearranged Monatomic Elements (ORMES) 337, 349

Order of Melchizedek 164

Order of Perfectibilists *see* Illuminati

Order of the Crescent (Order of the Ship) 174

Order of the Garter 123

Order of the Golden Fleece 123

Order of the Realm of Sion 95

Order of the Thistle 27, 95

Ordré de Sion (Order of Sion) 106

Origins of Freemasonry, The (Stevenson) 156

Ormus 334, 336–9, 342, 344, 347–8

Osiris 229

Ovason, David 312

Oxford University 41, 180

Paine, Thomas 30, 78

Palladism hoax 243–6

Paradise Lost (Milton) 224–5

Paris Grand Lodge 282

Parker, Samuel 215

Parkins, Thomas, Lord Rancliffe 78

Parzival (Wolfram von Eschenbach) 228

Paul, St 132

Payne, George 51

Pembroke, William, Earl of 253

Peninsula War 81

Pepys, Samuel 8, 53, 54, 58, 60–1, 66, 256

Perrière, Guillaume de la 259

Petrie expedition (1904) 208–12, 326–7

Petty, William 42, 56

Philadelphia Lodge of St John 287, 333

Philalethes, Eirenaeus (Thomas Vaughan) 40, 43, 183, 211, 227

Philip the Good 123

Philippe IV 112, 113, 114, 117

Philosopher's Stone 43, 55, 68–9, 146, 164, 182, 183, 188, 206, 211, 227, 228, 229, 230, 327, 336–7, 344, 347–8, 349

Philosophical Transactions (Boyle) 55

Philosophical Works of Francis Bacon (Shaw) 254

Phoenix (*benu* bird) 63, 69, 221, 223, 228, 230, 340

physical penalties 99

Pierre d'Aumont 116

Pièrre Yorick de Rivault 115

Pike, Albert 220, 242, 243, 245, 246

Pilgrim Fathers 235, 236

pillars and obelisks 194–8, 200–4, 207, 221, 222–3, 230

pineal gland 258–9

Pitt the Younger 79–80

Pius IX 88, 314

Plantagenet, House of 117, 118, 266

Plato 17, 24, 216

Pliny the Elder 205

Plot for the Intelligence out of Spain, The (Walsingham) 250

Plouden, Edmund 174

Poley, Robert 251

Pontefract Castle 323

Pope, Alexander 254

'powder of projection' 226–7, 325–7, 332, 337–8, 347–8

Prague fraternity 255–6, 267–8

Presbyterianism 218

Presbyterians 8, 214

Price, Henry 286, 287, 291

Primrose, Anne 74, 75

Principia Mathematica (Newton) 64

privileges, masonic 39, 264

Proctor, Edward 297

Proficience and Advancement of Learning, The (Bacon) 219, 220

Proofs of a Conspiracy Against all the Governments of

Europe (Robison) 309

Protestantism 218, 234–5

Protestants 14, 134, 236, 270

Ireland 15, 85, 236, 270

Proverbs of Solomon 70, 220, 227

Psalms of David 227

Ptolemy 43

Ptolemy I 199

Puritanism 165, 218, 224, 226

Puritans 41, 42

Puthoff, Hal 338

Pyramid texts 221

pyramids at Giza 341–2, 348

Pythagoras 17, 24, 32, 62, 307

Quator Coronati Lodge of Research 180, 278, 291, 292

Transactions 122, 123

Queen of Sheba 3, 182, 325

Quincy, Josiah 297

Ra 212, 221, 223

Rabanus Maurus 23

Radcliffe, Charles 276

Rameses I 209

Ramsay, Andrew Michael 282–4

Ramsay, George 170

Rawlinson, Henry Creswicke 192

Rawlinson, Thomas 274

Reformation 218, 234, 267

Regius Manuscript 21

Rehearsal Transposed, The (Marvell) 214–15

religion 9, 10, 15, 90, 91, 99, 217, 269, 284

Renaissance 40, 153–4, 215, 234

Restoration 8, 48, 153, 256

Revelation of St John 227, 325

Revere, Paul 292–3, 297

Revolution (1688) 6, 7, 10–15, 36, 182, 233, 257, 268, 298

Rhode Island, Newport tower 174

Ricoux, Adolphe 243

Rights of Man (Paine) 78

Robert II 7

Robert the Bruce 7, 49, 86, 115, 112, 116, 117, 162, 271, 278

Robinson, George, Lord Ripon 89, 91

Rohan-Stuardo, James de 71

Roll of the Newcastle College of Rosicrucians, The 322–3

Rollin, Charles 190, 191

Rollo the Viking 159

Roman Church 111, 218, 233

Romans 194–5

Rome 196

Rosarium Philosophorum 68–9, 344

Rose of Sharon 224

Rosetta Stone 154, 197

Rosicrucian fraternity 144, 233, 334

Rosicrucian Freemasonry 121, 188, 291

Rosicrucian Manifestos 49, 146, 147

Rosicrucian theatre 252

Rosicrucianism/ Rosicrucians 36, 45–6, 55, 147, 156, 182, 193, 214, 217, 218, 255, 257, 263, 273

and Freemasonry, Scotland 42–3

and Royal Society

48, 49, 59, 121, 145, 225, 324

symbols 198, 257, 305

Rosse, Richard, Earl of 84

Rosslyn Chapel 160–1, 162–72, 176, 180, 257

Rosy Cross, emblem and seal 234

Round Towers, Ireland 201–2

Roxburghe, Anne, Duchess of 52

Royal Arch Freemasonry 29, 89–90, 135, 148–9, 165, 170–1, 204, 254, 283, 291–3, 329–30, 333, 342–4

Royal Marriages Act (1772) 80

Royal Order of Scotland 118, 283

Royal Society 25, 33, 38, 40, 47–8, 53–4, 55, 56–9, 61, 62, 63, 66, 68, 72, 121, 127, 144, 145, 147, 148, 153, 154, 182, 211, 215, 224, 251, 256, 258, 262, 268, 274, 324, 336, 349

Rudolph II 68, 255

Rummer and Grapes, The 26–7

Rupert, Prince 255, 273

Russell, Arthur Oliver Villiers 248

ruthenium 338

Sacred Law 15, 68, 136, 258

Samaritan Magi 113

Sandilands, James 142

Satan 224, 225, 236–41, 301

satanism allegations 225–6, 242–7

'satans' 237

Saunders, Celia 80

Savage Club 96

Saxe Coburg-Gotha, House of 53

Scarborough, Lawrence, Earl of 99, 100
Schaw, William 150, 156, 153, 255–6
Schaw Statutes 150–1
School of Pythagoras 24
Scientific American 190, 338
Scota, Princess 202, 203
Scotland 7, 27, 37, 40, 85–8, 115, 143–4, 159, 203, 214–15, 219, 234, 235
Act of Union 27, 271–2
Highland Clearance 294
Knights Templars in 6, 108–9, 115–18, 141, 143, 267
see also Scottish Freemasonry
Scots Guard 116
Scott, Walter 88, 162, 166
Scottish Episcopal Church 235
Scottish Freemasonry 6, 27, 34, 36, 37, 42–3, 81, 82, 84, 87, 104, 115–16, 150–3, 159, 333, 343
Ecossais tradition 92, 113
Scottish Grand Conclave 82
Scottish Rite Freemasonry 10, 220, 233, 257, 276, 282–6, 313, 333
'exported' 233
Second World War 99
Secret Service 250–2, 320
Secrets Revealed (Philalethes) 211
Senusret obelisk 196, 201
Septuagint Bible 170, 229, 261, 325
Serâbît temple,

Mount Horeb 132, 181, 183, 208–12, 230, 326–7, 341–2, 344
Seton, David 143
Seton, Mary 143
Seven Liberal Arts 21, 22–4, 38, 56, 103, 137, 139, 223, 311
Shakespeare, William 248, 250, 253–4, 255, 257, 259, 263, 265, 318, 319, 320, 321–2
Shakespeare Memorial Theatre 96, 248, 263
Shakespeare's *Sonnets* 253, 321–2
Shaw, William 151
Shelêmôn, Bishop 240
shem-an-na (highward firestone) 229, 326, 342, 347–8
Shepheardes Calendar, The (Spenser) 319–20
Shroud of Turin 179
Sidney, Philip 250
signs, token and passwords 20, 33, 38, 39, 67, 71, 121, 138, 154–5
Sinai peninsula 207–8, 211
Sinclair Charter (1628) 151–2
Sinclair, Andrew 161, 166, 180
Sinclair, Elizabeth 175
Sinclair, Henry 173–5, 180
Sinclair, James 171
Sinclair, Niven 167–8
Sinclair, William 151–2
Sinclair, William, Bishop of Dunkeld 162
Sinclair, William, Earl of Caithness 150, 162–3, 167, 168, 169–70, 175
Sinclair, William,

Grand Master 153, 159
Sinclairs (St Clairs) 104, 150–3, 159–60, 161–2
Sir Thomas More (Shakespeare manuscript) 263
Sixtus V 196
Skeres, Nicholas 251
Sloane, Hans 57
Sloane Manuscript 3848 57
Smenkhkare (Smenkh-ka-ra) 202, 203
Smith, George 192
Sneferu, Pharaoh 208
Sobekhotep 211
Solomon 3, 17, 18, 25, 70, 71, 125, 126, 128, 129, 133–4, 148, 182, 183, 188, 227–8, 261, 268, 325, 326, 332
Solomon's Lodge of Savannah 290
Solomon's Seal 31, 71
Solomon's Temple 3, 17–18, 24, 30, 31, 32, 68, 72, 105, 106, 109, 110, 112, 121, 124–7, 128, 130, 133–4, 137–8, 145–6, 148, 163, 166, 169, 171, 194, 215, 221, 325, 328, 348
destruction (586BC) 113, 170–1, 194, 329
rebuilding 171
second temple 110, 340, 343, 344
Song of Solomon 224
Sons of Liberty 296, 297
Sophia 273
Sophia of Hanover 27, 33
speculative Freemasonry 26, 51, 66–7, 110, 140, 153, 215, 343

relationship with operative 19, 36, 87, 324
transition from operative 150, 152, 157–8, 217
Spenser, Edmund 250, 319–20
Speth, George 180, 181, 278
Spiritus Mundi 336
Sprat, Thomas 49, 252
St Clair, Henri de 159–60
St Clair, Henry de 160
St Clair, Oliver 170
St Clair, Rosabelle de 162
St Clair, William, Bishop of Dunkeld 162
St Clair, William de 162
St Leger, Elizabeth 84
St Paul's Cathedral 62, 65–6, 69, 145
St Peter's, Rome 196
Stamp Act (1765) 296
Steindorff, Georg 200
Stenographia (Trithemius) 250–1
Stephen, Comte de Blois 266
Stephen of Hungary 108
Stewart, James, 5th High Steward 118
Stone, Nicholas 19–20, 51
Strabo 31
Stuart (Stewart), House of 7, 18, 33, 34, 49, 48, 66, 71, 81, 92–5, 145, 180, 224, 257, 268, 319, 334
Stuart Masonry 35, 81, 275–9
Stuart Household Orders 118, 233
Stuart Papers 74, 298
Stuart, Charles Benedict 93–4

Stuart, Charles
Edward (Bonnie
Prince Charlie) 72,
73–4, 275, 276–9,
282, 283–4, 298, 334
Stuart, Elizabeth 27,
33, 49, 144, 156,
254, 255, 256, 273
Stuart, Henry 94
Stuart, James Francis
Edward 36–7, 270,
272, 273, 274, 276,
277, 278, 282
Stukeley, William 64
Sugar Act 296
Sun pillar 252–3
superconductors
202, 204, 337, 344,
347–8
Supreme Grand and
Royal Conclave 78,
80
Sussex, Augustus,
Duke of 33, 80–1,
88, 89

Tabernacle 132–3,
182, 200, 347
Taxil, Léo (Gabriel
Jorgand-Pages)
242–7
tchãm 204, 223, 340
tekhenu 223
Tempest, The 254
Templar Church
116
Temple Church,
London 111
Ten Commandments
227
Test Acts 9–10, 270–1
*Theater of Fine
Devices, The* (de la
Perrière) 259–60,
327
*Theatrum chemichum
Britannicum*
(Ashmole) 36
Theodosius 195, 218
Theophilus, Bishop
218
Therapeutate
(Karnak or White
Brotherhood) 200,
206, 227, 332, 337
Thompson, Charles
305

Thoth 32, 222
Three Great Lights
15–16, 67, 68, 105,
136, 207
Tiye, Queen 209
Tolpuddle Martyrs
79
Tories 65, 75, 76, 77,
273, 275
Tourangeau,
Sancelrien 336
Tower of Babel 26,
186, 188, 306
Townshend Acts 296
Tracing Boards
135–9, 156, 207,
212, 221
origins 176–9
Tree of Life 167
Trentaove, Gaetano
246
Trestle Board 177
Trismosian, Salomon
337
Truro Cathedral 96
Tubalcain 21, 32, 146,
188, 222
Turba Philosophorum
205
Tuthmoses III 184,
198, 200, 203, 206,
212, 227, 230, 326
Tuthmoses IV 210
Tyler 104, 177

United Grand Lodge
of England (est.
1813) 5, 19, 30, 35,
39, 63, 80, 89, 91,
98, 99–100, 165,
179, 230, 248, 329,
333
Unlawful Oaths Act
(1797) 79
*Unlawful Societies
Act* (1799) 79
Urqhart, Thomas
214
Ussher of Armagh
24
Uta-napishtim
(Zi-u-sudra) 186–7
*Utriusque Geomi
Historia* (Fludd) 46

Vatican Council 245
Vaughan, Diana

245–6
Vaughan, Thomas
see Philalethes,
Eirenaeus
Veitch, John 153
Veronica's Veil 164
Victoria, Queen 53,
92, 93, 95
Virgil 303, 306
Vitruvius 157–8
Vivian, Herbert 92,
93, 95
Voltaire 56
Vulgate Bible 221,
239–40

Waite, Arthur E. 245
Wales 234
see also Welsh
freemasonry
Waller, Edmund 56
Wallis, John 42
Walpole, Robert 72,
76, 273–4
Walsingham, Francis
250
Walter, Thomas 313
Walter de Clifton 117
Ward, Seth 42
Warren, Charles 109
Warren, Joseph 293,
297
Warrington lodge
149
Wars of the Jews 199,
200
Washington, DC 312
Washington, George
77, 291, 293, 298,
312, 313–14
Washington Capitol
312–13
Washington
Monument 313–15
Watcher, Baron 276
Watson, Robert 94
Wedel, Georges
Wolfgang 205
Weishaupt, Adam
302, 307–9, 310, 311
Welsh Freemasonry
73, 74–5, 84
Wesley, John 291
Wharton, Philip,
Duke of 28, 72, 274,
275, 334
Whigs 12, 14, 60, 66,

73, 75, 76, 77, 88,
273, 275
White Brotherhood
see Therapeutate
Wilkes, John 334
Wilkins, John 33,
41–2, 44, 45, 46–7,
55, 255, 262
William I 108, 159
William III of
Orange 10–11,
12, 13–14, 27, 66,
85–6, 171, 268,
270
Willis, Thomas 42
Windsor, House of
53
Wisdom of Lamech
222
*Wisdom of Ptah-hotep,
The* 228
Wolfram von
Eschenbach 228
women 84, 265–6,
280–1, 283, 308
Woodward, John
57
Wooley, Charles
Leonard 189
workers' (trade)
guilds 20, 72, 140–1
Working Tools 69,
105, 136, 137
Worshipful
Company of
Masons 68
Wren, Christopher
17, 28, 32, 33–4, 37,
41, 42, 44, 45, 49,
56, 58, 61–3, 64, 65,
66, 69, 71, 140, 145,
147–8, 153, 158,
224, 256, 268, 324,
349, 349
Wynn, Watkins
William 75

York, Edward, Duke
of 77, 275
Young, Thomas
197

Zeno, Antonio 173
Zerubabbel 110, 170,
171, 257, 340, 343,
344
Zohary, Daniel 191